3182

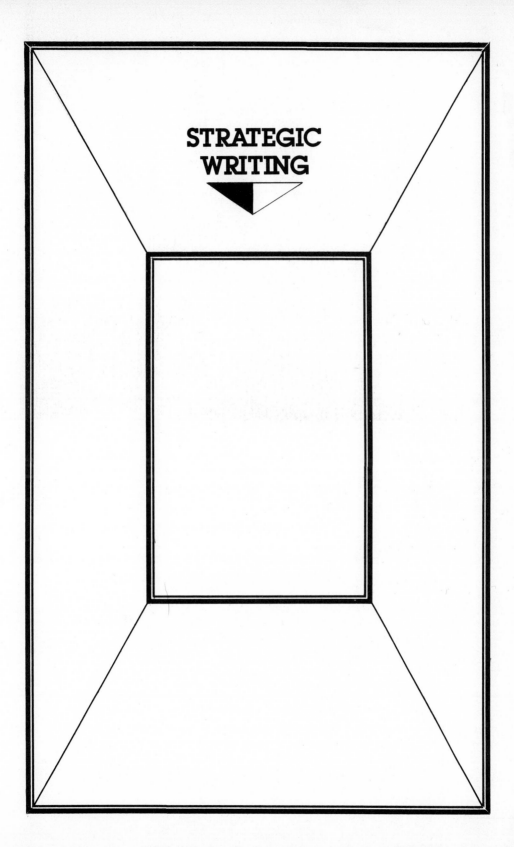

STRATEGIC WRITING

Lynn Z. Bloom

*Virginia
Commonwealth
University/
College of
William and Mary*

RANDOM HOUSE

New York

First Edition
9 8 7 6 5 4 3 2 1
Copyright © 1983 by Lynn Z. Bloom

Library of Congress Cataloging in Publication Data
Bloom, Lynn Z., 1934–
    Strategic writing.
    Includes index.
    1. English language—Rhetoric.
I. Title.
PE1408.B544   808'.042   82–3871
ISBN 0–394–31277–5   AACR2

Manufactured in the United States of America.

Book Design by Suzanne Bennett

Cover Design by Lorraine Hohman

Cover sculpture: Sidney Gordin. *Construction, Number 10.* 1955. Painted Steel. 36 x 41½". Collection of Whitney Museum of American Art, New York.

PERMISSIONS
AND
ACKNOWLEDGMENTS

P. 158. From *The Education of Henry Adams* by Henry Adams. Copyright 1918 by the Massachusetts Historical Society. Copyright 1946 by Charles F. Adams. Reprinted by permission of Houghton Mifflin Company; P. 162. "Private Lives" by John Leonard, June 18, 1977. Copyright © 1977 by the New York Times Company. Reprinted by permission; Pp. 162–3. "Politics and the English Language" from *Shooting an Elephant and Other Essays* by George Orwell. Copyright © 1950. Reprinted by permission of Harcourt Brace Jovanovich, Inc.; P. 163. From *Century Operating Systems Manual*, © 1973. Reprinted by permission of NCR Corporation; Pgs. 168, 169. From "Some Dreamers of the Golden Dream" from *Slouching Towards Bethlehem* by Joan Didion. Copyright © 1967, 1968 by Joan Didion. Reprinted by permission of Farrar, Straus & Giroux, Inc.; P. 177. "Carter's Gettysburg Address" by William Safire, December 12, 1977. Copyright © 1977 by the New York Times Company. Reprinted by permission; P. 178. From "God Helps Those Who Help Themselves," *Legislative News*, June 13, 1977. Reprinted by permission; P. 211. "38 Who Saw Murder Didn't Call the Police" by Martin Gansburg, March 27, 1964. Copyright © 1964 by The New York Times Company. Reprinted by permission; P. 216. From "Some Dreamers of the Golden Dream" from *Slouching Towards Bethlehem* by Joan Didion. Copyright © 1967, 1968 by Joan Didion. Reprinted by permission of Farrar, Straus & Giroux, Inc.; P. 219. From "Some Dreamers of the Golden Dream" from *Slouching Towards Bethlehem* by Joan Didion. Copyright © 1967, 1968 by Joan Didion. Reprinted by permission of Farrar, Straus & Giroux, Inc.; P. 221.

From "Walden" in *One Man's Meat* by E. B. White. Copyright © 1939 by E. B. White. Reprinted by permission of Harper & Row, Publishers, Inc.; Pp. 222–3. "Handcraft Swapping at Drive-Ins" by John Leonard, January 17, 1977. Copyright © 1977 by The New York Times Company. Reprinted by permission; P. 224. From "Marrying Absurd" from *Slouching Towards Bethlehem* by Joan Didion. Copyright © 1966, 1967, 1968 by Joan Didion. Reprinted by permission of Farrar, Straus & Giroux, Inc.; Pp. 235–6. From *Voyage of the Beagle* edited by Leonard Engel. Copyright © 1962. Reprinted by permission of Doubleday; Pp. 243–4. Lynn Z. Bloom, book review of Margaret Mead's *Letters from the Field*, Feb. 7, 1978, p. 3, Editorial Section. Credit to the St. Louis Post-Dispatch, copyright © 1978; Pgs. 246, 247, 248, 249, 250. "Immunization" by Donald Pelz. Published in *Human Factors*, 18:5 (1976), 465–476. Reprinted by permission of Donald C. Pelz; Pp. 276–7. "The Homosexual in the Classroom," October 24, 1977. Copyright © 1977 by The New York Times Company. Reprinted by permission; P. 278. Letter by Tim Manion in *Post-Dispatch*, October 24, 1977, Sec. A, p. 26. Reprinted by permission of the St. Louis Post-Dispatch; P. 279. Letter by Nancy Allen, October 14, 1977. Copyright © 1977 by The New York Times Company. Reprinted by permission; P. 279. Letter by Richard L. Day, October 22, 1977. Copyright © 1977 by The New York Times Company. Reprinted by permission; Pp. 278–9. Letter by Kate Roosevelt, October 7, 1977. Op-ed. Copyright © 1977 by The New York Times Company. Reprinted by permission; Pp. 287–8. "Standardized Tests: They Don't Measure Learning" by Edwin P. Taylor and Mitchell Lazarus, May 1, 1977. Copyright © 1977 by The New York Times. Reprinted by permission; Pp. 290–1. "How Not to Ease the Tuition Squeeze,"

To commemorate the continuity of generations of writers:

O. T. Zimmerman (in memoriam),

Martin Bloom,

Bard Bloom,

Laird Bloom

PREFACE: THE SIGNIFICANCE OF STRATEGIES

We live by strategies. Every plan with a purpose is a strategy—perhaps to promote our survival, everyday living, or enjoyment. Thus we use strategies to play games, hunt for bargains—or boyfriends, select teachers and courses, seek jobs, or public office.

We also use them, consciously or otherwise, as we write. *Strategic Writing* presents a series of strategies for writing through step-by-step analysis of the *writing process*, and its variations. These strategies begin with the search for a suitable place to sit and think about what to say and proceed through the proofreading of the final draft and its presentation to an audience. Every step of the way—forward, backward, or sideways—involves strategic plans and actions that can help you control your writing so that you can say what you want, the way you want to say it.

Strategies are inherently risky. Following a particular strategy does not necessarily guarantee success—at games, in love, or with writing. But strategies do provide direction and focus, an end to be accomplished, and some specific means by which to get there. If one strategy doesn't work, others may, as we shall see.

Becoming a skilled strategist, like becoming a good cook or a competent runner, requires time and many trials. Thought and practice are needed to try out various possibilities and see what works best with which subject and type of writing. The exercises throughout each chapter are designed to help you explore some of these alternatives; your instructor or supervisor may supply still others.

The strategies you will learn in the first eight chapters, Part I, provide an overall plan, with variations that you can adapt to suit yourself, for writing an entire paper. The plan is indicated by blocks 1-8 in the diagram somewhat resembling a Monopoly board that begins this book. Each of the first eight numerals (1, 2 . . . 8) on the diagram refers to a step in the writing process and corresponds to the identically-numbered chapter that discusses this step. The enlarged block in the diagram at the beginning of each chapter presents a brief outline of the chapter's main points, so you can see their relationship to the rest of the steps in the process identified in the diagram.

The reason for showing each part in relation to the whole is to emphasize that the writing process is fluid and that a person may move among the steps in a variety of ways; some chance event or attractive but random thought might prompt you to move two steps backward, or three jumps ahead. Nevertheless, there is an overall integrity to your strategy of composing everything you write, a game plan by which you eventually cover each of the basic steps and finally succeed in producing a written product that successfully accomplishes what you want it to do. That is why this book is titled *Strategic*

Writing—there is no single right way to write any given paper, but by using various tactics and alternatives, you can fulfill your goal.

Part II shows how to apply what you've learned about composing in general (Part I) to writing specific types of papers such as:

- ☐ descriptive—including descriptions that are scientific and technical, exploratory, persuasive, evocative, or some combination of these
- ☐ expository—including definitions, analyses, scientific reports, and essay examination questions
- ☐ argumentative—including classical and assertive arguments, arguments by cause-and-effect, analogy, or single case
- ☐ resource papers, with adaptations for the humanities, social, and physical sciences.

(How to write narrative is discussed throughout Part I, as illustrative examples.)

Thus the entire book has a practical as well as a literary focus, for it is intended to help you compose the kinds of writings that you'll need in school, on the job, and throughout life in general.

Premises: *Strategic Writing*

I would like to share some of the principles I followed in writing this book, so that you may better understand my purposes and how I tried to attain them—my strategies, in short.

1. *A book on how to write should be practical*, both in its general discussions of the composing process (Chapters 1–8) and in the specific applications of that process (Chapters 9–14). But, because nothing is as practical as a good theory (with its clear conceptual guidelines), I have tried to include both general principles and specific step-by-step instructions for carrying them out.

2. *Writers are made, not born.* Reading about writing is no substitute for actually writing. Practice and more practice, writing and rewriting, is the best way to learn to write.

3. *Writers need audiences*, real people, to read what they say. Although you'll be aiming each of your writings at a specific set of readers, you may intend each paper for a different audience.

4. *Writers need models.* Fortunately you don't have to re-invent the wheel (or the essay) each time you write. It helps, however, to see how other people have written the types of papers you're working on. That's why *Strategic Writing* is full of examples, many drawn from good and excellent student writing and the rest from the work of professionals.

5. *Writers should pay attention to the sense—the sound—of what they say.* Hearing your writing read aloud (by yourself or a sympathetic friend) may help more than arbitrary rules to tell you whether what you've said is clear, interesting, and in idiomatic English.

6. *Writers should develop their own style*, suitable to the subject and the writer's personality. Reread what you've written, listening for the sound of your particular voice. For example, the language of this book is intended to be clear and conversational, free from complicated terminology. You may want to write this way. But for formal papers you may wish to sound more formal.

7. *Writers should enjoy themselves while working*. This principle has governed the suggestions I've made for warming up, my selection of writing illustrations, and the way I've shaped the writing assignments.

8. *Writers should take risks*. If you stick to what's safe, what you already know how to do well, you'll stagnate and your writing will be dull. The exercises for thinking and writing are designed to suggest calculated risks—to offer chances to grow by trying techniques that are slightly new and that build on your previous writing, so you're not always grappling with the totally unfamiliar.

9. *Writing skills are transferable*. Many of the strategies and techniques that you learn while writing in one mode are applicable to other modes, as well.

10. *Writers need encouragement*—from their textbook, their teachers, their friends, other writers. If you don't get it spontaneously, ask.

ACKNOWLEDGMENTS

No one, especially a teacher of writing, is an island, nor does any book emerge in isolation, totally a product of its author's mind. If I began to acknowledge the influences of the thinkers, philosophers, linguists, scholars, and writers on this book, the list would stretch from Aristotle to Whorf. Although omitted here, many of these people are identified in the text itself.

The more subtle but most pervasive influence on *Strategic Writing* has been the many students, from basic to regular to honors writing students, including nurses, engineers, scientists, business and humanities majors, I have worked with over the past twenty years. Around 1970, having taught for a decade, I made a discovery that revolutionized my teaching of writing. As other teachers and researchers have also discovered, the best way to help people learn to write is to show them the steps (with variations) in the composing process and help them learn how to do them. This meant that I had to write along with the students, so that I could really understand the difficulties they were encountering, and could, as a result, try various writing strategies to see how well they worked. This book is in part a distillation of the collective learning of myself and my students at Butler and Washington Universities, Webster and St. Louis Community Colleges, the University of New Mexico, and the College of William and Mary.

Strategic Writing has also benefited from the careful, knowledgeable reading of various experienced scholars and teachers of writing. Among them are: Paul Eschholz, University of Vermont; Richard Gebhardt, Findlay College; Michael Hogan, University of New Mexico; Richard Larson, Herbert H. Lehman College of the City University of New York; Erika Lindemann, University of North Carolina at Chapel Hill; Lynn Mitchell, Indiana University-Purdue University at Indianapolis; Elsa Nettels, College of William and Mary; Carolyn Smith, St. Louis Community College; Joseph Trimmer, Ball State University; and Susan Waugh, St. Louis Community College.

The editorial advice from Steve Pensinger, Deborah Drier, Elisa Turner, David Rothberg, Richard Garretson, and Christine Pellicano of Random House has been appropriately rigorous and helpful, ever responsive to the needs of prospective readers, teachers and students alike. The text has also been aided immeasurably by the skilled typing of Kimberley Cross, Gloria Hall, Stephanie Hughes, College of William and Mary; and by the typing and careful proofreading of Mark and Maureen Orton. My children, Bard and Laird Bloom, have metamorphosed from junior high school to college students during the incessant writing and rewriting of this text and have often functioned as "typical"—and typically critical—student readers.

But my most profound gratitude is, as ever, to my husband, Martin Bloom—collaborator in our research with anxious writers, provocative reader of numerous drafts of the manuscript, provider of the serenity and stability so necessary for this—or any—writing.

Williamsburg, VA 1982   Lynn Z. Bloom

TABLE OF CONTENTS

PART II.
THE WRITING PROCESS IN PRACTICE

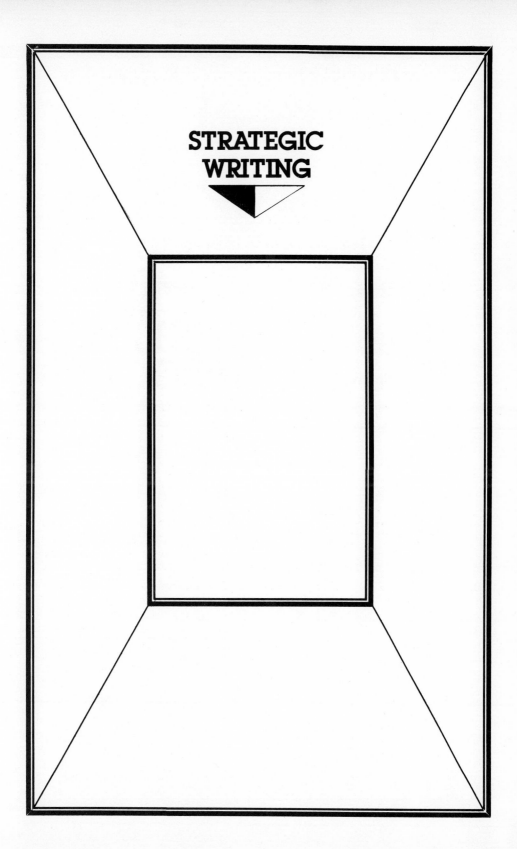

STRATEGIC
WRITING

GO

1
WARMING UP

8
REVISING, EDITING, AND PREPARING THE FINAL COPY

7
CHOOSING AND USING WORDS

1
THE WRITING PROCESS

The purpose of this text is to help students become confident and effective writers. This aim, we believe, is best accomplished by a clear focus on the *process* of writing—an orderly yet flexible sequence of interrelated tasks that leads from topic selection through revision to the finished composition.

Since the writing process involves a series of choices the writer must make, we offer clear and detailed analysis of what the important choices consist of, and we provide guidance and recommendations to help the writer reach the rhetorical decisions.

6
STRATEGIES OF SENTENCES

2
FINDING A SUBJECT, A FOCUS, AND AN AUDIENCE

Our organization should help remove the mystery from writing. We take little for granted. We begin (Chapter 1) with an overview of the essay, discuss the four types of nonfiction prose, and explain the elements essential to any discourse.

We then turn to the writing process. The chapters on prewriting (2–4) deal with planning: how to select a topic, create a thesis statement that will guide the rest of the paper, plan and organize the paper, and find a style suitable to a particular audience. The chapters on developing an essay (5–7) acquaint the student with the means for carrying out his or her intention as set forth in the thesis statement. Here, we discuss paragraphs, topic sentences, introductions, conclusions, and titles. These chapters on development provide an explanation of the ways of building and ordering content in both paragraphs and complete essays. Because revising a paper is an integral part of the writing process, we end with this subject in Chapter 8.

3
DEVELOPING IDEAS AND FORMULATING A THESIS

4
DESIGNING YOUR WRITING

5
STRATEGIES OF PARAGRAPHS

CHAPTER ONE
WARMING UP

Writing is a kind of double living. The writer experiences everything twice. Once in reality and once more in that mirror which waits always before or behind him.

—Donald Murray

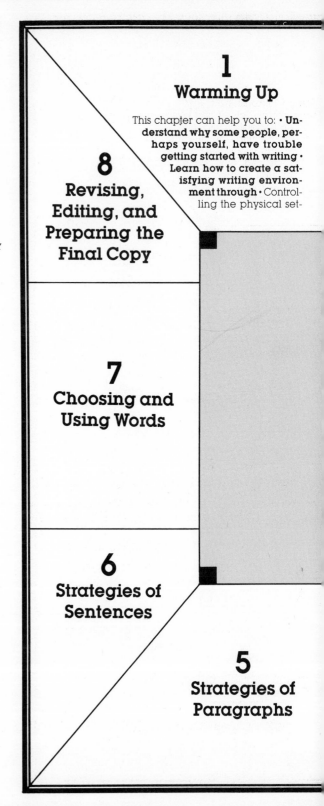

1
Warming Up

This chapter can help you to: • **Understand why some people, perhaps yourself, have trouble getting started with writing** • **Learn how to create a satisfying writing environment through** • Controlling the physical set-

8
Revising, Editing, and Preparing the Final Copy

7
Choosing and Using Words

6
Strategies of Sentences

5
Strategies of Paragraphs

2
Finding a Subject

3
Developing Ideas And Formulating a Thesis

4
Designing Your Writing

GETTING STARTED

Writers, yourself included, have their whole existence to draw upon—everything they've experienced, thought, felt, read, wondered. It's the mirroring of that existence, the translation or interpretation of that reality, into words that provides the chance and the challenge for people wanting to write. Sometimes the challenge is easily met. The right topic, words, techniques come together happily to help you say just what you want. More often it's not so easy, for you or for any other writer, amateur or professional, because with a universe of subjects and a world of ways to deal with them, there are so many choices. And there's so much to get under control. The mirrors seem to reflect each other infinitely.

Yet the subjects can be selected, shaped, controlled, and written about so that you can share with your readers the essence of reality as you see it, from whatever mirror angles you wish. This book can help you do this. It can help you draw upon what you already know—combined with what you are currently experiencing and learning—to write clear prose suitable for college, business, and other aspects of everyday living.

You've been speaking prose all your life. Ever since you learned to hold a pencil you've been writing it, too, in letters, memos, lists of things to do and things to buy, exam answers, applications for jobs or admission to college, school papers, diary entries of experiences to savor, to ponder. As a young child you may have cheerfully written all over the place—on sidewalks, on walls, on frosty windowpanes, even on paper. Teachers report that until the fifth grade or so, most children are eager to write. They write with enjoyment and absorption about what matters most to them—from the pleasures of pets, friendships, and family activities to fears of the dark, punishment, their parents' impending divorce.

But by the time they reach fifth or sixth grade, many children become self-conscious about their writing, as well as about themselves. And for many, writing shifts from being fun to being work; it's no longer enough just to capture reality or a glimpse from reality's mirror. There are rules to learn about How to Do It Right, and critics with red pencils are waiting to Make Sure That It's Done Right. As the pressures to Write Correctly increase, many writers become afraid to take risks, even though risk taking is the only way to really write anything well. You may have learned that if you didn't write with correct grammar, spelling, and punctuation you'd get zapped.

As a result, you may have decided to write safely, repeating the sentence patterns and vocabulary you already know because they wouldn't provoke the critics. If you were to continue to write safely for a long time (and research indicates that many people do), your writing would be likely to get duller and duller and require more and more of an effort, especially if you had to write for the seventh consecutive year about "What I Did on My Summer Vacation," even if on that vacation you went to China, fell in love, or qualified for the Olympics.

If you compared your work with published books or articles, you might have become further discouraged by your own attempts at writing, even on a subject you really wanted to discuss. The writing in a high-quality, finished book always appears effortless, as does a flawless half-gainer or a beautifully iced birthday cake. This seeming ease of writing is deceptive, for good writers don't want their readers to have to labor to read their writing, even though they've worked hard to produce elegant, engaging prose. Yet, what most of us get down on paper at first is rarely elegant or engaging; the mirrors have to be tilted, polished, and repositioned many times before they reflect the vision of reality that we want. And that takes work.

So you may have begun to avoid writing. Why not, if it's an effort, or dull, or likely to be met with negative criticism? Once you start to put off writing, it's easy to continue the procrastination; *mañana* may never come. Or it may come at the last minute. If you don't start writing until you're near a deadline, you won't have to spend much time on it. But if you write hastily, without time to think your subject through and then to refine it, you may not be doing justice either to what you want to say or to yourself.

There are a number of things, however, that you can do to make writing easier, more efficient, and more enjoyable for yourself, even if you have been plagued by procrastination or critics. What follows can help you to be true to that vision in the mirror.

CREATING A SATISFYING WRITING ENVIRONMENT

Some lucky people can write anywhere—on napkins in restaurants, on the back of envelopes while waiting in line at the bank, on lined pads in bus terminals; a few can even write in moving cars. Legend has it that determined newspaper correspondents can knock out stories in patrol cars, steaming jungles, or rowdy bars. But most of us work best in a place we find physically and psychologically satisfying.

The physical space in which you write can be measured and its dimensions recorded. But it is also a psychological space, full of objects arranged (or disarranged) in a setting of colors and textures. These may be comfortable—plump cushions on your favorite chair, an attractive painting or familiar photograph to cheer you up and cheer you on as you work, soothing background music. Or you may prefer an austere environment—blank walls, a cafeteria table cleared for study to shut out distractions, or a straight-back chair.

Here are some suggestions to help you determine the best writing environment for yourself.

The Physical Environment

How much space do I need? Do I need the space a big table will provide for papers, books, reference materials, a typewriter? Do I spread things out so that I can reach them when I'm writing? Do I like a room with a view of an even larger space outside? Or is that too distracting? Are bare walls better than walls with pictures?

How much comfort do I want? Do I like my setting lush, homey, or austere? Can I write best in a messy room or in a neat one? Do I like to write lying in bed or in a hammock? or sitting at a desk or table? Do I prefer a chair with arms? a straight back? lots of padding or none?

How much privacy do I need? Am I easily distracted? Or can I write in a room, such as a library, with other people nearby? If my best friend is at hand, can I concentrate?

How much noise can I tolerate? Must I write in total quiet? Do I enjoy subdued background music? (Loud music quickly becomes the foreground, and its words are bound to interfere with yours.) If the outside environment is full of the noises of traffic, construction, or people talking, will I want to block them out with the "white noise" of a tape deck with earphones? Or can I get my dorm council, or family, to establish "quiet hours" and enforce them?

What's the most comfortable climate for me? Do I work more efficiently in a warm room or a cool one? Do I like it humid or dry? To what extent can I control the temperature and moisture? Remember, even if you don't have access to a thermostat, you can put on or take off clothing to regulate your own body warmth. Some people who work in cold rooms to save energy even learn to type with gloves on.

How much light do I need? Is a "good light" a strong desk lamp? a bright ceiling fluorescent? or the natural light from a big window? You won't be able to write comfortably if you have to squint to see what's on the paper.

Your Own Writing Space

You will want to create and control the physical environment in which you'll be writing, to the extent that you can. If possible, you will also want the environment to be fairly constant, that is, a place you can depend on to be available and relatively unchanged each time you go there to write. The following questions indicate particularly important points to consider.

Is this truly a room of my own? Can I set aside a room, or part of a room, exclusively for my writing? Whether it's a section of a bookshelf by the chair in your dorm room, your own room or office, even a treehouse, try to mark it off as yours. That way you can leave your writing materials out, where they'll be ready when you need them. It's time-consuming and distracting to have to get out books, papers, typewriter, dictionary, pens, and other implements every time you begin to write, especially if you're writing something in short periods of time over several days or weeks.

Will others respect my privacy when I'm writing? They will if you insist, as long as you have not selected a writing spot in front of the family television set or in the middle of a busy kitchen. They will if you have either established a space or a time as "yours." You can work out a schedule so you have some time especially designated for your writing; if your roommate uses the livingroom for parties on Wednesdays, Fridays, and Saturdays, you get it to write on Mondays, Tuesdays, and Thursdays (and maybe you can join the parties on the other nights!).

Do I have my favorite writing materials at hand? Do I prefer felt-tipped pens or ball-points? Pens that write with wide or fine lines? In what color of ink? Or do I type my first drafts? or write in pencil? On what kind of paper, lined or plain, large or small, do I like to write? Remember to write on only one side of the paper; material on the reverse gets lost because you can't see it.

Do I have the resources I need? Besides the obvious writing materials, do I have a good, up-to-date college dictionary? a thesaurus, if I like to use one? any necessary reference books or supplementary readings? (Use library copies if you want to but make sure the necessary materials are nearby when you're writing.)

Establishing a Writing Time and Schedule

At what time(s) of the day or night am I most alert? most energetic? most likely to have good ideas? Do I work better in the early morning? midmorning? right after lunch? with a nap? without one? Or am I a "night person" who gets into high gear after dinner? or even after midnight? Can I work more easily just after I've eaten or when I'm hungry? Once you've recognized your best time for working, you can try to schedule part of that time for writing.

How can I tell how much time my writing will take? Although you can't clock it to the minute, you can make an educated guess. Estimate how long it takes you to write a page (ten minutes? an hour?), multiply that by the number of pages you expect the writing to be, and double that figure—to allow enough time for looking things up, revising, and typing or copying the final draft. So if you usually write a page in half an hour and have a five-page report due, multiply .5 (or 30 minutes) x 5 (pages) x 2 = 5 hours.

Even if you have a five-hour block of time for writing, it's better to schedule the writing over at least two periods, so that you can have a fresh look at your original draft before you revise it. In planning your week, allow two or more blocks of time when you're most alert and when there are fewest competing demands for your talents. A list of priorities can help you juggle the necessary tasks and still leave time for fun:

TUESDAY

Finish English paper	3–5:30
Play tennis	5:30–6:30
Dinner	6:30–7:30
Study for history test	7:30–10
Time out	10–10:20
Proofread English paper	10:20–10:45

Will others respect the time I've set aside to write? They will if you do. If you're in an office or a dorm, write with your door closed or post a "Writer at Work/ Please Do Not Disturb" sign. It won't keep out emergencies, but it should deter people with more casual intentions. It's helpful to get into the habit of the closed-door policy early in a semester or job, when you are not only training yourself to follow a routine but are teaching others to respect your writing pattern. To do this, you may have to be explicit with people who disregard your hints: "Sorry, Farrah, I can't talk now. I'm in the middle of an important paper. How about it if I call you when I get through, and we can go out then."

Understanding Your Writing Task

Obtain from your instructor, boss, or other intended readers whatever information you will need to accomplish the writing expected of you. Below are some specific matters you should consider before selecting a subject to write on. Answers to these questions can help you make some of the important preliminary decisions about your paper.

1. In what mode am I supposed to be writing? a report? (see Chapter 1) an argument? (see Chapters 11, 12) an explanation? (see Chapter 10) a summary? a memo? an exam answer?
2. What, precisely, is the topic? How much latitude do I have in interpreting it? Or do I have a totally free choice? (see Chapter 2)
3. Who will be reading what I write? (see Chapter 2)
4. Am I expected to draw primarily on my own knowledge in writing this? (see Chapter 2) If I consult outside sources, which ones should I use, and where can I find them? (see Chapter 13) May I use reference works? confer with instructors or supervisors? others?
5. Should the paper follow any particular pattern of organization? (see Chapter 14)
6. How long should the paper be? how detailed?
7. Do the spelling, grammar, and other conventions of standard English have to be followed all the time? (see Chapter 7 and Handbook) If there are any exceptions, what are they? Will I be penalized for departures from the conventions?
8. Should I be aware of any unusual or special aspects of this writing?

Once you know exactly what's expected you'll be better able to meet the demands.

Creating the Right Mood

Talking about writing always makes the process seem smoother than it really is, and our discussion here is no exception. What can you do if you're not in the mood to write during the time you've set aside? What if you don't like the type of writing or the subject? Suppose you just learned yesterday that the report is due tomorrow and you feel too pressured to write well?

Most professional writers stick to a schedule, particularly when they are working against a deadline. They keep at their work even when they don't feel particularly inspired or don't like the subject. They have to. It's the only way most writers, professional or not, can finish what they have started, for the muse may be out to lunch—and dinner and breakfast—during the time that you're obliged to get on with your task.

If you can't think of anything to say, try focusing on your subject and writing whatever comes into your mind until you latch onto some ideas that you can expand on (see the discussion of free writing below). Or talk to yourself, or another person, or read an article on the subject to get ideas flowing (see Chapter 3). If some parts are more difficult to write than are others, work first on the easy ones, which require the least concentration. You'll be getting something done, and that accomplishment may provide you with enough energy and ideas to finish the writing with more gusto. If it doesn't, and you're still in the doldrums with a deadline looming, jot down what you can and try to schedule some extra writing time before your deadline. Perhaps you can expand or revise what you've done. But even if you're dissatisfied with your results, you'll at least have something to turn in, and that's preferable to postponing the task indefinitely.

Even if it's hard to focus on your writing because of personal problems—or spring fever—you can try to compartmentalize your thinking. Force yourself to concentrate on the subject of your writing for fifty minutes of the hour, then take ten minutes out to rest or meditate, if you need to. Or write about what's bothering you, if the context permits. Even though you may be unable to solve the pressing problem, or to speed up its inexorable workings, you'll be getting some writing done in the meantime, and that in itself can be satisfying.

If on the other hand you're in a red-hot writing mood and don't want to stop to do other things, sustain the mood and the pace, even if it means rearranging the rest of your schedule. Write as long as you can; you'll be likely to get a lot done in a short time. Maybe you can convince your friends to go out for pizza tomorrow night instead of tonight when you're working efficiently. If, however, you can't change a commitment, keep your trusty note pad available so you can (unobtrusively, please) take notes on your thinking.

Rewarding Yourself for Writing

Why not? Finishing your writing, or a meaningful segment of it, is a reward in itself. The harder you've worked, the greater your satisfaction (or relief) may be. Knowing you've done a good job is even more satisfying. But perhaps most satisfying of all is having your own positive estimate of your writing corroborated by others—your classmates or colleagues, your teacher or boss. Yet additional rewards can be as pleasant in the anticipation as in the enjoyment, and they may be incentives to keep you writing.

You'll want to make the reward proportionate to the task at hand. Some rewards can even come while you're writing, for if you're working in long stretches you'll probably find that short breaks actually help you to think more clearly and write more efficiently. So allow yourself brief naps, short jogs, or snacks at intervals during your writing—enough to keep yourself happy and satisfied.

Other rewards come when you're finished. Perhaps seeing a long-anticipated movie would be a fitting way to acknowledge the completion of a ten-page paper you've worked hard on. Buying something you really want could be the reward for completing a term paper or major report. Or your reward might include having dinner with the people you haven't seen while you've been writing, or going to a party. When it's over you can begin planning for another—as you begin planning for your next writing!

FREE WRITING

Writing Freely: Without Focus

Once you've determined the most appropriate attitude, place, time of day, and routine for writing, you don't have to rethink these decisions each time you begin to write another paper; you can simply get on with your task.

A good way to get your mind working is to get your pen moving, through writing freely. *Free writing,* as defined by Professor Ken Macrorie,[1] is the act of putting down whatever comes to mind in ten or fifteen minutes in natural and comfortable language. You write as fast as you can, without stopping during this time. You're writing just for yourself, not for anyone else. So your writing should be thoroughly honest, full of specific details that capture the truth of your experience and opinions, and free of the abstract, vague, pompous, and often meaningless language that people sometimes use when they're trying to impress an outside audience.

If you can't think of anything to say, write "I can't think of anything to say" until a different thought comes to mind. Then write that down. Don't stop to meditate, don't correct the grammar or look up words or worry about making connections among the various topics you touch on. Just write. When the time is up, stop and read over what you've written.

This is a warmup process, like shooting baskets before the game starts. If you miss, it doesn't matter; you can always shoot some more. This relaxed writing practice should help you to overcome procrastination, and it may generate ideas to write about. It should help you develop the habit of writing honestly and specifically, which will carry over to your more structured writings for outside readers.

Be sure to save your free writings. You may find you've begun to explore a subject in them that you'll want to develop right away or in the future. Or you may simply like what you've written and the way you've said it. Like favorite memories, your free writings will be fun to contemplate later on.

Here's an example of free writing. A beginning freshman composed this in thirteen minutes.

> Running—I have been running for three weeks as of last Monday. I really like it. Surprising. Do anything to avoid taking gym. And when forced to take it, always the last one picked for the team. Paralyzing. Put downs and shame. However, I preferr to run in the early morning. If you run in the evening, you have to run
> 5 before supper or else wait about two hours after to run. Too late then. Also, there are people who turn and stare or want to make comments to you. Feel self-conscious when stared at. Formal dances are like that, everyone looking at everyone else. How much did their dresses cost? Do they look as glamorous as they think? One morning when I ran past the grocery store, Stan was out front talking to another
> 10 man. I said good morning as I ran past him. He did a double take and said "good morning, Nancy, Do you want a cup of coffe." Must mornings the only thing you ~~she~~ see is the Bi-State Buses going out west on Delmar. Bus exhaust is like breathing kerosene. However, one morning I pasted a lady put out her garbage and she

kept turning and looking at me as if I was ~~were~~ strange. Even when it dark out it is
15   nice, some morning you can still ~~sk~~ see the stars shining.

—Nancy Miller

Here, the author's general topic is "running." In free writing she's not obliged to stick to a single subject, and she doesn't. She also describes her feelings about taking gym, digresses on formal dances, and makes an observation on bus exhaust. Yet most of her comments pertain to either her actual experiences as a jogger or her reactions to that activity.

Her remarks occur in the order that she thinks of them, rather than in the order in which the events actually happened. This is natural and acceptable in free writing. It doesn't matter whether the writing is logical, and although Nancy's statements make psychological sense they are not always literally true. "However" (line 3) ordinarily signals a contrast with a preceding statement that is absent here. Nancy has omitted the logical first word of the sentence "Bus exhaust is like breathing kerosene"; she obviously understands that she means "Breathing bus exhaust . . ." but doesn't need to explain this to herself. In free writing the author is not tied to the usual obligations to check facts and correct inaccuracies. That Nancy associates bus exhaust with kerosene rather than with the diesel fuel on which buses actually run is a correct statement of her impression, regardless of the facts.

Nevertheless, despite its random order and some inaccuracies of fact and sentence construction, the writing is honest and interesting. Nancy admits she enjoys running and the early morning solitude and starlight. She acknowledges her self-consciousness, and she implies that she enjoys surprising Stan by running past him. Although Nancy would need to identify Stan and perhaps Delmar for readers who might be unfamiliar with each, she doesn't have to here because she is the only audience. The writing flows as the runner moves. Its pace is reflected in natural language, short sentences, and sentence fragments ("Put downs and shame."), which convincingly convey the fragmentary encounters with people and the environment as Nancy jogs past.

In free writing, too, the grammar, spelling, and mechanics may not be perfect; the writer doesn't have to demonstrate to an audience that she knows standard English. In this context the following mistakes are acceptable, although they would require correction in a more formal paper: spelling mistakes ("preferr"); careless substitutions of one word for another ("Must" for "Most" in line 11); mechanical errors ("good morning" instead of the conventional beginning of a quotation with a capital letter); grammatical errors (such as the use of a singular subject and verb with a plural object—"thing you see is . . . Buses"); and absence of paragraphs.

Writing Freely: With Focus

It is also possible to warm up with focused free writings. In these, you follow essentially the same process that you do with free writing except that you try to stick to a single topic in hopes of generating the basis for an essay to organize and develop later on. However, if you get sidetracked onto a related topic you should feel free to pursue it.

The same conventions apply to focused free writing that pertain to writing freely without focus. There are no rules. The writer, however, is continually encouraged to be honest, to use specific details, and not to worry about the conventions of logic, complete sentences, or standard English.

Here's an example of focused free writing that took a second semester freshman about twenty minutes. This was composed near the end of the term, after the author had produced a number of focused free writings and had transformed some into conventional essays. It is more philosophical and more stylistically distinguished than were many of the author's earlier attempts.

> How much further can I go—how much more do I deserve? How high in the tree can I really climb? How high is it necessary for me to go to feel content, secure; snug and out of the way of threats and disturbance. What I really like (I think) is challenge and ~~peace~~ Security.
> 5   The tree I refer to is a lovely large round staunch mulberry standing, when I was 9 years old, way back in our Atlanta backyard. In it I would take peacefully dreamy refuge from my childhood environment. I do not remember what it was like to be up there. As a teenager I still like to climb trees (to my little sister's frightened dismay, ~~she the~~ although great at sports she wouldn't save her kitty ~~from~~ stranded
> 10   to comrades. Declawed cats and I sit below. Both frustrated, not by limitations of of then, I do know now I am so jealous of the squirrels that rush with ease up 30′ and 40′ legs of giants; oaks in my yard. I take this personally as a confrontation/ slight to my abilities, they are playing on a vertical, more happily and gracefully than I can on the ~~ground~~ flat of ground. Tails twitching, waving; chattering away
> 15   to comrades. Declawed cats and I sit below. Both frustrated, not by limitations of our natures as much as culture's limitations. Cats with claws can climb. Can I? I have not been declawed—I am growing and maturing. I still have a desire to run, to challenge heights in college. But how does that fit with my need to be on the ground, reachable and findable?
> 20   What does this have to do with writing assignments, tests and letters? Challenges, all. Must I keep climbing higher than I can reach from the ground even though the ground is more secure?
>
> —Lou Hanson

Here, Lou is exploring the interplay between two values, challenges (which imply growth) and security (liking things as they are or used to be). These values are exemplified by the possibilities of either climbing the tree or staying on the ground. The author uses squirrels and cats, younger children and a college student, mulberry and oak to symbolize the issues involved and the juxtaposition of the past and the present. This exploratory writing raises questions but doesn't fully answer them—and it doesn't have to because of the tentative nature of free writing.

At one point Lou is imprecise, saying "I do not remember what it was like to be up there" (lines 7–8), when his previous sentence has clearly stated what it was like to be up in the "lovely large round staunch" mulberry. When free writing you don't have to worry about contradictions or inconsistencies. You may genuinely hold both views and not have thought through the implications of either. The free writing itself may be a way to investigate the implications of an issue or event, as Lou does when considering the relation of clawed and declawed cats (and their owners) to the culture they live in.

Some of Lou's expressions are unusual, either for writing or conversational use: "the feelings of then" (lines 10–11) and "the flat of ground" (line 14). But in free writings you, as the author, can say anything you want, as long as you understand what you mean. There's no point in writing nonsense, even if you're the only reader.

As in the free writing about jogging, there are some problems here with spelling, punctuation, and sentence construction. Again, in free writing, these do not need to be corrected.

These writers, intentionally or not, have employed four common aspects of free writing:

1. Write rapidly.
2. Write honestly.
3. Write abundantly, with specific details.
4. Write for yourself.

Their writings exhibit both the strengths and deficiencies of this process. They are honest, specific, personal, unpretentious, and free-flowing. They are also interesting, because the authors perceptively re-create their own experiences and thoughts as real people writing about matters of genuine concern. Because of these characteristics, the topics and treatment are likely to appeal to other readers, as well as to the writer. The free writings contain sufficient material for later development into full-fledged essays.

Avoiding problems with free writings   Like other free writings, these have problems. Parts of both are diffuse, illogical, incomplete, contradictory; both contain numerous errors of grammar, spelling, and mechanics. As long as the author remains the only audience, no corrections are necessary. But if the free writings were to be made into essays for a larger audience, they'd need to be revised and corrected, and they would no longer be free. Just as you may dress casually at home and more neatly for public appearances, you'll need to write more thoroughly and meticulously for an audience of other people. The body may be basically the same, but the presentation will be different.

If you're unaccustomed to writing, you may find that even free writing goes slowly at first. Don't let this disturb you; with practice you're likely to accelerate to a satisfying pace—perhaps a page or two in fifteen or twenty minutes. At least you're writing. If you customarily compose on the typewriter, try free typing—it's fast, produces lots of copy, and is easy to read.

As a result you will avoid a problem that plagues many writers, professional as well as amateur—getting stuck on the first sentence of the first paragraph, paralyzed by the fear that what they say has to be precise in meaning and letter-perfect before they can go on. With free writing there's no chance of that; you've discovered what experienced writers already know. Write fast to get down ideas, impressions, images. You can always go back and refine your writing. Or you can completely disregard the warmup. Just because they're written words, they aren't sacred. But the words are yours, and you're in control of them. Don't let them (or fear of them) control you.

If you have practiced what this chaper recommends, you should be fairly relaxed as you begin to plan and write an assigned essay. You will have established a comfortable environment, a writing space of your own, and a frame of mind conducive to writing. You will know what the writing task calls for and have determined to do your best. You will have set up a realistic, workable schedule, and allowed yourself some rewards. And you will have practiced writing in a manner over which you have had total control. If either your free writing or focused free writing has been on an assigned subject or project, you may find that you've already written a substantial portion of your essay.

EXERCISES FOR INVESTIGATION AND WRITING

1. Try free writing for ten or fifteen minutes in the best place and at the best time for you. This will be one way to test the decisions you made earlier.
   a. Be flexible enough to change your writing time, place, or schedule to see whether the change affects your writing—for better or worse. Feel free to experiment with free writing and the conditions under which you write. You may want to try free (or more highly structured) writings on several occasions before you decide what changes to make, for instance, to switch from writing at night to writing in the early morning.
   b. Read your free writing, decide what you think of it, and set it aside. If you had trouble with it, make a brief note of what the trouble was—for instance, lack of ideas, feeling of time pressure, or distraction.
   c. Read the free writing again the next day and see whether your original opinion of it coincides with your second look. What do you like about it? What would you change? Why?
   d. Then, either rewrite the original free writing or start again using the same general topic and see where you go today. Or try an entirely different free writing.
2. In the best time, place, and mood you can establish, practice a focused free writing for fifteen to twenty minutes on the subject of your next paper, or on another subject that interests you. If nothing comes to mind, try one of the following:

   foods—favorite, gourmet, junk, or fast
   love—parental, marital, religious, or patriotic
   sports—spectator or participant in a particular one
   education—vocational, technical, humanistic, or professional
   television—educational, entertainment, or timewaster

   After it's done, follow the same process (steps *a, b, c, d* above) as you did with your previous free writing.
3. Examine your free writing and focused free writing to see whether either contains a central idea suitable for a report or paper. If so, write out a sentence that incorporates your central idea and use it as the focus of your paper. Use the portions of your free writing that fit.

4. Imagine that you have to answer an essay exam question in a half-hour, or write an essay in class during a specified amount of time (perhaps forty-five minutes). As a trial run for what you can do to generate, develop, and organize ideas during the fixed time, try a focused free writing on the subject for the specified time limit. (Chapter 3 and later chapters will help you with this.)

NOTE

[1] *Telling Writing*, rev. ed. (Rochelle Park, N.J.: Hayden, 1976), pp. 5–12. See also Peter Elbow's encouraging book, *Writing Without Teachers* (New York: Oxford University Press, 1973).

CHAPTER TWO
FINDING A SUBJECT, A FOCUS, AND AN AUDIENCE

Have something to say, and say it as clearly as you can. That is the only secret of life.

—Matthew Arnold

2
Finding a Subject

This chapter will focus on:
• **Understanding your writing task** • **Finding subjects for writing through** • Keeping a

1
Warming Up

8
Revising, Editing, and Preparing the Final Copy

7
Choosing and Using Words

6
Strategies of Sentences

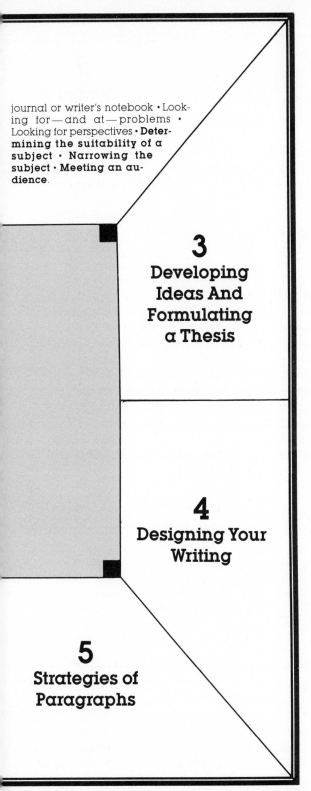

3

Developing Ideas And Formulating a Thesis

4

Designing Your Writing

5

Strategies of Paragraphs

UNDERSTANDING YOUR WRITING TASK

A Greek oracle told the king who consulted her, "If you go to war a great kingdom will be destroyed." So the king, interpreting this message as an assurance of victory, confidently waged war—and learned, too late, that it was the destruction of his own kingdom that had been ambiguously predicted. Though the message appeared so obvious to him that he never thought to examine it, it was clearly more complex than it seemed.

Likewise, many writing tasks can be interpreted in various ways. In a recent research project, a group of English teachers decided that each of them should write "an essay." When they compared what they'd done, to their amazement they found that one teacher had written an argument, another reviewed a book, a third reported on a recent soccer match, a fourth described her home town, and a fifth made up a test question and answered it. All defended their choices vigorously, and all, like the blind men identifying an elephant as a tree trunk, a wall, or a rope by feeling different parts of it, were partly right—but only partly.

These teachers learned a lesson they've passed along to their own students: *before you begin to write, make sure you understand the nature of your task.* This includes considering matters to be discussed in detail in later chapters:

1. The topic (see immediately below)
2. The audience for whom you're writing (see below, pp. 33–37)
3. The mode of writing—whether it's an examination answer (see pp. 65–68), a letter, a report, or an essay (see Chapters 9–12)
4. The conventions and techniques of those modes (see Chapters 9–12)

Sometimes you'll be assigned a specific topic—in English, history, political science, or chemistry, perhaps; as a reporter for your campus or local newspaper; in a research report; or almost invariably, on essay tests. In these instances, *make sure you understand both the literal meaning and the spirit of the assignment.* If you can't adequately paraphrase what you're being asked to do, or explain it to someone else, you probably need more information and should ask for it.

Even a straightforward-sounding assignment might have more possibilities than are apparent at first glance. If, for example, you were asked to write an essay on the significance of jobs for college students, you could interpret the topic in a number of ways. The topic might mean, "It is essential for students to pay their own way through college so they will appreciate the value of their education." On the other hand, it could imply that "College students who work more than fifteen hours a week are likely to jeopardize their academic standing." Or, "College students should seek work in jobs related to their major so they'll know whether their career choices are wise." An awareness of the alternatives can lead to more options in writing, as well as to a precise understanding of the assignment. Even if a specific topic is given ("Assess the consequences of the repeal of Prohibition"), you can usually restrict it or shape it to your liking ("The repeal of Prohibition has contributed to a devastating rate of alcoholism among American teenagers.").

TRY THIS

If you've recently been given a writing assignment, paraphrase it. Does the paraphrase mean the same as the original? Do you understand both the letter and the spirit of the assignment? How much latitude does the assignment allow? Compare your understanding of the assignment with that of another person assigned the same task. Do you both agree? If not, how can you resolve the discrepancy?

FINDING A SUBJECT

In many writing situations you will be free to choose your subject matter. Picking one subject among the many alternatives can by dizzying. You are, of course, ahead of the game if you already have a subject in mind. But what if you find yourself staring blankly at a blank paper? Three useful ways to think of subjects are to *keep a journal or writer's notebook, look for problems,* and *look for perspectives.*

Keeping a Journal, or Writer's Notebook

A journal, or writer's notebook (interchangeable terms, for our purposes), is the equivalent of an artist's sketch pad, a private place to explore your craft. Here you can talk to yourself about ideas for future writing and examine philosophical issues. Here you can record observations that you might eventually incorporate into your work: incidents, characters, settings, snatches of dialogue, arguments, conflicts, jokes. The notebook is also a good place to record provocative quotations and to file newspaper clippings or articles for further thought.

Because you're writing essentially for yourself, journal entries can be the most intimate and uninhibited of all your writings. You can release your emotions and your partisanship without worrying about whether you'll offend anyone. You owe no one an apology or an explanation; as long as your audience remains exclusively yourself, you don't even need to include definitions of terms, identifications of people, or background material. Furthermore, as with free writings, you can write journals quickly and freely, because you don't have to integrate the separate parts or set up a sophisticated literary style. The casual nature of notebooks makes such personal jottings easy to write and interesting, provided you don't keep saying the same old things over and over.

Here is a journal entry typical not in the life it represents, since each life is in some way unique, but typical in its somewhat random assemblage of diverse thoughts, cited briefly without elaboration:

> I have effectively avoided this assignment [to write in a notebook for ten minutes a day]. I wrote a five page letter to my boyfriend, a three page letter to my best friend, a letter to my boss, and a list of all I have to do to stay ahead of my homework. I also went swimming, did two loads of wash, made some iced tea, and found a fan to cool my room. So, here goes. What do I write, now that I'm started? What will my new teacher be looking for on the papers I'm going to write? Will she nitpick on sentence structure, vocabulary, grammar? Will she want fresh ideas? Theories? Experiences? She says she's not going to read this notebook. Does she mean it?
>
> I reread what I have written. So far, so good. Nothing earth-shattering, but clear. Two more minutes gone. What a screwy way to do an assignment, by time, not by content. If I were writing a paper on a subject, what would it be? Would I tell her about my summer, the friendships I made on my job with the Zion Police Department? Would I tell her about my ten-day vacation with my parents, and my new way of getting along with them? Would I tell her about the comfortable place I live, and how happy I am to be here? Would I tell her my views on nuclear power plants? No telling what I could have written. My ten minutes is up.
>
> —MARJORIE CLAY

In a writer's notebook you can tinker with scraps of poetry, tease and toy with names, make jokes, or use unusual words, rhymes, and rhythms, as Elaine Komorowski does here:

> I've got those Sunday night, paper-due-tomorrow blues,
> I got assignments hangin' over me like some old hangman's noose,
> Sometimes it leaves me wonderin' if college life'll ever let me loose.

You may find that you can work some of these jottings into more formal kinds of writing.

☐ A Checklist for Keeping a Journal, or Writer's Notebook

☐ *Write several times a week* (if not every day). You should average a minimum of ten minutes a day. Keep some scrap paper or a pocket notebook handy throughout the day so if something occurs you can jot down its essence for later elaboration.

☐ *Be selective.* Avoid an account of everything that happens or that you think about every day ("For lunch I had two tacos, rice, refried beans, and a double orange drink—and I'm still hungry."). Write about the interesting and unusual.

☐ *Concentrate on the content.* Record the specific and meaningful details but don't worry about spelling, punctuation, repetitive vocabulary, or other aspects of mechanics or style. As Lewis Carroll advises, in *Alice in Wonderland*, "Take care of the sense and the sounds will take care of themselves."

☐ *Use language that is comfortable for you.* Even slang, jargon, and abundant abbreviations are appropriate here as long as you understand what you mean when you reread your entries later. Remember, you're the main audience.

☐ *Don't let notebook-keeping become an obsession.* Some writers (such as Anaïs Nin, who kept minute track of her life in over 15,000 diary pages) become so preoccupied with elaborate entries that they write little or nothing else. Although keeping a journal may be an end in itself, it is a limited literary form. Notebook-keeping should be a stimulus to other types of writings, not a substitute for them.

EXERCISES FOR WRITING

1. Keep a writer's notebook for a week or two. Write in it every day for at least ten minutes. Try writing at different times of the day or night, under varying circumstances (in your room, in the library, with or without soothing background music) to see if you can determine under which conditions your writing flows most smoothly and easily.

Your entries might include:

a. People depicting different occupations, social classes, neighborhoods (with sufficient detail to indicate both their typicality and their individuality; interesting or unusual people you've observed, with enough detail to tell why.
b. Snatches of colorful, provocative, or otherwise memorable conversation.
c. Unusual or interesting words, names, jokes, or rhymes.
d. Attractive, startling, or repulsive sights, sounds, smells, tastes, textures.
e. Brief narrations of incidents, worth noting because of their vividness, humor, or typicality.
f. Controversial issues (see Chapters 11–12).
g. Unusual points of view on familiar issues (see Chapters 9, 10).

2. If you have kept a writer's notebook as indicated above, pick an entry on a particularly compelling topic and expand on it in an essay. When possible, provide the topic with a context—intellectual milieu, physical setting, description of someone's appearance, whatever background or other details will help to make it specific and meaningful.
3. Continue to write in your notebook throughout the term, or on your own, for enlightenment and pleasure. Dip into it from time to time for ideas to write about.

Looking for Problems

Problems are always with us—in the way we get along (or don't get along) with other people or other countries; in the way the government runs (or doesn't run); in the discrepancies everywhere between the way things are and the way they ought to be. Editorials, articles, debates, discussions focus on problems; you have but to browse or listen in to encounter some.

Some problems may prove intriguing enough for you to write about them from one or more of the angles suggested in the checklist below. Although not all the questions will pertain to every issue, writing out answers to a single question, or to related clusters of questions, can help you focus on an issue and develop ideas about it. Your answer can show what you know and what you can use. The sequence of questions may also help you organize your writing.

☐ A Checklist for Looking for Problems

☐ *Define the problem.* What is it? What major issue(s) does it contain? Are there any minor issues? Suppose, for instance, you wanted to write about the draft—a large subject. What about it? One major issue might be whether it is necessary. Another is whether certain groups—college students, married men, or parents—should receive preferential status.

☐ *Explain the key terms pertinent to the problem.* Sometimes an understanding of the terms focuses or even resolves the issue. What does "military preparedness" mean? "military weakness"?

☐ *Explain the problem.* What are the causes of the problem? What are its short-term and long-term effects? Is there disagreement over the alleged causes and effects? If so, what is the disagreement? Will the draft be reinstated to meet military needs? political pressure? Will it result in a larger standing military force? Will a corps including draftees be better prepared than an all-volunteer army?

☐ *What is the solution to the problem?* Are there alternative solutions? Can the problem be resolved at all? Should the draft be continued? on its present basis or on a different one? Or should we return to an all-volunteer military?

☐ *Which solutions are most necessary? desirable? feasible? likely to be put into effect?* Why? How can the possible solutions be effected? Are there any conflicts, actual or potential, among these alternatives?

☐ *Which individuals or groups favor which solutions?* Why? Are the groups united or in disagreement about these? Why? Which stands to gain the most from which solution(s)? Why? Which stand(s) to lose the most from which solution(s)? Why? Whose views should be given precedence? Under what circumstances? those of Congress? the military? men of draft age? women of draft age? parents of potential draft eligible men or women? students?

☐ *What will be the consequences of any given solution?* On what basis can you predict these? Will they be permanent? temporary? Are they contingent on still other factors, controllable or uncontrollable?

☐ *Are some consequences preferable to others?* on what basis? political? military? ethical? social? economic? religious? expediency?

EXERCISES FOR THINKING, DISCUSSION, AND WRITING

1. Think of a fairly serious problem that you or someone close to you has encountered recently. What major issues are involved? Do they include a conflict of opposing standards (say, between home and college, religion and business, government and private interests) or points of view (yours vs. a parent's, instructor's, employer's, friend's)? With the aid of the questions in the checklist above, think of possible approaches to the problem and ways to solve it. What will be the consequences of any given solution? Are these acceptable to you? Why or why not? If not, can you do anything to change the outcome?

2. Try a focused free writing or a notebook entry on one aspect of the issue you thought about in 1. If you wish, develop this into an essay.

3. Think of a serious problem affecting an occupational group or organization of which you are a member; or concerning your town, city, state, or country. Repeat the thinking procedure you used in 1. It may help to analyze this with your class, either as a whole or in small groups, using the relevant suggestions in the checklist above.

4. Write out the results of your thinking and/or discussion of the issues raised in 3.

Looking for Perspectives

Another way to find something to write about is to *look at a subject from various perspectives.* Upon careful examination almost anything can become fascinating. The famed naturalist Louis Agassiz once asked his students to examine a fossil fish for an hour. At the end of that time, the students thought they'd seen everything. But by the end of a week of scrutinizing the same fish eight hours a day, they realized how much more they had learned and how much there was yet to know.

It can be useful to consider *aspects of the static or dynamic characteristics of the object or phenomenon.* If you regard something as a *static entity,* you'll be concerned with describing it in detail, frozen in time and space just as it is. When you examine a birthday cake from this perspective, you'll be focusing on its size, shape, decoration, what it's made of, and whether it's intact or partly eaten. These descriptions are likely to be *literal,* although they can involve considerable *interpretation.* Will there be enough cake to satisfy all the people expected to eat it? Does it have too much frosting? not enough? Is it (oh, rapture) chocolate, or (alas) banana?

When you concentrate on the *dynamic aspects of an object or event, you may see it as part of a process that changes over time or space.* Thus, you might consider the process of making the birthday cake from start to finish. What were the ingredients? How were they combined? How long did the process take? Did the cake turn out as expected? Was it easy or hard to make? Does it require an expert's finesse, or can a novice count on a tasty product?

You might also consider the dynamics of the subject in relation to the various ways you view it. Would you have seen the same cake differently when you were a child from the way you do now as an adult? Would there be a difference if the cake had been baked for you from scratch or bought in a bakery? What if it were someone else's cake and someone else's birthday?

Analyses of the dynamic aspects may be symbolic or figurative, as well as literal. They may also involve a variety of perspectives. A particularly important one is *psychological distance:* How close am I to the subject? How much do I care about birthday cakes, in general or in particular? How affected am I by the threat of a nuclear war? too little (What, me worry?)? enough (And what does that mean? Will I lobby for peace? propose plans for evacuation?)? too much? (Am I writing letters to the President and Dr. Strangelove, urging them to build bigger bombs, faster?)

The perspective of *chronological distance* ranges on a continuum from the remote past (What were the redwood forests like after the last ice age?) to the nearer past (What were they like during the Gold Rush era?) to the present (What are they like now?) to the near future (What will they be like in the next century?) to the distant future (Will there be any redwood forests left by the twenty-fifth century?). You can focus on any part of the continuum, and omit those portions beyond the scope of your interests.

Physical distance is a familiar perspective—close up, middle distance, and farther away. Close up a helicopter may look like an awkward and menacing machine, but in the distant sky it may seem to metamorphose into a harmless dragonfly.

It is useful to consider your subject from the perspective of *figure/ground.* How does the object or issue appear in isolation? How does it appear in relation to others like itself? in relation to things different from itself? To what extent is it influenced by its context? Suppose you were to characterize your father. What is he like as an individual (see below, p. 27)? How does he compare with other fathers or other members of your family? How does he compare with people who are not fathers? Does he behave differently with the family and with others? You can ask similar questions of presidents and presidencies, states of the union, countries of the world, periods of history, and political movements, among others.

EXERCISES FOR THINKING AND WRITING

1. Look at something familiar for a few minutes, perhaps an object on your desk. Examine it close up and then farther away. How does its appearance change? What do you notice close up that is obscured farther away? Is anything, such as the shape or mass of the object, more prominent at a distance than at close range? How does the object look in isolation? How does it look in a context in which it belongs? in a context where it is not ordinarily found? Write a brief description of its appearance at two different distances or in two different contexts.
2. Consider another object, such as an article of clothing, a book, a person, a car, a building, as a static entity. Describe it briefly to someone who hasn't seen it. Is your description affected by whether you like or dislike it? by how involved with or remote you are from it psychologically? Then consider the object chosen as part of a dynamic process. Describe it.
3. Follow the same procedure as in 2 with an abstraction such as love, hate, indifference, independence, dependence, freedom, captivity. How does your attitude toward the concept affect your discussion?

IS YOUR SUBJECT SUITABLE?

Trying to decide whether to write on a new subject is like trying to decide whether to invest time or interest in a prospective friendship. Your approach may be tentative at first, until you've explored the subject sufficiently to determine whether it's congenial and worth the effort to continue the association. Answering some of the following questions should help you in your decision.

Does the topic interest me? Will I enjoy writing about it? If you have a strong interest in the subject you've been exploring, you may welcome an opportunity to discuss it. If you are concerned, for instance, that by the year 2000 600 million people will be living in absolute poverty, you may wish to write about the urgent need for worldwide population planning.

You may want to consider a subject in which you've long been interested but never have had the opportunity to explore. What do you read? What do you like to do in your free time? These may provide subjects. For example, if you're a film fan you should consider writing about films.

Your own interest is the single *most important* **consideration in choosing a topic.** If the topic does not attract you, abandon it *immediately.* If it bores you, it will surely bore your readers.

Is the topic of sufficient significance to be worth writing about? Will others want to read about it? One way to determine the significance of a topic is by a *quantitative* judgment. If it is a topic that will interest large numbers of readers, then it's probably suitable to write about. Inflation, taxes, and government spending influence many of us much of the time, as do parent-child relationships, and so would be appropriately significant. Jogging, tennis, and hero-worship of the late Elvis Presley, although they may be current fads, nevertheless involve a large number of people, and, therefore, qualify as "significant" enough to write on.

Another measure of a subject's significance is *qualitative*. A phenomenon might influence only one person, but if its impact is substantial you may want to write about it. For these reasons writers often discuss "the most unforgettable person in my life." As writers convey the essence of their relationship with Uncle Hector, they often capture elements of universal experiences through particular details. That not only makes their perspective understandable to others but gives it general significance. Thus E. B. White can write about the death of a "spring pig" he was raising to be butchered "when the solid cold weather" arrived, giving it epic proportions ("a tragedy enacted on most farms with perfect fidelity to the original script") and comic variations: "[When] my pig simply failed to show up for a meal . . . the classic outline of the tragedy was lost. I found myself cast suddenly in the role of pig's friend and physician—a farcical character with an enema bag for a prop."[1]

However commonplace the subject is, it can be shown to *have moral, philosophical, or human significance*. In *The Grapes of Wrath*, John Steinbeck spends a whole chapter on a turtle's struggle to cross the road. Its slow and painful progress symbolizes the difficulties the "Okies" (the main characters in Steinbeck's book) have in going West during the Dust Bowl era.

The significance of a subject can often come simply from your unique or imaginative way of looking at it. A single item out of place, like a Volkswagen amidst chauffeured limousines, can reveal a lot, as writers and readers of mystery stories, ever alert to the single clue, can attest. An unusual comparison, even between two ordinary things, can invest both with significance, as author John McPhee does in *Oranges*, explaining that "Citrus packinghouses are much the same wherever they are. In a sense, they are more like beauty parlors than processing plants."[2] Significance is in the eye of the beholder and exists, potentially, in any subject. You don't need to search for grandiose topics to find significance "in a grain of sand."

Do I know enough about the topic to write the paper? If not, am I willing to make the effort to investigate it? Can I get the information I need? As a consequence of your preliminary exploration you can probably answer the first two questions before you get very far into your writing. If you quickly run out of ideas or information, if your attempts to find problems or perspectives have drawn a blank, you may at the outset lack the knowledge to do an adequate job, even on a subject you like. These may be clues that you should find another topic. However, as this chapter and the next reveal, if you really want to write on a subject there are many ways to think of and develop ideas about it if you'll give your imagination free play.

A quick survey of your library, community, and personal resources for information (see Chapter 13) will also tell you whether what you need to know is available in print, photographs, documents, or your own life history. If the information is scanty, or too time-consuming to ferret out, you may decide to choose a more accessible subject.

Do I have enough time to write a reasonably thorough and convincing essay on the topic? On occasion, the answers to the questions above may tell you this. If your investigation will take a month and you have only a week to write the paper you'll either need to switch topics or simplify the one you have. On the other hand, if the information is abundant and easily obtained, or if you are already well-informed on the topic, the essay should be manageable.

How convincing you are may depend, in part, on whether you have enough ideas and evidence to present a solid discussion of your subject. This includes enough information to explain key issues and to accommodate and refute opposing positions or interpretations. How convinced are you of the merits of your stand? It's easier to convince your readers if your discussion is thorough-going and earnest. If you adopt a false or doubtful position, your uncertainty will probably be revealed, and it will undermine your credibility. If you're genuinely on the fence, write about the subject only if you can do justice to both sides.

EXERCISES FOR THINKING

1. Look over your recent free writings or notebook entries. Which particularly interest you? Which do not? Which do you think other people would most want to read about? Why? Do any of the subjects strike you as particularly limited or trivial? Can you think of ways to make them more interesting or significant?
2. Suppose you're searching for a subject and have to come up with a paper in three days. Could you examine any of the following topics and develop it so your paper would be interesting? Try it.

> a particular law   friendship   the U.S. immigration policy
> justice   fuel   shopping malls
> small cars   poetry   your best friend
> the contents of your closet, purse, wallet, or refrigerator

3. If you have been assigned a range of subjects (or a subject area with some latitude) to write on, examine the possibilities according to the criteria above (pp. 26–28) to decide which you can handle best. Then look at it from another perspective and try free writing to generate some ideas. Develop an essay from this, if you wish.

NARROWING THE SUBJECT

In many cases the subject is extremely broad (astronauts, peace, Vietnam), too far-reaching and vague to handle in an essay or report. If so, it will have to be made more narrow and specific before becoming manageable enough to use as a basis for writing. In these instances you will be working to narrow the main idea from a subject area to a topic to a thesis, as Figure 2.1 indicates.

Your subject may be so broad that it represents a *subject area,* the scope of all possible ideas on a given subject. Some subject areas are: food, religion, law, oceans.

Figure 2.1
CHOOSING A SUBJECT AREA, TOPIC, AND THESIS

First choice:
One subject
area among
many possible

Second choice:
One topic among the many possible in
the chosen subject area

Third choice:
The specific major point
to be made (the thesis)
among the many possible
points that could be
made on this topic

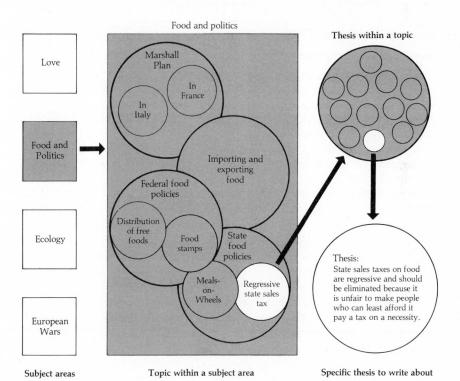

Subject areas

Topic within a subject area

Specific thesis to write about

Within each general subject area is a variety of *topics,* fairly specific aspects of the subject area. Because a subject area contains many topics, the easiest way to identify them is to break up the general subject area into smaller, more manageable portions and then to subdivide these into even more specific segments. One way to do this is to ask questions about the subject area. Each of the questions below represents a *type of essay* you might want to write. (For additional discussion of essay types, see Chapters 9–12.)

Agent (*or person*) *questions*
    a. Who is this person?
    b. Why is she or he significant, interesting, memorable, outrageous, despicable?
    c. What era, profession, activities, points of view, values does she or he represent?

Descriptive questions
    a. What is the subject?
    b. What are its various types? subtypes?
    c. How can it be described defined, or explained?
    d. How is it similar to or different from a related phenomenon/matter?
    e. What are its parts?
    f. How can it be made or done?
    g. How does it work?
    h. What are its functions?
    i. Who (individuals or groups) favors or opposes it?

Analytic and evaluative questions
    a. What are the causes of this?
    b. What are its effects? its consequences?
    c. What are its implications? (short-term? long-term? for a limited number? for a wider group of those affected?)
    d. What is the value of this?
    e. How can it be interpreted?
    f. Why should it be interpreted in this particular way?
    g. Under what circumstances is it feasible or unfeasible, desirable or undesirable?
    h. What arguments can be made for or against it?
    i. Why do people approve or disapprove of this? Why should your readers?
    j. What can or should be done to change this?

Suppose you decide to write about a subject you understand and that interests you, say, ecology. To narrow the subject and find possible topics that appeal to you, you might ask some of the following questions. These questions parallel the general ones listed above.

Agent (*or person*) *questions*
    a. Who is the country's (or world's, or local community's) foremost conservationist?
    b. What is the President's role in ecological issues?
    c. What are the significant ecological lobbying groups, and what do they do?

Descriptive questions
    a. What is ecology?
    b. What are the major ecological issues?
    c. What are the principal dimensions of the population explosion?
    c. What animal species are vanishing?
    f. How can we protect them? How can schoolchildren/students/homeowners/
       businesses conserve energy?
    g. How does solar heating work?

Analytic and evaluative questions
    b. What effects will the world's expanding population have on natural re-
       sources?
    c. What will happen when our supplies of fossil fuel and pure water run out?
    e. What lifestyles waste the most natural resources? What can be done to alter
       these lifestyles and conserve energy?
    g. Under what circumstances is solar heating or windmill power feasible?
    h. What arguments can be made for the construction of dams and artificial
       lakes, rather than leaving small waterways in their natural state?

All these topics are still broad, especially if you're trying to cover a large area in a short paper. To narrow the broader issues, you can apply the same general questions to some of the general topics you have already evolved. For instance, "What will happen when our supplies of fossil fuel and pure water run out?" can be refined still further: "What can the Western states do to ensure an adequate water supply for future generations?" This, in turn, can be narrowed to: "What can California do to minimize the effects of prolonged drought?" If this is still too broad, it can be compressed even further: "What types of citizens' campaigns can Los Angeles use to help conserve its water?"

Interconnecting Subject Areas

Another way to find topics is to *try to make interconnections between subject areas that seem related.* You could, for instance, connect food and religion, food and money, food and politics, food and friendship, food and cooks. You would then have to ask some of the agent, descriptive, analytic, or evaluative questions identified earlier to narrow the topic still further. Thus, some possible questions involving food and a related subject area could be:

What significance does food play in religious holidays? (or, narrower, in one or two specific holidays? weddings? funerals?)

Why do some states have a sales tax on food? (Narrower: Is such a tax regressive?)

Why was the Marshall Plan such an important part of United States foreign policy? (Narrower: between 1949 and 1952? Still narrower: in France between 1949 and 1952?)

Is it true that the person who loves to cook cooks to love?

Why are most of the famous chefs men?

You may ask yourself one such question, or fifteen, or twenty-five. You can stop asking these questions whenever you've settled on a topic, that, like the subject you originally chose, interests you, is significant, and can be discussed with reasonable thoroughness in the time you have for writing.

As rhetorician W. Ross Winterowd indicates, the interconnections among related subjects can sometimes be suggested, and signaled, by simple, linking words:

> *Subject plus and:* identifies what is similar to your subject and equivalent to it. "Food, sports, and sex remain favorite subjects of conversation among high school and college students." (Other signals are *too, moreover, also.*
>
> *Subject plus or:* indicates alternatives and choices, some or all of which your paper can explore. "A country at war has to choose either guns or butter."
>
> *Subject plus but:* identifies unusual aspects of your subject and exceptions to it. "Food is not a reliable instrument of foreign policy, but when a country has many hungry people. . . ."
>
> *Subject plus a colon:* signals a list, which could constitute the body of the entire paper and provide its organization. "A strong country is a country whose people are: well-fed, healthy, economically productive, active in their government, receptive to new ideas."

The more interconnections you make among subjects, the more choices you will have among alternative approaches to your topic and the better your chances of finding a congenial aspect of your topic.

EXERCISES FOR DISCUSSION AND WRITING

1. To the subjects below, or others of your own choosing, apply progressively more specific agent, descriptive, or analytic questions as suggested above.

love	peace	recreation
religion	friendship	the United States
war	psychology	travel

2. Try to make some interesting interconnections between two (or more) topic areas: love and religion, psychology and war, travel and recreation in the United States. Using some of the methods of linkage suggested above, focus the topic as specifically as you can: for example, to what extent has recreational travel in the United States been affected by the increasingly high cost of fuel?

3. Discuss some of these possible interconnections with a friend, preferably someone who has a special knowledge of one or more of the topics. Or do a focused free writing to see if more connections occur as you write. This could develop into the preliminary draft of a paper, a writing that explores various aspects of the subject in hopes of finding a specific direction. Try a preliminary draft on a subject of your choice.

MEETING YOUR AUDIENCE

"Dear reader, I *married* him," reported the nineteenth-century heroine, in quiet joy, confident that readers would empathize with her husband's progress from despair to happiness, recognize the bittersweet triumph of her marriage, and rejoice at this resolution of her previously painful situation. Such remarks reveal authors to be sensitive to their audience. For you, as for these writers, the intended audience may have an enormous impact on what you say, how you say it, and how you use the common heritage that you share. In theory, you can write on nearly any topic for almost any audience; books about the Holocaust have been written for young children, and volumes on gardening have been directed toward apartment dwellers. Once you choose an audience, however, you are obliged to accommodate your writing to the specific attributes of that readership.

One of your basic concerns with any topic you select will be, "For whom am I writing?" This consideration is central—even if you think your writing is for yourself. In one sense, of course, your writing is always for yourself, because you are writing to express your thoughts in ways that have to satisfy yourself first of all. But if you're communicating ideas in a medium more public than a private diary or a shopping list, the other forms of writing you choose imply an audience of other people.

If your writing is part of your course work, you may imagine that you are writing essentially for the teacher, who will, in fact, be reading your paper. In some ways you are doing just that, but if you think of your task as *only that*, the writing circuit becomes very short, a one-time message from you to a single, one-time reader. If your papers are for a writing course designed to help you communicate with others, you will function as a more mature writer if you broaden your audience to include a specified group of people for whom your writing will be of relevance, value, and interest, such as your community or fellow employees. If you're not writing for a class, you may be trying to reach these other readers directly, through a letter to a newspaper or by writing a newspaper article.

What Can You Assume About Your Readers?

It is commonly assumed that writing by nonspecialists is directed toward a "general audience" of rational, moderately well-educated people of good will (an English teacher often acts as their equivalent). If you are writing in America, your audience is thought to be Americans who represent either the people you are most familiar with (such as your classmates, friends, or hometown residents) or the broad range of people who read daily papers and popular magazines. Such readers, it is believed, will listen thoughtfully to defensible assertions, supported by accurate and appropriate evidence.

These assumptions are somewhat idealistic. A "general readership" is more likely to be composed of diverse people with special interests and biases. At the same time, the concept of "general audience" is so broad and vague it would be almost impossible to locate even two or three typical "general readers."

It is more realistic, therefore, to tailor your writing for an audience with identifiable and predictable characteristics. Communication is a two-way channel. You may write a perfect essay, but to ensure that it will be read in the spirit in which you wrote it, you will need to accommodate your readers' knowledge, interests, and prejudices. Once you determine the specific characteristics of your intended audience, especially their educational level, cultural background, special knowledge, interests, and biases, it will be easier to estimate their attitude toward the subject and to adapt your discussion accordingly.

Level of education Whether or not they have much formal education, your readers can be counted on to have common sense and a fund of common knowledge. One way to determine whether you've assessed your audience's general level of information accurately is to try to remember what you knew at a given age or particular stage of your education. When, if ever, did you learn why the sky is blue? or why the stars twinkle? Another way to assess the level of your audience is to examine some published writing aimed at the one you're writing for and see what general information the other writers take for granted. Always keep in mind your expectations of your readers: Do you expect them to have a minimum of fourth-grade education (the level the U.S. Army currently expects of its enlisted men) or an eighth-grade reading level (that aimed at by many general newspapers) or a high-school education (which you can assume of your college classmates) or a professional-level education in a specialized field which you share?

Cultural background Do you and your readers have a common heritage? How broad (all Americans) or how narrow (West Texans, Brooklynites)? Does your perspective encompass common features of particular religious, racial, or ethnic backgrounds? If so, are you justified in using yourself as a reference point; can you assume that what you know and take for granted (for instance, how to dance the salsa or what a blueberry rake is) your readers will, too?

Americans can be assumed to share a common cultural heritage, so the writer doesn't need to explain Lincoln (as long as it's clear which Lincoln you're talking about—the President or the car or the city) or the Mason-Dixon Line or McDonald's. The more provincial and limited the readers (Easterners who see the far West as a cowboy movie stereotype) the more limited—or explanatory—your writing may have to be.

Special knowledge or interests Do you and your readers have in common an occupation, hobby, activity, knowledge of a process? If so, you can write on such subjects for others with expertise, as well as for people who know little or nothing about such matters.

However, unless you have had medical training it would be inappropriate for you to write a specialized paper for an audience of surgeons. Generalists cannot easily or convincingly tell specialists more about their specialty than they already know.

Biases Do your intended readers harbor biases that will affect their reaction toward your interpretation or toward you as an author? They may react strongly if you're writing from a regional, religious, ethnic, or political perspective they do not share. Indeed, it would be unrealistic and somewhat dull to expect all your readers' views to be identical to yours. If you're trying to convince a fence-straddler or an antagonist to vote his rascal out and your knight in shining armor in, you may be glad to admit some differences of opinion. (Chapter 11 contains many suggestions on how to determine your readers' biases and how to accommodate these in your writing.)

It is useful to consider the relationship between writer, reader, and subject as three points on a triangle with sides of varying lengths that designate how closely any two points agree. As the writer moves closer to the reader (or vice versa), they look at the subject from more similar perspectives. The farther apart they are, the greater the disparity with which they view the subject, and the harder the writer must work to close the gap (see Figure 2.2).

Figure 2.2
THE RELATIONSHIP OF WRITER, READER, AND SUBJECT

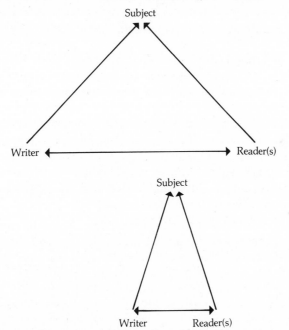

What Can Your Readers Assume About You as a Writer?

Your readers should be able to take for granted several things about you as a writer, whether they know you personally or agree with you about your subject. They should be able to assume, correctly, that:

You are honest. You say or strongly imply what you mean, either directly ("The Rocky Mountains are a hiker's delight.") or indirectly ("John Denver isn't alone on his 'Rocky Mountain High.' ").

You know what you're talking about. Why, otherwise, would you be writing and your audience be reading?

You are fair, to your subject and to your readers. You respect both enough to accommodate different views of the subject without distorting or suppressing unfavorable evidence (see Chapter 12). And you do not trick or force your readers into agreement with you.

You can establish all these qualities through essentially the same means. You do not need to assert "I am not a crook" or, "Now I'll be perfectly honest with you" to make your point. Telling people how fair you are may only arouse their suspicion. You will be most convincing if you demonstrate these qualities instead of merely talking about them. *Show, don't tell*, through specific details rather than generalizations, and support your case with illustrations, case studies, or references to other authorities.

For instance, instead of simply claiming that computer science is a desirable area to major in, and expecting your readers to take your word for it (why should they?), you can provide and interpret evidence to show why this is so. You could say that the art of programming a computer so it understands your directions [*evidence*] is intrinsically interesting [*interpretation*]. Because computers prepare payrolls, typeset news stories, and analyze complex scientific information [*evidence*], the demand for computer mathematicians is always expanding. You could supply additional information. The U.S. Department of Labor predicts that more than 25,000 computer mathematicians will be needed in the next five years [*fact*]. Salaries are high, ranging from $20,000 to $30,000 for a beginner with a bachelor's degree [*fact*] to double that amount for new Ph.D.s [*fact*], which is at least twice as much as new graduates in the humanities can command [*fact*]. Because it is a new and varied field [*fact*], computer math offers opportunities for imagination and advancement [*interpretation*].

A discussion such as this, illustrated with appropriate, accurate, specific evidence, demonstrates to your readers that you know your subject. Because your interpretation does not exceed the evidence, it will be clear that you are presenting the material honestly, without distortion. Your intent is to inform the audience—and you have done so. Your approach is straightforward and clear. Your readers know where you stand on the matter and why. They can now decide for themselves, on the basis of the evidence you have presented, whether to believe what you say and accept your interpretation.

Being specific has the further advantage of providing direction for your readers and control for you as a writer. Vagueness puts the burden of proof where it doesn't belong—on the reader rather than on the writer. Readers can supply whatever evidence they want and interpret it however they wish. You could assert, for instance, that "Cleveland, my home city, is the most wonderful place in the United States." But only if the readers are inclined beforehand to agree with you, or to accept your statement at face value, will your generalization be convincing. For the readers, if pressed, could supply their own corroborating evidence: "Oh, yes. There's the Art Museum, the Cleveland Orchestra, Little Italy, and Severance Center. Even Lake Erie is a lot cleaner than it used to be." But if your readers are indifferent to your subject, generalizations are likely to be a bore and insufficient to compel interest in the subject: "Cleveland, who cares?" If the readers disagree with your views on the subject, lack of specificity will allow them the latitude to support their contradictory opinions: "Cleveland? The police strike, the teachers strike; bankers control the city and pay no attention to the wishes of the people. It's still the mistake on the lake."

To attract the indifferent, and to anticipate antagonistic readers and evidence contrary to your position, *the more specific and focused you are in your writing, the more direction you will provide to guide your readers* **along the path of your own reasoning.** Thus a specific discussion of Cleveland could lead your readers to the shores of Lake Erie, and perhaps make them think, if you emphasized some of the following:

> Its business climate, and worker receptivity to new industry; its diverse ethnic strength, including sizeable numbers of Italians, Germans, Poles, Slavs, Asians, and Indians; its cultural attractions, among them Case Western Reserve and Cleveland State Universities, and the world-renowned Cleveland Orchestra, the oriental collections of the Art Museum; and its attractive residential areas, such as Lakewood, Shaker Heights, University City and Gates Mills.

EXERCISES FOR ANALYSIS AND WRITING

1. Here is freshman Mary Hannett's analysis of herself at eighteen in relation to her intended readers:

> I still have problems deciding whether I'm a delinquent or a convent candidate. In high school I ran wild with the worst of them and made A's with the best. I went out of my way to get into trouble and then couldn't lie about whether I had been truant or legitimately waylaid on the way to class or sick in the bathroom. My parents gave me everything I asked for and yet I was convinced that they wanted me placed in a home.
>
> I would like to be able to express these confusions and doubts to a group of people who might be in a position to better understand and alleviate them. My specific audience would consist of educators, parents, and teenagers; I would operate on the premise that everyone had experienced my problems and conflicts. However, this would probably mean that folks of my grandparents' generation would not necessarily understand.
>
> To make my tales of woe realistic, I would write in the language of the people I was attempting to portray. Hopefully, organization and sincerity would be good substitutes for an extensive vocabulary.

   a. What characteristics does Mary look for in an audience?

   b. Why does she think that "folks of my grandparents' generation would not necessarily understand" what she's talking about? Is she right?

   c. What do Mary's purposes as a writer seem to be? Identify some specific subjects she might write about, and the focus she might take for her intended readers.
2. Jim Keith, a classmate of Mary's, sees his readers this way:

> My ideal audience must be willing to work at my writing. Those who prefer to read with their minds in neutral are not for me. They must not have preconceptions about my writing. My audience must be able to "suspend disbelief" and approach me with an open mind. People who read me and find they either strongly agree or disagree with my ideas are part of my ideal audience. The lukewarm I do not want. Those who feel they are made wise simply by the collection of years are not for me, but one can have a fresh outlook at any age.
>
> I seek no audience with a leisure-suit. I do not aim my writings at war-mongers, phony liberals, California sophisticates who are utterly caught up in "selves," socialites who drop names from *The New Yorker* but do not read it, Communist-haters who don't know Marx from Stalin, capitalist-haters who eat caviar . . . .

   a. Is Jim's audience similar to Mary's? What are the similarities? What are the differences?
   b. What does Jim see as his relation to his readers? Do you see him the same way?
   c. Both Mary and Jim think in stereotypes about some of their intended, and excluded, readers. To what extent are such generalizations likely to help or hinder their writing?
3. Write a paragraph or a paper identifying the audience for your next paper. Specify the attributes of each of the following characteristics, if they are relevant:
   a. Minimum educational level
   b. National/racial/ethnic background
   c. Special knowledge or interests that pertain to your subject
   d. Biases, such as identification with a particular political, religious, age, or sexual group.
4. Write a paragraph (call it *A*) characterizing your favorite city for someone you think might agree with you.
   a. Now write a paragraph (call it *B*) characterizing the same city for someone you think will disagree with you.
   b. Have you included the same details in each? different ones? Have you included the same explanations in each? If one characterization is different from or more extensive than the other, explain why.
   c. Would readers of each paragraph think you knew the city well? Would they think you treated your subject and readers fairly? Without identifying which paragraph is *A* and which is *B*, trade paragraphs with a classmate and ask each other these questions.

NOTES

1 "Death of a Pig," *The Second Tree from the Corner* (1954; rpt. New York: Harper & Row, 1965), p. 229.
2 New York: Farrar, Straus, and Giroux.

CHAPTER THREE

DEVELOPING IDEAS AND FORMULATING A THESIS

How do I know what I think until I see what I say?

—E. M. FORSTER

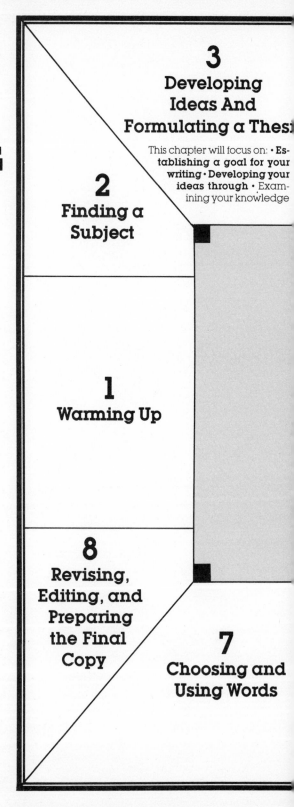

3
Developing Ideas And Formulating a Thesi[s]

This chapter will focus on: • **Establishing a goal for your writing** • **Developing your ideas through** • Examining your knowledge

2
Finding a Subject

1
Warming Up

8
Revising, Editing, and Preparing the Final Copy

7
Choosing and Using Words

and opinions • Holding a dialogue with yourself and others • Writing a zero draft • Playing with an analogy • **Formulating a thesis**.

4
Designing Your Writing

5
Strategies of Paragraphs

6
Strategies of Sentences

ESTABLISHING A GOAL

Each time you write you should have a goal, whether it's as general as "self-expression" or as specific as "I want to convince my state legislators to vote against a proposed sales tax on food." Although the purpose may not be stated explicitly in the first paragraph of the paper (or anywhere), you'll need to have it clearly in mind as you develop your topic.

Sometimes your purpose will be determined in advance. Or it can be built into the particular writing you're doing, if it involves explanation, description, or argument—for example, explaining to an admissions officer why you want to attend her college, or identifying and interpreting the results of your latest lab investigation, or demonstrating to a prospective employer why you are qualified for an advertised job.

At other times you will have to determine your own purpose or goal in writing. You can begin to identify your goal by asking yourself *Why am I writing about this?* and *What do I want to accomplish with this writing?* Some common goals for writers are to explain, report, describe, interpret, give directions, command, argue, or prove a point (see the Index for specific references to each of these). If, as suggested in Chapter 2, you have explored whether your subject is interesting both to you and your readers and whether it can be discussed through the use of agent, descriptive, or analytic questions, you will have already begun to consider your purpose. Or perhaps a purpose evolved gradually—or is still emerging—as you contemplate your topic. At any rate, focusing on a purpose will help you develop your ideas more effectively.

To provide specific answers to questions of purpose and audience, such as *For whom am I writing this?* and *Why should they want to read about it?*, writing researchers Linda Flower and John Hayes suggest including directions for accomplishing your purpose in your plan for discussing your subject.[1] Plans without built-in directions, they say, are vague and abstract: "I want to write about saving money." Asking agent, descriptive, or analytic questions, prefaced by *who, what, where, when, why,* or *how,* can make your focus more specific: Who wants to save money? How can they do it? Why should they? Questions such as these can be translated into a statement of purpose: "I want to demonstrate, through the examples of solar heating and windmills, how the average homeowner can save money and conserve scarce gas and oil." Here you've shown *what* you're going to do (demonstrate . . .), *how* you're going to do it (through the specific examples of solar heating and windmills), and for *whom* (homeowners who want to save money and who, presumably, are your intended readers).

EXERCISES FOR THINKING AND DISCUSSION

1. Select a topic you'd like to write about, following the suggestions in Chapter 2. To guide your thinking as you develop ideas, write out and put where you can see it a *statement of purpose*—the subject of your writing and what you hope to accomplish by writing about it. Include in your statement as many built-in directions as you can. Example: "Through three case histories of typical athletes, I want to dispel the myth that in this country athletic ability is valued more highly than is mental ability."

2. Which of the following goals contain built-in directions?
   a. I want to write about the importance of using renewable energy sources.
   b. I want to show, through examples of typical accidents and statistical information, why skateboarding is among the most dangerous of sports.
   c. I want my letter to the editor to be published.
   d. By ridiculing the city council's budget, with which I disagree ($30,000 for buried utility cables under Central Avenue? Why not $300,000 for pedestrian tunnels?), I want to make my letter to the editor unusual and amusing enough to be published.
   e. I want my readers to vote.

DEVELOPING YOUR IDEAS
Examining Your Opinions and Knowledge

Once you've picked a topic and begun to decide how you'll approach it to fulfill your goal, you'll need to think of what to say about it. Your *opinions about the subject* and your *knowledge of it* can often provide you with plenty of ideas. If you already have an opinion on the subject, you probably know more about it than you think you do.

It's useful to examine your opinions to provide your readers (and perhaps yourself) with explicit reasons for why you think the way you do. "I feel" or "I believe" or "Everybody knows" or "Of course" without supporting reasons usually aren't compelling enough to convince an audience. Skeptics can always counter your expression of belief with "So what?"; and "Everybody knows" is often a way to evade explaining what most people in fact *don't* know. To explore the bases of your opinions, ask yourself the three questions listed below. Write down your answers so you don't forget them; you may be able to use your notes in your paper. Here the questions illustrate how to find a way of discussing whether "Woman's place is in the home."

What are the bases for my opinion?

1. Long-established acceptance of someone else's (or my culture's) views on the subject?
   Only a mother can take care of her own children properly, so I don't want my woman (or myself, if writer is a woman) working outside the home.
2. Rebellion against the accepted views?
   "Woman's place is in the home" is as outdated as the buggy whip; woman's place is on the front line.
3. Habit or custom?
   Men should be society's principal wage earners. It's always been that way. When work is scarce, it's especially important for women not to take away jobs from men who must support their families.
4. Knowledge, either from personal experience or outside sources?
   Women should be as well-educated as are their husbands. Statistics show a much higher divorce rate among couples with a wide discrepancy in schooling. I know several doctors whose wives worked as secretaries to put them through medical school—and whose marriages broke up as soon as the men entered private practice.

Are any of these bases (specified in 1) for my opinions appropriate? inappropriate? Are my sources of information reliable? Am I relying heavily on custom? Have I analyzed this custom?

How much weight will I give to my opinion in comparison with the opinions of others?

Likewise, identifying and writing down what you know about a subject can help you focus on your topic and on possible ways to discuss it.

1. *What do I know about this topic from personal experience?*
   a. *Participation in an activity:* playing football or being an eyewitness to a newsworthy event
   b. *Knowing someone intimately:* self, parent, or friend
   c. *Performing a process:* cooking, playing a musical instrument, flying a plane
   d. *Living or traveling someplace and getting to know the people and the territory*
   e. *Working at a job*

    f. *Experiencing:*
      * *a condition:* illness, poverty, or affluence
      * *the law:* the Equal Opportunity Employment Act or the Bill of Rights
      * *a natural phenomenon:* tornado or extreme heat
      * *a circumstance:* your parents' divorce, a death, or an auto accident
      * *a crisis:* saving a life or nearly losing one

If you have personal knowledge of the subject, you can try to determine which aspects of your experience are relevant to your goal in the paper, and how much emphasis you wish to give them. In taking notes, it may help to underline or highlight the most potentially useful bits of knowledge and to put question marks by what is of dubious value or accuracy.

To supplement your personal information and experience, use points of view from other sources, such as books, articles, newspapers, films, television, radio, personal discussions, and courses in school.

You may find that several sources have contributed greatly to your understanding of your subject. Your next step would be to consider just how authoritative your sources are. A reliable source is worth its weight in footnotes; an unreliable source can undermine your discussion (see Chapter 13).

If you find yourself asking essential questions that you can't answer, or feel uncertain about what to say or about the truth of what you're saying, or if there appear to be gaps in your evidence or in your line of reasoning, these are indicators that you probably need to develop your ideas further by consulting other sources. Consider whether your paper will be improved by reference to any of the types of evidence listed below (see also the specific sources explained in Chapter 13).

1. *History* ("The fall of the Roman Empire shows us that a morally corrupt society will destroy itself.")
2. *Customs* ("Winners don't boast; losers don't cry.")
3. *Rules* ("Don't go out alone after dark.")
4. *Folk wisdom* ("Teenagers shouldn't eat chocolate or greasy food; they will ruin their complexions.")
5. *Maxims* ("Absence makes the heart grow fonder." or "Out of sight, out of mind.")
6. *Laws:*
   divine (the Ten Commandments)
   moral (Honesty is the best policy.)
   governmental (the Bill of Rights)

Are there other relevant perspectives? If you examine your topic from standpoints other than those you take for granted, you may see aspects of an issue that otherwise you would have overlooked. The word "PERSIAS" is a good device to help you remember some of the diverse possibilities. Its letters stand for points of view that are:

1. *Political* (What would a political scientist, a government official, a Republican, a Democrat, or a Socialist think about the topic?)
2. *Economic* (How would a banker, a consumer, a wage earner, a middle-income person, or someone temporarily unemployed respond to your subject?)
3. *Religious* (How might a theologian, atheist, or member of a particular religious denomination respond to your topic?)
4. *Social* (How would a member of your neighborhood, your town, your high school or college class, or a sociologist react?)
5. *Intellectual* (What are the views of a famous philosopher, say Plato, on your topic?)
6. *Aesthetic* (What might be the view of an architect, artist, city planner, or ecologist?)
7. *Sexual* (How might a male chauvinist—pig or piglet—feminist, or homosexual respond?)

Not all the perspectives raised here will be relevant either to your subject or to your purpose. Although you can eliminate those that are irrelevant, if you're arguing a point it will be important to acknowledge your awareness of alternative viewpoints and reply thoughtfully to them.

EXERCISES FOR THINKING AND DISCUSSION

When you try the following, take notes as a guide to later writing.
1. Choose a significant subject on which you have firm opinions and determine the bases for your views. Does your opinion reflect the views of others or your personal experience, knowledge of the matter from outside sources, or simply a popular view you've never analyzed? How long have you believed the way you currently do? If you've held your opinion for a long time, are you more firmly attached to it than you would be to an opinion of more recent vintage? Have you always taken your opinion on this matter for granted, or have you subjected it to reexamination? What has been the effect of either pattern on your thinking?
2. Discuss with one or more people the bases on which they hold opinions on a significant subject. Does your understanding of how and why they have arrived at their beliefs differ from their own? (Sometimes we can be clear-sighted about the opinions of others, even if we're nearsighted about our own.)
3. Pick a subject on which you might like to write, and a goal that you'd like your writing on the subject to accomplish. Think of the ways your knowledge or experience can supply you with ideas about your subject and your goal. Is your own information sufficient, or do you need to consult outside sources? which ones? How can you tell you're knowledgeable enough to begin writing an essay? Take notes on your thoughts to use as the basis of a paper.
4. Using the ideas you generated in 3, discuss the subject with someone else and see if you're able to accomplish your purpose orally. Then pay attention to your listener's commentary: Does your partner have a clear goal? Does he or she have enough information and ideas to start writing and to accomplish a purpose?

HOLDING A DIALOGUE WITH YOURSELF/ OR WITH OTHERS

Whether we admit it in public or not, all of us talk to ourselves at times. We play different roles, perhaps not to the extent that James Thurber's mousy Walter Mitty imagined himself a skilled surgeon or a stalwart ship captain, but roles that enable us to cope with actual or anticipated situations. Before asking for a raise, a mental rehearsal of the arguments for the extra money can help provide a necessary firmness to our request. Before erupting in righteous indignation, a silent recital of our grievances can help focus our anger. Such practice sessions are most fruitful when you also play the role of the other person and adopt that person's point of view and likely responses. This way you have a mental dialogue exchanged between yourself in whatever role you've chosen (mature and judgmental, innocent and inquiring, aggrieved and affronted) and someone else in an assigned role—such as a critical examiner, a curious but not knowledgeable listener, a dogmatic antagonist.

Such imaginary conversations can also help you develop ideas for writing. These dialogues will be most effective if you imagine various reactions from various people who might be interested in your subject. They should ask you to *define* ("What does that term mean?"), *explain* ("What do you mean?"), and *clarify* ("Which Roosevelt?"). They should question your *information* ("Are you sure that's right?"), your *sources* ("Who told you that?"), your *interpretations* ("Couldn't Hamlet have hesitated to obtain revenge from pity rather than from indecisiveness?"), and your *conclusions* ("That may be logical, but it's not true to life.").

For each of these questions, try to have an answer—or indicate that you will investigate the matter further. For each alternative interpretation, try to rebut it or offer a compromise. On the other hand, the new thoughts may cause you to change your mind and adopt the questioner's interpretation.

An actual dialogue with someone (your lab partner, for example) can be a particularly rewarding way to examine your topic. Then the dialogue will be real, though less predictable than when you're controlling all the voices, and it may provide you with material you'd never have thought of by yourself. Unlike a social conversation in which both speakers are presumed equal, in a dialogue to generate ideas, the person who chooses the topic is obliged to control the focus and emphasis.

Be sure to take notes or tape record these dialogues, whether with yourself or another person. Otherwise they, like the most brilliant of dinner table or telephone conversations, will be gone with the wind and of little help when you're trying to nail down ideas for a paper.

Suppose, for instance, that you were trying to decide which is better, life in a nuclear family or life in a communal setting. In the dialogue that follows, the speakers are *Ego*, representing yourself in your role as authoritative discussant of the issue, and *Alter*, you answering yourself from a variety of points of view intended to question your assumptions and make you think. However, *Alter* could just as well be another actual person performing the same functions. Square brackets [ ] indicate the principle or technique involved.

ALTER: Before you start your discussion, you'd better define "nuclear family" and "communal living." [*Define key terms wherever you first use them.*]

EGO: OK. (Picks up a pencil and takes notes at intervals throughout the discussion.) By "nuclear family" I mean a husband and wife living together in the same household for the purposes of mutual psychological, sexual, and economic support.

ALTER: Anything else?

EGO: Yes, the couple should divide labor for necessary household maintenance (cooking, shopping, cleaning, and so forth) and rearing children, if desired.

ALTER: Is that the whole family?

EGO: On occasion other blood relatives, such as aged parents, may be included. [*Definition of terms, to clarify the discussion and supply background information.*]

   "Communal living" consists of the same functions performed by people unrelated by blood or marriage living together in the same house or adjacent buildings. [*Definition of terms, on the basis of functions and relationships. Similarities and differences noted. Background information supplied.*]

ALTER: Because both nuclear and communal "families" do essentially the same things, is there a real difference between them?

EGO: Yes. Nuclear partners are related by a public commitment sanctioned by law (and sometimes religion) to live together in trust, sympathy, respect, and mutual assistance. Communes are much looser arrangements; people can join and leave easily. Because communal arrangements are not as binding, they require less commitment from their members than nuclear families do. [*Definition of the nature of the relationships, and the contrast between them.*]

ALTER: So what?

EGO: As a result, communes are more unstable. If people don't get along they can simply move out. [*Reference to customs of a small, communal society.*]

ALTER: What's wrong with that?

EGO: For one thing, the ease of moving in and out means that people in communes don't have to work very hard at living together, the way married people do. [*Conclusion derived from custom referred to in previous information.*]

ALTER: How do you know? [*The necessary question.*]

EGO: I lived in one for six months. But I grew up in a conventional nuclear family. [*Personal experience through participation in an event, living in relevant circumstances, and getting to know the people intimately.*]

   Although individual members may be more independent in a commune, they may also be more demanding, self-centered, and less involved with all the household duties that marriage partners have to perform. That was certainly true of the commune I lived in. [*Explanation based on limited experience and knowledge of members of both social groups.*]

ALTER: But you've only lived in one family and in only one commune—and that was for a *very* short time. How are you justified in making such a broad generalization on the basis of such limited evidence?

EGO: (Long pause for thought.) Well, I know people in other communes, too, and they behave pretty much like the people in the one where I lived. Oh, sometimes they're all involved with it when they start, but after they've been there awhile they often find that the group takes more of their time and effort than they want to spend on it. [*Generalization from limited experience.*]

ALTER: To be really convincing you should use some authoritative reference—a scholarly book or article that would provide some figures to support your restricted evidence.

EGO: OK. Good idea. I'll go to the library tomorrow. (Makes a note to do so.) [*Keep a list of matters on which to gather additional information later.*]

ALTER: Back to your last item. Can't commune members afford to be less involved with the total process than family members are? Communes permit a division of labor among many adult members so that no one or two people are burdened with everything, as they are in a marriage. [*Attempt to see another point of view, in this case the opposing perspective.*] "Many hands make light work." [*Maxim.*]

EGO: Well, that might be all right if shared work was the only factor involved. But suppose a commune member becomes ill, or disabled, or loses his or her job? If the other members don't want to help such a person, there's no way to make them. [*Social perspective. Logical extension of argument.*]

In the commune where I lived, when one guy lost his job we carried him for three months. But he stopped trying to find work, and with no bread coming in we just couldn't afford to feed him any longer, so we had to ask him to move out. [*Further example from personal experience.*]

ALTER: How far can you generalize on the evidence of a single case?

EGO: Not very far. Anyway, in a marriage the partners would take care of one another [*Reference to social custom.*] and the law would back them up on that. [*Vague reference to law.*]

ALTER: What laws? [*Appropriately pushing for the specifics.*]

EGO: Oh, there are laws saying that a husband has to support his wife.

ALTER: You'd better check on what they are so you can be more specific.
                    [The dialogue continues. . . .]

This process should continue until you have explored the subject sufficiently to write about it. You might need more than one session to pursue a complicated topic or to work through changes you made in your original topic.

Even this segment of a sample dialogue is only a partial representation of all the thoughts, fleeting and random, that occur when you try to develop a topic. Entirely omitted are the irrelevant thoughts, as well as the intrusions and distractions that occur when you're thinking or writing. These interruptions have to be coped with on the spot, but only briefly, so you can maintain your momentum. The checklist below makes clear the general principles for holding such a dialogue.

□ A Checklist for Holding a Dialogue with Yourself/or with Others

□ During the first stages of your dialogue, try to narrow your subject area, so you can treat your topic adequately in your assigned paper.

□ Determine your purpose.

□ Determine your intended audience.

□ Define your terms. Be sure to define whatever terms or concepts your audience might misinterpret, even if these are clear to you.

□ For the same reasons, supply background information where necessary for clarity or reference.

□ Keep track of definitions and information generated during the dialogue. Do this by taking brief notes on cards or slips of paper. Write on only one side; material on the reverse is likely to disappear from sight, and from mind. You can move these slips around later as you explore what's most important, and as you try out various organizational arrangements. During this process, you may reject some ideas as trivial or irrelevant.

□ Make notes of what additional information you need and, possibly, where to find it. Consult these sources later; do not interrupt your dialogue to do so.

□ Keep the intended length of your paper in mind, and gear the number and development of your ideas to it.

□ Don't stop if your dialogue is going along productively. If, however, your attention wanders or you're getting tired, take a break and come back to the dialogue when you're refreshed.

□ Examine your notes and dialogue to see if ideas cluster around a central point that identifies your subject and your attitude toward it. This could be your thesis and the focal point for your next draft.

□ Remember that while you're talking with yourself, you should be listening to yourself as well. If you're thinking clearly and using your reserves of knowledge and common sense, you will probably enjoy what you hear.

EXERCISES FOR DISCUSSION AND NOTE TAKING

1. To prepare for your next sustained writing, try a dialogue with yourself as a means of refining the topic and developing ideas. Follow the suggestions given in this chapter and in Chapter 2.

2. Try a dialogue with someone else to refine the topic and develop the ideas for a forthcoming writing. Take turns. First discuss the topic of your choice, in *Ego's* role, while your partner plays *Alter*. Then reverse roles and discuss the subject your partner wants to explore. Take notes while you're talking, if possible, to help remember what you said. Brief identifications of the main concepts and key words should be sufficient.

3. Try another dialogue, on the same or different subject, in which your partner (either yourself playing a role, or another person) has a different background, interests, or biases. How do these affect your choice of ideas? evidence? interpretations of evidence? language? Take brief notes as indicated in 2, above.

WRITING A ZERO DRAFT

Writing a *zero draft*—called "zero" because it's a free throw before your first draft—is similar to focused free writing. You write rapidly, honestly, abundantly, without stopping to edit or correct. However, it is different in that it is goal-directed: you have a topic and a purpose that you need to stick to. If you find yourself veering from these, you'll have to decide whether to allow yourself to explore the tangent. You can do so if it enhances your discussion, but not otherwise.

Other than that, there are no rules. You may want to have at hand the notes you've taken on your preliminary thinking, or you may prefer to set them aside and simply write what you know, trusting the preliminary thoughts to surface when they will. You can start anywhere you want, perhaps with the idea that interests you most or that you know best. If you push an idea, and look at it from some of the different perspectives identified earlier (such as political, social, or economic), you can develop clusters of related ideas: the economic significance of family units, the religious implications of families, and so on. As long as they relate to the same general topic, don't worry at this stage about which ideas you'll ultimately use or how to organize them. What you write first may turn out to fit best in the middle or at the end, but you can decide that after you've finished writing.

Giving It Some Structure

You may wish, however, to structure your writing of the zero draft somewhat more formally than the casual association of ideas suggested in the preceding paragraph. In this case, you can write by engaging in a dialogue with yourself as described above. Ask yourself the *Alter*-type questions. Then write down *Ego's* answers (and some of *Alter's* more provocative points), defining terms and supplying background information as necessary, noting where you will need to seek additional information later (don't stop to do it while you're writing rapidly). You will probably have a specific audience in mind—adapt the length and nature of your writing to it. Another approach is to engage in a dialogue first, either with yourself or with another. Take notes, and use them as the basis for your zero draft writing.

The reason for thinking of this writing as a *zero draft* rather than a *first draft* is to keep yourself feeling free about what you're writing and tentative about the content and organization. You should be willing to explore and experiment, add and delete, rearrange and rewrite what's down on the paper. If what you're saying at this stage turns out, happily, to fulfill your purpose, and to say just what you mean in exactly the right order, then this version may turn out to be both your first and final draft.

More likely, however, your zero draft will emerge in the state described by Donald Murray, the Pulitzer Prize winning author.

At that [initial] moment of composition all that [the writer] knows, and doesn't know, is there on the pages.

When he writes he discovers the holes in his argument, the logical steps which are passed over, the sentences which grow tang'ed upon themselves, the paragraphs which collapse, the words which are inadequate. But still he must push on through the [zero] draft. He cannot allow himself to be discouraged at this stage, or to be too critical. The happy accidents will be matched by the misfortunes, but still he must complete this piece of writing.[2]

When you finish this draft, look over what you've written to see whether your ideas have a central focus that could become the thesis of your next draft. Then, let it sit for awhile. Don't try to revise it immediately, but instead push the ideas that are still nagging to the back of your mind. They're likely to pop out, sharper and more provocative than before, while you're running or cooking or dozing off. If you keep a notepad handy, you can catch them before they get away.

EXERCISES FOR WRITING AND DISCUSSION

1. To prepare for your next sustained writing, write a zero draft according to the suggestions given here. When you're finished, examine it to see if you can find a thesis. Keep the draft for possible revision later (see Chapter 8 for suggestions on how to do this).
2. Exchange zero drafts with someone else. Examine your partner's draft to see:
   a. whether the ideas cluster around a central point;
   b. which sentences or paragraphs need additional information or ideas in order to be clear and convincing;
   c. which sentences or paragraphs are irrelevant.
   Explain to your partner what you've discovered and, if possible, make suggestions for improvement. You may find some of the ways of looking at topics discussed in "Examining Your Opinions and Knowledge," pp. 42–45, useful in accomplishing this.
3. Ask your partner to do the same for you. Take notes on the conversation to help you later if you decide to revise this draft.

PLAYING WITH ANALOGIES

An *analogy* is a comparison between two things or qualities that are similar in some respects but not all. Analogies are useful for explaining the unfamiliar, such as a place, object, quality, or process, in terms of the familiar: "Machu Picchu is the Mt. Everest of the Andes." "Racquetball is somewhat like tennis." Analogies are useful for making the abstract concrete: "Security is a down comforter on a frosty night." They can capture the elusive essence of a personality: with more than a hint of malice, philosopher Jean-Paul Sartre once described his life-long companion, Simone de Beauvoir, as "a clock in a refrigerator." Because they establish sometimes unforeseen connections among things, analogies are also useful in arguments: "If *A* and *B* are alike in certain significant respects, then what is true of *A* ought also to be true of *B*. . . ."

The comparisons in analogies may be *explicit* ("College students are like cattle. They are branded with numbers, prodded into lines. . . .") or *implied* ("the human zoo," "the blackboard jungle"). When you think in terms of analogies, whether they are overt or more subtle, you force yourself to examine each item being compared in ways that you might not ordinarily use. The simplest way to do this is to keep asking the question, "What is *X* like?" Your answers will either by structured "*X* is like . . ." ("Politics is like gardening . . .") or simply, "*X* is . . ." ("Politics is gardening . . .").

Generating Ideas

The process of making analogies can also be productive in developing ideas. Sometimes you can simply spin out a thought and see where it leads: "Our high school principal was a real Hitler, and he ran the school as if it were Nazi Germany. The teachers were the SS, and the students, all but a few, were Hitler Youth. . . ."

At other times you can explore what you know about the familiar to see if it will help you better understand the unfamiliar. One effective way to do this is by engaging in a dialogue with yourself, asking the same questions about the familiar and the unfamiliar aspects of your subject, and taking brief notes on your answers. Thus, to explore an analogy between government and business you might ask, "How is big government like big business?" You could then ask, "Are the leaders of each chosen in the same way? Should they be?" Then explore the possibilities of this aspect before moving to another subdivision of the main topic, "Do they obtain working capital the same way? Should they? Are they accountable to their constituencies, whether stockholders, customers, or citizens, in the same ways? Should they be?" This might lead to another fundamental consideration, "Are they accountable at all? What external forces operate to keep big government in line? Are these the same that influence big business?"

In discussing an analogy with yourself, you can play a number of roles, just as you would in dialogues with yourself on other subjects. As you do this, try to adopt the point of view, values, and language of the role you represent at the moment. For instance, in examining the analogy between big business and big government you might start with a familiar role, looking at both from the viewpoint of an ordinary citizen. In this role you could consider the aspect of size: "Big business and big government are so enormous that they are unresponsive to the needs of private citizens. Letters go unanswered, complaints are ignored, requests are simply shuffled from one person to another. Defective products and services from each are not corrected. . . ."

You might also compare big business and big government from the perspective of a middle management employee in each, concentrating on the organizational systems and bureaucratic hierarchy. Or you could view them as an economist might, considering the supply of goods and services, the efficiency of delivery, and the costs, in money, time, energy, human stress.

If you can find another person who fulfills one of the roles in your dialogue, see if she or he will examine your subject with you. That way you can experience the authentic perspective, judgments, and interpretations of someone who knows firsthand what you want to find out.

By whatever means you explore an analogy, stretch your thinking by pushing the comparison to the limits. Since analogies deal with phenomena that are similar but not identical, the inevitable differences between the two may eventually interfere and make the comparison seem ludicrous, irrelevant, or invalid. At some point you will have to acknowledge the differences, and at that point the analogy will break down, to be supplemented, perhaps, by points of contrast. Thus parents are quick to recognize the flaw in the child's standard argument by analogy, "But all the other kids get to do it," and reply, "You aren't 'all the other kids.'" Likewise, no matter how fruitful the comparison between big business and big government, some significant differences must be recognized. For instance, the board of directors of even a gigantic business has much narrower responsibilities than do the chief governmental policy makers. Each is elected by vastly different constituencies. In a capitalistic economy, most businesses are run to make profits; the government is nonprofit.

The more quickly the points of similarity in an analogy are exhausted, the less fruitful it is as a generator of ideas. Some analogies are best intended as brief illustrations rather than as panoramic murals. For instance, Tom Wolfe explains that drag racers' shirts with mottoes such as "born to lose" and "mother was wrong" are "'like a tattoo, only it's a tattoo they can take off if they want to.'"[3]; he then goes on to another point. If an analogy fights back, don't try to push it too far; stop before its brilliance fades.

EXERCISES FOR DISCUSSION AND WRITING

1. Either with a partner or in a group, examine one or more of the following analogies. How well does the analogy suit the author's purpose(s)? Could the point have been made equally well, or better, by using other analogies? Would straight explanation or discussion have been preferable? (For other analogies, see Chapter 12.)
   a. Happiness is a warm puppy.
   b. Kim is a Bo Derek, but Sandy is a Jane Fonda.
   c. Getting married at eighteen is like getting drafted at eighteen.
   d. We are the children who ride the horses on the merry-go-round in the amusement park. We pay a price to partake of the ride's inviting colors, music, pictures, and animals. We dream of reaching our goal by mounting the beautiful white steeds. But we riders soon find out that there is a constant battle between up and down, up and down; never an even gait. The continually circling ride makes matters worse. It will not slow down. Looking back is forbidden; we'll fall off if we turn around. We can't reach the goal; the little gold ring is frustratingly outside the ride's circumference. Only arms longer than ours can grasp it; we small people are seldom able to.

   —MELINDA WILSON, student

2. In a dialogue, either with yourself or with someone else, choose an analogy pertinent to your subject and explore it, taking notes on the points your dialogue generates. Push it until it becomes trivial, irrelevant, or until dissimilarities interfere with the comparison. At that point, however, continue to discuss the differences; recognition of these will help you develop new ideas.

   Identify a possible thesis, if one has emerged. Write an essay on the subject, if you wish.

3. In another dialogue, explore an analogy from the point of view of someone vitally interested in the subject but whose perspective is entirely different from your own. Try to adopt the point of view, values, and language of the role you represent at the moment. Follow the same procedure identified in 2, above.

   Then change roles, allowing your partner to enact the alternative part.

FORMULATING A THESIS

Thomas Edison defined genius as "one per cent inspiration and ninety-nine per cent perspiration." We can say the same about development of a thesis. Sometimes a good thesis will emerge quickly, almost spontaneously. But often, you'll need to expend a great deal of effort arriving at an acceptable one. Nevertheless, you should be ready by now to frame a *working thesis* on your chosen subject, a concise sentence that expresses the principal point of your essay and indicates your opinion about it. The working thesis will be a tentative statement of your main idea, and although it represents the focus of your current thinking, it can be changed at any time to conform to new ideas.

Your thesis, as it emerges, should be in statement form, an answer to the question or issue posed by the problem you've set out to solve. Depending on the type of writing you're going to do, the thesis can describe, define, or illustrate the topic, or it can analyze, criticize, or argue for or against it.

Suppose that you have narrowed the general subject area "housing" to the topic: "What is the relationship between a particular kind of housing and its inhabitants?" and have developed ideas on it, using some of the methods outlined earlier in the chapter. How would you begin to formulate a thesis? Depending on your stated purpose, many possibilities are open to you. The list below shows how each different purpose can lead to a thesis statement quite distinct from any of the others.

1. *General purpose:* I want to show why a particular person, place, or incident is significant to me; to others.
   Specific thesis: The six-bedroom baronial house in which I was reared in suburban Westchester County symbolized both my father's affluence and my family's disintegration.

2. *General purpose:* I want to describe, define, characterize, analyze, or otherwise explain the topic.
   Specific thesis: The amount of space that each person has in a household is directly proportional to how well the inhabitants get along.

3. *General purpose:* I want to provide directions on how to do something.

Specific thesis: Among the most important ways to make a house a home are the following: (a) devote thought and space to the preparation and eating of food; (b) have comfortable furniture for sitting and sleeping; (c) use plants, artwork, and personal objects to make the environment warm and human.

4. *General purpose:* I want to discuss or debate the causes, effects, or implications of something, or of some condition or phenomenon.
   Specific thesis: As the example of St. Louis's now-demolished Pruitt-Igoe housing indicates, replacing slum dwellings with high-rise apartment complexes causes more problems than it solves, such as rootlessness, lack of meaningful communication, and high crime.

5. *General purpose:* I want to extend an analogy to its reasonable limits.
   Specific thesis: People crowded into slums, like rats crammed into cages, turn vicious and destroy each other, and in the process destroy their society.

6. *General purpose:* I want to compare and contrast significant aspects of my topic.
   Specific thesis: Igloos are perfectly adapted to Eskimo culture; when Eskimos live in conventional Western dwellings they suffer physically and mentally.

7. *General purpose:* I want to present, explore, or solve a problem.
   Specific thesis: As housing prices continue to skyrocket, new means of financing must be made available to enable low-income and young people to buy suitable homes.

8. *General purpose:* I want to provide new information or a novel point of view about my topic.
   Specific thesis: Coed dorms should be abolished because they contribute to too much partying and too little studying.

Testing Your Thesis

Once you have arrived at a tentative thesis, you will want to see whether it works. It may survive the successive drafts you write and emerge unaltered. This is most likely to happen if you've completely thought through your subject before beginning a first draft, and if you know fairly precisely what you're going to say and what your line of reasoning will be.

However, your tentative thesis may change to reflect the alterations in your own thinking that can occur when you continue to examine your subject in detail as you write. The act of writing, as you have seen if you've written a zero draft or taken notes on the ideas arising from your dialogues, can help you discover new perspectives as well as new information. Or, as you write, you may find that the original emphasis of the thesis no longer reflects the proportioning of your paper as it grows. If you have become intrigued by a particular aspect of your topic, you may wish to concentrate on that and eliminate other aspects that you had initially thought you'd write on.

For instance, your original thesis might have been: "During World War II the Hollywood film industry manufactured extraordinarily effective films to promote the Allied war effort." If your investigation unearthed additional material about similar World War I films, you could expand the thesis to include World War I, as well. On the other hand, if your sources focused on World

War II documentaries your revised thesis might read: "During World War II the film documentaries about war-ravaged Europe and the Allied invasions in Normandy and North Africa were extraordinarily effective in promoting support of the Allied war effort."

Whatever thesis you finally construct should meet the following criteria:

1. The thesis should be interesting to yourself and your intended readers (see Chapter 2, pp. 33–36).

2. The thesis should be significant (see Chapter 2, p. 27).

3. The thesis should be clear, precise, and accurate. Try it out on a couple of sensible readers to see if they understand what you mean; you'll know it's clear if they can paraphrase it accurately. If you need to define terms or supply additional information, do so.

Suppose you're writing on "The government's housing policy is responsible for urban problems." You will need to specify which government—federal, state, or local. You will need to identify the specific housing policy or policies and to indicate the problems they cause. More meaningful theses would be more specific. Consider, for example:

> The federal government's urban renewal policy of replacing substandard housing with high-density high rise apartment complexes destroys established neighborhoods and causes enormous social problems.

or

> Federally guaranteed mortgages to low-income homebuyers drive up housing prices, contribute to defaults, and thereby cause urban decay.

4. The thesis should be emphatic. At times it might be tempting to use a vague, evasive, or ambiguous thesis, if you're still uncertain of what to say or if you're trying to avoid making a controversial statement that might antagonize some readers. But a wishy-washy thesis such as "Some people approve of integrated housing but others do not" is a losing strategy; it gives no direction to either your paper or your readers. A stronger thesis would forthrightly acknowledge the controversy: "Although the prospect of integrated neighborhoods still disturbs many people, in the long run it is the only effective way to eliminate ghettos and segregated schools."

You are most likely to state the thesis explicitly and early in your paper if you're writing a report, business memo, or a straightforward essay. At other times you may not want or need to be so direct. If you're building toward a climax, the thesis could come at the end. Or you might not state it overtly at all. Descriptive papers, character sketches, re-creations of a mood or atmosphere, or satires often imply their central point rather than state directly such sentiments as "How I loved the isolation—geographic and social—of my childhood in the Oregon backwoods." This is not to underrate the value of a working thesis; it simply means that you don't always have to let all the scaffolding show in the finished essay.

However, once you have a thesis that represents your thinking, write it out and place it prominently in your writing area while you're working on your paper. It will serve as both a guide and a reminder as you continue to develop ideas, organize them, and write and revise the paper itself.

EXERCISES FOR DISCUSSION AND WRITING

1. Which of the following are subject areas or topics (for definitions, see pp. 29–30)? Which are theses? Which theses would be suitable for a two- to five-page essay? Why or why not? For which audiences would each be most appropriate?
   a. Criminal justice in your home town
   b. Crime
   c. The U.S. courts are too lenient in prosecuting white-collar criminals.
   d. White-collar criminals
   e. What is white-collar crime?
   f. White-collar crime, its causes and costs
   g. White-collar criminals are more devastating to our society than violent criminals.
2. Frame suitable theses for the subject areas and topics listed in *1*, or choose a topic of your own. Make certain each thesis reflects one or another of the possible approaches you might take to the topic.
   a. Indicate its personal or general significance.
   b. Describe, define, characterize, analyze, or otherwise explain it.
   c. Provide directions on how to do it.
   d. Discuss or argue its causes, effects, or implications.
   e. Compare and contrast its elements, or the entire subject with another. Or encompass the subject in an extended analogy.
   f. Present, explore, and/or solve a problem.
   g. Provide new information or a novel point of view about the topic.
3. Exchange with a friend the set of theses you wrote in response to *2*. Evaluate each of your partner's theses according to the following criteria:
   a. Interest
   b. Clarity
   c. Accuracy
   d. Comprehensiveness
   e. Emphasis
   f. Originality
   Then evaluate your own according to the same criteria. Confer with your partner about your respective judgments of your own and each other's theses. How closely did you agree? Why?
4. Which of the following theses would be suitable for an essay of two to five pages? Which would not? In each case explain your reasoning.
   a. We should conserve energy because the world's irreplaceable natural resources are rapidly becoming depleted.
   b. The country needs strong laws to protect children against abuse, both physical and psychological.
   c. I'm afraid of heights, rats, and crime in the streets.
   d. The sores on the tops of the horses in the animal husbandry building are dreadful.
   e. College students should/should not be given academic credit for remedial courses.
   f. The most controversial character I've ever met is my great, great Uncle Julio.

If you are intrigued by any of these subjects, write an essay about it, based on your thesis and the ideas you develop to illustrate it.

NOTES

[1] Linda S. Flower and John R. Hayes, "Problem-Solving Strategies and the Writing Process," *College English*, 39:4 (Dec. 1977), 453.

[2] *A Writer Teaches Writing* (Boston: Houghton Mifflin, 1968), pp. 9–10.

[3] *The Kandy-Kolored Tangerine-Flake Streamline Baby* (New York: Noonday Press, 1965), p. 103.

CHAPTER FOUR
DESIGNING YOUR WRITING

Your form is your meaning, and your meaning dictates form.

— Joyce Cary

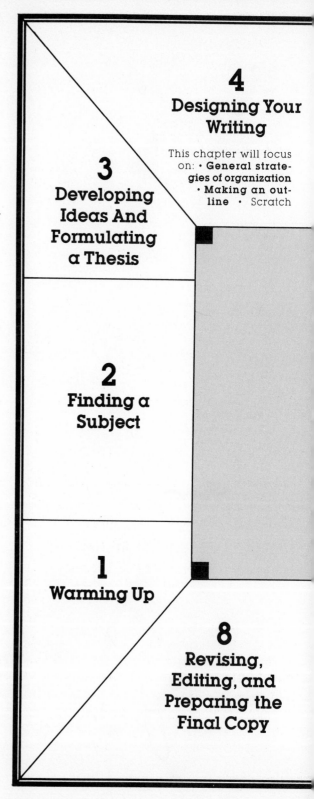

4
Designing Your Writing

This chapter will focus on: • **General strategies of organization** • **Making an outline** • Scratch

3
Developing Ideas And Formulating a Thesis

2
Finding a Subject

1
Warming Up

8
Revising, Editing, and Preparing the Final Copy

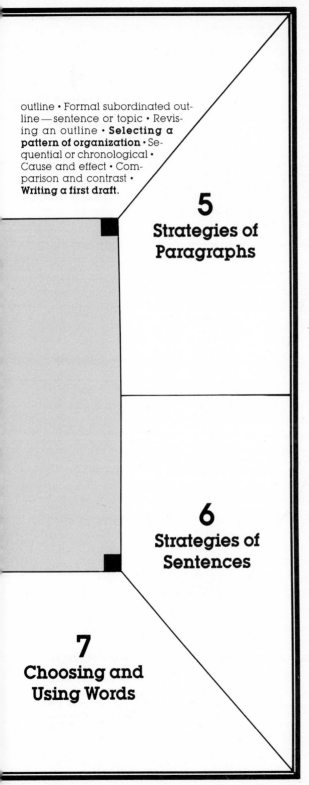

5
Strategies of Paragraphs

6
Strategies of Sentences

7
Choosing and Using Words

DISCOVERING A DESIGN

There are times when an absence of organization is fun. A single, spontaneous day spent in the sun, with no obligations, no set schedule, and nothing in mind to accomplish, can be delightful. So it is with writing. As you should be aware by now, writing freely can be enjoyable. You're playing with words and ideas, free to follow your train of thought as long as it holds your interest, yet equally free to switch to another subject or to stop altogether.

But totally free writing, like totally free living, has built-in limitations, the most obvious of which is that often it doesn't reach any effective conclusion. And, perhaps most important, its lack of structure may keep it from communicating very well.

When you are writing for an audience, as you will be with all but the most private pieces, it is a good idea to have a clear pattern of organization in mind. Among the many possible patterns of organization, this chapter will discuss some of the most common: sequential or chronological, cause and effect, and various arrangements of comparison and contrast.

If you can create an organizational pattern in advance, you can use it as a guide while you are writing. This will help you control your material instead of letting it dominate you. If, however, you need to write a preliminary draft in order to discover what you want to say, you may have to determine your organizational pattern *after* this is done, instead of beforehand. Then it can serve as a guide to the next draft.

GENERAL STRATEGIES OF ORGANIZATION

A basic question to consider in organizing your paper, any paper on any topic, is **What design will best accomplish my purpose?** What design will best provide directions on how to do something, for instance? Will the same or another design work better if I'm trying to argue the merits of a case? What pattern will best help me to explain how something works? Later this chapter will consider several common organizational patterns and indicate their advantages and disadvantages; Chapters 9–12 discuss other patterns.

A related and equally basic concern is **At what point in my writing do I want my readers to recognize what I'm driving at?** How you answer this will be likely to determine whether or not you make your thesis explicit and where you put it.

If you want your main point to be obvious from the outset, then you will want to state it near the beginning—not necessarily in the first paragraph, but certainly within the introductory section. A strong thesis statement will establish your point of view immediately and can function as a mini-outline to signal both the organization and emphasis of your paper. An early statement that "America's cultural values are most fully and fortunately manifested in fast food restaurants, professional sports, and television programs," would signal readers that the paper's three main divisions would be fast food restaurants, professional sports, and television programs, probably in that order. It would also indicate that these topics would be discussed approvingly in relation to how they expressed American cultural values. If, instead, you wanted to signal disapproval, your thesis could substitute *unfortunately* for *fortunately*.

In other cases you may prefer a more subtle approach to your subject, particularly if you want a light touch or if it's controversial and you know your audience to be unconvinced or hostile. In either case, you might want to work up to the thesis gradually and locate it farther along in your paper, after you have explored the subject, and the audience has gradually warmed up to it.

If your thesis is implicit, as it might be in the description of a place or person, or in the telling of a tale, it won't appear overtly in your paper at all. So its full importance may not be apparent until near the end, even though your entire essay will be working toward an expression of it.

Equally important to your ultimate design will be your decisions on **Which are my most important points in support of the thesis? Which are less important? Should they all be included?**

In a paper of limited length, you may want to select for development only the two or three most significant points that you generated when you wrote a zero draft or engaged in a dialogue with yourself or others (see Chapter 3) or when you did reading on the subject (see Chapter 13). *Don't feel that just because you've made a note on something you have to use it;* many preliminary ideas are discardable doodles. Even if all your ideas are good, in a longer paper you are still not likely to have enough space to devote to minor matters. However, you can save your notes on these in the hope that they may be suitable for another paper.

If you have taken notes while you were developing ideas, or if you have a zero draft, underline each topic and subtopic with a different color of ink and put check marks in the corresponding color beside related supporting items. The various colors will make related items visible at a glance, and you'll easily be able to sort out the main points and group the common subpoints. If you've written on only one side of the sheet, you can cut apart your notes so that a single point is on each slip of paper. If your writing is hard to understand, as scratch notes often are, you may wish to recopy the usable portions of your original notes on separate slips or index cards.

After you've organized your ideas into clusters, you'll want to determine **In what order should these points and supporting evidence be arranged?** There are many alternatives, depending on what you're trying to do, as later portions of this chapter and Chapters 9–12 will demonstrate. The movable slips or clusters of slips have the additional advantage of being flexible; you can rearrange them to try out different patterns until you arrive at the one that best suits your purpose and your subject.

You will also need to decide **Is it necessary to accommodate other ways of looking at my topic or to include arguments against it?** Your earlier investigation should have made these views apparent; your purpose and your audience will help determine whether to include them. **If so, where do these views belong in my paper?** Suggestions will follow later in this chapter and in Chapters 9–12.

As you're contemplating various arrangements, you will also need to think **How will I attract the readers' interest, right from the start, maintain it throughout, and provide a memorable conclusion?** Much of this book deals with various aspects of this issue; Chapter 5, pp. 111–119, focuses in detail on beginnings and endings.

TO OUTLINE OR NOT TO OUTLINE

If you've already thought through your subject and are holding in mind the main ideas in a suitable sequence, you may not need to write them down, especially if your paper is simple and short. Many writers don't. This is likely to be the case if the mode of your writing, say, a scientific report or a recipe, has a conventional format that you're following, which doesn't vary much for different subjects.

Or, if you followed the suggestions above, you may already have clusters of notes arranged in some recognizable fashion around main points and subpoints. In that case your paper is at least partially organized, and if the structure and emphasis are visible at a glance, you may not want or need to make an outline.

However, if you're having trouble organizing your ideas, an outline may be of considerable help, even if you have previously refrained from making outlines because they look as if they will involve more effort than they will save. Try a couple and see whether you're right. If they're more trouble than they're worth, you can always stop.

The principal justification for an outline is that it *makes visible the skeleton structure of the major and minor points of your paper.* You can refer to these while you're writing. Through the arrangement of points and evidence in major headings and subheadings, an outline indicates emphasis and subordination, showing which points are most and least important. At times, the outline also gives some indication of the proportioning of your paper by showing in more detail those parts that will receive greater development in the writing. If the proportioning reflects your emphases, fine; if not, you can add ideas or sub-points to the skimpy parts, or delete them from the sections that seem overly elaborate or repetitive (see "The Scratch Outline," below).

In theory, an outline can help you to write more efficiently. It can *save you a great deal of time.* Because it shows you where you're going and how you'll get there, you don't have to rethink your organization or identify your ideas anew each time you come to a new paragraph, as you may if your material is entirely in your head. Moreover, if you're following your outline and decide to add something new, you can compare it immediately with your thesis or subtopic to see whether you're sticking to the point. If you do discover a compelling idea to add, you can always alter your outline (and your thesis, if necessary) to accommodate it.

Indeed, if you find that your ideas are changing dramatically during the process either of outlining or of writing the essay, you are free to make radical alterations of your original pattern—including throwing the whole thing out and starting fresh. A rigid outline can be just as seductive as a random idea and can lead a writer just as far astray if it is illogical or otherwise inappropriate to the progression of its subject.

TRY THIS

Look at the ideas you've jotted down in thinking about what to write your next paper on. Do they cluster about topics? Are the main topics distinctive? emphatic? Is the relationship of the subordinate topics to the main topics clear? Can you identify the order in which each of the main topics (with its subordinate satellites) will appear in your paper? Do you have in mind the supporting evidence you'll use?

If you can answer *yes* to each of these questions, an outline may not be necessary. One or more *no* answers will tell you that you need to have a clearer pattern of organization before you can proceed. An outline can help to provide this.

WRITING AN OUTLINE

Outlines, like other architectural structures, can be plain or fancy, simple or complex. If you decide, either before or after writing a preliminary draft, that an outline can help to shape and control your writing, you will need to make some basic decisions about its nature.

If your writing is to be short and simple, perhaps an exam answer or an essay of a few paragraphs, then a *scratch outline*, consisting of informally grouped clusters of related ideas, may suffice. If, however, your essay will be longer and more complicated, then it is likely to benefit from the more thoroughly structured organization that a *formal subordinated outline* can provide. Through a system of numbers and letters, this outline will graphically indicate the relationships and emphases among major and minor ideas.

Whatever you have decided, as you use the outline to determine the emphases of your major and minor ideas, you will find the following questions useful in considering what to include or omit.

Does each item (an idea, detail, or necessary interpretation) support or illustrate my thesis or a subpoint of the thesis?

Are the items arranged in some order that

1. groups related matters?
2. emphasizes the most important?
3. subordinates the less important?
4. makes the interrelationship of each grouping clear, both within its own group and with relation to other groups?
5. satisfies some logical or psychological sense of progression from beginning to end?

To increase the emphasis on an item you can place it prominently as a topic or subtopic heading, and you can develop it more fully. To decrease its emphasis, you can put it in a less conspicuous spot and say less about it.

You will find that these general principles of outline construction suit a variety of contexts.

The Scratch Outline

A scratch outline is to a formal subordinated outline what a quick lunch is to a four-course dinner; both may help you fill up but take different amounts of preparation and thoroughness.

If you make notes while you're thinking of ideas to write about, a scratch outline may be the easiest way to organize them, especially if your writing will be brief—a paragraph or memo, a short essay, or an exam answer. The *scratch outline* is usually simple, a short, perhaps fragmentary listing of your main points in the order of their probable appearance. Beside or beneath each main point you might also note a few *key words* to indicate subtopics.

Suppose you were jotting down notes while thinking of ideas for an essay exam question that asked you to "Discuss and interpret two or three attributes of American culture as manifestations of the country's values." You probably can't color code them or cut up the bluebook to move them around, as you might in another context. But you could make a scratch outline to help you decide what's important, where it should go, and what needs more (or less) development as it pertains to your prospective thesis.

Let's say you've decided to focus on *professional sports* and *fast food restaurants* as attributes of American culture. In search of a thesis you might have clustered a number of ideas around these two topics:

professional sports
   superstars
   enormous salaries
   high-stakes gambling
   television viewers — millions
   large crowds
   athletic prowess
   drug use
   high pressure
   constant travel
   minority success
   young players
   strength
   glamor

fast food restaurants
   plastic — food, decor
   drive-in
   carry-out
   hamburgers
   tacos
   fish and chips
   litter
   hot-dog stands
   little packets of
      sugar, mayonnaise,
      ketchup
   teen-age hangouts
   families with little
      children
   cost
   cafeterias
   fried foods
   Chinese food
   artificial wood
   orange decorations
   nutrition
   pizza

A quick look would reveal that the items are grouped *only* under the principal categories *professional sports* and *fast foods*. Within each category, their emphasis, interrelationship, and subordination aren't yet clear, nor do you have a thesis that shows any connection between the two main groups. The number of items under each main heading indicates that you appear to have somewhat more to say about fast foods than about professional sports.

Your first task will be to determine a thesis that allows you to cover whatever of these main ideas you want to focus on. Because you're writing an exam question against a deadline, you don't have time to test out too many alternatives, so after a couple of tries you might come up with: "Professional sports and fast food restaurants are two attributes of American culture that manifest the country's overemphasis on speed, youth, and flashiness."

The thesis restricts your discussion of American culture to professional sports and fast foods. Moreover, its even more specific restriction to the attributes of speed, youth, and flashiness predicates the organization of the paper, for you can discuss each of these three characteristics in relation to both professional sports and fast foods.

Leave ample space between grouped items to accommodate later changes. Your revised grouping may look like this at first:

Thesis: "Professional sports and fast food restaurants are two attributes of American culture that manifest the country's overemphasis on speed, youth, and flashiness."

1. Professional sports
   speed—fast motion, high pressure, constant travel
   youth—young players, youthful physical ideal, American youngsters imitate
   flashiness—superstar players, glamorous lifestyle, media glorification, high-stakes gambling
2. Fast foods
   speed—hasty preparation, rapid eating, drive-ins
   youth—teenage hangouts, family restaurants, youth-oriented television advertising
   flashiness—plastic, bright colors, loud music, neon lights

Here the topics, with some indication of subtopics, are arranged in the order you intend to discuss them. The new listing has enabled you to *group many of the characteristics you had listed before*, to *add some new ones* (fast motion, media glorification, rapid eating), and to *eliminate some terms that were on your original list* (large crowds, minority success, hamburgers and other specific foods). However, the scratch outline doesn't reveal the emphasis you will give to each category, and this listing of topics still doesn't indicate what you're going to say about the meaning of the individual items as they relate to American culture.

Some sense of these relationships can be provided by adding explanatory words or phrases to each category [additions italicized]:

1. Professional sports
   speed—fast motion, high pressure, constant travel *promote hyperactive American image, but passive—millions of spectators, few adult players*
   youth—young players, youthful physical ideal, American youngsters imitate— *physical fitness desirable; athletic success undervalues intelligence, creativity, sensitivity*

flashiness—superstar players, glamorous lifestyle, media glorification, high-stakes gambling—*media glorification of superstar players' glamorous lifestyle encourages superficiality*

2. Fast foods

speed—hasty preparation, rapid eating, drive-ins, *reflect America's obsession with haste and mobility; indigestion*

youth—teenage hangouts, family restaurants, youth-oriented television advertising, *highway centered rather than home centered*

flashiness—plastic, bright colors, loud music, neon lights—*focuses on appearance rather than nutrition*

This outline still doesn't indicate the subordination or proportioning of the ideas as they will appear in your essay, but it does show the arrangement and gives many specific details. It might be too ambitious to try to cover all the ideas in an essay written in an hour; if so, you could eliminate some of the details or some of the subcategories, perhaps *flashiness*. The key words in the outline will serve as cues for your more extensive thinking on the subject, but you won't have wasted valuable time making an elaborate outline. It's better to spend most of your limited time writing the answer itself.

The Formal Subordinated Outline

If you want to write a longer essay and have ample time to work out the relationship among ideas in advance of your writing, you can construct a *formal subordinated outline*. This more elaborate form of outline not only groups the main ideas but indicates which are most (or least) important and will consequently receive the most (or least) emphasis. Formal subordinated outlines also show the interrelationship within and among groupings and indicate the progression of ideas from beginning to end. Consider the model below of a formal subordinated outline:

I. First main idea of division of topic
   A. Idea, information, or interpretation necessary to discuss I
      1. Idea, information, or interpretation necessary to discuss I.A
      2. Idea, information, or interpretation necessary to discuss I.A
         a. Idea, information, or interpretation necessary to discuss I.A.2
         b. Idea, information, or interpretation necessary to discuss I.A.2
            1. Idea, information, or interpretation necessary to discuss I.A.2.b
            2. Idea, information, or interpretation necessary to discuss I.A.2.b
            [additional enumerated points as needed]
   B. Idea, information, or interpretation necessary to discuss I
     [other subdivisions as needed, on the same format as I.A]
II. Second main idea or division of topic
    [other subdivisions as needed, on the same format as I]

(This format may be continued with as many Roman numerals for main ideas as necessary.)

As you can see, there are conventions to be met in writing such an outline. Notice that:

Numbers and letters alternate, beginning with Roman numerals and capital letters. These are followed by Arabic numerals and lower case letters from then on.

Major divisions result in two or more subdivisions—a I requires a II, an A requires a B. You cannot subdivide a section into only one part, so if you find that you have a single letter or number, incorporate that point into the larger unit that immediately precedes it.

Points made at the same level are approximately equal in importance. Thus in the essay to be derived from a formal outline, points I, II, and III are equivalent; I.A and I.B are equivalent in their significance to the discussion of I, and so on.

The greater the elaboration and development of subpoints in the outline, the more fully developed the corresponding section of the paper is likely to be. Nevertheless, the divisions of your outline will not necessarily correspond to the paragraphs in the paper derived from it. In other words, point I.A.1 won't necessarily be a paragraph, nor will point I.A.2; the two points could be combined in a single paragraph, or each point might require several paragraphs to discuss. However, the portion of your outline that is the most fully developed is likely to project an equivalent development in your paper.

TOPIC OUTLINE OR SENTENCE OUTLINE

When you're making an outline you have a choice of how complete or fragmentary you want the statements of your ideas to be. You will also have to decide how fully developed each item in the outline will be. You can ask, "Will I know what I mean if I write in sentence fragments or key words? Or do I need whole sentences to jog my memory?" Your answer will determine whether you write a *topic outline* or a *sentence outline*. In either case you will want to decide whether the main and subordinate ideas are expressed in sufficient detail so that you know exactly what you mean when you look at them. If you don't, you may need to add modifiers or even additional subpoints to clarify what you want to say.

The Topic Outline

The *topic outline* consists of concise phrases that contain *key words* central to your discussion. Because of its abbreviated format, you can write it quickly, and arrange and rearrange its parts with dispatch. If each phrase in the outline is sufficient to jog your memory while you're writing the paper, then this format will be sufficient.

Here is the first part of the topic outline Jennifer McBride prepared for her paper "The Rock Fantasy," printed on pp. 239–241. [Note: Key words are italicized in the thesis and in the outline.]

I. Thesis: *Rock concerts attract young people* because of their *magical, otherworldly atmosphere,* in which the performing *idols manipulate the audience* into *defying convention, sexual fantasies,* and *hero worship* of the stars.
II. The *nature* of *rock concerts*
  A. *Music*
    1. Very *loud*
    2. Pulsating *rhythm,* pronounced *beat*
    3. *Out of tune*
    4. Sexy *lyrics*
  B. *Unusual stage effects* create *otherworldly atmosphere*
    1. *Bizarre lighting*
    2. *Mock hangings*
    3. *Fire breathing*
  C. The stage is the stars' habitat [transition to next section]

Heading I is simply a statement of the thesis. A thesis statement is useful to help you direct your thinking as you begin to draft an outline or an essay, even if it won't appear as the first sentence (or even in its original form) in your finished essay.

Heading II represents the first major topic area of the discussion, in this case, "The nature of rock concerts," divided into its major subtopics, A "Music," and B "Unusual stage effects." Appropriate key words have been employed to indicate how each subtopic will be developed. Other headings and subdivisions for later sections would be determined in the same way. It is not always necessary to include headings for transitions, as C ("The stage is the stars' habitat") does here, unless you particularly want to emphasize the connection when you write about it.

TRY THIS

Outline the rest of Jennifer McBride's essay, using I and II of her topic outline as a guide. Underline the key words.

The Sentence Outline

A *sentence outline* states each point and subpoint in complete sentences. The sentence form obliges you to say something *about* each of the points on the outline. Its greater length, which makes it longer to write than the topic outline, is some insurance against memory lapses or topic outlines so vague as to be meaningless.

The following is an outline of the topic explored in Chapter 3 in the dialogue with yourself or others.

TITLE: NUCLEAR FAMILIES OR COMMUNES?

Thesis: "The nuclear family is better than communal living for its members and for society."

I. The introduction is a definition of terms.
   A. The nuclear family consists of a husband and wife living in the same household, possibly with other blood relatives.
   B. Communal groups consist of multiple adults living in the same household, married or otherwise.
      1. Communes may also include other blood relatives, possibly the members' children.
      2. Some communes include visitors, too.

II. The advantages of nuclear families outweigh the disadvantages.
   A. Nuclear families offer several advantages to their members and to society.
      1. The sanctions of law and custom protect the interests of family members.
         a. Welfare and social security laws pertain to legal members of families.
         b. Family members have a strong commitment to their family unit; it's hard to disband.
      2. Children in nuclear families are likely to have a stable and secure environment.
         a. The parents provide love.
         b. The parents provide role models.
         c. The parents set rules and provide rewards and consistent discipline.
      3. Nuclear families provide extended care and support for the weak and dependent: children, sick, disabled, elderly.
   B. The major disadvantage of nuclear families is the enormous responsibility placed on the parents.
      1. The parents bear the family's financial burdens.
      2. The parents bear the family's psychological burdens.

III. The disadvantages of communal living outweigh the advantages.
   A. Communal groups have two major advantages.
      1. Their members have more independence and less responsibility for the total functioning of the group.
      2. Their members can be more specialized in their contributions to the group.
   B. Communal groups have several major disadvantages.
      1. They have no legal sanctions and little community support.
      2. Commune members have a weaker commitment to their group than members of nuclear families do; it's easy to leave and for the group to disintegrate.
      3. Children in communes are likely to be victims of an unstable, insecure environment.
         a. Their caretakers are diverse and changing.
         b. Consequently, their caretakers provide shifting and inconsistent role models.
         c. Their caretakers provide inconsistent application of rules, rewards, discipline.
      4. Communes, inherently unstable, offer no guarantee of extended care and support for the weak: children, sick, disabled, elderly.

IV. Conclusion: The nuclear family is better than communal living for its members and for society.

The completed outline should give you a sense not only of the major points you want to make and their supporting ideas but also should clue you in to the proportioning of those points—how much emphasis each will get. Will you devote a single paragraph to each major heading and include all its related subheadings within that paragraph? If you were using the outline presented here, that would mean spending one paragraph on the advantages and disadvantages of nuclear families, and another on communal living, resulting in either very crowded paragraphs or a very short paper. Or does the complexity of the subject warrant discussing each of the main advantages and disadvantages in a separate paragraph? A third possibility is to compress some of the ideas in the outline into a single paragraph and to expand others by elaborating on many details in several additional paragraphs.

In addition to using the outline as the basis for determining the emphasis and proportioning of your paper, you can also use it to examine your organization. Does the pattern you've come up with represent the best possible arrangement of your ideas? Or would a reorganization of the main ideas or subheadings make your presentation more logical, compelling, or emphatic? What, for instance, would the effect be in the outline above if the sections on nuclear families and communal living were reversed? Or if the disadvantages of nuclear families were discussed before the advantages? Outlines are easy to cut up and rearrange. You can play around with the headings in an outline the way you can play around with pieces of a jigsaw puzzle, moving them in different combinations until you hit upon the one in which the pieces fit perfectly.

Does It Work?

You'll find your outline most helpful if you think of it as a slender support of slightly flexible bamboo rather than a massive, rigid steel framework. For it bears a tentative relation to the essay you will ultimately write. It provides support and offers direction but remains capable of change if you wish to alter the pattern of your paper or to expand or condense any of your major points or illustrations. You will want to examine your outline, whether it is in sentence or topic form, to see

1. whether it is organized logically and in some appropriate pattern
2. whether there are any serious omissions in the line of reasoning
3. whether the proportioning reflects what you want to emphasize
4. whether or not you have stuck to the subject.

If the outline doesn't reflect what you want your paper to emphasize, in the order you want to say it, change it *before* you start to write. This will save you a lot of time later on.

SUGGESTIONS FOR OUTLINING AND WRITING

1. Imagine that you have to write an exam question or in-class essay on one of the following subjects. Jot down topics and subtopics, develop a thesis, and write a scratch outline in preparation for what you will ultimately say. Allow yourself only as much time to do this as you would have to do it in class.

co-ed dorms	military service	Olympic games
easy courses	the draft	world population
for athletes	television programs	control
welfare reform	cloning	

2. Expand your notes for the subject you developed in *1* into a sentence outline suitable for an out-of-class essay.
3. Write a subordinated topic or sentence outline of the ideas developed when you explored your subject through a dialogue, writing a zero draft, or playing with an analogy, as suggested in Chapter 3. You should already have a thesis, but if not, frame one before you try to make the outline. You can always adapt the thesis to the outline if new ideas arise while you're working on it.
4. Arrange whichever of the following items you find appropriate to form a subordinated sentence outline that discusses the following thesis: "America's character is manifested in its fast food restaurants." You may add or delete items or modify those listed, as you wish.

hot pretzels	plastic or cardboard	family restaurants
tacos	fish and chips	pizza
delicatessens	litter	cafeterias
orange	hotdog stands	nutrition
decorations	fried foods	Chinese food
hamburgers	odor	eat in your car
artificial	advertising	teenagers
wood	drive-in	cost
carry-out		

little packets of sugar, mayonnaise, ketchup

5. Identify what is wrong with the following outline for an essay.

Thesis: Commercial television has not fulfilled its potential to educate and inspire the American public.

  I. Was there life before television?
    A. Libraries
    B. The Chatauqua lecture circuit brought culture to millions in American small towns.
      1. Concerts
      2. Lectures and plays
      3. Thomas Ingersoll and William Jennings Bryan were especially popular.
  II. Definition of commercial television
III. Most prominent types of programs
    A. Sports—football, baseball, Olympics

    B. News takes up much prime time.
      1. Newscasters emphasize the visual but do not explain the causes and effects of what they show.
      2. Beautiful people
      3. Game shows make the participants look like fools.
        a. Honeymooners on vacation
      4. Fat people exploited
IV. Adventure programs
    A. Action
    B. Sex
    C. Violence is condoned and people are degraded.
      1. It is the same in children's cartoons.
V. Conclusion: The American public gets what it deserves.

6. Using what you can salvage of the above ideas, revise the outline in 5 into a subordinated sentence or topic outline designed to produce a good paper.

SELECTING A PATTERN OF ORGANIZATION

"Form follows function," the precept of master architect Frank Lloyd Wright, applies equally well to organizing writing. This does not mean that there is only one form for one function. Nevertheless, certain forms accommodate certain purposes of writing better than others do, although they permit many variations and combinations. Some types of writing, such as analysis or argument, permit more organizational options than do types with a more restricted range, like technical reports or job application resumés. Yet even in those cases where your options are most numerous, the organization will depend in part on your purposes, your emphases, your audience, and how you think you can best handle the subject. We will consider here several of the most common forms as they fulfill their particular functions; other organizational patterns will be discussed in Chapters 9–12.

Sequential or Chronological Organization

The events of our lives unroll according to clock, calendar, and biological programming as we are born, mature, and die. Processes begin, operate, and are completed. To the extent that time rules our lives and governs such sequences, it determines our presentation of time-bound phenomena. For *in sequential or chronological organization the main points are usually arranged to correspond to the order in which the process, event, or phenomenon they describe would normally occur.* First things come first, second things come second, and so on to the last, though there are variations on this tidy scheme.

    Sequential organization is often used to *explain a process or phenomenon,* how something was created (a volcano) or made (paper); how it behaves (the Legionnaire's Disease virus), works (LED watches), or ought to work (representative democracy). This pattern is conspicuous in the how-to-do-it essay, whether it tells how to make rabbit pie, rebuild a Cadillac engine, or write a computer program.

In such essays the thesis is likely to be stated explicitly near the beginning, or to be implied by the title ("How to . . ."), and followed by the main points and related supporting evidence in sequence (see Figure 4.1 on p. 76). It starts with the beginning of the process ("First, catch your hare.") and proceeds, step-by-step in sequence, to the end ("Let it cool in the pan and voilá! the perfect rabbit pie."). Because each step builds on those that have preceded it, once you have set the process in motion you cannot easily depart from the procedural sequence without confusion. However, every step may not need equal explanation. You might want to spend more space on the steps that are more unusual, harder to understand or perform, or that permit alternative interpretations. For instance, in an essay on "How to Play Baseball," if you wanted to emphasize pitching you could explain the various styles at the point in the sequence where pitching is most important.

Chronological organization can, like the progression of the calendar, move inexorably forward from beginning to end, just as the organization of a process is likely to do. This pattern is particularly appropriate for narrations and the telling of tales: "*Then* Red Riding Hood reached her grandmother's house, and *then* she went in and saw the hulking shape in her grandmother's bed, *after which* she. . . ."

Chronological organization is also a commonly used pattern for the narration of the full or partial life stories of ourselves or others, real or imagined. Chronology forms the organizational basis of many interviews, biographies, autobiographies, as well as diaries and personal letters. Thus in "Confessions of a Compulsive Overeater," student Carolina Broccardo invites readers to eavesdrop on her running debate with herself over whether "To overeat or not to overeat?" (italics supplied to denote time words and other indications of time):

> *Eleven a.m. The third day* of my semester break. I am home with nothing to do, so I decide to bake chocolate chip cookies. *Two hours later* I am still baking. I have snitched so much dough from the first batch that I *have to bake another* or run the risk of having my mother ask me how it is that a full, twelve-ounce bag of chocolate chips yielded so few cookies. But the dough is *so* tasty.
>
> *Twelve midnight. The end* of another uneventful party. A bowl half filled with peanut M&Ms beckons me. I sit by the bowl and *begin* downing the candy. Why not? The party's *almost over* and no one's said more than "hello" to me all night. I might as well save the hostess the chore of putting the M&Ms away.
>
> *Eight p.m.* A family birthday party. I nonchalantly pass up the cake and ice cream. *Three hours later, when* no one is looking, I cut myself a "sliver" of cake. And another. And another. And still another. . . .

Historical events or phenomena that occurred in a particular sequence, such as meetings, courtroom trials, riots, and political conventions, are also reported chronologically (italics supplied to indicate words denoting chronological sequence):

(*text continues on page* 77)

Figure 4.1

A TYPICAL PATTERN OF SEQUENTIAL OR CHRONOLOGICAL ORGANIZATION*

* (The numbers and letters refer to entries on an outline.)

I. Introduction: The thesis (if explicit) is likely to appear in the introduction or shortly thereafter.

II. Major point 1
   A. That which occurs first in the process or chronological sequence
      1.
      2.
   B. Details explaining or illustrating major point 1
   C.

Logical or chronological progression
to the next point

III. Major point 2
   A. That which occurs second in the process or chronological sequence
   B.
      1. Details explaining or illustrating major point 2
      2.
      3.

Logical or chronological progression
to the next point

IV. Major point 3 . . . and so on until the process or sequence is completed
   A.
   B.
   C.
      1.
      2.   } This complicated step required
        a.   extra explanation.
        b.
   D.

V. Conclusion: Represents the completion of the process. Might include an overview of the finished product, or a prediction about its future performance.

completely. But in spite of its imperfections, the bracelet could not be any more perfect to me than it is because of the sentimental value it holds.

I will always remember the first time I saw a jade bracelet of this kind, when I was eight. It was in a museum collection of Chinese jewelry. I found it amazing that the bracelet could be a perfectly polished ring carved from one single piece of jade, and thought it must be very valuable.

I went home and told my mother, who explained to me that such bracelets were quite common among Chinese women, and varied greatly in expense and quality. Some women would get jade bracelets when they were very young and wear them until they died. Since jade is a soft stone, it can break very easily when treated roughly. My mother told me that if a bracelet did break, the woman would wrap all the fragments up in a handkerchief and save the pieces for the rest of her life, for even the pieces would bring good luck. This gave me an image of the Chinese woman, and having my bracelet will always remind me of my culture and the individual that I am.

I remember very clearly the night my parents gave me the bracelet. It was in my sophomore year of high school, and I had stayed out past my curfew of midnight. When I got home that night, my parents gave me a lecture on responsibility. I expected to be placed on restriction, but instead they gave me a jade bracelet. I was totally shocked . . . but when I went to bed that night I was supremely happy.

The next morning, my father told me that because they had gone shopping for the bracelet, he had not gone to the racetrack and had missed out on winning $20,000 because of me. However, he said that I was worth it.

The bracelet will always remind me of those two days and the love that exists in my relationship with my parents, even though nothing is ever said. I know that no matter what I may do, my parents will always love me and accept me the way I am.

Since I got the bracelet, I have not taken it off—mostly because I don't want to, but also because my hand has outgrown the bracelet and therefore it is stuck on permanently. My bracelet means so much to me that if it should ever break I would be enormously upset. But then, I could always save the pieces for good luck.

4. Identify an incident or object in your own life that is as important to you as Lai Lee's bracelet is to her. Explain its history and its current meaning by writing your main points and subpoints on index cards or slips of paper. Move these around to arrange your narrative in various ways, through telescoping or skipping events, or using one or more flashbacks. When you've found an organization that best expresses your sense of the material, use that as the basis for an essay.

Cause and Effect Organization

An examination of a phenomenon or condition in terms of its causes and effects can help you and your readers to understand it better. Because many phenomena have more than a single cause and produce multiple effects, showing some of these in your discussion will help you to avoid oversimplifying the issue and to present its full significance.

Consider, for example, the fact that American schoolchildren and adults are estimated to watch television an average of four hours a day. Why do they do this? You could examine many actual or probable causes, no one of which would be a sufficient explanation. Does television satisfy an American craving for news and good drama? or for sports and other entertainment? Or do Americans watch television from boredom? lack of resourcefulness to try other pastimes? habit? its inexpensive cost? or the convenience of having a television set at home? You could also examine some of the alleged effects of this phenomenon. Does television watching create a greater awareness of people, places, and events around the world? an unprecedented opportunity to see major events live—the moon landing, the Olympics, political conventions? an acceptance of newscasters' overly simplified explanations for complicated events? a nation-wide lowering of reading ability? a greater tolerance of representations of sex and violence? inflated revenues for television advertisers? a new class of pseudo-heroes—prominent entertainers and sports stars?

As you note possible causes and effects, you will reject some as obvious, trivial, unprovable, or too distracting to the focus of your discussion. You may decide to restrict the scope of your paper by concentrating exclusively on several of the causes (or effects). What you decide will help to determine how you organize your discussion.

Once you decide to treat the causes and the effects of a phenomenon, you may organize it according to the *chronological sequence* of the causes: if A has in fact caused B, which caused C, and so on. (In this pattern the first effect be-comes the second cause which produces the second effect, and so on. . . .) You could do the same with effects.

But not all cause and effect relationships are sequential. The extensive watch-ing of television might have many simultaneous causes (or effects). You may be aware that readers of essays, like listeners to speeches, tend to pay attention to the first and last points in a series but at times let their attention stray from what's in the middle—as the snores during Sunday morning sermons testify. So, since you want to arrange your points not only to attract your readers' attention but to keep it, you may decide to discuss the most significant or star-tling causes first, and to develop them the most fully. The lesser points could come later, if at all, and be discussed more briefly.

A discussion of the effects of a phenomenon, Z, would be arranged in the same way as in Figure 4.2, except that the introduction would probably begin with a thesis statement that said, "Phenomenon Z produces the effects A, B, C, D. . . ."

SUGGESTIONS FOR DISCUSSION AND WRITING

1. Find an article describing a situation with which you are familiar that probably has several causes. Through discussion with a partner or your class, identify as many causes for the situation as possible. Which seem the most likely? the least likely? Rejecting the least feasible causes, outline the major points you would discuss in an essay explaining the causes of this event. Write the essay, if you wish.

2. Examine, in discussion or in writing, your decision to attend the particular college or university in which you are now enrolled. What were the causes of your decision? Was the choice a wise one? the best possible one you could have made?

3. Think of a mistake in judgment you have made, or a disagreement you have had with someone, that you now regret. What were the probable causes of this (Did you, or your antagonist, make a misjudgment from ignorance? prejudice? habit?)? What have

Figure 4.2
AN ALTERNATE PATTERN FOR DISCUSSING THE CAUSES OF A PHENOMENON

I. Introduction: Identifies the phenomenon, Z. May or may not contain the thesis.

II. Major point 1: Explanation of Cause Q (involving, perhaps, still other causes)
    A. Interpreted evidence for explanation of Cause Q
    B., C., D. Same as A
    E. Relation of Cause Q to the phenomenon, Z

Transition

III. Major point 2: Explanation of Cause R
    A. Interpreted evidence for explanation of Cause R
    B., C., D. Same as A
    E. Relation of Cause R to the phenomenon, Z

Transition

IV. Major point 3: Explanation of Cause S
    A. Interpreted evidence for explanation of Cause S
    B., C. Same as A
    D. Relationship of Cause S to the phenomenon, Z

Transition

V. Major (or minor) point 4: Minor causes T, U, V
    A. Causes identified; perhaps explained as a group; little individual explanation
    B. Relation of Causes T, U, V to the phenomenon, Z

VI. Conclusion: Phenomenon Z is the result of Causes Q, R, S (and, optional, T, U, V). This may be the thesis.

the short-term effects been? If there have been any long-term effects, what were they? How can you avoid a subsequent mistake? Write an essay on the subject, organizing it according to either of the patterns suggested above.

4. In discussion or in writing, examine a campaign promise by an elected official for or against whom you have recently voted. What was the promise? Why was it made? (Identify as many causes as possible, from the most obvious to the more subtle.) If the promise is honored, what will its immediate and more remote effects be?

Organization by Comparison and Contrast

Deliberate choices involve comparison (pointing out similarities) and contrast (identifying differences). Do you prefer chocolate or vanilla? Will I major in architecture or journalism? Should I get married or not? to Sandy or Terry? Will we vacation in Greece, Italy, or Spain? Whenever you use *more* or *most*, *better* or *worse*, any comparative or superlative adjectives, you're implying comparison—and creating a context for contrast, as well.

Comparison and contrast also enhance the way you explain and interpret things. When you compare or contrast two phenomena, for instance, city dwelling and suburban life, one provides the setting or context for the other. You no longer have to examine city dwelling in isolation. You can, for example, play off your analysis against life in the suburbs and so enrich your readers' understanding of each. Or you can play with analogies, as indicated in Chapter 3.

Block Design   There are three common ways to organize comparisons and contrasts: block; point-by-point; and comparison first, followed by contrast, or vice versa. In a *block design*, you first present all the material about one item and then all the material about the second. If you organize the points within each block in the same order, the essay will be easier to follow; the first block sets the pattern for what is to come. Parallel organization within each block also helps to emphasize the implicit comparison and contrast between the two things being compared, which readers must make explicit for themselves while following the essay.

For instance, student Conrad Dechiara wrote a comparison and contrast of two dwellings as reflections of their occupants, his two grandmothers. He began his first block with a discussion of the dominant motif:

> "Bright" is the best adjective to describe Grandmother's apartment. Walking into her Florida home is like walking into sunshine. The visitor enters immediately into a petite, L-shaped kitchen lined with vivid yellow cabinets. . . . Adding to the brightness of this contemporary compartment are bar stools with thin yellow cushions. Because the room is small, my thin Grandma is the only one who does the cooking—when she cooks (she usually eats out).

Lightness and vividness integrate the room-by-room tour of his Grandmother's dwelling and its relation to her activities, which concludes with an analysis of how the house mirrors her values and ways of life:

For a woman of 67 she is very vibrant and active. She and her husband lived in New York City and worked very hard until he died, five years ago. Now she is fulfilling her ambition to live comfortably and have a good time. As my father says, admiringly, "She's a swinger."

Conrad makes the transition to his other Grandmother's dwelling by beginning with his impressions of its atmosphere, the opposite of the Florida home:

My Granny, on the other hand, is practically a recluse and her house in Queens reflects this. As soon as you enter the front hall from the outside, you are momentarily blinded by the extreme interior darkness, even on the brightest of days. Even when you regain your sight, you are likely to lose your balance on the unusually steep staircase that leads up to Granny's upstairs half of the duplex. When we visit her I still have to climb the stairs practically on all fours to avoid falling backwards. Because Granny has arthritis she cannot walk very well; the only way she can navigate the stairs is to be carried.

This house, too, is seen from the viewpoint of the visitor upon entering, and its physical characteristics are related to Granny's energy level and way of life:

Granny's kitchen is her place to cook, to eat, to think, to pray. She spends a lot of time making pretty pot holders of various sizes, colors, and patterns. They are everywhere—in drawers, on walls. . . .

Conrad's description of the rest of the house ends with a dim, faded living room, rarely used except for annual family visits, for Granny has no other callers: "You can almost feel the solitude that engulfs this dark house."

To integrate the separate blocks, Conrad provides an interpretive concluding paragraph, characterizing the friendship between the two grandmothers, who "keep in touch through letters, phone calls, exchanges of gifts, and occasional visits; and they help each other in times of illness or depression."

It's possible, of course, to keep adding blocks onto such a pattern, if you wish to compare and contrast more than two things, like stringing beads of a similar size. In block organization, the more you add, the more complicated the implicit connections become among all the items being considered, and the harder the reader may have to work to keep them straight. But you may need lots of blocks to represent a complex subject adequately, such as relations among foreign countries, even if the analysis becomes difficult. Figure 4.3 on p. 84 indicates the typical block organization in an essay of comparison and contrast.

The major advantage of block organization is that it provides the format for an integrated discussion of each unit as a whole and thus enables the reader to get a sense of each major unit. A major disadvantage of this organizational pattern is that unless you repeat in later blocks much of what you've said in earlier sections, the comparisons and contrasts remain implicit and may get lost. And if you repeat too much, even to clarify, you may become redundant or boring. So block organization is often most effective in short papers, where

(text continues on page 85)

Figure 4.3
COMPARISON AND CONTRAST USING BLOCK ORGANIZATION

I. Introduction: Thesis may appear here. Will probably identify the subjects to be compared/contrasted and the specific dimensions of the comparison.

Transition

II. Item A
   A. Dimension 1
      1. Explanation
      2. Illustration
   B. Dimension 2
      1. Explanation
      2. Illustration
   C. Dimension 3, 4, 5 . . .

Transition

May or may not involve reference to analogous dimensions in Item A

III. Item B
   A. Dimension 1
      1. Explanation
      2. Illustration
   B. Dimension 2
      1. Explanation
      2. Illustration
   C. Dimension 3, 4, 5 . . .

Transition

Additional items to be compared could be inserted here, each to be discussed in a block with organization comparable to the above.

Transition

IV. Conclusion: May state or restate the thesis. Makes explicit the comparisons and contrasts implied by the material in each of the blocks; integrates these; analyzes and draws conclusions.

readers can keep in mind what you've said in one block as they proceed to the next. In your conclusion you can integrate the discussions of the individual blocks, as Conrad did, and make explicit whatever comparisons and contrasts implied throughout need to be emphasized.

Point-by-Point Design Conrad could also have organized the essay *point-by-point*, comparing and contrasting the arrangement of his grandmothers' dwellings, the styles and condition of the furnishings, the color schemes, and the activities of the inhabitants. His organization might have looked like that in Figure 4.4 on p. 86:

The advantages and disadvantages of this format are the opposite of those in block organization. Point-by-point organization offers an opportunity for immediate comparison and contrast of each item. Because each major idea will be treated in a separate unit, you won't need to repeat what you've already said—an efficient process, especially when the subject is complicated and each point needs considerable elaboration. If you have large quantities of material to present, point-by-point makes it easier for you to analyze and simpler for your readers to follow. Somewhere, however, you'll have to integrate what you've said, probably at or near the end, so that your readers can see the forest as well as the trees.

Similarities/Differences If you offer a *comparison among the similarities of two (or three or more) entities first,* before considering their differences, you establish their relationship: "Happy families are all alike," said Leo Tolstoy. By discussing their differences as a group, you can more easily play the components off against one another: "But every unhappy family is unhappy in its own way." In this format, whatever you discuss last will be most emphatic (if you treat it fully); if you want to emphasize the contrasts (or the likenesses), put them last.

These patterns of organization provide good ways to develop ideas as well as to organize them—whether in whole essays or in paragraphs. As will be discussed in Chapter 5, other methods of organizing paragraphs also work well with whole essays—and vice versa. Chapters 9–12 discuss how to organize and develop material by means of description, analysis, the format for a classical argument.

Organizational patterns do not have to be used in isolation. One pattern may be dominant, for instance, comparison and contrast, and contain within it a number of other patterns. If you were showing why your college is superior to its traditional rival, you could compare and contrast their major similarities and differences. In the course of that discussion you could also demonstrate why some causes, say excellent faculty and well-stocked library, produce a particularly desirable effect—highly stimulated, successful students—which contributes to your college's superiority.

Figure 4.4

COMPARISON AND CONTRAST: POINT-BY-POINT ORGANIZATION

> I. Introduction: Thesis may appear here. Will probably identify the subjects to be compared/contrasted and the specific dimensions of the comparison.

Transition

> II. Point 1
>   A. Subpoint A
>   1. Comparison (or contrast) S and T
>   2. Contrast (or comparison) S and T
>   B. Subpoint B
>   1. Comparison (or contrast) S and T
>   2. Contrast (or comparison) S and T
>   C. Subpoints 3, 4, 5 . . .

Transition

> III. Point 2
>   Same organizational pattern as Point 1
>   And so on for however many points discussed

Transition

Thesis may appear or be repeated here

> IV. Conclusion: Integration of points previously made, possibly including summary comparison and contrast.

SUGGESTIONS FOR DISCUSSION AND WRITING

1. Discuss with a partner or on paper your possible choices of a major or career. Identify the similarities and differences among your choices, and organize your presentation in a way that will emphasize the one you prefer.
2. Think of several vacation possibilities: the mountains or the seashore, a glamorous city or a tranquil rural area, a foreign country (which one?) or your home state. Imagine what activities you would do in each of two desirable alternatives (exercise? rest? sightsee? work?). Write a paper that will ultimately lead you to an appropriate selection and that will convince your readers to want to try it too.

3. Write a paper of comparison and contrast on a subject similar to Conrad's paper on his grandmothers. Pick two houses (or churches, schools, restaurants, or stores) that you know well. Identify and analyze selected characteristics of the buildings themselves (such as size, design, construction, maintenance), their location and setting, their furnishings (what kind, quality, condition) and other artifacts (books, paintings, food, recreational equipment, religious articles) to tell as much as you can about the people who live in or otherwise use the two buildings regularly. Which of the comparison-and-contrast organizational patterns will best represent your ideas?

THE FIRST DRAFT

By now you should be ready to write the first draft of your paper. You should have a manageable thesis (pp. 54–56)—though it can still be changed; some ideas to express (pp. 42–49); a zero draft or a network of notes or both to illustrate your points (pp. 50–53); and a plan for organizing them (Chapters 4–9, Chapter 12). If you need a refresher on any part of this process, refer to the appropriate preceding pages.

Although the preliminaries may seem elaborate, they are logical; after you've written a few essays, many of them will probably take less time to accomplish than to read about. Nevertheless, even eager writers, like swimmers, often hesitate to take the initial plunge. The water will be cold, the activity will require some effort—perhaps more than you want to expand at that particular time, in spite of the prospective accomplishment once you've begun.

If you have trouble actually beginning to write a first draft despite your careful preparation, try writing a focused zero draft on your thesis or a second zero draft, if you've already written an earlier version. Just sit down, fix your thesis clearly in mind (keeping it visible on your desk is even better), and write for fifteen or twenty minutes without stopping. If you get stuck, write out your thesis or the idea you're stuck on over and over using different words each time, until you can go on. You may find, after doing this, that you have unconsciously followed the plan of your preliminary thinking—whether it's in your mind or down on paper. Or you may find at this stage, as throughout the process of writing, that as you write you come up with new ideas that improve or supplement what you originally intended to say.

Another way to begin writing your first draft is to jot down—or tape record—anything that seems possible for an introductory paragraph, just for a warmup. If you do this, don't linger over the introduction or you may wind up spending more time on it than is profitable at this stage. You will need to rewrite the introduction later to adapt it to the rest of your paper, anyway. So save for revision the polishing of each word.

Still a third way to get started is to begin writing on the *second* major point of your outline, instead of the first, since the first is probably the introduction. As you write rapidly to get down the thrust or essential argument of your essay there's not so much pressure to be scintillating. In the body of the paper you have more latitude; presumably, if you've induced your readers to get beyond the first paragraph they're willing to hear what you have to say. After you have developed the body of your paper and have reached a conclusion, you will have a better idea of what to say in the introduction and how to tailor it to fit your entire paper.

Use whichever of these ways best helps you to get started—or use anything else that works. If you should have a happy inspiration and find that a ripe, delicious introduction has just dropped onto your writing desk, serve it up intact (see "Effective Introductions," pp. 111–114).

Every time you stop writing and start in again later you have to get warmed up all over again, and try to re-create your original mental set. That's hard and sometimes frustrating to do, whether you're using an outline or not. So try to avoid distractions and interruptions as you write the first draft. Put the cat out and the dog in (or vice versa), stock an ample supply of food or other creature comforts within easy reach, take your phone off the hook, close the door, and begin.

Once you've started, keep on writing—and writing—and writing. If you have the momentum and you're attuned to your subject, it's far more efficient and effective to write as much of your draft as possible in a single sitting (or two, at the most) than to try to write it in small batches, a paragraph or even a sentence at a time.

You're writing the first draft to get the ideas down, or to refocus and refine the ideas of your zero draft, or to generate still more ideas. You won't want any to escape, so write as fully as possible, putting in whatever seems appropriate. Don't worry about conciseness, spelling, punctuation, the precise choices of words, or total clarity at this stage; you'll be attending to those matters in later drafts.

In writing, as in driving a car, you usually look ahead to see where you're going, as well as paying some attention to your current surroundings—with an occasional backward glance to make sure you haven't overlooked something. *So although it's customary to say that you're "following an outline," you're much more likely to be anticipating it.* A scratch outline, in particular, is often a casual guide that will be receptive to adaptation. If your mind races ahead of your pen, jot down fragmentary notes on your outline, on notecards, or on the zero draft where they seem to fit. If you can develop them on the spot without getting too distracted, go ahead. But if stopping to expand on each new idea as it occurs to you bogs you down in digressions, you will want to wait to work on the new ideas at the points where they fit into your original design. Anticipation of what's coming will help you to make transitions from one idea to another. It should also help to lead you out of the paragraph you're currently writing and into the next.

What happens, however, if you find that you've become so absorbed in an idea that's just come to you while you're writing that your earlier thoughts seem trivial or uninteresting in comparison? If the new thought is really good and fits into your existing structure, perhaps it will be an appropriate substitute for the original one. This may mean that you'll change the emphasis in your paper; additions or supplements to your plan will show you where the changes belong.

But what if your new idea is out of place in your original structure? Do you abandon your initial design and run off with the attractive newcomer? There's no absolute answer to that question. It all depends on how logical, integrated, thorough, and convincing your original conception of your topic was. If it was done very well to begin with, then you may be going off on a tangent and should simply keep the new idea in reserve for another paper. But if your initial thinking could use improvement, perhaps your new idea is just what it needs. If the new is so remote from the original that you appear to be ending up with an entirely new topic, you will have to decide which will produce the most compelling essay—and make your choice.

You should find the checklist on pp. 23–24 helpful as you write the first draft.

SUGGESTION FOR WRITING

1. Imagine that you are trying to develop an essay on one of the topics below, or on another that you have chosen:

independence	slob movies (like *Animal House*)
the sexual revolution	airplane hijacking
taking risks	quitting
computers	
values vs. costs of higher education	

Try a dialogue with yourself or write a zero draft to help you think of ideas. As you do so you might explore the possibilities of an extended analogy, comparison and contrast, cause and effect, or sequential pattern. After you have a network of ideas, organize them according to a scratch outline or more formal outline, and use this as the basis for writing a first draft by one or another of the methods suggested above.

Write a second (or final) draft if you wish.

NOTE

[1] Rosalyn Baxandall, Linda Gordon, and Susan Reverby, eds., *America's Working Women* (New York: Random House, 1976), p. 3.

CHAPTER FIVE
STRATEGIES OF PARAGRAPHS

In Miss Brill I chose not only the length of each sentence, but even the sound of every sentence. I chose the rise and fall of every paragraph to fit her, and to fit her on that day of that very moment. After I'd written it I read it aloud—numbers of times—just as one would play over a musical composition—trying to get it nearer and nearer to the expression of Miss Brill—until it fitted her.

—KATHERINE MANSFIELD

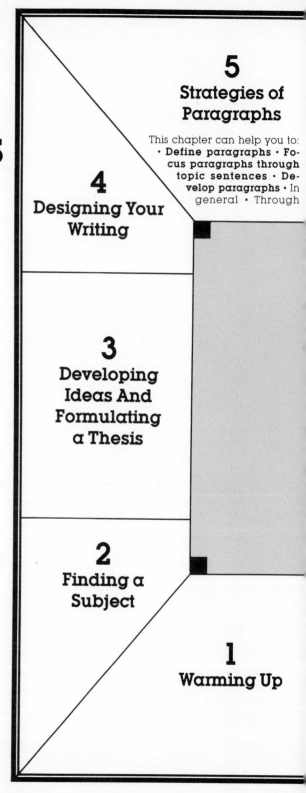

5
Strategies of Paragraphs

This chapter can help you to:
• **Define paragraphs** • **Focus paragraphs through topic sentences** • **Develop paragraphs** • In general • Through

4
Designing Your Writing

3
Developing Ideas And Formulating a Thesis

2
Finding a Subject

1
Warming Up

6
Strategies of Sentences

7
Choosing and Using Words

8
Revising, Editing, and Preparing the Final Copy

WHAT IS A PARAGRAPH?

Making paragraphs when you write may not be a wholly conscious act any more than choosing the right word is. Yet research indicates that readers "intuitively" recognize where paragraph breaks should occur, just as writers have an instinctive sense of where to put the indentation or to skip the line that indicates a break. Part of that sense is visual, for paragraphs serve an important function as punctuation. The indentations at the beginning of paragraphs or the skipped lines between units provide a visual respite from what would otherwise be long and densely packed pages of uninterrupted print, hard to follow and hard to remember. Newspapers, in particular, paragraph to enhance the appearance of the column. They insert indentations every inch or so on the theory that the readers can follow the writing more easily if they can pause often. Lists are sometimes punctuated the same way, with each item indented to give it prominence.

Most other paragraphs, the kinds we will be focusing on throughout much of this chapter, represent divisions of material that signify a shift in topic, tone, or technique from one paragraph to the next. Below are some of the reasons for paragraph divisions.

1. A major change in the topic.
2. A shift of focus to a major division or subdivision of an existing topic.
3. A change in the author's point of view or opinion about the topic.
4. A change of approach to the topic, such as a shift from statistical analysis to anecdote.
5. A change in level of generality, from the more general to the more specific, or vice versa.
6. A shift in time or place. Or a shift of speakers, as in the alternation of speakers in a dialogue.
7. Division of material to set off a point or points for emphasis.
8. Division to make the material easier to follow.
9. Division to provide variety and interest. (This often prompts an alternation of short, medium, and long paragraphs.)
10. Norms of the culture or the literary mode, or the author's stylistic sense that says a given paragraph is long enough and that if it continues it will be too long. Modern readers prefer shorter paragraphs and sentences than did nineteenth-century readers; readers of scholarly journals tolerate longer paragraphs than do readers of sports and human interest magazines.

Your sense of such shifts, whether deliberate or intuitive, will often tell you where to make paragraph divisions in your writing. If you're reading your writing aloud and come to a place where you pause longer than usual, you may be responding to signals indicating where a paragraph should be. Your sense of the total pattern may also tell you where paragraph breaks should occur. We have assumed in discussing the writing process that you'll be starting with an overview of the whole, through either an outline (on paper or in your mind), a zero draft, or a first draft. As you think of the total design, you'll have been thinking of where its parts will go and how they will highlight what you want to say. The divisions of the parts will probably determine where the paragraphs will come.

Paragraphs are the major constituent units of essays. In effect, many paragraphs may be regarded as miniature essays, with *the controlling idea—the paragraph's main point—either implied or stated overtly in a topic sentence, and with integrated supporting sentences that carry the development of the main idea to some tentative sense of closure, pause, or change of direction.* Such paragraphs are relatively self-contained; each makes sense as a unit, but each gains in meaning through its place in a planned sequence of paragraphs. The combination of paragraphs that makes up the essay is indeed greater than the sum of the individual parts.

SUGGESTION FOR DISCUSSION

1. See if you can tell where this article should be paragraphed, using one or more of the reasons for paragraph divisions identified in the list and some of the signals of paragraph indentation discussed immediately above.

   Compare your conclusions with those of your classmates. If you get into disagreements about where the paragraph divisions should come, be of good cheer. There are a number of logical possibilities and no single "right" way to divide them.

IT'S HELLO, CLEMSON, GOODBYE COLUMBUS

(1) His hero, George Patton, lost a chance for promotion to major general after a moment's indiscretion.   **(2)** Now Woody Hayes has been drummed out of the Ohio State football coach's job for a similar offense.   **(3)** Patton slapped a hospitalized soldier for not measuring up to the general's idea of courage.   **(4)** Hayes fell upon a Clemson player, fists flying, when the young man made a terrific play that beat Ohio State.   **(5)** The Ohio State athletic director, High Hindman, said Hayes' firing was the toughest decision he'd ever made.   **(6)** It should have been the easiest.   **(7)** Hayes preached discipline but practiced tantrums.   **(8)** Any university that hopes to teach lasting values would have been ashamed of a professor who, when his students failed, fell upon them in a fistfight of frustration.   **(9)** Yet Ohio State tolerated Woody Hayes through years of shameful behavior.   **(10)** Only Muhammed Ali, and perhaps Billy Martin, threw more punches in the last decade than Hayes.   **(11)** He aimed at a photographer during the 1975 Rose Bowl, at a TV cameraman in the '77 Michigan game, and at a student reporter in the '77 Oklahoma game.   **(12)** He once punched his own fullback and last January even hit a goal post in the Superdome. . . .   **(13)** A common thread weaves these moments into the whole fabric of a man's failure.   **(14)** Hayes always lashed out when he was losing, when his omnipotence was questioned.   **(15)** Charm he has, and he can be warm and witty.   **(16)** Without his intelligence and creativity, Ohio State and college football would have been poorer.   **(17)** Ohio State chose to let pass the earlier indiscretions—one of the perquisites of eccentric genius— but the university could not abide this childish, even irrational, foolishness forever.   **(18)** At 65, Hayes had run out of time to grow up.   **(19)** Churchill said, "Success is never final, failure is never fatal."   **(20)** Intercollegiate athletics often seems without value.   **(21)** Hypocrisy reigns as surely today as it did 50 years ago when the University of Chicago quit the game in disgust at what it had become: a commercial circus with hired hands posing as students.   **(22)** If the college games have a redeeming value it is that they teach well the truth of Churchill's memorable line.   **(23)** That was Hayes' real transgression.   **(24)** He taught Ohio State to win, but not to lose. . . .[1]

THE COMPONENTS OF PARAGRAPHS

Most paragraphs, other than some short paragraphs of dialogue on transitions from one longer paragraph to another, provide within their indented boundaries *focus, development,* and *movement.* Through a *topic sentence, expressed or implied, they focus on a single main point, the controlling idea to which everything else in the paragraph relates.* Through two or more *supporting sentences* they *develop* that central point, and through a *transition sentence, phrase,* or *word* they provide *movement* from one paragraph to the next.

Topic Sentences

Initial Topic Sentences   When a topic sentence is stated explicitly, it is likely to come at or near the beginning of the paragraph, though, in theory, it may come anywhere. As perhaps the first or second sentence, the topic sentence can work like a miniature thesis sentence to establish not only the subject of the paragraph but the pace, tone, and sometimes the organization of what is to follow in that unit. An early topic sentence may amplify the discussion and viewpoint of the preceding paragraph, through introducing another subpoint or illustration of what has been talked about earlier. Or the topic sentence may make a new point in an argument, set a new scene, introduce a new character, comparison, or contrast, or signal a shift of time, place, or approach to the topic (see the list on p. 97).

If you are writing your paper from a formal subordinated outline (see Chapter 4, pp. 68–72), you will have already worked out a sequence of main headings that can easily become your topic sentences. Or, if you've written a zero draft, even if you didn't paragraph it, you can go through and underline the main ideas as potential candidates for topic sentences.

In the paragraph below, which appears one-third of the way through science writer Daniel S. Greenberg's "Scientists Wanted—Pioneers Needn't Apply; Call A.D. 2000," the opening sentence states the topic and provides the controlling idea on which the rest of the paragraph focuses, the "progressive mechanization of scientific research."

> *The next 25 years will also produce further changes in the internal affairs of the scientific community, largely as the result of the progressive mechanization of scientific research.* The conduct of most kinds of research is impossible without the use of highly expensive facilities—computers, particle accelerators, space satellites, oceanographic vessels, huge banks of experimental animals. There is and always will be a market for the breakthrough genius, but without the assistance of sophisticated apparatus, genius will be to science as expert archery is to modern military affairs— admirable, but ineffective by itself. Theoreticians may still use their traditional tools, paper and pencil, but to test their work they like to have a powerful computer which can race through calculations that would require weeks, even years of hand computation.[2]

The topic sentence refers in general to changes that will occur in scientific research as a result of its "progressive mechanization." The other three sentences of the paragraph develop it by identifying some specific types of scientific mechanization, "computers, particle accelerators, space satellites, . . ." and spelling out the essential relationship of this "highly expensive" apparatus to individual scientific research.

Typical of many paragraphs that open with a topic sentence, this paragraph starts with a general statement and narrows with each succeeding sentence (except the third, which offers an explanatory aside about the relative ability of the "breakthrough genius" to work with and without "sophisticated apparatus"). The paragraph moves from "the progressive mechanization of scientific research" (sentence 1) to "highly expensive facilities" (sentence 2), specified more explicitly later in the same sentence as "computers, particle accelerators, space satellites, oceanographic vessels. . . ." Here these are treated as a general group of "sophisticated apparatus" but are not elaborated on until the more detailed, specific example in sentence 4, of the "powerful computer which can race through calculations that would require weeks, even years of hand computation."

Internal Topic Sentences   The topic sentence can also come *somewhere in the middle of the paragraph, transforming what is usually a less emphatic spot to the focal point.* In writing such a paragraph, you are likely to start with the topic sentence (derived, perhaps, from your outline or a preliminary draft) and cluster the ideas around it as they come to mind, always moving in the direction they will be read, from the beginning to the end. Peter Elbow does this in his paragraph explaining the process of editing:

> Editing is almost invariably manipulative, intrusive, artificial, and compromising: red-penciling, cutting up, throwing away, rewriting. And mostly throwing away. *For this process, follow all the standard advice about writing: be vigilant, ruthless; be orderly, planned; keep control, don't lose your head.* At last it is appropriate to sit, ponder, furrow your brow, not write, try to think of a better word, struggle for the exact phrase, try to cut out "dead wood," make up your mind what you really mean: all the activities which ruin your writing if engaged in too soon.[3]

Elbow begins by identifying in the first sentence the activities that editing involves, "red-penciling . . . throwing away." Repeating "throwing away" in the second sentence emphasizes its appearance in the first. In the topic sentence (italics supplied for identification) he explains the best way to do this: "follow all the standard advice about writing: be . . . ruthless . . . planned, . . ." The following sentence, the longest and last of the paragraph, illustrates some specific applications of his general advice: "struggle for the exact phrase, try to cut out 'dead wood.' "

You are most likely to use such an internal topic sentence when you need a *pivot, to cause a shift from one aspect of a topic to another.* A pivot pattern is useful in constructing an argument. You begin the paragraph by dealing with the objections you or others might have to a point, in order to treat your audience fairly; then you state the point and follow it with evidence in its favor. You can also use a pivot topic sentence in a paragraph of comparison and contrast, where the pivot marks the change from examining the similarities to scrutinizing the differences between two items, or from analyzing one item to analyzing the other.

Margaret Mead and Rhoda Metraux use such a pivot paragraph in their discussion of the erroneous concept of egalitarianism that many Americans hold, which denies "any significant differences among human beings":

> For many Americans, a related source of confusion is success. As a people we Americans greatly prize success. And in our eyes success all too often means simply outdoing other people by virtue of achievement judged by some single scale—income or honors or headlines or trophies—and coming out at "the top." Only one person, as we see it, can be the best—can get the highest grades, be voted the most attractive girl or the boy most likely to succeed. Though we often rejoice in the success of people far removed from ourselves—in another profession, another community, or endowed

with a talent that we do not covet—we tend to regard the success of people close at hand, within our own small group, as a threat. *We fail to realize that there are many kinds of success, including the kind of success that lies within a person.* We do not realize, for example, that there could be in the same class one hundred boys and girls—each of them a "success" in a different kind of way. Individuality is again lost in a refusal to recognize and cherish the differences among people.[4]

For the first two-thirds of the paragraph the authors discuss the erroneous American conception of success, "outdoing other people" (sentence 3), for "only one person . . . can be the best" (sentence 4). This belief makes Americans feel threatened by successful people within their own groups (sentence 5). Then comes the pivotal topic sentence (6), in which the authors offer a new, pluralistic definition of success, "many kinds . . . including [that which] lies within a person." Sentences 7 and 8 illustrate this new definition, focusing on the possibilities of acknowledging as successful a variety of individual "differences among people."

Final Topic Sentences   Though it is less frequent, the topic sentence may also come at or near the *end of the paragraph*, in which case the last or next-to-the-last sentence condenses the essence of the writing into a single, memorable statement. Or the paragraph can supply progressively more significant evidence to lead to its culmination in the topic sentence. See the discussion of concluding paragraphs, below (pp. 118–119).

Your writing will be more interesting if the topic sentences appear in various places in your paragraphs rather than if they always come at the beginning. Except for making lists or itemizing the points or steps in a process, variety is the antidote to monotony.

Implied Topic Sentences   Occasionally, a single topic sentence may serve as the focal point for two or more consecutive paragraphs, especially if they are short. This is characteristic of much newspaper paragraphing. Or the topic sentence may be *implied* and never be exactly stated. When you are working on a paragraph without an explicit topic sentence, it's helpful to have a topic sentence written out (perhaps in your outline or in a zero draft) to help control your focus, even if you don't use it in the paragraph. A precise and explicit statement will keep you from wandering away from the subject. A paragraph that describes, defines, illustrates, compares and contrasts, or tells a portion of a tale is more likely to have an implicit topic sentence than is a paragraph that identifies steps in a process or points in an argument.

Mary McCarthy's description of the room in her grandmother's house in which she and her orphaned brothers slept when visiting is an interpretive rendering of details:

Whenever *we children* came to stay at *my grandmother's house,* we were put to sleep in the *sewing room,* a bleak, *shabby, utilitarian* rectangle, more office than bedroom, more attic than office, that played to the hierarchy of chambers the role of poor relation. It was a room seldom entered by other members of the family, seldom swept by the maid, a room without pride: the old sewing machine, some cast-off chairs, a shadeless lamp, rolls of wrapping paper, piles of cardboard boxes that might someday come in handy, papers of pins, and remnants of a material united with the iron folding cots put out for our use and the bare floor boards to give an impression of intense and ruthless temporality. Thin white spreads, of the kind used in hospitals and charity institutions, and naked blinds at the windows *reminded us of our orphaned condition and of the ephemeral character of our visit;* there was nothing here to encourage us to consider this our home.[5]

The topic sentence here, as in many other paragraphs with an implicit topic sentence, can be constructed in part from key words and phrases central to the paragraph, which are italicized in the above illustration: "The inhospitable, shabby, utilitarian sewing room in which we children slept at my grand-mother's house reminded us of our orphaned condition and of the ephemeral character of our visit." At other times, the implied topic sentence may be so obvious that to make it explicit would be unnecessary: "This is what we did on our first afternoon in Washington, D.C."; "Here is a definition of *language.*"

You will find it helpful to use your topic sentence, implicit or explicit, as a guide to constructing a unified paragraph. The following checklist suggests how to do this.

☐ A Checklist for Achieving Paragraph Unity

☐ Make sure you have only one major point in the paragraph.

☐ Check each sentence in it against your topic sentence, explicit or implied, to be certain they are related.

☐ Stick to the point. No matter how fond you are of an observation or detail, if it's irrelevant, eliminate it.

☐ Group the evidence supporting your topic sentence into unified categories. Put steps in a process or in an argument into logical sequence; group all the negatives together, and all the positives; finish talking about one point of view before you proceed to another, and so on.

☐ Other ways to achieve paragraph unity are discussed below, on pp. 107–108.

SUGGESTIONS FOR DISCUSSION AND WRITING

1. The following sentences, from W. Nelson Francis's "Usage and Variety in English,"[6] are out of order. Rearrange them to form an effective, coherent paragraph. Explain the rationale behind your organization.

   a. An expression like *I ain't got no time for youse* may be most effective in the situation in which it is used and, hence, "good English" in the first sense.

   b. Applied to language, the adjective *good* can have two meanings: (1) "effective, adequate for the purpose to which it is put" and (2) "acceptable, conforming to approved usage."

   c. On the other hand, the language of a poorer writer, which does not meet adequately the demands put upon it, might be called "bad English."

    d. The second meaning of *good* is not really a judgment of the language itself but a social appraisal of the persons who use it.

    e. The first of these is truly a value judgment of the language itself.

    f. In this sense the language of Shakespeare, for example, is "good English" because it serves as a highly effective vehicle for his material.

    g. But most people, including those who naturally speak this way, will call it "bad English" because grammatical features like *ain't, youse,* and the double negative construction belong to a variety of English commonly used by people with little education and low social and economic status.

2. As a class, play "The Paragraph Game." It works this way. The teacher brings to class a number of paragraphs of approximately equal length, with each sentence pasted separately on a strip of heavy paper. The class is divided into groups of three or four students each. Excluding the topic sentence, the instructor shuffles the sentences from as many paragraphs as there are groups, mixing up the sentences from all the paragraphs together. The instructor then distributes a topic sentence and an equal number of other sentences to each group.

    The object of the game is for each group to trade sentences with other groups until it secures all the sentences to which its topic sentence pertains, and then to construct the paragraph in its most appropriate order (which may duplicate the original, though the group might provide a convincing rationale for other structures). The group that successfully completes its paragraph first wins.

    If desired, a paragraph tournament could be played.

3. The following are notes for the paragraphs in a potential essay, by student John Reilly (the essay is reprinted in full on pp. 232–234, that is attempting to define the term "human." Arrange them in a plausible order, and identify the organizational pattern you are using, as well as your reasons for organizing the notes as you have done. You may want to cluster several of the ideas in a single paragraph. If so, indicate in what order these would appear within the paragraph.

    a. Chimpanzee Sarah has a language system.

    b. Feral men ("wolf children") aren't human.

    c. One is human if he is "civilized."

    d. Humans are capable of rational thought.

    e. "I'm only human" is a defense against imperfection.

    f. Humans use language to communicate effectively with each other.

    g. Sarah combines symbols to form sentences.

    h. Sarah's symbols have an arbitrary relationship with the things represented, as do humans' symbols.

    i. "Human" implies such qualities as honor, loyalty, compassion.

    j. "Human" implies moderation; "animal" behavior is excessive.

    k. A man with an extraordinary sexual drive or gross behavior is an "animal."

    l. The *human*ities connote a human response to beauty and subtle emotions.

4. Select a sentence from the list in *3* as the topic sentence for a paragraph. Write a paragraph using that sentence at the beginning and then write another paragraph using the same sentence at the end. How does the organization of the two paragraphs differ? If you like the subject, write an essay on it.

5. Write a paragraph identifying a step in a process or describing or defining a particular quality. Frame a topic sentence to guide you as you write, but do not include it in the paragraph. If desired, use this as one paragraph in an essay on that process or quality.

6. Select two friends, favorite places, or possible careers that are somewhat similar but that also have significant differences. Take notes identifying their major points of similarity and difference. Then write a sequence of three paragraphs, in which the first emphasizes the similarities, the second focuses on the differences, and the third ties together what you've said in the first two paragraphs. If you wish, transform these paragraphs into an essay. Or try a condensed version in which you encapsulate the essence of your three paragraphs in a single paragraph.

PARAGRAPH DEVELOPMENT

Cultural norms for appropriately developed paragraphs vary from one era to another. The Victorians valued abundance, so their writings, like their furniture, were well-upholstered—ample sentences and rotund paragraphs abounded. Today's era of physical fitness has its analogue in writing. Many believe that thinner is better (short of emaciation). Predictably, our sentences are shorter, as are our paragraphs. A long, formal paragraph today is about 350 words long; in some contexts a short but acceptable paragraph might be a single brief sentence.

Since paragraphs are so diverse, it's hard to tell in the abstract when a paragraph is developed sufficiently. As this chapter (and others) will indicate, paragraphs serve a variety of purposes in a multitude of contexts. Furthermore, the relationship of any particular paragraph to its neighbors will vary, being more intimate and, therefore, dependent in some cases and more casual and independent in others.

However, there are some useful ways to handle even as protean a shape as the paragraph. The process of developing a paragraph is analogous to the process of developing a whole essay (as discussed in Chapter 3 as well). At any given stage in the writing process you can always initiate a dialogue with yourself or write a sample paragraph draft to develop one or more ideas, or to help yourself rethink familiar ones. You are always free to discuss a point with other people or to consult outside sources, and thereby to provide additional subordinate ideas to buttress the development of any given paragraph.

As you begin to develop a particular paragraph, you may find that asking some of the following questions about purpose, topic, organization, or content will help you write more effectively. If you have already written a sample draft, examine it by asking yourself those questions pertinent to your subject.

1. *Purpose/Function:* What do I want this particular paragraph to accomplish?
   To introduce a topic or conclude the discussion? (see pp. 111–114, 116–118)
   To define—a term, issue, or larger concept? (see pp. 229–232)
   To describe or characterize? (see pp. 102–104)
   To compare and contrast? (see pp. 82–85)
   To classify? (see pp. 100–102)
   To analyze a process, a relationship, or the nature or function of something? (see pp. 236–239)

   To provide a step in an argument, by presenting a proposition, anticipating a
   disagreement, objecting, or conceding? (see pp. 259–309)
   To supply an illustration (see pp. 306–308), analogy (see pp. 283–284), anecdote
   (see pp. 104–107), or characterization? (see pp. 102–104)

2. *Location:* Where will this paragraph come in the essay?
   What, if anything, will precede and follow it?
   How will this paragraph be related to its environment in content and style?

3. *Topic sentence:* How will I express the topic idea?
   Should it be explicit? or can I merely imply it?
   If it's explicit, where will it go?
   (When you've figured out what it is, make sure it's relevant to your thesis.)

4. *Organization:* How do I want to organize this paragraph?
   In sequential, spatial, or chronological order? (see pp. 74–78)
   Through cause and effect? (see pp. 79–81)
   Through comparison and contrast? (see pp. 82–85)
   Through classification? (see immediately below)
   Through building to a climax, whether intellectual or emotional? (see pp. 116–
   118, 287, 293
   Other ways (specify)?

5. *Content:* What evidence or illustrations can I offer to demonstrate my point?
   What can I use to develop it:
      analysis? (see pp. 245–250)
      definition (see pp. 229–236)
      description? (see pp. 205–224)
      analogy (see pp. 51–53)
      anecdote or incident? (see pp. 104–105)
      characterization? (see pp. 102–104)
      statistics, numbers, graphs, diagrams, tables? (see pp. 245–250)
      illustration, example? (see pp. 205–224)
      symbol (p. 220) or metaphor? (see pp. 169–170)
      negation? (see p. 173)

Many of the techniques discussed in this chapter concerning the purpose,
organization, and development of single paragraphs will be useful to you when
you write longer sequences of paragraphs or even whole essays. Obviously, many
techniques are best used in combination; they are separated here for simplicity
of discussion. In this chapter, we will consider how to develop paragraphs
through classification; narration of an anecdote, incident, or relationship; and
characterization. (Additional techniques are discussed in other chapters.)

Classification

Although we may like to think of ourselves as unique individuals, we are more
often than not known by the company we keep, the classification into which
we are put. We can be identified by social or economic class, academic or marital
status, country or region from which we come, or where we live. At the same

time, we are known by our ethnic group, race, religion, and sex. We can also be categorized in many other ways—by our occupation; political affiliation; whether or not we smoke, drink, vote; own a television set, car, or boat (and how many); whether or not we traveled during the last year, and, if so, where we went; and so on.

When you write a paragraph (or an essay) depending on classification, you are concerned with *categorizing the individual units to emphasize their common features, and with setting them apart from units that do not share these characteristics (division).* (You follow the same processes in making an outline.) Once you've decided on a topic, you should try to identify its major characteristics and then make lists of their main attributes. Suppose that your thesis is, "Love is the most powerful human emotion." First you can subdivide *love* into smaller categories: romantic, filial, religious, patriotic. Each of these would (or could) be treated in a paragraph, which you could develop by identifying (and explaining, where necessary) its appropriate characteristics, again through the use of classifying lists. The process is delineated in Figure 5.1 below.

Figure 5.1
DEVELOPING A PARAGRAPH OF CLASSIFICATION

Thesis: Love is the most powerful human emotion.

Subjects of separate paragraphs	Romantic	Filial	Religious	Patriotic

two types

Classification of the paragraph on romantic love	Casanova	Sentimental
Possible details to use to illustrate each category	insincere, flatterer rapid conquest	sincere focuses energy, effort on the beloved
	makes no commitment—love 'em and leave 'em	makes an emotional commitment to the beloved, presumably long term
	wants no commitment from partner plays the field	wants commitment from partner concentrates on one person

A paragraph developed from these lists might read as follows:

> When we think of lovers we think of romance; poets write about it, pop stars
> sing about it, at least one war (the Trojan War) was fought over it. Yet as song
> and story reveal, there are at least two types of romantic lovers, the Casanova
> and the sentimental lover. The Casanova makes his many conquests quickly—
> through flattery, insincere protestations of undying love, and his own personal
> charm. But his love 'em and leave 'em attitude prevails. He makes no commitment
> to his partner and wants none from her. The sentimental lover, on the other hand,
> focuses his whole attention on his only beloved. He is the passionate and gener-
> ous wooer, bestowing upon her undying attention and gifts, whether daffodils or
> diamonds. Fully committed to her, he does everything he can to encourage her
> commitment to him.

This classification also serves to contrast the types of lovers, presenting them
along parallel dimensions (for example, how they relate to their partners, how
exclusively, for how long, etc.)—a useful technique in classification, as well as
in comparison and contrast. Each type gets equal emphasis, in this case, three
sentences of approximately equivalent length. Yet this classification, like many,
oversimplifies its subject for ease of presentation. Though "at least two types
of lovers" allows for the possibility of more, only two are presented—and with
stereotyping generalizations. If the paper is short and the stereotyping intentional, it may be acceptable that the subject is not explored further.

But a more thorough discussion of the topic would examine some related
questions: Do all sentimental lovers focus exclusively on one person? Are Casa-
novas always insincere? If both types of lovers are considered *romantic*, in
what ways are they similar? (The classification here has not included common
characteristics, though it could have done so.) Because the essay is short and its
subject ambitious, the writer cannot spend more space on different categories
of romantic lovers. To treat the subject more fully, the writer could narrow the
paper's focus even further and write exclusively on *sentimental* love, a subcategory of *romantic love*.

The same technique is, of course, applicable to other categories. In each case,
you will figure out the major subcategories and then make lists for each. If the
categories or subcategories can be discussed along parallel dimensions, so much
the better for the development of your classification.

Characterization

If you want to talk about someone in an essay, you'll need to introduce him or
her to your readers, just as you would if they were meeting face to face. The
extent of that introduction or characterization will depend on the prominence
that person assumes in your writing. If you're merely referring to Dickens's
Mr. Venus, a character in *Our Mutual Friend*, it might be sufficient to *identify*
him by his occupation, a taxidermist, or by the description he provides of himself on his business card, "Preserver of Animals and Birds, Articulator of hu-

man bones." But if the person is more central to your focus, you'll need to say more about him, perhaps through a paragraph or two of characterization. A more extensive character sketch might develop into a paper in itself.

Whatever your approach, you will want to identify or describe some of the following characteristics in developing your characterization:

Physical appearance:
　　body size, shape, condition, age range
　　attractiveness, grooming
　　clothing—type, suitability to wearer and occasion, condition

Behavior:
　　actions performed—habitual or unusual, manner of performing them
　　facial expressions, posture, gestures

Way of talking:
　　level of language used
　　typical words, phrases, accent
　　amount of talking or silence

Manifestations of roles:
　　occupation—what does the person do, and how well?
　　relationships with others—family, friends, colleagues, antagonists
　　objects or artifacts associated with roles—carpenter's tools, college student's books

Typical milieus:
　　job setting
　　home
　　recreation or entertainment areas (restaurants, vacation spots)
　　urban, suburban, or rural environment preferred

Manifestations of values:
　　characteristic point of view—liberal or conservative, humanitarian or selfish, nationalistic or international, male or female chauvinist (pig or piglet)
　　important decisions made—reflecting the above, or other clues about what's important to the person—family, job, status, money, intellectual life, travel, religion, etc. (For instance, an athletic person might look trim, dress casually, and exercise regularly.)

When you're writing a single paragraph, you'll have to be highly selective and choose only the most revealing or characteristic details. In a longer paper your characterization could be more elaborate. In either case, the *dominant impression* you have of the person is probably what you'll want to convey to your readers.

Student Steve O'Connor conveys the dominant impression of his boss, Red, in a paper on his summer in Texas as a worker on a crew that built oil storage tanks. He describes their first meeting:

The huge, jacked-up green Chevy pick-up roared in through the mud tracks left by the derrick-tractor. I could see a Confederate flag decal on the back window and a fat, freckled hand grabbing the can of Skoal off the dashboard. The truck skidded to a stop beside me, and when I introduced myself, Red seemed glad to see me as he smothered my hand when I shook his beefy paw. He was a short man, but built like a tank, with forearms as thick as telephone poles. With his fiery orange hair and sharp, inspecting eyes riveting me over his barrel chest, I hoped that I would never be the object of this man's anger. Opening the can of Skoal and, to my shock, shoving the entire contents into his fat cheek, Red called the attention of the crew. "Men, this here's Steve. He's a college boy from New Mexico State, the Aggies, and he's gonna be with us for the summer." Bits of powdered tobacco were flying out of his mouth. "Now I want you all to go easy on this boy for the first couple days, so's we can show him we got nuthin' against Yankees."

We'd know Red anywhere from the vigorous, vivid portrait that Steve paints. Red, nicknamed because of his "fiery orange hair" [*physical appearance*] drives not merely a truck, but a "huge [*size*], jacked-up [*unusual feature,* a clue to the way Red drives, and where], green [*color*] Chevy [*brand*] pick-up [*model type*] that roars through mud [*manner of driving, job setting*]. . . ." Red himself is a Southerner (he identifies Steve, a Southwesterner from New Mexico, as a Yankee!) and proud of it, judging from the "Confederate flag decal on the back window" [*indication of Red's values and region*]. Although Red is "short" [*height*], he is a giant of a man, "built like a tank, with forearms as thick as telephone poles," a "barrel chest," and a "beefy paw"; these indications of *size and bulk* also imply that he is enormously strong [*physical condition*]. Perhaps his *most unusual characteristic* is his ability to chew a whole can of tobacco at once, "shoving the entire contents into his fat cheek" [*behavior*]. This *action* strikes the readers (and Steve) as unusual, but is clearly *habitual* to Red, who performs it so casually.

Narration of an Anecdote, Incident, or Relationship

A narrative is a story (whether truth or fiction) told by a *narrator*, who may or may not be a character in the tale. It has one or more main *characters* who are involved in an *action or series of actions that have a beginning, a progression, and an end.* It occurs in a particular *time* and *setting* (place), and may or may not involve dialogue. Even in a single narrative paragraph you will want to include these features; it's easy to do if you think of writing a narrative as a way of telling a story.

A narrative is sometimes *told for its own sake:* it's interesting or exciting or frightening or sad. And a narration is sometimes *told to make a point external to the tale itself,* in a more immediate, dynamic, or otherwise memorable way than an analytic essay or other form of writing might do. Fables and parables do this in order to make a moral point. So do essays that begin with a paragraph or two narrating an anecdote, incident, or relationship and then move to a more general, objective, or theoretical discussion of the narration's theme.

The following paragraph is a brief example of two narratives of one sentence each; each contains many of the principal elements of a longer narrative. Here, freshman Diana Chang parodies her expectations of finding a compatible college roommate and living happily ever after:

> now every dream i'd ever dreamed about college roommates said they are your best friends and the two of you fall in love with two men who are best friends and you get married after college to the best friends and you move to minneapolis or new rochelle and live next door to each other and you have kids who grow up to be best friends with your best friend's kids. but kim was coolish and i was warmish and kim loved beethoven and i loved the beatles and kim was neat and i was sloppy and kim was quiet and i was noisy as all hell broke loose. so much for the dream.

Diana, as author, has efficiently, if unconventionally, narrated two stories. The first, a unified chronological progression, tells the myth of a college girl's stereotyped life history. The second, variations on the theme of incompatibility, is the story of the actual relationship between the author and her roommate. The first story has two main characters: Diana's idealized version of herself and her roommate. The two characters of the second story are the actual Diana and the actual Kim. Each story has a setting: college and the suburbs for the first, college for the second. And each has a time—in the first, the whole life span; in the second, the recent past. Here, the narrative's second sentence negates the first and leads to the emotional climax, "so much for the dream." (If you are writing a paragraph of negation, the best strategy is to put the positive first, so the negative can counteract it.)

This paragraph also shows that a narrative can be both brief and meaningful. Three sentences, two stories, and a vigorous five-word interpretation provide a witty and integrated overview of the contrast between the narrator's expectations of what it would be like to have a college roommate—and the reality. This paragraph, which comes early in an essay entitled "Great Expectations," prepares the readers for an extended discussion of the general subject of discrepancies between expectations and reality.

SUGGESTIONS FOR DISCUSSION AND WRITING

1. Here is a single-paragraph answer to an essay examination question, "Identify a pressing social problem and offer a solution." The first sentence implies that the answer will be based on classification. Is it? Rewrite the paragraph (or discuss how you would do it) to make the classification clearer and to provide necessary information, eliminating irrelevant material in the process.

> The poor people in this country are suffering from many things, but the three that are most prominent are inequalities in job opportunities, inequalities in educational opportunities, and inadequate housing. The word ghetto comes from the Hebrew word "ghet" meaning separation, and in the United States this word has taken on added significance as it is now used to describe the areas where low-

income groups dwell. Upon seeing these areas, compassionate people unacquainted with them are often overcome with anxieties concerning the American social structure. They find it hard to understand why these people, products of the American way of life, are not being helped. The inequalities in job opportunities are directly associated with the inequalities in educational opportunities, because money is necessary to receive an adequate education. The lack of money to "buy" sufficient training has forced most of these people to retain their low-paying jobs. The fact that some of these people have low-paying jobs and often a large family also serves to preclude the opportunities for receiving enough education to allow them to have a better way of life, because if they leave their jobs, their families would probably starve.

2. What elements of narrative does the following one-paragraph student essay exhibit? Does it gain or lose from being a single paragraph? If you think it should be broken up, where would you divide it? Why?
3. What is the author's tone? Does his exaggeration help or hinder the narrative?
4. After you have completed the revision, write a narrative paragraph about an episode in which you experienced some painful discrepancy between appearance and reality, as Diana Chang does, on p. 105, or in which you were the victim of an institution or organization, as Alfred Dow narrates below:

EMERGENCY

I was sent to the hospital one time with a badly twisted ankle. After taking a rollercoaster ride on a wheelchair with only one wheel, I was left off in a cold room full of medical supplies, much like a closet. And as I sat there on the table with only one shoe on and my right foot swollen like a watermelon, in walks good ole Marcus Welby Jr. Then he's got the nerve to ask me, "Where does it hurt?" The man with the coke bottle bottomed glasses didn't even notice my foot. All he did was press a stethoscope up against my chest, the kind they keep stored in freezers. After a couple more hours of joyriding on the rollercoaster and having had x-rays taken of my x-rays, the good ole doc decided that the problem must be in my foot. After agreeing with his wild guess I proceeded to go to the nurse's desk at the entrance. Over here is where you tell your life history. It helps if you tell them you can't read or write. Then they'll fill out the forms for you and all you have to do is make your little x where it says signature on the bottom. It's nice seeing people turn from federal agents to social workers. Overall it's quite an experience. It's not as frightening as going to a dentist who wants to try out his new Black and Decker variable speed drill, but it is quite an experience.

3. In this two-paragraph essay the student author, Audrey Meadows, relates a narrative and characterizes herself in the process. Analyze her writing to determine the aspects of narration and characterization that she uses. Is the writing self-contained? Do you want to know more about either Audrey or her story?

After you have examined this writing, try writing a one- or two-paragraph narration about a memorable person, event, or period in your life in which you convey the essence of both your experience and yourself.

AUTOBIOGRAPHY OF AN AUTUMN

There were so many firsts that fall: first semester of college, first long-lasting love affair, first time I was in the South, first time I was ever so unabashedly happy. I can't remember how I did it, whether I was drugged by something in the air or whether it was the spice in Steve's cooking or some magic combination of everything, but the problems of existence didn't confront me.

One day walking back from classes I looked up at one of the flaming trees along the path. In a burst of glory I set up shop by the tree to offer a leaf to everyone who passed. This was euphoria for me, to open up fully like a flower on the sunniest day of fall and simply present myself to the world. I could do it then and not worry about how it would look. But I am no longer in my first semester and I feel too battered to risk somebody knocking off a petal, so I no longer offer leaves or petals to strangers. But the smell in the air is the same as ever this fall, and I recall the story to offer to you.

PARAGRAPH COHERENCE AND MOVEMENT

A paragraph divided against itself cannot stand; its ideas and its style need to be integrated so they will work together. In addition to the unity of topic and pattern, there are other ways to provide integration within individual paragraphs and among paragraphs in sequence. One group of integrating devices might be called *signals of continuity*, words or phrases that show the reader you will continue to discuss a given matter.

The repetition of previously used *key words*—nouns, verbs, adjectives, or adverbs—or *key phrases* can provide both unity and movement, as can the substitution of *synonyms* for key words or phrases previously introduced.

> In the language of screen comedians four of the main grades of laugh are the titter, the yowl, the bellylaugh and the boffo. The *titter* is just a *titter*. The *yowl* is a runaway *titter*. Anyone who has ever had the pleasure knows all about a *bellylaugh*. The *boffo* is the *laugh* that kills.[7] (italics supplied to emphasize repetition)

> On my last visit to New York, I took an enormous bite out of the *Big Apple*. And *the Big Apple took a big bite out of* me.

Integration can also be provided by *pronouns* that refer to nouns or phrases already used.

> The children from town let us know immediately of our inferior position. *Their* fathers were businessmen, while *ours* were farmers, laborers, and the unemployed.

Demonstrative pronouns (this, that, these, those) functioning as modifiers enhance unity. An example of these so-called *demonstrative adjectives* is provided in the following note a maid allegedly wrote her employer upon discovering an alligator in his bathtub:

> I cannot work in a house where there are alligators. I would have told you before, but I didn't suppose *this* matter would ever come up.

If you're writing in the first person (*I*), don't lapse into the second person (*you*), or the third person (*he, she, this writer,* or other synonyms). *Consistency of person* is easier to understand and to follow. Shifting from the first to second person often sounds awkward or unnecessarily self-effacing:

> In August I returned to a disaster of bugs. I knew it was my fault. I called the landlord who called Bah, Humbug! Exterminators who came quickly—even before *this writer* had unpacked *her* bags and reordered the camping gear in the closet.

It sounds better to say, "even before *I* had unpacked *my* bags. . . ."

At other times, if you shift from first to second person in the same paragraph, you will appear to be preaching to your readers (the *you*) by removing yourself (*I* or *we*) from the message you're delivering:

> It we have the freedom to make choices, we also have the responsibility to accept the consequences of these choices. If *you* don't like the results *you* have only *yourself* to blame.

If this is intentional, and it may be if you're giving advice to readers who need it, keep the pronoun shift. Otherwise, include yourself and your readers in the comprehensive pronouns *we* or *our:* "If *we* don't like the results *we* have only *ourselves* to blame."

Other unifying devices, such as sentence patterns, tone, and levels of language, will be discussed in Chapters 6 and 7.

Transitions

Transition *words or phrases* can also integrate ideas *within or between paragraphs.* They help to show the connection between what comes first and successive statements or paragraphs and show how these will extend, develop, qualify, or contradict it. Among the common types of emphasis and connection that transition words and phrases provide are the following:

sequence: first, third, last

time: meanwhile, thereafter, before, next, during

cause and effect: because, therefore, consequently, for example

coordination, amplification: and also, in addition, not only . . . but

qualification, contrast: but, nevertheless, moreover, however

restatement: in other words, that is to say

Transition paragraphs, more extensive than the transition words or phrases they may incorporate, *are usually short but firm bridges between major blocks of ideas.* Set off by space, they call attention to themselves and what they say. They may, for instance, signal the shift from cause to effect, from comparison to contrast, from problem to solution. Sometimes a transition paragraph will take the form of a question:

> What will happen if the property tax is reduced? Let us look at the possibilities.

At other times, a transition will appear as a single sentence:

> But since I am not an anthropological linguist, I will simply go on to my second observation, which is that women are expected to play a passive role while men play an active one.[8]

Or transitions may consist of longer groups of two or three sentences, but still shorter than neighboring paragraphs or blocks of paragraphs. Because they signal a shift, rather than elaborate on a point, transition paragraphs may lack topic sentences. Many could be easily incorporated into the paragraphs that follow them. Whether you set them off as separate paragraphs depends on whether you want the extra emphasis that such paragraphing will provide.

SUGGESTIONS FOR DISCUSSION AND WRITING

1. Analyze the following paragraphs to determine how each is integrated. Consider the various elements contributing to this integration: ideas, expression (including parallel sentence structures and repeated words), and other devices of connection, subordination, and transition. How successful are they?

a. Some people say the business about the jolly fat person is a myth, that all of us chubbies are neurotic, sick, sad people. I disagree. Fat people may not be chortling all day long, but they're a hell of a lot *nicer* than the wizened and shriveled. Thin people turn surly, mean, and hard at a young age because they never learn the value of a hot-fudge sundae for easing tension. Thin people don't like gooey soft things because they themselves are neither gooey nor soft. They are crunchy and dull, like carrots. They go straight to the heart of the matter while fat people let things stay all blurry and hazy and vague, the way things actually are. Thin people want to face the truth. Fat people know there is no truth. One of my thin friends is always staring at complex, unsolvable problems and saying, "The key thing is. . . ." Fat people never say that. They know there isn't any such thing as the key thing about anything.

—SUZANNE BRITT JORDAN[9]

b. But our greatest delight in all seasons was "delicatessen"—hot spiced corned beef, pastrami, rolled beef, hard salami, soft salami, chicken salami, bologna, frankfurter "specials" and the thinner, wrinkled hot dogs always taken with mustard and relish and sauerkraut, and whenever possible, to make the treat fully real, with potato salad, baked beans and french fries which had been bubbling in the black wire fryer deep in the iron pot. At Saturday twilight, as soon as the delicatessen store reopened after the Sabbath rest, we raced into it panting for the hot dogs sizzling on the gas plate just inside the window. The look of that blackened empty gas plate had driven us wild all through the wearisome Sabbath day. And now, as the electric sign blazed up again, lighting up the words JEWISH NATIONAL DELICATESSEN, it was as if we had entered into our rightful heritage. Yet *Wurst* carried associations with the forbidden, the adulterated, the excessive; with spices that teased and maddened the senses to demand more, still more. This was food that only on Saturday nights could be eaten with a good conscience. Generally, we bought it on the sly; it was supposed to be bad for us; I thought it was made in dark cellars. Still, our parents could not have disapproved of it altogether. Each new mouthful of food we took in was an advantage stolen in the battle. The favorite injunction was to *fix yourself,* by which I understood we needed to do a repair job on ourselves. In the swelling and thickening of a boy's body was the poor family's earliest success. "Fix yourself!" a mother cried indignantly to the child on the stoop. "Fix yourself!" The word for a fat boy was *solid.*

—Alfred Kazin[10]

2. The following paragraphs are from a newspaper column. Regroup them as if they were to appear in a magazine that permitted longer paragraphs. Justify your new grouping.

Some quite reputable hospitals have gone so far as to establish marketing departments. Hospitals are merchandising their wares like businesses—and in many ways businesses are what they are.

That is plainly true of the one hospital in seven now run for profit in the country. But it is also true of most of the rest, as they increasingly will tell you.

They make unusual businesses in one sense. As an officer of Humana, Inc., the nation's largest for-profit hospital company, put it not long ago, "our definition of a sale is a patient stay."

But in other respects they are ordinary. Most, nonprofit as well as investor-owned, are constantly trying to increase "sales."

And as in other businesses, some kinds of sales are highly profitable, some not.

The profit-generating patient, the kind whose arrival makes a hospital administrator smile secretly into his adding machine, tends to be one who:

• Is well-insured by a large commercial insurance company like Aetna or Prudential, and is not a Blue Cross-Blue Shield, Medicare or Medicaid patient.

• Will need lab tests and/or X-rays or other so-called ancillary services.

• Will end up having a fair-sized operation.

• But basically is not that sick. This perfect patient, whose surgery was probably elective, will be able to go home by the weekend, or, in the best of all possible worlds, will stay in the hospital over the weekend but by then require little care.

The reason this last is a desirable quality from the hospital's point of view is fairly obvious. A hospital administrator wants, insofar as he safely can, to skeletonize his staff on the weekend to cut costs. And to the extent that he can do that and still keep paying patients around, he wins on both sides of the ledger.

The other points are more complicated. They have to do with the convoluted way a hospital bill is constructed.[11]

3. After you have written a first draft of your next paper, examine each paragraph to

see what devices of coherence you have used. Is each paragraph effectively unified? If not, can you rewrite it, using a more consistent tone, level of language, or
person? Will repetition of words or sentence patterns help you achieve greater coherence?

EFFECTIVE INTRODUCTIONS

The introduction can make or break your writing, whether it's an essay, a report, a letter of job application, a grant proposal, a speech, a newspaper article,
or a book. The price for a lame introduction is sudden death, for you either capture your readers in the first few paragraphs of a short piece of writing (or the
first chapter of a book), or lose them altogether.

Writing the introduction can take more than its share of the effort—one
author estimates as much as 85 percent,[12] though that's considerably more time
than you're likely to spend. If done well, an introduction can establish the limits
of your paper, its tone, language, structure, and perhaps even its length. If you
can control the lead, you can control the rest of the paper—and you can control
your audience. So it's worth the writing and rewriting and rewriting again to
produce an attractive introduction that not only does all of these things but
also captures your readers' attention and makes them eager to go on.

Let's see how this would work in a paper on *Robert's Rules of Order*. Although many a meeting or debate you've attended has been influenced by this
classic, you—and your readers—have probably taken its existence for granted
and have never thought of wanting to learn more about it. Consequently, the
first paragraph of an essay on this subject would have to attract a possibly indifferent audience, as well as set the boundaries for the ensuing discussion. It
should be written in the language that the rest of the essay will adopt. Given the
less compelling nature of the subject (unlike, say, sex or love, which will attract
curious readers no matter what), the thesis should probably be stated near the
beginning, so readers will know what they're getting into.

Here's the way the essay starts:

A reviewer of *Robert's Rules of Order* wrote in 1881: "In a country where every
school has its debating society, every village its lyceum, and every man—and woman
too, for that matter!—cherishes the hope of some day shining in the deliberative
assemblies of the land, a reliable manual of parliamentary practice is as indispensable as
was the catechism in more ecclesiatical times." This early assessment of Robert's famous
little book hardly overstated the importance it was to claim in American life. The one
hundredth anniversary of its publication in 1976 passed without notice amid the hoopla
of the bicentennial, but not because of its obscurity. On the contrary, *Robert's Rules of
Order* had long since become an accepted commonplace, an ultimate source of unquestioned authority ingrained in most Americans by the time they leave high school. The
rules are adopted routinely and obeyed thoughtlessly in American organizations of
every kind.[13]

We can tell from this introduction that the essay will discuss how *Robert's Rules of Order* came to be an "accepted commonplace, an ultimate source of unquestioned [parliamentary] authority ingrained in most Americans by the time they leave high school." We know, because first and second person pronouns are absent here, that the *voice* will be impersonal. The objective, thoughtful tone leads us to expect that the rest of the essay will be expressed clearly in an educated but not stuffy language. The choice of expressions like *famous little book* and *hoopla* keeps the language lively. Of the five sentences in this paragraph, the shortest is fourteen words, the longest (the quotation), seventy-four. The writer's own sentences average twenty-two words apiece, and alternate between short (fourteen words), medium (nineteen and twenty-three words), and long (thirty-one words). They are counterbalanced by the complicated quoted sentence that is nearly as long as all the rest combined. We can probably assume, since this paper depends on outside sources, that the writer will follow this practice throughout. We can expect his own writing to have medium-length sentences, but that the sentences he quotes will be much more elaborate and formal, perhaps because they were written for the more formal tastes of a century ago. A reading of the essay reveals that the promises implied by this beginning have been fulfilled.

Choosing Your Approach

Whenever you begin to write you will be looking for ways to engage your readers' attention honestly and to encourage them to continue reading. Obviously, some types of attention-getting devices fit a particular topic or treatment of it better than others. For instance, it might take an extraordinarily intriguing opening to entice even a selected audience to read a paper with the thesis, "Every college freshman should take at least one course in composition." You would want to try out various alternatives to see which ones might best fit your views and be most effective at attracting your readers. The list below illustrates the multitude of approaches you might consider. Each example could be the focal point for one or more introductory paragraphs.

1. *A forceful statement of the thesis or topic.*
   A course in composition can make the difference between success and failure for most freshmen.
2. *A controversial statement of the thesis or topic.*
   Johnny can't write because Johnny can't read; Freshman English should be a course in reading instead of writing.
3. *A witty or dramatic statement, observation, or epigram.*
   Some students swear by Freshman English; others swear at it. Nevertheless, all should swear to take at least one semester.
4. *A reference to past or present events.*
   In the shouting '60s, student advocates of the Free Speech Movement quickly realized that they didn't have to know how to write a syllable; they could simply talk their way through courses—for college credit. But no more.

5. *A compelling illustration from real life.*

   "One feature of life in college that I feeled need to improved is Flunking. The rate of flunking has been going up repedly in the past decay in C.U.NY." So began a typical English placement essay of a new member of the Class of 1984.

6. *Narration of the writer's (or another's) personal experience.*

   For the first eight weeks of the semester I remained unconvinced that Freshman English would do me any good at all. Monday, Wednesday, and Friday at 8 A.M. I slogged through rain, hail, sleet, and snow to confront The Thesis Sentence, The Paragraph, The Outline. I lost; they won. But then. . . .

   Caution: Avoid the forced joke, "A funny thing happened on the way to my 8 A.M. English class," unless it fits naturally with the topic.

7. *Reference to authority.*

   Although the Kitzhaber report on Dartmouth students, *Themes, Theories, and Therapy* (1963) showed that the ability of students to write well declines significantly after they've left Freshman Composition, more recent research contradicts this.

8. *A provocative quotation.*

   "And how is clarity to be acquired? Mainly by taking trouble; and by writing to serve people rather than to impress them."[14]

9. *A statistical interpretation.*

   It is alleged that three-quarters of the college freshmen who take composition eventually earn a degree, as opposed to only one-quarter of the freshmen who avoid learning to write.

   This is interesting, but readers may well wonder who made this statement. An anonymous allegation is not nearly as convincing as the citation of a specific, authoritative source would be.

10. *An appeal to potential antagonists.*

    Even freshmen who hate to write would love composition if they realized how much it would improve their chances of academic success.

11. *A metaphor, analogy, symbol, or other figure of speech.*

    Taking Freshman Composition during the first semester is like taking a cold shower first thing in the morning. The prospect of either may not be very appealing, but they're good for you—and they can really wake you up.

12. *An indirect approach.*

    Traditionally, sports has received tremendous emphasis at America's colleges, with the best efforts culminating in Bowl and tournament games and invitations to the Olympics. Imagine how writing could improve if there were intercollegiate writing teams, for which every freshman writing student was in training.

As you decide on a suitable method of introduction, you will also be determining how long it should be. This depends, in part, on how long you expect your paper to be. The length of your introduction should be proportionate to the paper's total length; 10 to 20 percent or less seems to be about right. Just as an elaborate facade of columns, balconies, and porticoes would be an inappropriate entrance to an adobe residence, a two-part introduction to a three-page paper would throw the emphasis off balance. Yet an introduction of that length might be just right for a twenty-page term paper. A book might warrant an entire introductory chapter.

As your paper changes during successive revisions, you will need to revise your introduction—and conclusion—to accommodate the changes.

INEFFECTIVE INTRODUCTIONS

Not all introductions are likely to work as well as those identified above. Humorist James Thurber offers some indirect advice on how to begin an essay. In "University Days" he tells the story of the unfortunate Haskins, a shy journalism student at Ohio State whose beat on the student newspaper was the agricultural school. Haskins persisted in writing dull, colorless stories, to the great frustration of his editor. Finally, in response to the editor's admonition to " 'Start [your story] off snappily. . . . something people will read,' " Haskins labored for two hours and produced "a two-hundred word story about some disease that had broken out among the horses. Its opening sentence was simple but arresting. It read: 'Who has noticed the sores on the tops of the horses in the animal husbandry building?' "[15]

In beginning his essay, Haskins used the time-honored device of asking a rhetorical question intended to compel the readers' attention. Yet instead of encouraging his readers to pursue the topic, Haskins led them to a dead stop. It's dangerous to ask a question to which you don't really expect an answer, especially at the start of an essay, before your readers have warmed to your presentation. Although your own interest in the subject may lead you to think that even from the outset the readers share your concern with the issue, this is not necessarily so. Avoid asking questions of readers either uninterested in the topic or unsympathetic to your perspective; their answers may undermine your purpose.

Other ineffective introductions belabor the obvious, show the writer as self-conscious or floundering, or are misleading. They can be painful to write—and to read—if they:

State the assigned topic. In this paper I am going to argue that every college freshman should take at least one course in composition.

State the obvious, a truism already well known to your audience. Everybody needs to know how to write.

Use a dictionary definition. According to the *Random House College Dictionary,* a composition is "a short essay written as a school exercise."

An introduction is particularly dead—and inaccurate—if you begin with the cliché "As Webster says . . . ," for if you're using a current standard college dictionary you are not quoting from Noah Webster, who died in 1843, well before the current dictionaries were written.

Emphasize the writer's ignorance or lack of expertise on the subject. Until I started taking Freshman Composition two weeks ago, I had never thought much about it. I still haven't had enough experience to claim to be an expert, but. . . .

Tell the reader of the writer's problems in getting started. It was hard to find much of the research on Freshman Composition because it's mostly in periodicals that don't leave the library. The library closes before I get off work in the evenings, and. . . .

Use an irrelevant opening sentence or paragraph, which may itself be catchy, but which has little or nothing to do with the topic. Stories of sin, seduction, and betrayal! Freshman Composition is loaded with them, if you know where to look! Take Hawthorne's *Scarlet Letter*, for instance.

All of these methods of introduction defeat its basic aims—attracting the readers' attention appropriately and making them want to continue reading. Even if the subject and thesis are compelling, the paper will have no impact at all if the readers give up before coming to terms with them. Chances are that if you write an introduction that appeals to you, it will appeal to other readers as well and will encourage them to keep on reading.

SUGGESTIONS FOR DISCUSSION AND WRITING

1. Here are three introductions to student papers. Can you tell what each paper will be about on the basis of the introduction? If not, why not? If so, why? Do any of the introductions make you want to continue to read? Which techniques of introduction do they illustrate? Do any of the introductions combine more than one technique? Which introductions are the best? Why?

Women are obviously superior to men. Even from childbirth, females are maturing faster than males. Women reach maturity, mentally and physically, faster than males, who sometimes never grow up.

I need these!!! They're for a gum wrapper chain that I'm gonna make if that's O.K. with your majesty. For your information, the egg shells under my bed are for my plants. I'm gonna break them all up and put them in the pot with the dirt and I haven't thrown away those other plants yet because I'm not sure they're dead.

We used to drive twenty-eight miles north of town, turn west at a nondescript gate, and then drive another fifteen miles to the Sanger Ranch. It belonged to my great-grandfather. By driving forty-three miles I would change time zones, and I would go back in time about fifty years. Upon arriving at the ranch the car was garaged and never used until the return trip to town and the then present time.

2. Using one of the topics below, write three different introductory paragraphs employing a different technique of introduction for each. Which of the techniques fits your topic best? Which of your paragraphs do you prefer? Why? If you wish, use that paragraph as you write an essay on the topic.
   a. My favorite symbol
   b. The army—draft or volunteer?

   c. How to make/repair _____

   d. Nuclear reactors—blessing or menace?

   e. My trip to _____

   f. Television—preserver or destroyer of culture?

   g. Our forgotten aged/retarded/gifted/poor

   h. Is affirmative action discriminatory?

   i. The joys of _____

EFFECTIVE CONCLUSIONS

In listening to symphonies, as in reading essays, we like to know when we've reached the end, so we're alert for signals. The symphony may slow down, get louder, and conclude with several emphatic chords. The tempo, volume, and music combine to end with a bang, not a whimper. They tell us we can stop concentrating (or they wake us up if we've slept through the last movement) and start clapping. Likewise, in reading we don't want to turn the last page, anticipating more, and encounter a blank and a letdown.

Conclusions signal readers that the end is approaching; meaningful conclusions also leave the readers with a memorable thought or image. As in music, the conclusion should not be long; a short, brisk farewell is preferable to a lingering departure. "Amen" says it in a single word. The conclusion to Gay Talese's portrait of Mafia boss Frank Costello says it in a single sentence: "And he will die thinking he has done no wrong."[16] A book, of course, will have a concluding chapter, but that, too, is likely to be much shorter than the rest.

Beginning writers are sometimes given the safe but dull advice to end their essays with a summary. However, unless the summary provides something new or memorable, it is unnecessary in an essay short enough for the readers to remember what you've already said. However, summaries are often useful in examination answers to bring together diverse points that you've made or in longer papers where these points may have been widely separated in the discussion. In many types of scientific and report writing, a summary is the standard conclusion.

Another way to end an essay, and one that is usually more interesting, is to focus on an anecdote that illuminates or illustrates its central point. In a brief essay, "Goodbye to All T- -t," Wallace Stegner makes the point that literary decorum, the right word in the right circumstances, is violated when writers use more profanity than the situation warrants; the excess undermines the effect. He concludes with an anecdote to illustrate his argument:

> I remember my uncle, a farmer who had used four-letter words ten to the sentence ever since he learned to talk. One day he came too near the circular saw and cut half his fingers off. While we stared in horror, he stood watching the bright arterial blood pump from his ruined hand. Then he spoke, and he did not speak loud. "Aw, the dickens," he said.
>
> I think *he understood* better than some *sophomore girls* and *better than some novelists the nature of emphasis.*[17] (italics supplied)

With restraint, Stegner lets the action and his uncle speak for themselves, rather than loading the writing with unnecessary description and interpretation. Readers can imagine the situation better if it is sketched sparingly, as Stegner does, and the emotions are more powerful. The extreme understatement of "Aw, the dickens" is so unexpected that it is almost comic, but the grimness of the situation converts it into sardonic humor.

Stegner's concluding sentence interprets for his own purposes the implication of his uncle's subdued expletive, and integrates his point about "the nature of emphasis" with the rest of the essay's content, as the italicized words indicate. He accentuates "emphasis" by making it, memorably, the last word of the last line.

Choosing Your Approach

There are several other effective ways to end essays, which can be used either individually or, sometimes, in combination. The following list shows a number of the more compelling techniques available to you.

1. *Refer to the introduction, either in content or by the use of a significant symbol, figure of speech, or key word or phrase.*

    Just as *the engagement ring needs the wedding ring to complete it,* so the effectiveness of premarital counseling needs the validation of marriage. That is why the ultimate proof of the effectiveness of such counseling may not show up until the couple's first, or fifth, or even tenth anniversary! (Italics refer to repetition from the introduction.)

2. *Discuss the implications of the thesis.*

    Premarital counseling can be accomplished with minimum cost, approximately $10 per couple per session. Compared with the high human costs of marital disharmony and divorce, this is an extraordinarily inexpensive ounce of prevention.

3. *Propose ways to implement the thesis.*

    The people with whom engaged couples are likely to be talking are in the best position to provide the premarital counseling described here. So youth workers, clergy, teachers, and physicians should pay particular attention both to the couples and to this thoroughgoing program.

4. *Specify the possibilities for further investigation or application of the central idea. Project into the future. This is often a fitting way to conclude research reports, after the results have been summarized.*

    Once the rationale of premarital counseling has been accepted, the next steps are to hire a good counselor; establish a series of counseling sessions, to be offered at regular intervals, in a high school, community college, church, or other accessible community location; enlist the support of people likely to refer couples to the program, such as youth workers, clergy, teachers, and physicians; inform the prospective users about the program; and, finally, do such a good job that satisfied "graduates" will tell their friends, who in turn will come in for counseling.

5. *Specify the logical conclusion to an argument or the logical outcome of a process. (See illustrations above.)*
6. *End with a memorable quotation or authoritative statement from another writer.*

The research of renowned psychologist Jessie Bernard has demonstrated that there are "two marriages in every marital union,"[18] the husband's and the wife's, and that these may be very far apart. As this paper has demonstrated, one of the major goals of premarital counseling is to help bring them closer together.

Who gets the last word is essentially a matter of your preference as an author. Do you want readers to finish the essay with your own impressive words, or someone else's, reverberating in their thoughts? Your overall intentions should help you decide.

INEFFECTIVE CONCLUSIONS

Ineffective conclusions sometimes mirror the writer's too-evident fatigue; he or she is tired of the subject and limps to the finish line with a cliché, an unnecessary repetition of previously stated material, or an apology. The following examples are characteristic, and are calculated to bore or confuse readers.

Use of cliché expressions: "In conclusion," or "To summarize."

In conclusion, I have proved my point.

A restatement of the thesis. This is simply a repetition of concepts or language already familiar to your readers.

In conclusion, we have seen that every engaged couple should have premarital counseling.

An apology or qualifying remark that undermines the readers' confidence in what has preceded.

My remarks on premarital counseling apply only to people under 25; older people have already thought through the issues.

Grandiose but unfulfilled claims for either your thesis or your proof.

I have demonstrated that if engaged couples don't have premarital counseling, not only will their marriages suffer, but family relationships throughout the country will be dealt a crushing blow.

Significant new material that is unrelated or tangential to the thesis and will cause the paper to change direction suddenly.

Furthermore, every engaged couple should also live together for at least two months before marriage.

Because they're in an emphatic location, conclusions, like introductions, can leave a lasting impression—positive or negative. It's worth taking the time to write and rewrite your conclusion until it is memorable.

Having considered paragraphs in various ways, it is now appropriate to think again of the quotation from Katherine Mansfield at the beginning of this chapter. As she wrote each sentence and paragraph she read them aloud to hear their rhythm and determine whether they fit the subject, "just as one would *play over a musical composition.*" Try reading your sentences aloud. And your paragraphs. Tinker with them for length, for sound, for flow. Read them again, aloud. When they sound right, stop.

SUGGESTION FOR DISCUSSION AND WRITING

1. Here are the conclusions to two of the essays whose introductory paragraphs are on p. 117, though presented in a different order. Match the endings with the beginnings.
   Which techniques of conclusion do they illustrate? Do any combine more than one technique? Which conclusions are the best? Why?

The summers spent at the ranch make very pleasant childhood memories for me. The lack of modern conveniences was not really noticed at the time. Years later I asked my great-grandmother how she managed to raise a family under such "awful" conditions. She smiled and cheerfully replied that it had been easy because she knew of no other way.

Papa has his own collections out in the garage. "You had better not throw it away!!!! I save this stuff so I can tell what to buy when something wears out." I guess that's why he has seven cracked Delco spark plugs, three heat-warped black rubber radiator hoses, miles of unravelled rope he constantly tries to tie together and use, and four jars of rotten plastic washers that came out of some drippy faucet. In the corner, stacked one inside the other, are empty milk cartons and a six-foot stack of yellowed newsprint all waiting to be put to some useful purpose. Exactly how and when these things will be pressed into service no one knows. But to Dad, their value is universally recognized and "it would be a real pity to throw it all out."

NOTES

[1] Dave Kindred, "It's Hello, Clemson, Goodbye Columbus," Washington *Post*, December 31, 1978, H 1, cols. 1–2; H 5, cols. 2–4.

[2] *Smithsonian* (July 1976), p. 61.

[3] *Writing Without Teachers* (New York: Oxford University Press, 1973), pp. 38–39.

[4] *A Way of Seeing* (New York: William Morrow, 1970), pp. 74–75.

[5] *Memories of a Catholic Girlhood* (New York: Harcourt Brace Jovanovich, 1957), p. 29.

[6] *The English Language: An Introduction* (New York: W. W. Norton, 1965), p. 245.

[7] James Agee, *Agee on Film* (New York: Grossett & Dunlap, 1958), p. 438.

[8] Alleen Pace Nilsen, "Sexism in English: A Feminist View," *Female Studies VI: Closer to the Ground* (Old Westbury, N.Y.: The Feminist Press, 1972), p. 104.

[9] "That Lean and Hungry Look," *Newsweek*, October 9, 1978, p. 33.

[10] *A Walker in the City* (1951; rpt. New York: Grove Press, 1958), pp. 33–34.

[11] "In Hospital 'Marketing,' A Patient Stay Is a 'Sale,'" Washington *Post*, January 10, 1979, A 6.

[12] Donald Murray, *A Writer Teaches Writing* (Boston: Houghton Mifflin, 1968), p. 7.

[13] Don H. Hoyle, "Rules of Order: Henry Martyn Robert and the Popularization of American Parliamentary Law," *American Quarterly*, 32:1 (Spring 1980), p. 3.

[14] F. L. Lucas, *Style* (1955; rpt. New York: Collier, 1962), p. 74.

[15] From *My Life and Hard Times* (1933), in *The Thurber Carnival* (New York: Harper, 1945), p. 227.

[16] "The Ethnics [sic] of Frank Costello," in *Fame and Obscurity* (1970; rpt. New York: Bantam, 1971), p. 146.

[17] *Atlantic Monthly*, 215:3 (March 1965), p. 119.

[18] *The Future of Marriage* (1972; rpt. New York: Bantam, 1974), p. 4.

CHAPTER SIX
STRATEGIES OF SENTENCES

There is the first satisfaction of arranging it on a bit of paper; after many, many false tries, false moves, finally you have the sentence you recognise as the one you are looking for. . . .

—VLADIMIR NABOKOV

6
Strategies of Sentences

This chapter can help you to: · write better sentences through learning strategies for · Making sentences longer · Making sentences shorter · Emphasizing sentence

5
Strategies of Paragraphs

4
Designing Your Writing

3
Developing Ideas And Formulating a Thesis

2
Finding a Subject

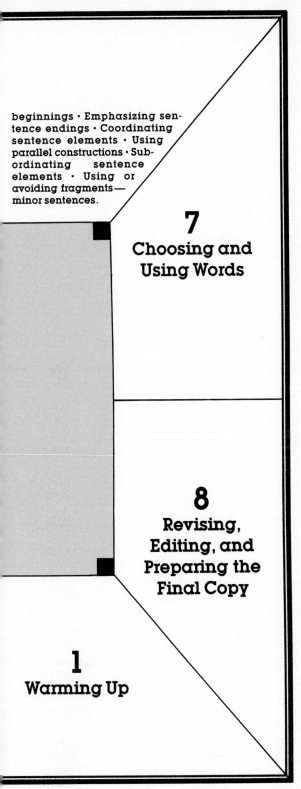

WHAT IS A SENTENCE?

Many of us learned in elementary school that "A sentence is a complete thought." Yet this definition is both perplexing and inadequate. The meaning of a drowning swimmer's cries of *Help!* are clear and complete to the lifeguard who hears the shouts and comes to the rescue. Yet the very people who use the above definition would not consider *Help!* a sentence. Others, however, might disagree if they defined a sentence as a unit beginning with a capital letter and ending with a period, exclamation point, or question mark. On the other hand, to explain the thought *I love you* thoroughly might require a poem or a song or a book, each composed of a number of sentences. Yet everyone would agree that the statement *I love you* is a sentence, whether or not its thought is complete.

For the purposes of this discussion, our definition of a sentence will rely on grammar instead of meaning. Thus the basic sentence pattern in English is the *simple sentence,* which consists of one *independent clause*—that is, a *subject* and a *verb*—often followed by a *complement* (S-V-C pattern) or an *adjunct,* an optional element (see the chart that follows). In *I devoured the pizza, I* is the subject, *devoured* is the verb, *the pizza* is the complement. In this case, *the pizza* is a direct object. Table 6.1[1] represents common sentence patterns, including a variety of verb forms, complements, and adjuncts.

Table 6.1
COMMON SENTENCE PATTERNS

SUBJECT (S)	VERB (V)	COMPLEMENT (C)	ADJUNCT (A) Optional; not necessary to basic sentence pattern
I	devoured (transitive verb)	pizza (direct object)	greedily. (*manner*)
Henry	gave (transitive verb)	the dog (indirect object) pizza. (direct object)	
The gorilla	scratched. (intransitive verb)		
The encounter group	seemed (linking verb)	unhappy (adjective)	in its mountain retreat. (*place*)
Calamity Jane	was (linking verb *be*)	a powerful woman. (predicate noun)	
The townspeople	elected (transitive verb)	a dog (direct object) as dogcatcher (object complement)	in 1984. (*time*)

Sentences, even simple ones, can vary considerably, as this chart implies. *Many sentence parts are movable.* It is possible to write a draft sentence and then rearrange it to change its emphasis, meaning, and length. For instance, you can *reorganize* sentence components by shifting the position of subjects, verbs, complements and adjuncts: "Pizza I devoured greedily." You can *expand* sentences through the addition of modifying words, phrases, or clauses: "*With unbecoming haste,* I greedily devoured the *giant* pizza," or "*Passing over the many gourmet delicacies,* I devoured the pizza." You can *join* sentences with other sentence elements: "Yesterday afternoon I devoured the pizza and *washed it down with lukewarm root beer.*" Or you can *delete* sentence elements: "I washed down the pizza with lukewarm root beer."

This chapter is concerned with several of the basic strategies of composing sentences. We'll focus essentially on the question of how you can best use these fundamental units of expression—and their many variations—to say what you mean in the most appropriate and interesting fashion. Recognizing the various attributes of sentences and what you can do with their components—words, phrases, clauses, and so on—will help to give you the ability to control your writing. Such control places you in a far stronger position as a writer than you would be if you simply let the words flow and were stuck with whatever landed on the paper. Let us examine some of the ways you can vary the form of your sentences to make them say exactly what you want them to.

MAKING SENTENCES LONGER

Combining Short Sentences or Sentence Elements into Longer Ones

Short sentences are often effective because they stand in isolation and thereby call attention to their meaning, or because they break up strings of longer sentences, often by signaling shifts of tone or topic (see Chapter 6). However, a series of short, repetitive sentences, or a paragraph written primarily in short sentences can seem underdeveloped, jumpy, or childish, as if it were written by someone incapable of greater complexity of thought or expression. Consider, for example, this series of sentences about the effect of Mack Sennett's comedies on his audience:

Millions of unpretentious people loved Mack Sennett comedies.
These comedies were very popular during the era of silent films.
The people loved their sincerity and sweetness.
They loved their innocence, like that of wild animals.
They loved their glorious vitality.

If, however, we combine the short sentences into one longer sentence, the writing flows more smoothly:

> Millions of unpretentious people loved the Mack Sennett comedies, highlights of the silent film era; they loved their sincerity and sweetness, their wild-animal innocence and glorious vitality.
>
> —adapted from JAMES AGEE[2]

The longer sentence *integrates ideas that logically belong together, indicates the relationships among them,* and it *eliminates unnecessary repetition* (the people, they loved).

Long sentences are not necessarily preferable to short ones. You don't want to combine shorter sentences just for the sake of making them longer. However, if the resulting combination can provide advantages lacking in a series of shorter sentences, such as economy, unity, and a clearer relationship among the ideas, then you will want to use it.

Expanding Short Units to Make Longer Sentences

Short sentences can sometimes be very effective. *Jesus wept. Familiarity breeds contempt. Gentlemen prefer blondes.* These sentences are self-contained, provocative, and to the point, though for the sentences to have their full impact, readers will still need to supplement the words with their own understanding. *Jesus wept,* for instance, means considerably more in its biblical context than it does in the abstract, out of context.

You may wish to control more fully your readers' understanding of the meaning of individual sentences and not leave so much to their imagination. There are a number of effective ways you can do this.

For instance, adding modifiers, whether single words, phrases, or clauses, can greatly clarify your writing. To write "The Great Depression of the 1930s was devastating" doesn't say enough to be meaningful. You could add, "The Great Depression of the 1930s, *when 20 percent of the work force was unemployed, banks failed, and millions' life savings were wiped out,* was *the most* devastating *period in American history*" and be certain your readers will get your point.

If you have trouble thinking of what kinds of explanations to add, consider the ways of developing thesis sentences or topics discussed in Chapter 3 and Chapter 5. Asking of a single sentence the same questions you would ask of a thesis or topic can be very helpful.

Consider also changing the sentence structure to emphasize one or more aspects of the coordination or subordination of its parts (see below, p. 127). This may involve the addition of more material, along with words that indicate coordination or subordination. For instance, in revising "The Great Depression of the 1930s was devastating," you could indicate causality by saying, "*Because 20 percent of the work force was unemployed, banks failed, and millions' life savings were wiped out,* the Great Depression of the 1930s was *the most* devastating *period in American history.*"

Expanding both the sentence and its context is a third possibility. The latter is a matter of paragraph development and is discussed in Chapter 5.

MAKING SENTENCES SHORTER

Dividing Long Sentences

As we have seen, long sentences have some advantages over short sentences when they integrate logically or thematically related ideas, indicate their interrelationships, and eliminate the monotonous choppiness that a series of short sentences can create. There are times, however, when you may want to break up even a perfectly good long sentence.

You can break up a long sentence to provide variety. For instance, in "A Declaration of Interdependence," historian Henry Steele Commager wrote:

> We affirm that the resources of the globe are finite, not infinite; that they are the heritage of no one nation or generation, but of all peoples and nations and of posterity; and that our deepest obligation is to transmit to that posterity a planet richer in material bounty, in beauty, and in delight than we found it.[3]

This is a strong sentence, with the interrelationship among its independent clauses enhanced by the fact that they are linked by semicolons rather than broken up by periods. The author could have decided, however, that in the context in which this sentence occurred, there were too many long sentences in a row, and so have broken this one up to provide variation in sentence length. With a single division it would look like this:

> We affirm that the resources of the globe are finite, not infinite, and that they are the heritage of no one nation or generation, but of all peoples and nations and of posterity. It is our deepest obligation to transmit to that posterity a planet richer in material bounty, in beauty, and in delight than we found it.

You can break up a long sentence to call attention to its separate points. This can be particularly effective if you use repeated vocabulary and parallel construction (see below, pp. 133–137). Thus Commager might have divided the original long sentence into three shorter ones, repeating *We affirm that* at the beginning of each new sentence to emphasize his personal endorsement of his position, as well as to focus attention on each of the points he was trying to make:

> We affirm that the resources of the globe are finite, not infinite. We affirm that they are the heritage of no one nation or generation, but of all peoples and nations and of posterity. We affirm that our deepest obligation is to transmit to that posterity a planet richer in material bounty, in beauty, and in delight than we found it.

No one of these three variations is intrinsically better than the others. Each has its advantages, depending on whether the writer wants to stress the interconnectedness of ideas, variety of sentence length, or emphasis of each point.

Long sentences may also be condensed. Some sentences are flabby from a surfeit of words. They have taken more words than necessary to get their point across and need pruning to get in trim. This can be done by *reducing clauses or phrases to single words.* Or, you can *substitute a simpler, shorter synonym for the wordier expression.* Or both.

Consider, for instance, this sentence by a student writer, Lisa, who is trying to define the ideal audience for her writing:

> Having an intense nature, with leanings toward cynicism on one side and empathic subjectiveness on the other, I like sensitive readers who are aware of the many possibilities of human expression, perceptive, intelligent readers who have experienced some of life's apportioned joys and sorrows, readers who can challenge my material and find its contents enticing.

There are definitely too many words here, though the author's ideas are good. Let us examine the steps Lisa could go through to condense this sentence without loss of meaning.

First, it would be necessary to identify the sentence's main ideas or topic divisions:

1. Definition of Lisa's personality
2. Definition of Lisa's ideal readers
3. Identification of how Lisa wants her readers to react to her writing

Then, related ideas should be grouped under the main headings. This grouping could resemble an abbreviated outline; in fact, you might think of it as an outline of the sentence.

1. Lisa's personality: intense nature, leanings toward cynicism, empathic subjectiveness
2. Readers: sensitive, aware of the many possibilities of human expression, perceptive, intelligent, have experienced some of life's sorrows and joys
3. Reactions to Lisa's writing: challenge my material, find its contents enticing

If the related ideas are written down, it will be easier for you to recognize and delete redundancies. When you see the parts in isolation, it is also easier to think of synonyms and shorter ways to express longer phrases.

Next, unnecessary repetitions should be deleted. You can do this quickly by finding duplicate items on your list of grouped ideas and crossing them out on the list and in their corresponding places in the sentence.

Finally, synonyms, words or phrases that include several of the original meanings, should be substituted for wordier expressions. For instance, without loss of meaning Lisa can simply define herself as *intense*, rather than as *having an intense nature. Empathic subjectiveness* is difficult to define, but in context it is evidently intended to mean the opposite of *leanings toward cynicism.* An appropriate and less wordy translation would be *I am both cynical and sensitive.*

She could repeat the same process in analyzing the definition of ideal readers and identifying her readers' prospective reactions. Her revised scratch sentence outline might look like this:

Lisa's personality:

    intense ~~nature~~

    ~~leanings toward cynicism~~   cynical

    ~~empathic subjectiveness~~   sensitive

Readers:

    sensitive   range

    aware of the ~~many possibilities~~ of human expression,

      including its ←

    perceptive

    intelligent

    ~~have experienced some of life's~~ (sorrows and joys)

Reactions to Lisa's writing:

    ~~challenge~~ (my material)

    find ~~its contents~~ enticing and challenging

She might eventually end up with a sentence like this:

> Because I am an intense mixture of sensitivity and cynicism, I like perceptive, intelligent readers who are aware of the range of human experiences, from joy to sorrow, for they will find my material challenging and exciting.

This is considerably clearer than the original version, more precise, and 25 percent shorter. Yet the reduction from fifty-five words (a very long sentence by today's standards) to thirty-seven words (still fairly long) has not changed the meaning but merely sharpened the focus.

Loose Sentences

By tradition, sentences with the main idea presented first and the lesser ideas following are called *loose sentences.* Americans like loose sentences, in writing as in speaking, because they like to get to the point quickly. In a loose sentence *the main subject, verb, and complement come near the beginning and can stand independently;* everything else comes afterward. (The two preceding sentences are loose.) Loose sentences are flexible because the additions can be so varied; they are comfortable because we use them so often that they seem the natural way to write. In conversation or informal writing, most of your sentences will automatically be loose.

Stringing a number of loose sentences in a row will set up a pattern with repeated emphasis on the beginnings of the sentences. Such emphasis is useful for definitions or other writing in which you want to *call attention to a number of separate, but equivalent, related points of information.* Student Karl Jennings uses three loose sentences (in a four-sentence paragraph) to define a political meaning of *landslide.* The *sentence bases*—subject-verb-optional complement—are italicized.

>   s   v   c
> An election *landslide is* a *victory* overwhelming, one-sided, unequivocal. In recent state primary elections for the Presidency, no single candidate has received an
>   s   v
> overwhelming majority of the votes. However, *"landslides" have been claimed*
>   s v   c
> by some commentators. Perhaps *this is* a public relations *device* to make small victories seem like major triumphs.

Because of their structure, loose sentences are particularly appropriate for *making lists or otherwise putting items in series* because you can make them as long as you need to to hold everything. (The sentence base is italicized.)

>   s   v   c
> The *food is unsurpassed:* Vienna pure beef hotdogs, cradled in steamed poppyseed buns, smothered with mustard, relish, chopped onions, peppers, sauerkraut, long slabs of dill pickle, tomato slices and topped with a sprinkling of celery salt.[4]

Loose sentences are also *useful for narrations*, because their rhythm is often conversational and because the narrator can continue to add elements and after-thoughts to the sentence base. Student Sandra Richardson's narrative of her attempt as an adult to escape the influences of her mother's traditions begins with two loose sentences:

> I knew the sinfulness of walking with toes pointed out, cutting the sandwiches horizontally, saying *icebox* instead of *refrigerator, you guys* instead of *y'all,* and *Louweesianna* instead of *Louisiana,* hating the animal books mother believed in but getting in trouble for reading *Travels with Charley* (who was very much a dog, I did want to please, but who belonged to John Steinbeck who swore and believed in integrating Little Rock). Furthermore, I more often than not forgot to dust the baseboards, the bottom rungs on chairs, and behind the books on the bookshelves.

The sentence rhythm moves the story along by reflecting the pace and movement of the action, and it prepares the readers for more to come.

Periodic Sentences: Putting the Emphasis at the End

A *periodic sentence* is the reverse of a loose sentence; the major point and at least some of the principal grammatical elements (subject-verb-complement) *come at the end rather than at the beginning.* You can use a periodic sentence to *create movement and suspense* by putting the subject near the beginning and withholding the verb and the complement until the end. In anthropologist Desmond Morris's sentence

> $\overset{\text{s}}{}$
> Each *event,* such as eating a meal, visiting a theater, taking a bath, or making
> $\overset{\text{v}}{}$ $\quad \overset{\text{c}}{}$ $\overset{\text{c}}{}$ $\overset{\text{c}}{}$
> love, *has its own special rules and rhythms*[5] (base italicized).

the subject, *event,* is introduced early. Readers then have to wait until after the intervening explanation of what events are (*such as eating a meal, visiting a theater, taking a bath, or making love*) to find out the author's main point, that each event *has its own special rules and rhythms.* This periodic sentence structure puts the emphasis where Morris wants it, at the end.

You can also use a periodic sentence to *drive home a point.* The sentence rises to a crescendo of emphasis, aided by the weight of such sentence elements as modifiers and clauses (a cluster of words containing a subject and a predicate) that have preceded it. Such is the case in this example, again by Desmond Morris:

If one's attacker is too strong to be challenged, there is nowhere to flee or hide,

               s   v   ·   c

and no one to come to his aid, then *appeasement is the only solution.*[6]

The initial *If* puts the sentence in suspension until the *then* appears, three-quarters of the way through. Only after the *then* is the meaning completed and the point made emphatically.

On the average, periodic sentences are longer than loose sentences because they are structured toward a climax. They are particularly suitable when you want to provide extra emphasis—to the point of the sentence, or to the paragraph in which the periodic sentence occurs, especially if it's the last sentence. In the essay "Notes of a Native Son" James Baldwin achieves such a climax when speculating about the outcome of Harlem race riots:

If ever, indeed, the violence which fills Harlem's churches, pool halls, and bars

                              s   s   v

erupts outward in a more direct fashion, *Harlem and its citizens are* likely *to*

 v

vanish in an apocalyptic flood.[7]

The climactic impact of *in an apocalyptic flood* is reinforced by its conspicuous terminal position in the sentence. The same point would not be nearly as impressive if the sentence order were reversed:

Harlem and its citizens are likely to vanish in an apocalyptic flood if ever the violence which fills Harlem's churches, pool halls, and bars erupts outward in a more direct fashion.

The point of the sentence isn't the *fashion* but the *apocalyptic flood.*

A few words of caution are in order here. Long sentences with suspended meanings are sometimes hard to follow, because the readers don't always know what to expect. As Mark Twain said, "Whenever the literary German dives into a sentence, that is the last you are going to see of him till he emerges on the other side of his Atlantic with his verb in his mouth."[8]

Furthermore, because of the delayed emphasis of periodic sentences, a paragraph composed entirely of them would have a rhythm at variance with the emphasis of most American writing, for it would seem to progress by a series of delayed explosions rather than in a smooth flow. So use periodic sentences with restraint; a single explosion can make more of an impact than a string of firecrackers.

SUGGESTIONS FOR WRITING

1. Combine the following groups of short sentences into longer sentences, either loose or periodic.
   a. I had many adventures during the summer.
      I flipped over on a motorcycle.
      I shot myself in the chest with a firecracker.

The firecracker was illegal.
I leaned against an electric fence.
Unfortunately, it was during a rainstorm.
b. I am dining with a close friend in a New York restaurant.
We eat our steaks.
We drink our brandy.
We smoke our fat cigars.
He tells me that the world is obviously overpopulated.
He says that somebody must starve.
He explains that we as a nation must decide who it will be.
c. A prince should seem to be all mercy.
A prince should seem to be all faith.
A prince should seem to be all integrity and humanity.
A prince should seem to be all religion.
This last quality is especially important.
Everybody sees what you appear to be. Few feel what you are.
—adapted from NICCOLÒ
MACHIAVELLI, *The Prince*

2. Break up the following sentences from student writings, eliminating unnecessary words where necessary. Make a scratch sentence outline, if that will help.
   a. The two important elements of writing, and perhaps the most basic, are the author and audience, primarily because the written words mean nothing without readers; which is indeed a sad prospect when you consider how many ways it it possible to interpret an author's thoughts, as many ways as there are readers, critics, scholars, and reviewers.
   b. I don't concern myself with whether my readers are well educated nor with their social or ethnic origins, but only with whether or not they have sufficient background to understand and evaluate what I'm saying with some objectivity, for I often treat my topics with biases that I do not expect my readers to share.
   c. The comforts that we surround ourselves with, whether they be formal, informal, rugged or convenient, are the thumbprints of a uniqueness involving separate human conceptions of territory, the solutions to which are quite diverse.
3. Write a paragraph in which you have at least three loose sentences and one periodic sentence, of different lengths. Where will you place the periodic sentence? Why?

TRY THIS

In the next essay you write, consciously vary the structure of your sentences. Make some of them loose and others periodic. Try writing some that are long and others that are short. You may be surprised with the results.

COORDINATION AND ITS USES

In speech, we naturally use compound sentences and, consequently, a great deal of *coordination*, through which equal weight and emphasis are given to various units within a sentence by the use of words, phrases, clauses, or punctuation. We can also coordinate sentences within paragraphs or paragraphs or longer sections within whole works. Children use a lot of coordination when they first begin to talk in sentences: "I went to the store, *and* saw Santa Claus *and* I sat on his lap *and* told him I'd been good, *and* he asked me what I wanted for Christmas, *and* I told him a hammer *and* a box of real nails *and* some boards *and* especially a dog." Of course, we continue to use coordination even as sophisticated adult speakers and writers, both to express equivalence and to give fluency to our utterances. Overdependence on it would produce a tedious flat effect, but when used judiciously coordination has definite functions that you should be aware of as you are writing. The following list will give you some sense of these functions.

Coordination can indicate an equivalence or equality among elements or ideas under consideration:

> Hitler overran Poland, Czechoslovakia, France, and Belgium.

The coordinate structure implies that you consider each country equivalent for the purposes of the discussion you're conducting. Likewise, Ben Franklin must have considered each alternative equivalent when he said, at the signing of the Declaration of Independence, "We must all hang together, or assuredly we shall all hang separately." Putting the ideas in parallel form reinforces the pun on the two senses of *hang*.

Coordination can be used to group ideas in order to demonstrate their relation clearly and conspicuously:

> The Kiowas are a summer people; they abide the cold and keep to themselves, but when the season turns and the land becomes warm and vital they cannot hold still; an old love of going returns upon them.[9]

In this example, each semicolon signals a clause of equivalent importance.

Coordination can signal cause and effect. The proximity of the coordinated units of the sentence implies that the first caused the second which caused the third, and so on. Thus Browning's Duke tells succinctly how he disposed of his friendly wife, his "last Duchess," whose innocent attentions to others made him jealous enough to have her murdered:

> This [her indiscriminate smiling] grew; I gave commands;
> Then all smiles stopped together.

Coordination can emphasize a crowding of events, an abundance of happenings or things. In Dickens's *Great Expectations*, an unsophisticated character, Joe Gargery, describes how the robbers treated the pompous merchant Pumblechook:

> . . . and they took his till, and they took his cash box, and they drinked his wine, and they partook of his wittles [food], and they slapped his face, and they pulled his nose, and they tied him up to his bedpust, and they giv' him a dozen, and they stuffed his mouth full of flowering annuals to perwent [prevent] him crying out.[10]

This quoted portion of a very long sentence contains eight independent clauses of the basic simple sentence pattern (subject-verb-complement). The ninth segment follows the simple sentence with an infinitive phrase ("to perwent him crying out"). Each clause begins with "and they," followed by a verb. This highly coordinated sentence is full of events and vigorous action that builds to a climax in the last clause, the longest.

Coordinating Devices

There are a number of devices for indicating coordination. Some, *coordinating conjunctions*, or pairs of conjunctions, and *coordinating punctuation*, go in between the elements that are to be coordinated as a signal of their equivalence. Among the most common coordinating conjunctions are *and, or, nor, but, yet, for:*

Wine *and* cheese have replaced cake *and* ice cream as adult party fare.

Every man desires to live long, *but* no man would be old.

—Jonathan Swift

Coordinating pairs of conjunctions set up the expectation that when the first element of the pair appears, the second must inevitably follow, as in either/or, neither/nor, both/and, not only/but also.

To celebrate the New Year I will *not only* make good resolutions, *but* I will *also* keep them.

Coordinating punctuation is of two sorts, commas and semicolons. *Commas* separate *words in series:* "Coffee, tea, soda, or milk?" They can separate short unpunctuated *phrases* (groups of words that function as a single part of speech but lack a subject or predicate): tart red apples, sweet yellow pears, succulent crimson pomegranates. And they can also separate *a series of clauses* (word groupings with a subject and verb): I came, I saw, I conquered.* *Semicolons*

* Technically, these are comma splices (see p. 385). However, custom and a desire to integrate the separate, short parts of a larger sentence into an intimate unit, dictates the use of commas here instead of semicolons.

separate whole series or longer, punctuated phrases or clauses: We consumed a succulent breakfast of Danish pastry, Irish marmalade, and English tea; and we devoured an equally international lunch of French cheeses, Italian sausage, and Greek olives.

Repeated words and *repeated grammatical structures* can also provide coordination. To illustrate her opposition to the dictatorships taking power just before the outbreak of World War II, writer Gertrude Stein repeated one sentence and the words *fathers, depressing, and* each twice:

> There is too much fathering going on just now and there is no doubt about it *fathers are depressing.* Everybody nowadays is a *father,* there is *father* Mussolini *and father* Hitler *and father* Roosevelt *and father* Stalin *and father* Lewis *and father* Blum *and father* France. . . . *Fathers are depressing.*[11]

Repeated clauses with a parallel structure and rhythm function in the same way as repeated words or phrases in providing both sentence coordination and sentence unity: It's a bird, it's a plane, it's Superman!

Such coordination can also provide emphasis. For instance, in "Radical Chic," author Tom Wolfe gives a satiric account of a party that composer Leonard Bernstein and his wife gave to raise money for the revolutionary Black Panthers in 1966. He uses the coordinating devices of repeated words and repeated grammatical structures to point out (and poke fun at) the way the hostess treated everyone, irrespective of social status:

> *She greets* the Black Panthers with *the same* bend *of the* wrist, *the same* tilt *of the* head, *the same* perfect Mary Astor voice with which *she greets* people like Jason, John and D.D.[12]

In this particular sentence, the repeated words also signal repeated grammatical structures; the same pattern of subject (*she*), verb (*greets*), and object (*the Black Panthers/people*) is used for both the first and second halves of the sentence.

Parallelism

Parallelism is the strongest and most effective means of emphasizing coordination. *It is an expression of coordinate ideas in the same grammatical form*— whether that form is two or more words, phrases, clauses, or whole sentences or paragraphs.

Parallelism emphasizes *the relationship or the equivalent importance of two or more ideas, sentence elements, sentences, or paragraphs* (see paragraph coherence, pp. 107–108): As the patrons emerged from the Woody Allen movie, they *tittered, snickered,* and *guffawed.*

Parallelism can also *smooth the flow of words*, because the matched elements are structurally equivalent. For instance, nouns match nouns or noun phrases; verbs match other verbs in mood, tense, or sentence position; clauses must be roughly equivalent in structure and in length. Thus *Newsweek* uses parallelism to describe conductor Zubin Mehta's "habit of squiring around expensive women in fast cars—or perhaps it was fast women in expensive cars."[13] The structure of each of the last two phrases is identical: adjective, plural noun, preposition, adjective, plural noun. Indeed, the basic terms, "women in . . . cars," are identical; only the adjectives are switched in the successive phrases:

expensive	women	in	fast	cars
fast	women	in	expensive	cars

The switch emphasizes the equivalence of both the adjectives and the nouns they modify; it makes women and cars seem equivalent in their relationships to Mehta; it is a daring play with words that creates surprise and humor.

When you're using parallelism, you must be certain to keep both the ideas and the syntactic relations equivalent. Keeping the following principles in mind will help you in creating parallel constructions or in revising your writing to make the constructions parallel:

Use language of an equivalent level (equally formal or informal) **to emphasize the equivalence of ideas for each item or statement in a series.**

Make pairs or series parallel (i.e., match nouns with nouns, verb form and tense with verb form and tense, etc.).

When you have a coordinating word in a series (*to, for, because* . . .), **either use it once to precede the entire series or repeat the coordinator before each item in the series.** Either:

Rosy Grier likes to play football, appear on television, and do needlepoint.
> or
Rosy Grier likes to play football, to appear on television, and to do needlepoint.

There are times, however, when you may consciously choose to leave an element in a series *out of parallel*, thereby calling particular attention to it. Witness the effect of the following extract by writer Dick Gregory:

When I played the drums in high school it was for Helene *and* when I broke track records in college it was for Helene *and* when I started standing behind microphones and heard applause *I wished Helene could hear it, too*[14] (italics added).

Gregory sets up the parallel pattern in the first two clauses of the sentence (coordinated by *and*) which he begins to repeat in the third (also coordinated by *and*). But instead of saying again, *it was for Helene,* he offers the variation, *I wished Helene could hear it, too*—which calls attention to the end of the sentence—the most emphatic position and provides a pleasant change from the predictable.

On the other hand, in Lincoln's "Gettysburg Address" we appreciate the cadence and emphasis of the triple rhythm in "that the government of the people, by the people, for the people, shall not perish from the earth." Saying *the people* three times reinforces the weight of the message that variation would only undermine.

SUBORDINATION

We have already seen how coordination and parallelism can be used to establish or demonstrate equivalence among the parts of a sentence. But you may not always want each part of a sentence to carry equal weight, if one part is more important than another, or if you want to emphasize one part more than the rest. In these instances, you may decide to use *subordination,* in which one sentence element is placed so that it depends (because it cannot stand alone grammatically) on another. The subordinate element works to restrict, explain, or substantiate the meaning of the main element.

This can be seen more clearly if we look at the grammar of subordinated sentences. Usually, the *independent clause* of a sentence is the main element. The subordinate elements are one or more *dependent clauses, phrases, or words,* often signaled by a subordinating preposition (therefore, whenever, etc.). A *complex sentence* consists of one independent clause and one or more subordinate clauses. Compare the following two examples:

                     independent clause   independent clause

Coordinate sentence: My money was stolen and I couldn't take a long-anticipated trip to Tahiti.

                     dependent clause   independent clause

Subordinate senence: Because my money was stolen, I couldn't take a long-anticipated trip to Tahiti.

The coordinated sentence simply equates the two elements. The subordinated sentence removes the equivalent emphases on the stolen money and the trip to Tahiti and establishes a causal relationship between the two—the theft prevented the trip. By putting the trip to Tahiti last, the sentence gives it greater importance than the theft.

The Functions of Subordination

Subordination, as we've seen, can help you express both the dominant and the dependent relationships among the elements of sentences. Use of subordination will also reveal your judgment, for when you subordinate one element to another, you are implying that it is less important or secondary. Subordination is not to be thought of as superior to coordination—each has its own merits—but, as the list below illustrates, it can help you accomplish several different and important aims in your writing.

   Subordination can establish cause and effect relationships among the sentence elements. Whereas coordinated sentences sometimes do this simply by placing items together, with or without extra coordinating words, subordinated sentences use key words or phrases such as *because, consequently, as a result of, in order to*, and *for* to establish the dependence of one element on another.

   Coordinate: The weather is unusually dry, and Santa will arrive by camel caravan.
   Subordinate: As a result of unusually dry weather, Santa will arrive by camel caravan.

Your purpose and your judgment will determine which sentence pattern you will choose. A coordinate sentence will suffice if you merely want to call attention to two phenomena—here, the unusual weather and Santa's unusual mode of transportation. But if you want to make a causal connection emphatically clear, you will choose a subordinate pattern.

   Subordination can establish the time sequence in which events occurred. Again, what coordination does by proximity (I came, I saw, I conquered) subordination does by establishing grammatical relationships signaled by key words such as *when, whenever, while, then, thereupon, before, until, after.*

   Coordinate: The gourmand consumed an entire submarine sandwich and polished off a quart of strawberry ice cream.
   Subordinate: After the gourmand consumed an entire submarine sandwich, he polished off a quart of strawberry ice cream.

The coordinate sentence itemizes the gourmand's meal but doesn't identify the order in which he ate it. If it seems important to establish a particular sequence (you're the judge), you'll need to use the subordinate pattern.

   Subordination can indicate exceptions, qualifications, or concessions. Typical key words/phrases—*except, except for, in spite of the fact that, yet, although, nevertheless*—signal the exceptional or qualifying portion of the statement.

   Not subordinate: Claude weighed 330 pounds. He ran four miles every morning.
   Subordinate: In spite of the fact that Claude weighed 330 pounds, he ran four miles every morning.

Or, for a different emphasis, you could write, "Claude ran four miles every morning in spite of the fact that he weighed 330 pounds."
   If you expect readers to make the connection between the two phenomena, Claude's weight and his running, you could leave the sentences as independent

units. But if you want to imply that for such a heavy person to run that far was unusual, the subordinate structure would better serve your purpose.

Subordination can indicate a condition or alternative contrary to the state being identified or described. This is signaled by such key words/phrases as *if, even if,* and *unless.*

> *Not subordinate:* Kelly keeps on missing her eight o'clock classes. She can't seem to get up on time.
>
> *Subordinate:* Unless Kelly can make herself get up on time, she'll keep on missing her eight o'clock classes.
>
> or
>
> If Kelly doesn't get up on time, she'll continue to miss her eight o'clock classes.

The form you use will depend on whether you expect your readers to make the necessary connection between the two independent sentences, or whether you want to offer the more overt interpretation that the subordinate forms provide.

Subordination can designate a relationship between two places, or between something else and a place. Typical key words or phrases indicating such relationships are *where, here, beside, inside,* and *on the spot that.*

> *Not subordinate:* Jonah was inside the whale. Jonah felt cramped.
>
> *Subordinate:* Inside the whale, Jonah felt cramped.

In this case the subordinate construction is preferable to the short sentences side-by-side because it more clearly shows the relationship between the two and eliminates unnecessary repetition of the subject.

As the above examples illustrate, the use of subordination can help eliminate sentences with monotonously repetitive patterns (such as S-V-C, S-V-C, S-V-C, S-V-C). Subordination is also helpful in transforming longer, overcoordinated sentences full of too many equivalent constructions into sentences that differentiate more carefully among their parts.

SUGGESTIONS FOR DISCUSSION AND WRITING

1. Combine each of the following clusters of sentences or fragments into a single sentence, using appropriate subordination or coordination.
   a. Rock music. Teens listen to it. It comes on strong and heavy. It beats to the rhythm of cars, drugs, and sex.
   b. Country music talks of aching hearts. Faithless lovers are another subject of country music. It also sings of driving the big rigs.
   c. As a group, truck drivers are probably country music's most dedicated listeners. Country music makes a man's life on the road a mite easier. It can also make one homesick.
2. In the passage below, student Steve Arata describes the effect of an afternoon on the beach. Analyze this description for elements of coordination. What is their

cumulative effect? Should there be more subordination? What is the impact of the continual repetition of *I*?

> As I lie on the beach, I feel the sand. It molds itself to me and I feel as if I become part of it, connected to the entire beach. The beach is a whole, an eternity, and I am part of it, lost in it. I feel engulfed in something that is larger, more important than I am. I lose myself. I feel the sand, and I feel each individual grain touching my skin. I know an infinite number of points of feeling. I concentrate and am aware of each grain being separate, distinct from every other grain. I feel immense as I think of all the unique grains of sand that surround me. I am whole, made up of countless grains of sand. The beach is whole, made up of countless grains of people.
> I close my eyes and listen. I hear the people, because the beach is crowded. Separately, I hear the purr of the ocean. The two sounds never mingle; they are always separate. I hear one or the other, but never both together. I listen to the ocean, my thoughts standing beside the sound of the waves. Slowly, the two intertwine, moving in and out, knit together in my mind until I cannot tear them apart. I slide into a state of half-consciousness, aware of nothing but the sound. The entire ocean is only a part of my thoughts. I encompass it all. I feel lost in the ocean, floating helplessly in the immensity of the sound of the waves. My mind and the ocean melt together until they become silence, complete and total. There is nothing. I revel in the silence and the emptiness. I feel exhilarated, exalted— and then unbearably alone. I become frightened, and fight to come back. I shudder, open my eyes, and sighing, bask in the dullness and security of conversations and a.m. radios.

3. For each category below, compose a sentence that places the items in a series that is consistent in level of usage (i.e., don't mix highly formal and highly informal language—change some terms to have them conform to the others). Arrange each series so that the items proceed from the least to the most emphatic or important.
    a. tops   better   OK
    b. pride   having a swelled head   arrogance
    c. daytime   darkness   eventide
    d. war   civil disturbance   riot
    e. superhighway   a littered alley   a clean street
    f. stumbling   to walk   to run
    g. shouting   yakking   to whisper
4. Each pair or group of sentences below is related. Combine them using subordination. First subordinate sentence 1 to sentence 2 or to sentences 2 and 3; then reverse the subordination. What is the difference in emphasis (and grammar, if necessary) between the two versions?
    a. 1. Garbo hasn't appeared in a film since 1940.
       2. Garbo's beauty continues to be the standard by which every other film actress is measured.
    b. 1. Fred Astaire and Ginger Rogers were a superb dancing team.
       2. Their musicals are a popular art form.
       3. The main value of the Rogers-Astaire movies lies in their charm as escapist entertainment.

c. 1. The public has demanded disaster movies.
   2. Disaster movies concern large-scale floods, mammoth fires, crashes, or invasions of terrifying insects, animals, or monsters.
   3. In disaster movies, the disaster itself is the "star."
5. Identify the elements of coordination, subordination, and/or parallel construction in the following article by Washington *Post* reporter Lou Cannon:

> Little over a year ago he was "Stevie Wonder," the 16-year-old Cinderella kid of horse racing. Fresh from taking New York by storm, winning three Eclipse awards and setting an all-time record for purse earnings, he had come to California to seek the good life and the laurels that went with it.
>
> Now, at 18, Steve Cauthen is the snake-bitten ex-wonder of Santa Anita. The laurel has turned into hemlock, the prince has become a frog. After 126 races this season at this tough, competitive Southern California racing showplace, Cauthen has only four winners. On Saturday his losing streak reached 89 consecutive mounts.
>
> Cauthen has changed agents, testily rejected interviews, decided one day to abandon Los Angeles for New York and two days later to stay here. He seems confused and says he is "disgusted" with his showing. The boos of the crowd ring in his ears.
>
> But in this winter of Cauthen's discontent, the prevailing view on the Santa Anita backstretch is that he is as good as he ever was and maybe even an improved jockey. The general opinion here when Cauthen was the toast of the nation was that he was not yet a finished rider, a contention seemingly supported by the number of stretch drives Cauthen lost to top rider Darrel McHargue or the veteran Bill Shoemaker, the all-time leading jockey.[15]

TRY THIS

In the next essay you write, consciously try to vary your sentences through use of coordination and subordination to achieve unity and/or emphasis precisely where you want to.

FRAGMENTS/MINOR SENTENCES

Sentence fragments look like sentences because they begin with a capital letter and end with terminal punctuation—a period, question mark, or exclamation point. However, they usually lack one of the two major ingredients of a sentence—either a subject or a verb, or both. Like this.

Believing fragments to be incomplete expressions of meaning or of grammar, teachers have for centuries tried to drive them out of the language. Without success. For they're too useful in speech and writing to disappear. Research indicates, in fact, that nearly all professional writers use what are conventionally called *fragments* to *avoid wordiness,* to *break up complex sentences into simpler segments,* to *sound informal,* or to *make transitions from one point to the next.*

Researchers Kline and Memering call these *minor sentences* (as distinguished from major sentences, which have subjects and verbs), and divide them into two basic types, *independent* and *dependent.*[16] For the practical purposes of most writers and speakers, *independent sentence fragments are those that function as complete sentences,* even though they are not grammatically complete. You can recognize many of them by their context:

Commands: Sit down!

Exclamations: Man overboard! Danger!

Single-word questions: Who? Why?

Answers to questions: Whose paper deserves an A? Mine. Why? Because I worked hard and stayed up all night to finish it.

Transitions: Now for the other side of the problem.

Some expressions of feeling: Oh, for a hot shower.

Items in lists or free-standing series: The catalog looked particularly enticing. Skis. Stereos. Camping equipment. Even a speedboat with a 225 h.p. inboard motor.

The fragments that teachers and some critics object to most vigorously, though research again indicates that professional writers often use them, are what Kline and Memering call *dependent minor sentences.* Because they are tied through both grammar and meaning to the preceding sentence, they look incomplete or sloppy as free-standing units. Hence the advice to "complete" them.

A typical construction using a dependent minor sentence is the following:

On a whimsical impulse, the interior decorator threw out all the modern furniture and replaced it with antiques. *Antiques that were so expensive that his clients couldn't pay for them.*

The fragment (italicized) is a noun phrase modifying *antiques* in the first sentence. Conventional usage says that it isn't complete because the fragment breaks up the sentence flow with punctuation that is too strong. The period makes the readers stop where they should pause—as a connecting comma or dash would indicate.

Conventional advice would also insist that subordinate clauses, with their subject-verb-[complement] structure, be tied to the preceding sentence:

Not: Brigita wore a wide, gold wedding band. Although she wasn't married.
But: Brigita wore a wide, gold wedding band, although she wasn't married.

Conventional advice also dictates that constructions containing *-ed* or *-ing* verbal forms,

Being of sound mind and body . . .
Sitting, fully clothed, in the middle of the swimming pool . . .

be included in either the preceding or following sentence.

Research evidence notwithstanding, as long as your writing is being judged according to these conventions, you will want to avoid the use of a fragment if:

Its meaning is not fully apparent. If the fragment is unclear, you should probably supply the missing elements and make it a full sentence.

It looks or sounds isolated, as many of the S-V or S-V-C fragments do that are separated from the main clause. In such cases, the fragment should probably be attached to the independent clause that immediately precedes or follows it and completes its construction.

SUGGESTIONS FOR DISCUSSION

1. The following description by student Stacey Ponticello contains a number of sentence fragments. Which function as independent sentence fragments, and which do not?

> The inevitable guitar. The inevitable banjo. Perhaps a bass and fiddle thrown in for good measure and, of course, every once in a while an organ or piano. Country-western, the twangiest music in the whole world with singers and lyrics to match. For the most part the music drones. It is sad music of loneliness and death. The chords repeat themselves frequently as the general tone of the song comes to the fore. Some of the lyrics are ridiculous. The twang distracts from the depressing tone of the song and it begins to be like waiting for the other shoe to drop. To drop and drop again. Speed enters into the dancing music. Fast paced plucking and a quick but steady beat. You can hear the handclapping and foot-stomping. Still the twang. The nasal sound. The high pitched screams. The guitar becomes a slicer that grates on the nerves.

2. Examine some published writing, perhaps a newspaper feature article or editorial, or an essay you particularly like, to see whether it contains sentence fragments (minor sentences). What is the purpose of each that you find? Does each function effectively in its context, or do some need to be integrated with what precedes or follows?

SENTENCE VARIETY AND RHYTHM

You will want to vary the lengths, rhythms, and constructions of your sentences to suit your message, your approach to your subject, your audience, and your general stylistic preference. If you're writing formally, especially about a serious subject, your sentences, like your paragraphs, may be on the average longer and more complicated than they would be in informal writing. If you're writing informally, your sentences may be shorter, simpler, and more numerous, as you divide or subdivide your material into more free-standing units for simplicity of expression or ease of understanding. Yet even informal writing will be likely to contain some long sentences, and even in the most formal writing you will use shorter sentences to break up a series of long ones, or for contrast, emphasis, or transition.

To discover the rhythm of your sentences, read them aloud. If they seem to jerk along they may be too short or be broken up by punctuation into too-brief segments, inhibiting the narrative flow. If they leave you gasping for breath, they may be too long. If the emphasis of your meaning doesn't coincide with the emphasis of your sentence structure, you'll want to rework the sentence to make the two congruent. In reading aloud you'll also be able to hear alliteration (similar initial consonants), rhyme (is it intentional? does it really fit?), and (for better and worse) repeated sounds. Do you have a lot of words ending in -tion or other tongue-twisters that make your sentences hard to say? In writing sentences, it is at least partly true that if you take care of the sound the sense will take care of itself. For in good sentences, sound and structure reinforce the meaning and collaborate to attract and hold your readers.

Revision Through Sentence Alteration

Taking care of the sounds turned out to be a good way for student Phyllis Kaplan to approach her revision of "The Tooth, the Whole Tooth," an account of her too-long-delayed trip to the dentist. Indeed, when she read the original version (see below) aloud, she realized that it contained some short, choppy sentences of a similar pattern; a number of overcoordinated sentences; and many excess words. Once she could *hear* the problems, it was easy for her to alter the sentences to provide greater variety of length, structure, and rhythm—and to remove the deadwood.

Original:

I found myself in a dentist's office last week. I hadn't been to the dentist's in nearly five years. I hated the thought of going. This is because dental care is so expensive these days, and I get upset at the thought of paying all that money.

The last time I permitted myself to be exposed to the gymnastics of dental hygienics I just saw the dentist. This time was different. A whole team was there. Two people placed me, a grown up type adult person, in a dentist's chair and put a bib on me and it wasn't even decorated with a lobster. And if that wasn't enough I had to listen to the usual fundamentalist sermon about the virtues of proper tooth care and get a bag of goodies. It contained a little "illustrated" handbook of the "how-tos" of teeth brushing, and a plastic toothbrush, toothpick holder, and a little just-like-the-dentist's mirror to look at your teeth with, and some red spy pills. These stain the stuff on your teeth you don't remove with the newly taught method of super tooth brushing. All this happens very quickly. It is done with sweet and slightly detached efficiency.

Revision:

Although I hadn't been to the dentist in nearly five years, I finally went last week. I found the thought of going very painful, in spite of the fact that I didn't know which would hurt more—the anguish of the dental work or the agony of paying the bill.

The last time I permitted myself to be exposed to the gymnastics of dental hygiene I saw only the dentist. This time I was at the mercy of a whole team. Two people placed me, an adult, in a dental chair and tied a bib (not even decorated with a lobster) around my neck. Then they forced me to listen to the usual fundamentalist sermon about the virtues of proper dental care, and rewarded my patience with a bag of "goodies." This contained an illustrated handbook on tooth brushing, a plastic toothbrush, a toothpick holder, a little imitation dental mirror, and some red spy pills, which stain your teeth red where you haven't brushed thoroughly with the newly taught method of super tooth brushing. All this took place with a sweet, swift, slightly detached efficiency.

The first paragraph of Phyllis's revision combines the four original sentences into two, without changing the meaning. In fact the new, subordinated sentences (with the subordination signaled by *Although* and *in spite of the fact that*) make the meaning clearer than it was in the original because the subordination shows relationships among ideas that had been previously isolated in separate sentences. She eliminates one of the two repetitions of *the thought of* that appear in the first version and alters the lengthy last sentence of the original to a memorable parallel construction, *the anguish of the dental work or the agony of paying the bill.*

In the second paragraph, Phyllis's new version combines the original second and third short sentences (totaling eleven words) into one eleven-word sentence that has a more pointed meaning than the first account because of her interpretive *I was at the mercy* . . . She leaves out some of the too-cute words of the original, substituting, for example, simply *an adult* for *a grown up type adult person.* The rather aimless *and it wasn't even decorated with a lobster* is appropriately put into parentheses (*not even decorated with a lobster*) that accurately convey the impression that this is a humorous afterthought rather than the main point of the sentence.

The fourth sentence (*Then they forced me* . . .) is coordinated in both versions. The revision is far more emphatic, however, because there the hygienists, who had been absent in the first version, inflict two unwelcome actions (preaching, rewarding with unwelcome goodies) on the wretched victim. The fifth sentence in the revision eliminates some of the *ands* in the original to tighten the parallelism, combines two sentences into one, and emerges with a single, coordinated sentence of forty-one words in comparison with the fifty-seven words of the original. In the revision, Phyllis combines the last two sentences of the first version into a single, fast-moving concluding sentence that ends with a brief swish of alliterative s's, *sweet, swift, slightly.* . . . The original version has thirteen sentences, one of which is periodic; the revised, eight-sentence version has two periodic sentences, one to begin each paragraph. Thus Phyllis has shifted the ratio of loose to periodic sentences from 12:1 in the first version to 3:1 in the second—a possible clue to her greater control over her sentence structures. The kinds of questions that Phyllis asked herself as she was revising her writing, as presented in the checklist below, should also prove helpful to you when you are contemplating sentence revision.

☐ A Checklist for Sentence Revision

☐ Do I have too many short sentences?

☐ Can I combine any sentences to make longer ones?

☐ Do I have too many long sentences?

☐ Would any of the long sentences be clearer or more emphatic if they were broken up?

☐ Would any of the long sentences be clearer or more emphatic if repetitive or unnecessary words were deleted?

☐ Is the emphasis in my sentences where I want it to be—presumably, at either the beginning or the end? If not, would revision to make the problem sentence subordinated rather than coordinated, or would rearranging the subordinated elements help to change the emphasis?

☐ Would changing a sentence from a loose to a periodic construction help to change the emphasis?

☐ Have I used any fragments? If so, are they independent sentence fragments? Or should they be integrated with the preceding or following sentence?

☐ Do my sentences have the right flow, rhythm, and sound when read aloud in sequence? If not, what words or sentence patterns do I need to change?

SUGGESTIONS FOR WRITING

1. In student Romy Gaida's description of her childhood visits to her Italian grandmother's apartment in Verona, the original sentence structures have been deliberately altered to simplify their construction and minimize their variety. Using the Checklist for Sentence Revision, rewrite the passage to make the sentences more varied in emphasis, pattern, and rhythm. You may alter the wording, if necessary.

My grandmother always welcomed us children in the kitchen. My mother did not. So we congregated in grandmother's bedroom. This room was always a special place for us. Every time I enter it I recapture the special but trivial events of my childhood. The big, soft, dark brown wooden bed many times lulled us to sleep while we listened to my grandmother's soft voice. She told us ballerina and fairy stories. Many times we left open the polished, wooden closet doors. We took down all my grandmother's clothing and had fashion shows. The two mirrors reflected back hazy misty images. This was because the glass of the early 1900's wasn't made well. Nevertheless, I thought it gave us an aura of mysteriousness and fascination. In the middle of the wall over the big bed was a beautiful oil painting. It showed Jesus on the cross. We always kneeled respectfully in front of it when we passed from one side of the room to the other. That was when we were pretending we were nuns. On the walls were framed portraits of my grandmother's relatives. One was of her as a seven-year-old child in Yugoslavia. All these portraits were in the traditional brown and white of early turn-of-the-century photographs. The windows in the bedroom opened onto a courtyard. A breeze came in through the venetian blinds. This was different from the kitchen windows. These opened onto a busy street, letting in smoke and noise. The mementos of the past are reminders of my great-grandmother's and grandmother's days. Once the objects were thought of as old and useless. Now they are priceless and sought after.

2. As you write your next essay, use the checklist as the basis for revising your own sentences and paragraphs.

NOTES

[1] See Michael Adelstein and Jean Pival, *The Writing Commitment* (New York: Harcourt Brace Jovanovich, 1980), p. 65.

[2] "Comedy's Greatest Era," *Agee on Film* (New York: Grossett & Dunlap, 1958) p. 443.

[3] *Today's Education* (March–April 1976), p. 86.

[4] Diana Granat, "Dog Days on the Potomac," the *Washington Post*, September 11, 1980, E 1.

[5] Desmond Morris, *Manwatching: A Field Guide to Human Behavior* (New York: Harry N. Abrams, 1977), p. 11.

[6] *Manwatching*, p. 142.

[7] *A Connecticut Yankee in King Arthur's Court*, Chapt. 22.

[8] *Notes of a Native Son* (Boston: Beacon Press, 1955), p. 100.

[9] N. Scott Momaday, *The Way to Rainy Mountain* (New York: Harper & Row, 1968), p. 123.

[10] Charles Dickens, *Great Expectations* (1860; rpt. New York: Rinehart, 1948), p. 474.

[11] *Everybody's Autobiography* (1937; rpt. New York: Vintage Books, 1973), p. 133.

[12] *Radical Chic & Mau-Mauing the Flak Catchers* (1970; rpt. New York: Bantam, 1971), p. 6.

[13] Hubert Saal, "Macho Maestro," *Newsweek*, December 18, 1978, p. 72.

[14] *Up from Nigger* (New York: Stein & Day, 1976), p. 6.

[15] "Peers Predict Better Times for Cauthen: Luck Now All Bad for 'Stevie Wonder,'" the *Washington Post*, January 29, 1979, D 1.

[16] Charles R. Kline, Jr., and W. Dean Memering, "Formal Fragments: The English Minor Sentence," *Research in the Teaching of English*, 11:2 (Fall 1977), 97–110. Their reasoning and explanations have been simplified and adapted for the purposes of this discussion. They do not share the conventional views identified in this section, which most critics and teachers still hold despite the merits of Kline and Memering's research.

CHAPTER SEVEN
CHOOSING AND USING WORDS

Hemingway: I rewrote the ending to Farewell to Arms, *the last page of it, thirty-nine times before I was satisfied.*

Interviewer: Was there some technical problem there? What was it that had you stumped?

Hemingway: Getting the words right.

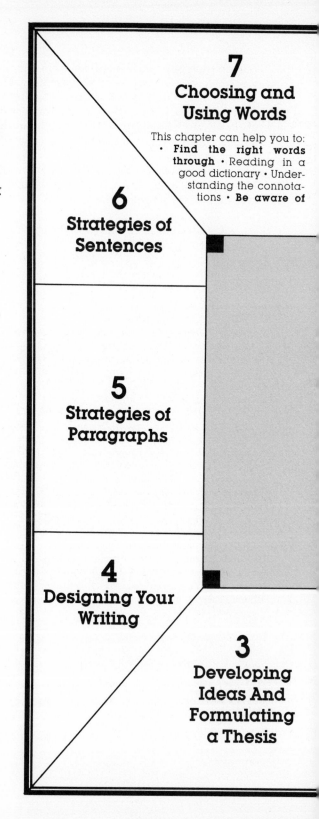

7
Choosing and Using Words

This chapter can help you to:
· **Find the right words through** · Reading in a good dictionary · Understanding the connotations · **Be aware of**

6
Strategies of Sentences

5
Strategies of Paragraphs

4
Designing Your Writing

3
Developing Ideas And Formulating a Thesis

special adaptations of language ·
Technical language · Slang · Dialect ·
**Improve your word usage
through** · Concrete language ·
Figures of speech · Conciseness
· Clarity · Consideration for
your readers.

8
Revising,
Editing, and
Preparing the
Final Copy

1
Warming Up

2
Finding a
Subject

FINDING THE RIGHT WORDS

Encountering an essay is like meeting a person for the first time: an unappealing first impression may be your last impression, but love at first sight will lead you to read on. In many cases you make your decision quickly, on the basis of various clues of which you may not be consciously aware. You may be responding not just to the overt message but to the language—verbal or nonverbal—in which it is expressed.

Readers of your work will be doing the same. So it will be helpful to consider what kinds of messages you're sending in addition to those that are the explicit content of your essay, and whether these reinforce or undermine it. As we have seen in earlier chapters, the length and arrangement of sentences, paragraphs, and the entire paper can strongly influence the reactions of readers. This chapter will examine how and where to find the right words and how to use them in your writing with clarity, conciseness, precision, and sensitivity to your readers.

Where to Find the Right Words

We live in a society that bombards us with words. Although we probably don't talk as much as we listen, we do spend considerable time conversing with different people in varying degrees of formality or informality, using varying amounts of slang or technical language or dialect. At the same time that we are adapting our tone and vocabulary to each conversation, we are also picking up new words, expressions, and nuances from the people we talk with—a process that is intensified when we read challenging literature with its enriched vocabulary and ever-new ways of saying things. Even if our language had only a thousand nouns and a thousand verbs we could make a billion different three-word sentences. The infinitely creative possibilities of language are not only astounding but overwhelming!

Listen and Read: This lifetime immersion in a world of words can give you many sources of words to write with. The best ways to learn new words are to *listen carefully to spoken language* and to *read widely*, especially imaginative, technical, or otherwise thought-provoking literature that has a large and varied vocabulary. You will understand and remember words better if you *learn them in context* rather than if you try to memorize vocabulary lists. Make note (a pocket or purse-sized pad will do) of unfamiliar words when you encounter them, and then look them up in a dictionary when it's convenient. Keeping a notebook with one page for each letter of the alphabet is a good idea. As you discover new words, write each one down with an abbreviated definition of it or a sentence using the word in context. This notebook should be kept at hand for easy reference. Or collect new words or usages in your writer's notebook (see Chapter 1).

A typical entry might look like this:

adulterate: make impure by adding inferior materials.
The conniving cook *adulterated* the hamburger with horsemeat.

If there's anything else you want to remember about the word, include that here too:

not to be confused with adultery

You can also keep lists of words you misspell. To make it easier to learn them, do not group these words alphabetically but according to the correction for the problem they represent (see *Handbook,* pp. 375–379).

ei	ie
rec**ei**ve	fr**ie**ze
conc**ei**ve	n**ie**ce
	bel**ie**ve
	gr**ie**ve

Use a Good Dictionary: Dictionaries are also a good source of words—not just the words you look up to find the spelling, meaning, or pronunciation, but of synonyms (words with similar meanings) and antonyms (words with opposite meanings). A *full-sized college dictionary* (not a small, abridged paperback) is probably the best for your purposes, for it will explain the word's history and its various shades of meanings, and it will show how it is used in different senses. Because the language is changing continually, you will want to get an up-to-date edition of the *Random House College Dictionary,* the *American Heritage Dictionary, Funk and Wagnalls Standard College Dictionary, Webster's New Collegiate Dictionary,* or *Webster's New World Dictionary.* All of these dictionaries are *descriptive* (describing how real people *actually* talk) rather than *prescriptive* (telling what people *should* say). Although some people still prefer to believe that what "Webster says" is an authoritarian command rather than a reflection of actual usage, in fact, not all dictionaries agree on every definition, etymology, or even pronunciation.

From a typical definition you can learn a great deal about the word. Here, for instance, is a portion of the definition of *person* from the *Random House College Dictionary.* Its particular features are identified in the margins.

Capitalization (if any) would also be identified here

Syllable
Accent division

Part of speech

In most dictionaries (except Webster's *Collegiate*) the most common meaning; Webster's *Collegiate* usually puts oldest meanings first

Word (Spelling; any alternate spellings would also be given)

Pronunciation

Illustration of the word in sense 3 used in context

Specialized meanings

Explanation of grammar

Slang or dialect usages, if any, would be provided here

Synonyms [antonyms sometimes identified, too]

Synonyms used in context to aid in discriminating among them

per·son (*pûr'sen*), n. 1. a human being. 2. the actual self or individual personality of a human being. 3. the body of a living human being, sometimes including the clothes being worn: *He had no money on his person. . . . 6. Law.* a human being, a group of human beings, a corporation, an estate, or other legal entity recognized by law as having rights and duties. 7. *Gram.* a category used to distinguish between the speaker of an utterance and those to or about whom he is speaking. In English there are three persons in the pronouns, the first represented by *I* and *we,* the second by *you,* and the third by *he, she, it,* and *they.* Most verbs have distinct third person singular forms in the present tense, as *writes. . . .* [ME *persone* < L *persona* role (in life, a play, a tale), LL: member (of the Trinity), orig. actor's mask, prob. < Etruscan *phersu*] —Syn. Person, individual, personage are terms applied to human beings. Person is the most general and common word: *the average person.* Individual views a person as standing alone or as a single member of a group: *the characteristics of the individual.* Personage is used as an outstanding or illustrious person: *a distinguished personage.*[1]

The second most common meaning

The third most common meaning

Specialized meaning

Etymology—word history, listed with most recent sense first, moving back toward oldest sense

The abbreviations, such as those used in the etymology (ME—Middle English, L—Latin, LL—Late Latin), and the symbols (< derived from), are identified at the beginning of the dictionary; a pronunciation key is provided at the beginning and at the bottom of every other page.

In addition to their primary function as definers of words, dictionaries also serve as abbreviated reference works, providing lists of abbreviations and symbols (pharmacy, proofreading, meteorology, and so on), tables of weights and measures, biographical and geographical names, small maps and illustrations of unfamiliar animals or objects, occasional portraits, population figures, lists of proper names, and identifications of American colleges. Some dictionaries also contain brief handbooks of grammar and usage. For enriching your vocabulary and flexibility with words, the definitions, synonyms, and antonyms will probably be the most useful aspects of your dictionary.

UNDERSTANDING THE CONNOTATIONS OF WORDS

Many words have two kinds of meaning, the *denotation*, the relatively straightforward, objective, unemotional definition that a dictionary provides; and the *connotation*, the more subjective definition that individuals or groups associate with a word because of their personal or collective experiences with it. One denotative definition of *maturity*, for instance, is "the state of being mature . . . full development." Yet *maturity* to a sixteen-year-old might mean the chance to drive the family car on weekends; to her older brother it might mean the opportunity and common sense to make major decisions for himself; to her parents it could be the obligation to pay the family bills. And as used in the magazine *Modern Maturity* it means *anyone fifty-five or older*. Likewise, *middle class* is defined, denotatively, as "a class of people intermediate in social, economic, and cultural standing." Connotatively, however, there are probably as many definitions available as there are members of that vast middle class extending from Archie Bunker to members of Congress. Still other definitions could be provided by people who are not middle class.

In spite of our enormous freedom to interpret words in a variety of senses or to invest them with special or private meanings, none of us has the total license to assign arbitrary meanings to words that Humpty Dumpty claims in *Through the Looking-Glass*:

> "But 'glory' doesn't mean 'a nice knock-down argument,' " Alice objected.
> "When *I* use a word," Humpty Dumpty said, in rather a scornful tone, "it means just what I choose it to mean—neither more nor less."
> "The question is," said Alice, "whether you *can* make words mean so many different things."[2]

The answer is, of course, that you can't. As a writer you are responsible for the meaning your words convey—their connotations as well as denotations. And as a writer, you must meet the twofold challenge of connotations, to make sure that you understand the connotative meanings of the words you use and to make sure that you have conveyed these meanings to your readers. "Account executive," "salesman," and "huckster" may have similar denotative meanings, as may "spinster" and "unmarried woman," or "relaxed" and "laid back," but their connotations are *very* different.

The most reliable way to learn the connotations of a word is to encounter it in context often enough to verify your understanding of the term. You are doing much of this already as you read and converse. If you're in doubt about the connotation of a word, ask someone. The answer you get, subjective though it may be, will give you a point of reference against which to test your understanding.

SUGGESTIONS FOR DISCUSSION AND WRITING

1. Identify the differences in the connotations of the words in each of the following groups:
   a. meeting, rendezvous, assignation, conference
   b. dwelling, house, home, pad
   c. child, youth, kid, juvenile
   d. trip, journey, peregrination, sojourn
   e. die, pass away, decease, croak, kick the bucket
2. For this comparison and contrast of dictionaries, each member of the class should bring his or her dictionary.
   a. Are the following proper names included? Where? What does your dictionary say about each?
      Jesus Christ, Susan B. Anthony, Jimmy Carter, Jane Fonda, Malcolm X, Cyril Henshilwood
   b. Which of the following abbreviations does your dictionary include?
      NF, nF, n/f, N.F., NFD., NFL, NG, N.G., n.g., NH, nH, N.H., NHI, N.H.I., Ni, N.I.
   c. Are the following places included? How much information (including maps) is provided? Do the dictionaries agree on the area, population, principal products of each?
      New Amsterdam, Newark, Newark Bay, New Britain, New Caledonia, Newcastle, Newcastle-upon-Tyne, New Hebrides
   d. What definitions does your dictionary provide for Chicano, Ku Klux Klan, Vietnam War, special education, sexism, racism, feminist?
   e. Does your dictionary include any slang meanings for the following? How recent or out-of-date are these?
      laid back, grass, pot, tomato, streak, screw, skunk
   f. Does your dictionary include the meanings of such specialized scientific, technical, and business terminology as software, hardware, PKU, money market certificate, CAT scanner, hadron, no-loan fund, synchrotron, degree of freedom, opisthognathous?
   g. What etymologies does your dictionary provide for the following?
      OK, quark, arroyo, peach Melba, daft, Dada, sideburns
   h. What does your dictionary say about the uses of the following?
      ain't, shall/will quotation marks, it is I/it's me, kike, wop, quoth, ope

Write a few paragraphs identifying the significant features of your dictionary as indicated in a-h above.

3. Skim a newspaper, read an advertisement or the lyrics of a popular song, or listen carefully to a friend's conversation. Write down five to ten words (slang or not) that seem to be used in new or unusual senses and a sentence in which each appears, so you can tell how it's used.

Then, look up each word in your dictionary. Does it list the meaning you've discovered, or not? If not, make up a definition for your meaning. If the word is listed, but not in the sense you've found, how does the meaning differ from the more established sense(s) of the word? Has the word become more general? more specific? acquired a more pleasant meaning? a more derogatory one? Has its usage become more or less formal over time? (You might also consult the *Oxford English Dictionary* or Wentworth and Flexner's *Dictionary of American Slang* to help answer these questions.)

Discuss your findings either in class or in an essay.

4. All of the following words have undergone changes in meaning over the years:

alibi	cattle	corn	chivalry	curfew	cute
dollar	foil	gossip	hussy	knave	lady
lord	lust	machine	mice	pride	salary
salt	sand	simple	starve	wench	worm

Pick one and first look it up in

a. The *Oxford English Dictionary*
b. *Webster's New International Dictionary*, second or third edition
c. A reputable, current, standard college dictionary (not an abridgment). Any of the following is suitable: the *Random House College Dictionary*, the *American Heritage Dictionary*, *Webster's New World Dictionary*, *Webster's New Collegiate Dictionary*, or *Funk and Wagnalls Standard College Dictionary*.

Then, write a brief report on the word. It should include:

a. The word's etymology (the source or sources from which modern English derives it).
b. The historical changes in the meaning of the word.
c. Its current meaning or meanings, both denotative and connotative if applicable.

At the end of your paper give full bibliographical information about each of the three references you have used (see Chapter 13).

ESTABLISHING THE LEVEL OF LANGUAGE

To express ourselves we can choose from a wide range of words, from casual to very formal, from the language of everyday conversation to the language of specialists. As a consequence, writings, like writers, have personalities that range from breezy and boisterous to somber and stately. Your chosen *level of language*, spanning this continuum from *informal* to *middle level* to *formal*, reflects not only your personality as a writer but judgments you make about your subject, the way you will discuss it, and the audience you will address, as the following considerations reveal.

Does the subject dictate or restrict the attitude you'll take toward it? If so, in what ways? For instance, it would seem pompous to treat the death of a rat in a trap with the same dignity you'd accord to a discussion of military heroism under fire. And your humaneness would prohibit you from writing flippantly about the Holocaust.

Within the limits (if any) established by your answers to the first question, how lightly or seriously do you want to treat the subject? For instance, you could treat an event from your childhood soberly and analytically, or with nostalgic humor, or even with weighty symbolism. Which way will best accomplish your purpose?

Does the mode or audience of your writing restrict or otherwise influence the possible range of expression? In a formal essay or scientific report the conspicuous intrusion of your personality would be out of place; conversely, a letter to a friend would seem oddly distant without indications of the writer's personality.

Within the restrictions (if any) established by your answer to the question above, how personal or impersonal do you want to be? On what terms do you want to meet your readers: as an intimate friend? or a distant acquaintance? as a colleague? or as an advisor or superior who expects to be treated with respect and obedience? Which approach will best accomplish your purpose?

Voice, Tone, Vocabulary, Sentence Structure

The degree of formality or informality that you decide on will be controlled to a large extent by decisions you make about the *voice, tone, vocabulary,* and *sentence structure* of your writing.

Voice, for our purposes, pertains to the pronouns you use to refer to yourself and to your readers. If you write in a *personal voice,* when you're on fairly intimate terms with your audience, you would speak of yourself as *I* and of your readers as *you.* As you move toward an *impersonal voice,* you are more likely to call yourself and your readers *one* or *we:* "One must do as one's conscience dictates" creates a greater distance between writer and reader than "Let your conscience be your guide," even though the message is the same. You're likely to do much of your writing in the personal voice, as examples throughout this book illustrate, even on subjects that aren't personal. But there are many exceptions: writing highly formal speeches, research papers, sermons; issuing orders, making judgments, or offering advice when it's clear that the writer knows better than the reader, will clearly demand a more formal voice.

The *tone* of your writing reveals its mood or emotional coloration, and this can vary as widely as your moods vary. A given piece of writing will usually have a dominant tone. It can be objective, serious, angry, sarcastic, argumentative, pleading, flippant, playful, or relaxed. Or it may have a combination of compatible tones, like adjacent shades on the rainbow, somber and sad, moderate and thoughtful, up-beat and cheerful.

Consider the differences in tone in the following presentations of information. The first is a description, from *Consumer Reports*, of how soft contact lenses work: "Soft lenses fit snugly on the cornea, keeping out the dust and soot particles that can cause so much discomfort to people wearing hard contact lenses. The snug fit also means that soft lenses are unlikely to be dislodged from the eye, so they are especially suitable for athletes."[3] The second is the beginning of a review of a concert performed by the U.S. Army Band:

> There was a massacre on the Mall Tuesday night, leaving several composers dead, including Hector Berlioz and Barry Manilow. The sole survivor was identified in the program as Peter Ilich Tchaikovsky, who sustained critical injuries. The source of the musical violence in front of the Washington Monument was the annual concert of the United States Army Band featuring the 1812 Overture.[4]

The tone of the *Consumer Reports* article is factual, objective, reasonable. The writer is not telling readers what kind of lenses to wear but is merely providing information and letting them make up their own minds. In contrast, the review of the band concert is amused and tongue-in-cheek; readers are expected to know that the reviewer is speaking figuratively in referring to the deaths of Berlioz and Manilow and the injuries of Tchaikovsky. Once in on the joke, they can enjoy the reviewer's playful exploitation of the military metaphor, as the band attacks the music and massacres it. The humor allies writer and reader in their criticism of the poor concert.

If you choose to write informally, you will probably select more common words than if you write in formal or technical English. Informally you'd say *use* instead of *utilize, get* rather than *procure, a cold sore* rather than *herpes simplex.* On the whole, the words of informal English seem shorter than those of formal English, and a higher proportion are of English origin. In writing informally, you will probably use shorter, more simply constructed sentences than the longer, more complicated sentences typical of formal English. You might write informally, "Researchers suspect a connection between love and chocolate. People in love produce the same chemical that is in chocolate" (19 words, 33 syllables). In a more formal paper you might combine the sentences, subordinating the meaning (and grammar) of one element to the other and use more elevated or technical language: "Researchers, suspecting a correlation between the chemical composition of chocolate and the biochemistry of people in love, have discovered that lovers secrete the same chemical that is an active ingredient of chocolate" (32 words, 64 syllables).

In contrast to the relative casualness of informal English, formal English appears in full regalia to suit the occasions on which it is used—in sermons, ceremonies, and important speeches; in legal, business, and governmental transactions; in some technical papers, textbooks, and other writings requiring a more thoughtful response. Formal English treats weighty matters seriously. Its many long, complicated sentences look serious; its high proportion of long words (many borrowed from other languages), ornate phrases, and specialized vocabulary sound serious. As a consequence, it can be a challenge both to the reader and to the writer.

Let us see how voice, tone, vocabulary, and sentence structure combine to contribute to the level of formality of the passages below.

The Informal Level

"Tastes like *ice cream!*" my mother exclaimed, as she dipped her spoon into a carton of plain yogurt. "Try some."

"*Ugh*," I said, and made a face at her. "I bet it's like sour cream."

"No, *try some!*" my mother protested loudly. She thrust a spoonful of yogurt towards my mouth.

"No!" I squealed, pushing her hand away.

"You don't know what you're missing," my mother told me.

After my mother left the room, I tried a half a spoonful of plain yogurt. It tasted like sour cream.

—MYRNA GREENFIELD

Student Myrna Greenfield used this dialogue to begin an essay describing her mother and analyzing their relationship. Because the relationship was an intimate association, loving but sometimes stressful, she decided to write about it informally and humorously. She felt she could distance herself somewhat from this potentially problematic subject if she treated both her mother and herself with slightly sardonic humor, rather than if she played it straight and serious or used a more penetrating satire that would cut too close to the bone. She wanted to express her personality so the readers, college students, would know and like her. She wanted them to be her allies in her one-sided war of independence from her mother—who would not be reading the paper.

Myrna chose a dialogue, an obviously conversational form, and accented this by recreating the manner of spoken speech through italics for emphasis, exclamation points, and the choice of specific words—*exclaimed*, *protested loudly*, and *squealed*—to indicate the conversation's loud volume. She and her mother speak a simple, conversational language, its informality indicated by the contractions, *it's*, *don't*; by words omitted but understood (*Tastes like* instead of *It tastes like*); and by the plain *I bet* instead of the more elevated language, *I imagine* or *I surmise that*. The language into which the dialogue is set is also down-to-earth; the vocabulary and sentence structure are simple and the voice personal as Myrna refers to herself as *I* and lets her own personality emerge. She can argue with her mother, squealing and making a face (childish actions, which imply that she was fairly young at the time), but she candidly admits to the inconsistency of tasting the yogurt even after having refused it so violently. By acknowledging this she enters into a conspiracy with her readers, inviting them to share her secret exploration of the yogurt and her triumph—the yogurt *did* taste like sour cream, just as she had predicted. She can tell the readers what she can't admit to her mother, and she can invite them to participate in her enjoyment. Myrna writes with an appropriate tinge of self-mockery, however; the taste of yogurt is too insignificant to fight a major battle over, and so her victory is minor, as well as private.

The Formal Level

In contrast, consider this typically formal passage from Henry Adams's autobiography, *The Education of Henry Adams*. In this section his childhood self is about the same age as Myrna's:

> The atmosphere of education in which he lived was colonial, revolutionary, almost Cromwellian, as though he were steeped, from his greatest grandmother's birth, in the odor of political crime. Resistance to something was the law of New England nature; the boy looked out on the world with the instinct of resistance; for numberless generations his predecessors had viewed the world chiefly as a thing to be reformed, filled with evil forces to be abolished, and they saw no reason to suppose that they had wholly succeeded in the abolition; the duty was unchanged. That duty implied not only resistance to evil, but hatred of it. Boys naturally look on all force as an enemy, and generally find it so, but the New Englander, whether boy or man, in his long struggle with a stingy or hostile universe, had learned also to love the pleasure of hating; his joys were few.
>
> Politics, as a practice, whatever its professions, had always been the systematic organization of hatreds, and Massachusetts politics had been as harsh as the climate. The chief charm of New England was harshness of contrasts and extremes of sensibility—a cold that froze the blood, and a heat that boiled it—so that the pleasure of hating—oneself if no better victim offered—was not its rarest amusement; but the charm was a true and natural child of the soil, not a cultivated weed of the ancients.[5]

Throughout his life story Adams adopted the unusual technique of referring to himself in the third person, as *he* or as *one*; or by his developmental stage in life, as *the boy, a student*; or, as here, as part of a group of which he is a member, *the New Englander*. These terms distance the autobiographer from his subject, himself, for they give the impression that he's talking about someone else. And so that most personal of forms, the autobiography, becomes through this device quite impersonal, as Adams treats himself and his life as fit specimens for the dissection provided by his thorough analysis.

His language, too, is formal. Although most of the words are familiar, their general tone is elevated: *as though he were steeped . . . in the odor of political crime, numberless generations, extremes of sensibility*. Some of the words allude to people, practices, or events of historical significance (*Cromwellian, colonial, revolutionary*). Other phrases are deliberately from an earlier time (*a cultivated weed of the ancients*), which make them quaint but hard to understand for readers without a sense of the older meanings. Throughout, the language presupposes an educated reader who not only understands history, politics, and the older senses of the words, but who can follow with ease the complicated sentences.

In Myrna's eleven-sentence, eighty-eight-word passage the sentences range in length from two to eighteen words; their average is eight, four less than the average sentence length in the editorials in today's newspapers, which are geared for people with a seventh- or eighth-grade reading level. In contrast, Adams's 237-word passage contains—surprise—only six sentences, which are not only formal, but formidable. The shortest (sentence 3) is twelve words; the longest (sentence 2) is sixty-four words; the average is thirty-nine. All of Myrna's sentences are simple in structure; only one of Adams's (sentence 3) is. Although Myrna uses exclamation points, the other punctuation consists of commas and periods. Adams indicates the complicated subordination and co-ordination of his sentences by intricate punctuation, including a high proportion of semicolons and some dashes. Yet both Myrna and Adams are writing for general, nonspecialized readers. Each has chosen the style most suitable for the purpose of his or her writing.

The Middle Level

Much of your writing will probably be in level of formality midway along the continuum of extremes represented by Myrna Greenfield and Henry Adams. The following excerpts from student papers indicate just two possibilities among many. In her essay on the history and usage of the word "salt," Nora Palmer writes:

> Telling someone he's "not worth his salt" is not only rude but downright cruel, too. People have various amounts of pride in their work, and any endeavor should be taken seriously—with more than a grain of salt, if you please.
>
> "Salt" has been the base for many words and phrases. A few examples are: "salt of the earth," "salt away," "saltines" and the ever popular "Epsom salts." One more form of the word is a common term: "salary." The original meaning comes from Rome when soldiers were given money to buy the "salt," hence, their pay.

And Willard Porter describes his favorite place, a canyon in Arizona:

> Into the broad open desert flood plain the long boulder-strewn arms of the mountain reach out. Drawing me in, they seem to hold me close to the valley's life. The immense granite domes loom upward; their light tan and gray faces peer down on me. I feel the focus of the great rocks' power. The sound, the heat, and the light are all reflected toward the valley's center by the encircling rock guards. The gentle flow of cool water beneath the shady protection of an old scrub oak forms a shallow pool which offers refuge from the sun's burning intensity.
>
> Here are the healthiest of any desert plants in southern Arizona, because the domes nourish and protect them from too many intruders. They fill the valley with their thick, sweet odors of sap, blossom, and bark. If I hurry, they begin to pull and tear my clothes as if to get me to slow down and notice them. To me, the most outstanding plants are the saguaros, which stand forty to fifty feet high and are surrounded by an aura of pale yellow sunlight and needles.

Both Willard and Nora speak thoughtfully, without pompousness. Willard is serious, awed ("I feel the great rocks' power"); he appreciates the immensity of the desert and the beauty of its vegetation, especially the impressive saguaros, "surrounded by an aura of pale yellow sunlight and needles." Nora straightforwardly conveys information about salt but does so with a touch of humor: "any endeavor should be taken seriously—with more than a grain of salt, if you please."

Yet Nora's writing is impersonal; she removes herself from her essay and focuses on the subject. Willard uses the personal voice, but his *I* is less intimate, less identifiable as a personality than is Myrna Greenfield's. Although he presents a speaker with identifiable perceptions ("If I hurry, [the plants] begin to . . . tear my clothes") and reactions ("I feel [the rocks'] power"), he focuses not on himself but on the canyon. His feelings add human interest to a description that could stand independently of his personal responses.

Both writers use standard English and vocabularies familiar, but not slangy, with an occasional formal-sounding word (*encircle, endeavor*) for variation. Willard's metaphor of the rocks standing guard over the plants in the valley reinforces the awesome atmosphere of the setting.

Most of Willard's and Nora's sentences are simple in structure but nevertheless varied in length and form. Nora's sentences range between eleven and twenty-seven words in length; Willard's vary from nine to twenty-eight. In both instances the sentences are less than half the average length of Henry Adams's sentences. The average length of Willard's sentences, 18.7 words, is almost identical to Nora's, 19.4 words—over twice the length of Myrna's informal sentences.

The table on p. 161 summarizes the differences among the levels of language discussed here. It should be useful in helping you determine how to construct the level of language you wish for any given writing. You can also use it to analyze the writings of others.

SUGGESTIONS FOR DISCUSSION AND WRITING

1. Examine two or three of the following passages and analyze their voice, tone, vocabulary, and sentence structure. Which level of language is each written in? Are there varying degrees of formality or informality within each category?

    Some of these passages are easier to understand than others. Is this because of the formality of informality of their language? the complexity or simplicity of their sentence structures? the difficulty or ease of their ideas? Is formal writing necessarily more difficult to understand than informal writing?

    The selections below have been considered models of good writing. Would you agree or disagree? Why or why not? Be prepared to discuss your opinions either in class or in an essay.

    a. To every thing there is a season, and a time to every purpose under the heaven:
       A time to be born, and a time to die; a time to plant, and a time to pluck up that which is planted;
       A time to kill, and a time to heal; a time to break down, and a time to build up;
       A time to weep, and a time to laugh; a time to mourn, and a time to dance. . . .

A time to get, and a time to lose; a time to keep, and a time to cast away;
A time to rend, and a time to sew; a time to keep silence, and a time to speak;
A time to love, and a time to hate; a time of war, and a time of peace.

Ecclesiastes 3:1–4, 6–8[6]

b. A man may take to drink because he feels himself to be a failure, and then fail all the more completely because he drinks. It is rather the same thing that is happening to the English language. It becomes ugly and inaccurate because our

Table 7.1
LEVELS OF LANGUAGE

CHARACTERISTIC	MOST INFORMAL Informal Level	Middle Level	MOST FORMAL Formal Level
voice	personal—pronouns are *I*, *you*; author's personality and personal reactions prominent	somewhat less personal, may or may not use personal pronouns *I*, *you*; author's personality and personal reactions more subdued	impersonal—pronouns are *one*, *we*, *he*, or may be absent if passive voice is used; little or no direct representation of the author's personality
tone	wide range of tones possible, usually expressed conspicuously, sometimes without restraint	wide range of tones possible, expression more subdued	in theory, a wide range of tones is possible, but the expression is highly controlled
vocabulary	informal, conversational; may include slang, profanity, dialects; fairly simple vocabulary	ranges from conversational to more formal standard English; vocabulary varies from common to unusual; some figurative language	formal standard English, much more likely to be written than spoken except in oratory, speeches; more foreign and archaic words
sentences	short, simple, with less variation than in middle or formal levels; see Chapter 6	wide range of lengths; average length in middle range; some variation in patterns and construction.	wide variation in lengths; longest average number of words; most complex construction

thoughts are foolish, but the slovenliness of our language makes it easier for us to have foolish thoughts. The point is that the process is reversible. Modern English, especially written English, is full of bad habits which spread by imitation and which can be avoided if one is willing to take the necessary trouble. If one gets rid of these habits one can think more clearly, and to think clearly is a necessary first step toward political regeneration: so that the fight against bad English is not frivolous and is not the exclusive concern of professional writers.

—GEORGE ORWELL, "Politics and the English Language"[7]

c. Fourscore and seven years ago our fathers brought forth on this continent a new nation, conceived in liberty, and dedicated to the proposition that all men are created equal.

Now we are engaged in a great civil war, testing whether that nation, or any nation so conceived and so dedicated, can long endure. We are met on a great battlefield of that war. We have come to dedicate a portion of that field as a final resting-place for those who here gave their lives that that nation might live. It is altogether fitting and proper that we should do this.

But, in a larger sense, we cannot dedicate—we cannot consecrate—we cannot hallow—this ground. The brave men, living and dead, who struggled here, have consecrated it, far above our poor power to add or detract. The world will little note, nor long remember what we say here, but it can never forget what they did here. It is for us the living, rather, to be dedicated here to the unfinished work which they who fought here have thus far so nobly advanced. It is rather for us to be here dedicated to the great task remaining before us—that from these honored dead we take increased devotion—that we here highly resolve that these dead shall not have died in vain—that this nation, under God, shall have a new birth of freedom—and that government of the people, by the people, for the people, shall not perish from the earth.

—ABRAHAM LINCOLN, "Gettysburg Address"

d. In a month or so, he will be 15, which is absurd. I never intended him to be old enough to contemplate driving a car or applying to college. He was supposed to stay 8, or maybe 12. I examine him for stigmata of sullenness: no, merely the clouded look of afternoons with books, and, where the light collects—at the rims of his aviator glasses, in the braces on his teeth—some fire. His feet are huge; I have ordered seven-league boots.

—JOHN LEONARD, "Private Lives"[8]

2. Pick a subject that you know well, whether vegetarianism, oil spills, or photography, or a controversial subject dear to your heart, and write two or three paragraphs about it in a highly formal level of language. Then rewrite the paragraphs, using either an informal or middle level of language. Is each suitable for the same audience? What adaptations have you made in voice, tone, vocabulary, and sentence structure between the first and the second version?

3. Rewrite one of the passages quoted in *1* in a level of language different from the one its author used. What are the differences between the two versions? Have you improved upon the original? Why or why not?

SPECIAL ADAPTATIONS OF LANGUAGE

In addition to determining whether your language in any given writing will be informal, middle level, or formal and to deciding how personal or impersonal your authorial voice will be, you may at times have to consider other aspects of writing that depend on specialized word usage. Those types that you are most likely to have to deal with are technical language, slang, and dialects.

Technical Language and Jargon

Sometimes you will find yourself writing for an audience of specialists: teachers and students in specialized courses; or, perhaps, bosses, co-workers, or members of professional, trade, civic, or hobby groups. For such selected readers you will probably write in *technical language*, which is characterized by a high proportion of specialized words or of common words used in restricted senses to express concepts or other elements particular to a trade, profession, or group. Because scientific or technical writing is often objective, impersonal, and full of complicated concepts expressed in uncommon, elaborate terms, it may sound very formal.

For instance, consider this paragraph explaining to aviation scientists how a spacecraft's baseband processor works:

> The *executive software* controls all *program-related functions*, such as handling *input and output operations*, *interpreting* and *executing macro instructions*, providing *format and translation capabilities*, and handling *error conditions*. To conserve valuable *memory space*, only the pertinent *software overlays* are *memory-resident* during *program execution*; all other *software overlays reside on disc* and are *called into memory* only when needed[9] (italics supplied).

Those familiar with computers would follow these directions easily; in fact, they have been commended as a model of clarity for technical writers. The italicized words have precise technical meanings here, but somehow different meanings in other contexts, both technical and nontechnical.

Technical language is sometimes known as *jargon*, with no derogatory connotations. But *jargon* can also mean vague, abstract, unintelligible, or meaningless writing. Social scientists, academics, and government bureaucrats are particularly susceptible to jargon, under the mistaken impression that if they call a spade a spade it won't sound as authoritative as calling it a *portable, manually operated, human-powered, soil-transferring instrument.* Language analyst Stuart Chase illustrates the problems that such jargon, which he calls gobbledygook, can cause:

> A New York plumber wrote the [National Bureau of Standards] that he had found hydrochloric acid fine for cleaning drains, and was it harmless? Washington replied: "The efficacy of hydrochloric acid is indisputable, but the chlorine residue is incompatible with metallic permanence."

The plumber wrote back that he was mighty glad the Bureau agreed with him. The Bureau replied with a note of alarm: "We cannot assume responsibility for the production of toxic and noxious residues with hydrochloric acid, and suggest that you use an alternate procedure." The plumber was happy to learn that the Bureau still agreed with him.

Whereupon Washington exploded: "Don't use hydrochloric acid; it eats hell out of the pipes!"[10]

If you are writing for nonspecialists, it's best to explain technical concepts in ordinary language. You should define any terms that they may not understand or will find ambiguous, preferably the first time you use such words, abbreviations, or concepts. For instance, the following would need to be defined for general readers:

words—such as ametropia, rad
foreign terms—Weltanshauungen, mazel tov
abbreviations—QSRS, T-unit
concepts—ontogeny recapitulates phylogeny, Gresham's law

Although you won't want to belabor the obvious, you can assume that if you wonder whether readers will understand your terminology you will probably need to define it.

Slang

At the opposite extreme from technical or bureaucratic language is slang, though it, too, is sometimes used to convey the impression that the writer is a member of the inner circle, one of the up-to-date group that knows and appreciates the words' current connotations. When you use slang you're also indicating that you're willing to exaggerate, startle, joke, or sound irreverent.

Some slang has become standard English (*mob*, *jazz*) through constant usage; other expressions remain slang—and nonstandard—for centuries (*bones* for *dice*, *kick the bucket* for *die*). Most slang expressions have a limited life span: *twenty-three skidoo* and *cool cat* are dead clichés, and even *far out* isn't very far in these days. On the assumption that your writing will last longer than the next month or so, it's wise to avoid much slang except in dialogue or quotations from conversations. You won't want to sound dated.

Dialect

A dialect is a variety of a language characterized by unique combinations of words and meanings, grammatical forms, pronunciations, and emphases that are common to a region or group but not to the standard language used by the nation as a whole. A dialect in itself is neither bad nor good; it is simply a way a group of people speak. Here are some synonyms in different dialects:

submarine, poor boy, hero, hoagy (or hoagie), grinder

parkway, parking strip, devil strip, berm, boulevard, sidewalk plot, tree lawn, tree belt

sneakers, sneaks, gym shoes, tennis shoes, tennies

Consider this translation of "The Night Before Christmas" into Black Idiomatic English, a dialect spoken throughout the United States by many blacks who are not middle class:

It's the night before Christmas, and here in our house
It ain't nothing moving, *not even no* mouse.
There *go we-all* stockings, hanging high up off the floor,
So Santa Claus can *full them up,* if *he walk* in through our door.[11]

This example typifies the ratio of standard English to dialect features. Although most of the words, many of the phrases, and much of the grammar are standard English, the departures from the standard, italicized here, characterize the dialect.

Dialects can usually be understood by readers who speak a different variety of the same language, but it's still preferable to write in standard English, the language used by the largest possible number of readers. If everyone wrote in his own dialect every region, perhaps every city or town, would have its own variations in vocabulary, grammar, and spelling, and the possibilities of written communication would be severely limited.

Nevertheless, even when you're using standard English it is acceptable to employ some dialect or regional words if there is no generally used synonym available. And you may wish to use the dialect common to a particular area or group if you're writing exclusively for them, or if you're trying to convey a "down home" flavor, or if you're quoting people who speak that way.

In his moving analysis of the Pine Barrens, an enormous wilderness area in the midst of highly populated New Jersey, author John McPhee counterpoints his own middle-level standard English with quotations in dialect and slang from the people who live there:

The people have no difficulty articulating what it is that gives them a special feeling about the landscape they live in; they know that their environment is unusual and they know why they value it. Some, of course, put it with more finesse than others do. "I'm just a woods boy," a fellow named Jim Leek said to me one day. "There ain't nobody bothers you here. You can be alone. I'm just a woods boy. I wouldn't want to live in a town." When he said "town," he meant one of the small communities in the pines. . . .[12]

McPhee conveys the flavor of the people through the flavor of their language; when they use a word in a special sense, as *town* above, he explains it so that the "outsiders," his readers, will understand.

SUGGESTIONS FOR INVESTIGATION AND WRITING

1. In order to discover how people actually use words, pick several of the words or phrases below to investigate according to the method described following this list:

   fewer/less (The mangy dog had fewer/less flea bites than we'd expected.)

   guys/gals; boys/girls; men/women [when speaking of adults] (All of the guys/ boys/men from the office went to the races, and some even took gals/girls/women with them.)

   alot/a lot (He who eats alot/a lot of cookies gains alot/a lot of weight.)

   shall/will (On our way to the Empire State Building we shall/will stop at the Whitney Museum.)

   utilize/use (We must utilize/use all available manpower.)

   OK as a verb (She OK'd the check.)

   myself/I/me (That is a matter strictly between him and myself/I/me.)

   criterion/criteria [for the singular usage] (The criterion/criteria for an A grade was not clear.)

   Smith's/Smiths [punctuation for the plural] (All the Smith's/Smiths have the measles.)

   -wise [as a suffix] ("What's your persuasion, Godwise?" said Bunny, in John Guare's *House of Blue Leaves*.)

   Ask two teachers, or other people who are concerned with writing and usage, and two friends (not in your English class), or other people who are not professionally concerned with language which alternatives they would use in speaking and in writing, and why. Ask them to use their preferred versions in a sentence and copy down the sentence.

   Be prepared to discuss your evidence and conclusions about the usages of these words or phrases in class. You could summarize your findings in a chart to use as the basis of either an oral or a written discussion.

   Does your mini-panel agree or disagree on usage? What are their reasons? Do you agree with the majority in each instance? Why or why not? Does the usage recommended in your college dictionary or reference Handbook (pp. 369–375) corroborate any or all of your findings?

   What can you conclude about the usage of these terms, based on your evidence?

2. Write a paper presenting the results of your investigation.

3. Pick a controversial topic that interests you and write two or three separate paragraphs on it. Each paragraph will present an argument for or against the same point but will be written for a different audience. Adapt your language and perhaps your illustrations to your particular audience. Choose two or three of these alternatives:

   a. Discuss the point in a letter to your best friend.

   b. Discuss the point in a letter to your local newspaper.

   c. Discuss the point in a letter to a scholarly journal devoted to your subject. (Your librarian can direct you to journals to look at as models of the kind of language and tone you should use.)

   Then, write an analytic paragraph in which you identify the language and tone of each of your two or three letters. In which is the language most formal? least formal? (Consider such matters as sentence and paragraph length, complexity, structure, and variety; presence or absence of slang, jargon, technical or specialized language; proportion of abstract to concrete words, figurative to literal language (see p. 161); and any other relevant matters.) Is the tone of each letter the same? If not, why not? Is the arrangement of your points the same? Have you used similar or different evidence in each argument? If so, why? If not, why not? How have you adapted each letter to fit the context and the intended audience?

ABSTRACT VERSUS CONCRETE LANGUAGE

In much of your writing, you will be free to express your points in words ranging on a continuum from *highly abstract and general* to *very specific and concrete*. You can talk, for example, about *fun*, or the somewhat more restricted *summertime pleasures*, or the more specific *fishing, hiking, and travel*, or the even more specific *surf casting, backpacking in the Colorado Rockies, or exploring the Amazon jungles.*

Some of your writing, such as a description of a particular place, or a character sketch of a person, or a lab report about a given experiment, will focus primarily on the specifics of the subject in question, concentrating on the trees to the exclusion of the forest. Other writing, however, will require you to combine theory and practice, general principles and applications to provide a necessary overview of the forest as well as of the trees that compose it.

You will probably find when you write a first draft that your statements tend toward the general: *college students are overworked.* As you revise you'll have to make them more specific to be sure that you're communicating exactly what you mean instead of leaving a wide open framework into which your readers can insert whatever meanings they want: *college students have a difficult balance to maintain among the demands of studying, working, and personal life.* An illustration would make this even more pointed: *college students carrying a full load of fifteen hours, and working between twenty and forty hours a week, have time commitments upwards of sixty-five hours a week, leaving far too little for personal life, let alone sleep.*

Your finished essay will probably include a mixture of the general and the specific, as in this paragraph from an article in *Science News* discussing the general idea that there is growing evidence that alcoholism may "run in the family":

> Recent studies have shown as much as a fourfold increase in alcoholism among children of alcoholics over children of nonalcoholics. Other studies indicate a 25 to 50 percent lifetime risk for alcoholism in the sons and brothers of severely alcoholic men, and twins of alcoholics have about twice the chance of becoming alcoholics as do two non-twin brothers or sisters.[13]

Yet even this paragraph is not as specific as it could be; *recent studies* and *other studies* are identified by their results but not by title or by the names of the researchers. This is because the article is short and appears in a general publication for nonspecialists. A college resource paper or a paper for a more knowledgeable and specialized audience would have to specify the references in full (see Chapters 13 and 14).

Although abstractions in themselves are not necessarily unclear (*Power to the people!*), the more abstract the writing, the harder readers must work to interpret its meaning. This paragraph by sociologist Talcott Parsons should give you some sense of the forbidding effect produced by highly abstract language:

> All *institutionalization* involves *common moral* as well as *other values. Collectivity obligations* are, therefore, an aspect of every *institutionalized role.* But in *certain contexts of orientation-choice these obligations* may be *latent,* while in *others* they are *"activated"* in the sense that the *actor faces the choice either of choosing the alternatives which conform* with *these values* or of *accepting* the *negative sanctions which* go with *violation* (Italics supplied to indicate abstractions or references to abstractions).[14]

Nearly 50 percent of the sixty-seven words above are abstractions or references to unspecified antecedents (*certain contexts*). Even the explanation (the last half of the last sentence) is so full of abstractions that it's hard to understand. As is typical of abstract writing (see Table 7.2), the language here is clogged with prepositions (17 percent) and with general nouns or combinations of nouns modifying other nouns (e.g., "orientation-choice"). These total 43 percent of the words. Verbs (12 percent) and adjectives (10 percent) are scarce, concrete illustrations nonexistent.

There are significant differences between Parsons's difficult abstractions and the much more specific, active writing of Joan Didion, who concretely illustrates an equally abstract principle. In "Some Dreamers of the Golden Dream," Didion generalizes about Southern California, "The future always looks good in the golden land, because no one remembers the past." She then goes on to illustrate this generalization with many fewer abstractions (italicized in the quote from the same page below—13 percent to Parsons's 50 percent), nouns and noun-noun combinations (20 percent to Parsons's 43 percent). She uses a higher percentage of verbs (17 percent to 12 percent) and adjectives (15 percent to Parsons's 10 percent). The results are summarized in this table:

Table 7.2
**A COMPARISON OF ABSTRACT AND
CONCRETE WRITING STYLES**

CHARACTERISTICS	*PARSONS*	*DIDION*
Total words	67	116
Percent of abstractions	50	13
Percent of nouns and noun–noun combinations	43	20
Percent of prepositions	17	6
Percent of verbs	12	17
Percent of adjectives	10	15
Number of concrete illustrations	0	11

The most striking difference between the two writers, however, is revealed by Didion's use in the following passage of concrete illustrations, bracketed below, in eleven instances, to none at all for Parsons.

[after a] [Tijuana divorce] and a [return to hairdressers' school,] ["We were just crazy kids,]" they say without regret, and *look to the future.* . . . [Here is where the hot wind blows] and the *old ways* do not seem relevant, where [the divorce rate is double the national average] and where [one person in every thirty-eight lives in a trailer.] Here is the [last stop for all those who come from somewhere else,] for [all those who drifted away from the cold] and the *past and the old ways.* [Here is where they are trying to find a *new* life style,] trying to find *it* in the only places they know to look, the [movies] and [the newspapers].[15]

Didion does not just mention divorce; the divorce is in Tijuana, with connotations of haste, if not sordidness—and, again specifically, at a rate double the national average. Didion does not say explicitly that the values in Southern California are superficial and the way of life impermanent. Instead, she specifies the transitoriness (one person in thirty-eight lives in a trailer) and the shallowness: people find their values not in religion or philosophy but in "the movies and the newspapers."

TRY THIS

To find out whether you're communicating exactly what you mean in your writing, ask a friend or other typical member of your intended audience to read one or more paragraphs, or even the entire essay, and tell you what she thinks you mean. If she understands, your other readers probably will, too. If she doesn't, find out why not and continue to revise until your meaning is sufficiently specific to be clear.

Figures of Speech: Metaphors and Similes

Among the most memorable ways to make your writing specific are the appropriate uses of figures of speech, particularly metaphors and similes. A *metaphor* is an implied comparison of two things that are literally unlike:

Each rich nation is a lifeboat full of comparatively rich people. In the ocean outside each lifeboat swim the poor of the world, who want to get in, or at least to share some of the wealth. What should the lifeboat passengers do?
—adapted from Garrett Hardin, "Lifeboat Ethics: The Case Against Helping the Poor"[16]

Each rich nation is identified as a lifeboat full of affluent passengers; the rest of the less affluent world is compared figuratively to an ocean, with poor people swimming in it. The explicitly comparative terms *like* or *as* are not used in a metaphor.

In a simile a direct comparison is made between two unlike things:

> The earth is like a spaceship, in which energy and resources have to be conserved by all and the environment kept free from pollution if we are to continue on a safe course.

Here the earth is openly compared to a spaceship, with similarities between the environments and resources of the earth and a spaceship emphasized in the course of the comparison. *Like* or *as* is the comparative word in a simile.

A good metaphor or simile has the following characteristics. It must fit the subject in some reasonable, appropriate, or natural way. In the above examples, both the lifeboat and spaceship comparisons with earth are sufficiently obvious to keep the readers from mental strain, and neither comparison is pushed to extremes. A fruitful metaphor or simile permits comparison of more than one aspect of the two phenomena under consideration, but at some point the dissimilarities will become apparent, if not overpowering, and the figure of speech will have to stop or lose its effectiveness. The spaceship simile above, for instance, would lose its point if the writer extended the comparison to talk about weightlessness versus gravitational pull. A good metaphor or simile should be alive and lively, original or vigorous enough to cause readers to pay attention to the comparison rather than to overlook it.

We have already talked about the use of analogies (which similes and metaphors are) to develop ideas (see Chapter 3). You can employ them to explain, to clarify, or to argue—and at the same time to add color and flavor to your writing.

A couple of cautions. *Avoid an excessive number of metaphors in any given paragraph or longer writing.* Like spices, a little figurative language is powerful and goes a long way; too much is overwhelming.

Mixed metaphors, images that pertain to more than one thing, should also be avoided because they are confusing and sometimes unintentionally humorous. Consider this passage, which a student wrote on an essay examination: "He leaves his emotional well-being as healthy as a beached whale. He takes a pitchfork to his love-life as if it were only a helpless jellyfish rather than crediting his loss and swimming back into the social life with Cupid's arrow." This conglomeration of ill-fitting images can only leave readers puzzled and grasping for meaning. Is the writer intending to be ironic when he says *as healthy as a beached whale,* since a beached whale would presumably be either sick or dead? Would anyone take a pitchfork to either *a helpless jellyfish* or to *his love-life?* It would seem more suitable for stabbing the beached whale, but unnecessary (if the whale is dead) or unkind (if it is merely ill). What has *crediting his loss,* a business metaphor, to do with *swimming back into the social life,* an aquatic metaphor that, relating to the earlier images, bestows upon the hapless lover the image of either a jellyfish or a beached whale? And how does one swim with an *arrow, Cupid's* or anyone else's?

Personification, giving human attributes to abstractions, inanimate objects, or animals, is another common figure of speech: the door groans on its hinges, the fire hisses; Cupid stands for love, the Grim Reaper for death. Personification, like metaphors and similes, can make your writing memorable if used with restraint. Too heavy a dose of it will make your writing seem too cute or inappropriately human-centered: "The breeze tiptoed in through the window, pulled back the curtain, scampered across the room, and ran its gentle fingers through her hair."

OTHER SUGGESTIONS ABOUT WORD USAGE

Be Concise

Today, lean, muscular prose is considered the essence of good writing, and English teachers have become the leaders of Word Watchers, trying to help writers take off flabby phrases. The general recommendation is: "Write concisely." Use as few words as possible to communicate your exact meaning. Your readers will pay more attention to a taut, well-shaped body of prose than they will to one that bulges and sags with excess verbiage. This does not mean that you must use only short words in short sentences or that all your essays should be short. It does mean that every word should count. The principles presented in the following checklist can help you choose your words wisely.

□ A Checklist for Writing Concisely

□ **Substitute short, simple words for equivalent longer, murky, or redundant words or phrases.**

Instead of using	substitute
herein, therein, hereinabove	here, there, above
prior to	before
in order to	to
at this point in time	now
interface with	meet
cognizant	aware
a query relative to the status of	a question about[17]
great big, little tiny, enormously large	one word or the other—big, little, enormous

□ **Substitute single words or short phrases for longer phrases, whole sentences, or possibly even whole paragraphs, when you can do so without loss of meaning.**

Instead of writing
   Management has become cognizant of the necessity of eliminating undesirable vegetation surrounding the periphery of the facility.

say
  Please kill the weeds around the building.[18]

☐ **Avoid expendable redundancies, words or phrases that repeat the same meaning unnecessarily.** Watch out especially for such common but wordy phrases as *which is, who was, in the area of, in regard to, in relation to.* Most of them can simply be omitted.

  Instead of writing
    The spider *which is* crawling over my foot has hairy legs that tickle.
  say
    The spider crawling over my foot has hairy legs that tickle.
  Instead of writing
    R. Van Winkle was eighty *years of age.*
  say
    R. Van Winkle was eighty.

☐ **Avoid meaningless qualifiers.** These are such extra words or phrases as really, very, definitely, of course, basically, rather, quite, honestly, between you and me, you know what I mean, I'll be honest with you. These fill up blank spaces in conversation, instead of pauses, while you're groping for something of more substance to say. Because they're so common in conversation, people tolerate them, if you know what I mean. But I'll be honest with you, they're less acceptable in writing because basically they take up space and really don't change the meaning very much. Delete them.

  However, not all qualifiers are meaningless. Chances are that if you make a general, unqualified observation ("Everybody likes children."), you will draw the distrust, if not the anger, of those readers who can think of exceptions to it ("Anyone who hates children and dogs can't be all bad."). So unless you're discussing a universal law, it's more accurate and strategically safer to qualify your generalizations through using such qualifiers as many, most, some, often, or usually: "Nearly everyone likes some children." or "Nearly everyone likes children." This is not being wishy-washy, it's being accurate.

☐ **Avoid padding, extra words or phrases that fill up space without adding meaning.** If you're assigned a 500-word essay, it's tempting to fill up that frightening blank space with whatever comes to mind. To avoid padding:

1. Eliminate unnecessary repetition of ideas.
2. Eliminate words, phrases, sentences, or paragraphs that do not add meaning, color, or interest to your writing.
3. Substitute short expressions for long ones when you can do so without changing the meaning.
4. Combine sentences to eliminate repetition or recurring words or phrases.

When you're writing the first draft, don't worry about padding; you already have enough to concentrate on. But as you're revising either the first draft or later versions, ask yourself: *Does each word or phrase contribute clearly and specifically to the meaning of what I'm saying?* Eliminate those to which your answer is *no*.

Use the Active Voice

To keep the emphasis on the action and the actor, use verbs in the active voice: "I came, I saw, I conquered." Continual use of the passive voice slows down the pace and makes writing colorless and vague: "The conquering was done by one who came and saw" (note ten words vs. six in the active voice). Because the passive voice disguises the actor, or removes the action from the actor, it can be a way of concealing responsibility. If you don't say who did it, maybe no one will know. Perhaps this is why bureaucrats so often hide behind the passive voice, making such announcements as "It is hereby ordered that everyone's tuition will be raised by 15 percent as of July 1."

If, however, you want to emphasize the object of the action or its passivity, or both, you would choose the passive voice:

> Fifteen houses were smashed to kindling by the tornado.
> Open heart surgery was performed on our distinguished senator, full of acupuncture needles and smiling the whole time.

In the first sentence, the emphasis is on the action and the number of houses being smashed and less on the tornado. In the second, who performed the surgery is not as important as the person who was operated on, the operation itself, or the accompanying circumstances.

Eliminate Unnecessary Negatives

Sometimes you must say "No" or make other emphatic negative statements: "I will not run for Vice-President." "We disagree." These are forceful and to the point. But negative expressions are frequently less forceful in effect than their positively worded counterparts. You will want, therefore, to avoid using negatives unnecessarily. Be careful, though, not to change the meaning in the process of rephrasing your statements.

NEGATIVE: Our Mercedes does not have air in the front tires.
POSITIVE: Our Mercedes has two flat front tires. (Unless you mean, "The tires of our Mercedes have not yet been pumped up.")
NEGATIVE: He is not a good American; he does not like baseball, apple pie, or his own mother!
POSITIVE (even though the sentiment is negative, the grammar is positive): He's un-American—he dislikes baseball, apple pie, and his own mother!

AVOID CLICHÉS AND EUPHEMISMS

Clichés are overworked, thoroughly familiar expressions that conceal the real meaning by keeping you and your readers from thinking about the implications of what you're saying. People have heard clichés too often to do more than yawn (*wearily*) or smile (*knowingly*) when they encounter language that in *time immemorial* was *forged on the anvil of creativity* in the *white-hot excitement of the moment.* Believing that they already know what the *stock phrases* mean, they *don't give them another thought.* So cliché-laden writing, *comfortable as an old shoe,* becomes *dead as a doornail.* In the last analysis, your readers have already *been there and back.* Baseball writing is riddled with such clichés, as Frank Sullivan's Cliché Expert testifies:

> Big-league baseball is customarily played by *brilliant outfielders, veteran hurlers, powerful sluggers, knuckle-ball artists, towering first basemen, key moundsmen . . . ace southpaws, scrappy little shortstops . . . sterling moundsmen, aging twirlers,* and *rookie sensations.*[19]

An overdose of clichés can also lead to a jumble of mixed metaphors, humorous or otherwise, that can undermine your point. Former New York Mayor Abraham Beame once observed, "The biggest challenge was to *come into the harbor safely.* I think we've *met that challenge.* . . . we've *turned the corner* and *seen the light at the end of the tunnel*" (italics supplied).

Some euphemisms originate from the noble attempt to avoid offending readers through substitution of a vague or indirect or even favorable expression for a harsher one. Mentally retarded children are placed in ambiguously labeled *special education classes,* a term that could and does also apply to education for the gifted. Some police departments now refer to juvenile parole officers as *aftercare youth counselors,* in order not to jeopardize the delinquents' chances for work after imprisonment.

At best, euphemistic terms are ambiguous or unclear. How many of us would know what an aftercare youth counselor was unless we were told? At worst, euphemisms become the deceptive packaging of our language and take advantage of the neutral or favorable connotations of words to conceal poor quality, dubious motives, and debatable or immoral actions. For a college athletic coach to *take care of* a star player can mean anything from finding him an easy job or easy courses to paying him for a nonexistent job or faking a transcript for courses he never took.

Two student veterans of the Vietnam War, Karl Klankwski and Terry Moore, defined the following euphemisms from firsthand observation:

> *police action:* This commonly connotes response to a small civil disturbance. In reality, it is a polite term for an undeclared war, as in Vietnam.
>
> *lost:* In general usage, this means "misplaced." In war, when you lose five thousand men through death ("battle casualties" is too casual a term) or a dozen $5 million aircraft (through destruction) they're much further gone than "lost."

preemptive strike capability: Literally, the ability to initiate an attack. The U.S. and Russia strive to maintain a preemptive strike capability, the power to destroy another country before it can react effectively.

neutralize: In advertising, a way of relieving excess stomach acid. In war, to kill or otherwise render your enemy ineffective. "Napalm neutralized the gun emplacement."

You will want to avoid such ambiguous and misleading usage in your own writing. Say what you mean in your own words, and always select language that is:

Honest. Say *war* rather than *police action, kill* instead of *neutralize.* Some initial shock at your candor is preferable to the outrage and loss of confidence in you as a writer if your deceptive language were exposed.

Clear and unambiguous. Instead of using the pseudoauthoritative term *educational administrator,* specify the particular job: *college president, dean of students, high school principal, truant officer.* (Of course, if you were referring to administrators as a group, the general label would suffice.)

Straightforward, instead of falsely delicate. Avoid the cute and coy: in adult language, *bathroom* is preferable to *potty.*

Avoid the inaccurate and misleading; if you mean *rape,* say *rape* instead of *assault.*

Original. Avoid clichés (many euphemisms are also clichés—*to pass away* instead of *to die*) and other tired ways of saying things.

Don't worry about eliminating clichés or euphemisms or finding original expressions when you're writing the first draft. But when you're revising, look carefully for expressions that you may have used automatically, or that sound right because you've already heard them so often or because they conceal something you'd rather not confront. If you look up the too-familiar words in the dictionary, you will find appropriate synonyms either incorporated into the definitions or identified as synonyms after the main entry. (Since many euphemisms are heavily connotative, you may not find their meanings in the dictionary at all.)

Be Considerate of Your Readers

Readers, like writers, have the right to be treated with respect. A variation of the Golden Rule applies here: *Use the language in relation to your readers that you would have them use in relation to you.* This is easy enough to do if you pay attention to the following points:

Avoid deliberately denigrating terms or labels, such as *gook, wop, honky, nigger.*

**Avoid depersonalizing language that refers to human beings in nonhuman terms—as animals, objects, or machines for example—or which totally elimi-

nates references to them. *Hunk, piece of meat, dog, bitch* for *man* or *woman* are depersonalizing and demeaning. The language of war, as we've seen above, can be particularly dehumanizing, when *kills* mask *deaths,* often of innocent civilians, *body counts* substitute for *human deaths, protective reaction strike against a hamlet* conceals *total destruction of a rural village.* Part of the danger with such language, as George Orwell demonstrated in the novel *1984,* is that your thoughts can change to fit your words. If your thinking becomes dehumanized, it's easier to authorize or condone crimes and violence against people, such as exile, imprisonment, murder, war, genocide.

Use equivalent terms for equivalent categories. If you say *men* you should say *women,* not *girls* or *gals.* If you say *Einstein,* say *Dickinson,* not *Miss Dickinson* or *Emily.* Or, say *Mr. Einstein* and *Miss* (or *Ms.) Dickinson.*

Be sensitive to changing practices concerning the indefinite person. For centuries custom dictated using the masculine gender to mean either an indefinite person (*he or she*) or a group composed of both men and women (All *men* are created equal). This could have ridiculous implications, as when the Ohio General Assembly passed a law that stated, "No person may require another person to perform . . . or undergo an abortion of pregnancy, against *his* will." Although custom declares that readers should understand that *he or she* is meant when *he* is used, research indicates that in fact a significant proportion of schoolchildren think that *he* means *men* exclusively.

There are as yet no wholly satisfactory solutions to this problem. Substituting *he or she* or *men and women* for the general *one* or *he* or *men* can become wordy, awkward, and self-conscious. Here are some suggestions for temporary solutions until new and satisfactory usages have become established:

Change the singular to the plural when the meaning will permit. Instead of writing, "The exhausted traveler will find his spirits soaring when he reaches Papetee, Tahiti," say "Exhausted travelers will find their spirits soaring when they reach Papetee, Tahiti."

Use he or she **or the combined** s/he **form occasionally to let your readers know you're aware of the issue.**

Use she **when the indefinite person is likely to be female.** "A sensitive nurse doesn't crack sick jokes where her patients can overhear."

Try to find nonsexist substitutes for words that incorporate the generic man: *chair* or *head* for *chairman, letter carrier* for *mailman, humanity* for *mankind.* Some writers substitute *person* for *man,* but others find *chairperson, mailperson,* or *personkind* too clumsy and conspicuous to be effective.

If you follow the suggestions given in this chapter, you will learn to write in clear, concise, honest standard English that expresses your own unique perceptions and personality. If you choose your words as carefully and consciously as you select your clothing and your way of life, they will reflect your own dignity and reserve, or daring adventuresomeness, or as many other alternatives as there are thoughtful writers. In combination, your words can become as identifiable as your signature; your way of writing, like that of James Baldwin, Virginia Woolf, George Orwell, Maxine Hong Kingston, and all other distinguished writers, will be distinctively your own.

SUGGESTIONS FOR DISCUSSION AND WRITING

1. Rewrite the following portion of William Safire's parody of "Carter's Gettysburg Address" to improve its style and clarify its point. Take out all the unnecessary or redundant words and phrases, eliminate the clichés, make the vague language more specific. Then, rewrite it in your own words to retain the message (if you can find it) and provide more verbal color and interest. Do not copy Lincoln or look at the original until you have finished your version.

Exactly two hundred and one years, five months and one day ago, our forefathers—and our foremothers, too, as my wife, the First Lady, reminds me—our highly competent Founding Persons brought forth on this land mass a new nation, or entity, dreamed up in liberty and dedicated to the comprehensive program of insuring that all of us are created with the same basic human rights.

At the present moment, our nation clearly seems to be gathered up in a period of great disharmoniousness, testing whether our country, or homeland, can achieve an increasingly stable relationship and at the same time balance the budget by the end of my first term, which is my present intention.

We have come together at one of the great scenes of that disharmoniousness. We have come to dedicate a portion of that field, within adequate parameters, as a final resting place for those whose lack of compatibility led to this unfortunate conflict. . . .

I have taken a leadership role in strongly supporting initiatives for national survival that contain three basic elements and are fair. When my comprehensive reform proposals are adopted, and we have fruitful exchanges between North and South, then I think it is accurate to say that this government of the persons, by the persons, and for the persons shall not vanish in a highly erroneous display of incompatibility and disharmoniousness.[20]

Then, compare your version with Lincoln's "Gettysburg Address," above, p. 162. Are both equally clear? precise? memorable? The same in tone and length? What are their similarities and differences?

2. Choose one or more of the samples below and rewrite each to eliminate bias, unnecessary jargon, passive construction, or any other stylistic problems you notice, such as too many negatives or unnecessary words.

As an alternative, find an example of such writing in a newspaper or magazine. Government or other bureaucratic or legal documents and reports, political speeches, some specialized technical or other professional journals are good places to look. Sometimes for laughs the *New Yorker* reprints particularly murky writing at the end of its regular columns.

a. As a result of the sale and subsequent transfer of governmental customers to PANSY [Power Authority of the State of New York], Con Edison will no longer receive the revenues these customers formerly paid. This loss will be offset in part by the revenues Con Edison will receive from PANSY for delivering electricity from these plants to PANSY customers, and because it no longer must generate the electricity used by the PANSY customers.

However, after subtracting these offsets, there will still be a net revenue loss to Con Edison.

—Bill insert to customers from Con Edison Power Company

b. Considering the advancements made by mankind in the last 100 years, it is quite amazing to think what could have happened had humankind been involved.

—Teheran *Journal*

c. God Helps Those Who Help Themselves

It is so easy to cry over spilled milk and blame our misfortunes on the politicians, or the lobbyists, or some other straw man we set up to take the blame for our own failings. Let's face it, with only hours to go until the Constitutional cut-off time of midnight 12 p.m. the 15th of June for the Missouri Legislature, MASW has experienced a debacle in the field of social legislation. The only successful bill in our package was the Parent Locator Bill. We really can't take much credit for that because it wouldn't have passed either except for the multi-million dollar arm twisting engaged in by the federal government expert authorities.

We must look now to the future with fortitude and courage. We must plan intelligently and then roll up our collective sleeves and go about our business. Politics is both an art and a science and we must learn the rules in order to play the game. We must be dead serious in our game. We must be dead serious in our approach because the welfare of the people is at stake. Sometimes their very lives may hang in the balance. . . .

—LEGISLATIVE NEWS, Missouri Association for
Social Welfare, June 13, 1977

3. From newspapers, political speeches, conversations, advertisements, or other sources pick out eight to ten euphemistic words or phrases. Write a brief paragraph about each word, indicating:
   a. How it is used.
   b. What its ostensible meaning is and what this meaning connotes.
   c. What its real meaning is; what is behind the meaning indicated in *b*.
   d. Why you think it's used as it is in the context in which you found it.
   Example: *Body count:* "The body count was Americans 723, North Vietnamese 1,438." Ostensibly, *body count* means the number of bodies counted. As used in the Vietnam War, however, it meant *deaths*—of soldiers and civilians, adults and children. The term dehumanized the deaths by reducing the dead person to a body and a number, in an attempt to make the war seem less personal and less brutal.

4. Create a dialogue (in the manner of Frank Sullivan's Cliché Expert dialogues) in which at least one of the two speakers characterizes himself and his subject through an extensive use of clichés.

5. Examine your local newspaper, a textbook, or a popular magazine (an older one would be particularly revealing) to find eight to ten instances of language that shows lack of respect for people. Discuss your findings and how these could be corrected. Do you find:
   a. Derogatory or depersonalizing terms (specify)?
   b. Lack of equivalent terms for different races, sexes, backgrounds, cultures (such as identifying a woman's marital status or age without doing the same for a man, or identifying a person's race or background when it's not relevant to the point)?

c. Discriminating clichés, whether overt or subtle ("She's free, white, and twenty-one!")?
d. Does the publication always use masculine pronouns for the indefinite person? If not, what accommodation does it make to changing usage?

NOTES

1 (New York: Random House, 1975), p. 990.
2 Lewis Carroll, *Through the Looking-Glass* (1872; rpt. New York: Macmillan, 1966), p. 79.
3 "Contact Lenses," *Consumer Report* (May 1980), p. 290.
4 Octavio Roca, "Victims of the U.S. Army Band," the *Washington Post*, Aug. 28, 1980, F 10.
5 *The Education of Henry Adams*, ed. Ernest Samuels (1918; rpt. Boston: Houghton Mifflin, 1973), p. 7.
6 Ecclesiastes 3:1–4, 6–8, King James Version.
7 In *Shooting an Elephant and Other Essays* (New York: Harcourt Brace, 1950), pp. 77–78.
8 The *New York Times*, June 8, 1977, C 12.
9 *NCR Century Operating Systems Manual*, NCR Corp., 1974, n.p.
10 "Gobbledygook," *The Power of Words*, in collaboration with Marian Tyler Chase (New York: Harcourt Brace, 1954), p. 259.
11 Tr. William A. Stewart. Italics supplied. Quoted in William Raspberry, "Should Ghettoese Be Accepted?" *Today's Education* (April 1970), p. 61.
12 *The Pine Barrens* (New York: Farrar, Straus, and Giroux, 1968), p. 56.
13 "Alcohol Metabolism: All in the Family," *Science News*, 115:1 (January 6, 1979), 6.
14 *The Social System* (Glencoe, Ill.: The Free Press, 1951), p. 99.
15 *Slouching Towards Bethlehem* (1968; rpt. New York: Delta, 1968), p. 4.
16 Garrett Hardin, "Lifeboat Ethics: The Case Against Helping the Poor," *Psychology Today* (September 1974), p. 38.
17 Adapted from the 1977 directive of Alfred Kahn, Chairman of the Civil Aeronautics Board, to his staff to avoid bureaucratese. Quoted in the *Washington Post*, September 18, 1980, D. 5.
18 Plain Talk founding president Albert Joseph, quoted in the *Washington Post*, September 18, 1980, D 5.
19 "The Cliché Expert Testifies on Baseball," in *The Night the Old Nostalgia Burned Down* (Philadelphia: Curtis, 1948), p. 72.
20 "Carter's Gettysburg Address," the *New York Times* (December 12, 1977), 39M.

CHAPTER EIGHT
REVISING, EDITING, AND PREPARING THE FINAL COPY

The last act of . . . writing must be to become one's own reader. It is, I suppose, a schizophrenic process. To begin passionately and to end critically, to begin hot and to end cold; and, more important, to try not to be passion-hot and critic-cold at the same time.

—JOHN CIARDI

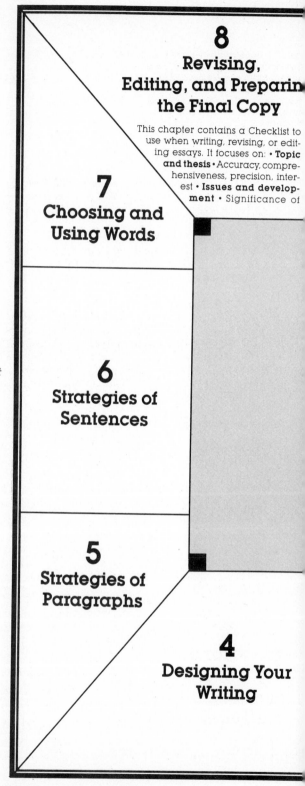

8
Revising, Editing, and Preparin[g] the Final Copy

This chapter contains a Checklist to use when writing, revising, or editing essays. It focuses on: • **Topic and thesis** • Accuracy, comprehensiveness, precision, interest • **Issues and development** • Significance of

7
Choosing and Using Words

6
Strategies of Sentences

5
Strategies of Paragraphs

4
Designing Your Writing

subject • Coverage of the issues • Accommodation of the intended audience • **Organization — beginning, middle, end, proportioning** • **Style** — clarity, conciseness, variety, level of language, word choice, figurative language • **Grammar** — parts of speech, sentences • **Mechanics** — spelling, punctuation • **References** • **It illustrates revision of:** • Introduction • Tone • Focus and structure • Verbal expression • **It shows how to select a title** • **It shows how to prepare the final copy.**

1
Warming Up

2
Finding a Subject

3
Developing Ideas And Formulating a Thesis

REVISING: MOVING FROM PRIVATE TO PUBLIC COMMUNICATION

The act of revising moves a paper from being a private expression to being a public document. Revision is the acknowledgment that you are not writing a memo to yourself (whether or not you were doing so in the first draft) but a presentation for an external audience.

Even if you have a specific audience in mind when you write your first draft, the first time you tackle a subject you will be preoccupied with deciding what to say and how best to say it. So, though the first draft may exhibit a frame of reference that is clear to you, it may not make sense to anyone else.[1] A first draft may focus on the writer's enjoyment of or surprise in exploring the subject or on the difficulties in finding materials. First drafts may also contain a number of false starts, redundancy of evidence or argument (because you've found your material after some labor, perhaps, and can't bear to leave it out), or excursions into byways beloved by the writer but irrelevant to the subject. Such manifestations of the composing process, signs of the effort of writing or of lack of authorial control, are likely to occur, for better or worse, in a first draft.

But such evidence of your search and struggle needs to be removed in revision to let the solid substance of the actual essay emerge clearly. The second, third, or even subsequent drafts need to be oriented to the essay's prospective readers, no matter who the initial version was geared to.

To do this effectively you need to have a perspective on your writing that may not be possible immediately after you've finished the first draft of an essay. You may be so tired of it at that point that you simply want to hand the first draft in so you can stop thinking about it for a while. Or you may have invested so much of yourself in the paper that you can't read it with detachment right away.

To gain the distance necessary to become an objective reader and reviser of your own writing, try to finish the first draft of your paper, report, or article at least two days before it's due. That way you can let it sit undisturbed for twenty-four hours before you revise it and hand it in. (If you have the time, it's even better to wait a bit longer.) However, even if you have to rush through a midnight-to-4 A.M. version of your paper the night before it's due, you will need to examine your first draft as objectively as possible so you can revise it.

If possible, arrange to have a friendly critic whose judgment you trust read your paper also. Perhaps you can trade drafts with someone else who's working on a similar task; a writing "buddy" can be a valuable friend. Whether or not you do this, one of your aims in learning to write should be to become your own most reliable critic. You won't always have an English teacher to make marks in the margins and put comments at the ends of your papers. Perhaps you don't now, if you're writing on the job, for yourself, or for an organization to which you belong. As you examine your own writings you'll be functioning as a critic, and in the process of becoming your own critic you'll become your own teacher. In learning to write and to revise and edit, you're developing a lifetime skill.

Here is a checklist of points to consider as you work on your revisions. It summarizes many concerns discussed in the preceding chapters, as the page numbers in parentheses indicate. Use the individual sections of the checklist as they apply to the current stage of your writing: I in determining what to write on and in framing a thesis; II (and VII, if necessary) in developing your ideas; III in organizing your materials; IV to VII in evaluating style, mechanics, and outside sources. Part VIII and the checklist as a whole provide an overview of the first or successive drafts of your paper as well as a set of criteria for evaluating the papers of other writers. You and your instructor or writing buddy may also use relevant portions of the checklist as the basis for discussions about your writing.

☐ A Checklist to Improve Your Essays [2]

I. Topic and thesis

    A. Is the exact point I wish to make clear to me? Is there an exact point? (pp. 54–55)

    B. Have I framed this point accurately, precisely, and clearly in my thesis? (pp. 54–55) Or have I used vague, ambiguous, or misleading words? (pp. 54–57)

    C. Does my thesis cover the entire essay? (pp. 55–57)

    D. Does my thesis express my opinion about the subject? (pp. 54–57)

    E. Is my thesis interesting? emphatic? (p. 56)

II. Issues and development

    A. Have I limited the topic sufficiently so that it can be treated thoroughly and adequately in my paper? (pp. 29–32)

    B. Does either the issue itself or my treatment of it have enough significance to justify this paper? (pp. 26–27)

    C. For what audience am I writing? (pp. 33–35) Have I supplied the necessary background information so my readers can understand what I'm talking about? (pp. 33–37)

    D. Within the limits I've established, have I covered the issues adequately?

        1. What sources have I used?

            a. Personal experience? (pp. 42–48; 102–107; 269–270; 311–312)

            b. Printed sources, films, or other authoritative informants? (pp. 313–321)

            c. Relevant political, economic, religious, social, intellectual, aesthetic, or sexual perspectives? (pp. 43–45; 323–324)

            d. History, customs, rules, folk wisdom, maxims, laws? (pp. 44; 311–312)

        2. Do I need additional illustrations of any sort?

        3. Can anything be omitted without doing violence to my viewpoint? (pp. 186–194)

    E. Have I acknowledged and accounted for exceptions or alternatives to my point of view? (pp. 189–190; 211–212)

    F. Have I considered how the opposition will react to each of my points? Have I built my answers into the discussion? (pp. 259–309)

III. Organization

    A. Beginning

        1. Is the central issue defined fairly early in the paper? (pp. 62; 74–78) If not, should it be?

        2. Will my topic, tone, and style attract the readers' interest? (pp. 111–116)

    B. Middle

        1. What are my strongest points? Where are they? Are they made emphatically enough? (pp. 74–78; 85)

        2. Is there a pattern to the arrangement of the points? (pp. 61–63; 74–88) If so, what are my reasons for using this pattern? If not, why not?

        3. Have I slid over or ignored important points?

        4. Where are the minor points (if any) mentioned?

        5. Does paragraphing help make the points stand out clearly? (pp. 93–97) Is each paragraph coherent? (pp. 101–109)

        6. Are there false generalities, missing steps, or interpretations or conclusions that don't fit the evidence? (pp. 107–108; 109)

C. End
   1. Does the ending follow easily and necessarily from the strongest point(s)? from all the points? (pp. 118–119) Does the essay flow smoothly from beginning to end? (pp. 116–119)
   2. Is it possible to make a fresh observation to add interest to my conclusion? (pp. 116–118)
   3. Does the tone of my conclusion fit the tone of the paper?
   4. Have I claimed to have proved more than I've actually demonstrated?
D. Proportioning
   1. Have the ideas and materials in the beginning, middle, and end received about the right amount of emphasis? (pp. 190–194)
   2. If not, what can I do to make the parts balance more pleasingly?

IV. Style
A. Is my writing clear and unambiguous? (pp. 159–169)
B. Is my writing suitably concise? (pp. 125–129; 171–172)
   1. If it's too wordy, what can be omitted without loss of meaning? Have I cut as much as I can?
   2. If it's too concise to be meaningful, what needs to be added?
C. Have I used the active voice primarily and avoided the passive? (p. 173).
D. Are the sentences and paragraphs of varying lengths and structures, rather than monotonously uniform? (pp. 125–146)
   1. Do their structures clarify and emphasize what I want them to? (pp. 125–146)
   2. Have I kept parallel elements parallel? (pp. 133–136)
E. In general, what level of language am I using? (pp. 155–161)
   1. Are its level and tone appropriate to my intended audience? (pp. 155–163)
   2. Are its level and tone appropriate to my treatment of the subject? (pp. 155–163)
   3. Is my vocabulary appropriate to the level of language I'm using? (pp. 155–163)
   4. Is my vocabulary consistent and harmonious? (pp. 163–169) Or do I mix formal and informal usages? or technical and nontechnical usages? With what effects?
F. Diction
   1. Do I know the meanings of all the words I'm using? Will my readers? Are specialized or unfamiliar terms identified in the text? (pp. 163–164)
   2. Is my language suitably varied?
   3. Is my language sufficiently precise and specific? (pp. 167–177)
   4. Do my words have the connotations I intend them to have? (pp. 174–177)
G. Symbols, metaphors, and other figurative language; dialogue; dialect

1. If I've used such language, is it relevant to my presentation of the subject? in nature? in quantity?
2. Does such language enhance my presentation or detract from it? (pp. 164–165)
3. If I haven't used any figurative language or dialect, should I have done so?

V. Grammar
   A. Parts of speech
      1. Do the subjects and verbs agree?
      2. Are the verb tenses congruent? Or, if I've used the past tense in one portion and the present tense in the next, is this justified?
      3. Are the pronoun referents clear? (If I say "it" or "that," can the reader tell what I'm referring to?)
   B. Sentences
      1. Do my sentences have an emphasis and variety that enhances their meaning? (pp. 125–146)
      2. Have I coordinated and combined groups of sentences that were too short? (pp. 133–137)
      3. Have I broken up long and cumbersome sentences? (pp. 127–129)
      4. Have I used independent sentence fragments? (pp. 126–129) If so, would it be better if they were incorporated into other sentences? (pp. 141–143)

VI. Mechanics
   A. Spelling
      1. Have I checked the spelling of all words:
         a. of which I am doubtful?
         b. that I had to sound out to spell?
         c. whose meaning is unfamiliar?
         d. that I have previously misspelled?
      2. Have I divided words properly at the ends of lines?
   B. Punctuation
      1. Have I used punctuation in accord with the accepted conventions? (pp. 380–389)
      2. If not, have I good reasons for breaking the rules?

VII. References
   A. Have I used outside sources when necessary? (pp. 312–324)
   B. Are my quotations, paraphrases, or other references relevant? Are they excessive? too difficult or obscure?
   C. Have I acknowledged outside sources accurately? (pp. 327–330) Have I used appropriate footnote and bibliographic form? (pp. 328–333)

VIII. Overall
   A. Have I said what I mean?
   B. Am I satisfied with this draft of my paper? Is this the best I can do?
   C. If not, am I willing to work to remedy my dissatisfaction by revising one or more sections *before* I turn in the paper?

D. What would it take to write a better paper than I usually write?

E. Could I have expressed myself in different and better ways—with greater color, precision, or suitability to my audience?

F. Have I felt free to break any of the rules or to disregard any of the suggestions for good writing if I felt it would make my paper more effective? (This independence, handled knowledgeably, can be one of the major attributes of creativity. A rule broken at random is caprice; a rule broken effectively and to good purpose is creative.)

If you are writing a technical paper for a specialized audience, you will want to check with your supervisor or instructor about adaptations you may need to make in this Checklist to accommodate both a specialized readership and a technical format.

In the analyses of revision that follow, portions of the outline will be referred to in parentheses by number and letter.

THE SECOND DRAFT

In a utopian world you'd have as much time as you wanted to write as many drafts of a paper as necessary to make it ideal. How many would that be? That would depend—on the condition of the first draft, on what you're aiming for, on what your readers and critics expect, and on how much energy you're willing to expend. Professional writers often rewrite their works, or the troublesome spots, many times before submitting them for publication. Novelist John Nichols explains that he completely rewrote *The Sterile Cuckoo*, originally a 450-page manuscript, ten times in two years before he created a version that satisfied him.[3]

For most students or writers on the job so prodigious an effort is simply not possible. Realistically, given the pressure of competing demands, a second or third draft may be the best you can hope for. You will find, if you go over your paper objectively, considering the various points on the Checklist, that a second look will reveal all sorts of things you missed the first time around. In this process of *re-vision*, literally "seeing the topic anew," you will have the chance to rethink and test alternative ways of expression and organization of your existing material.

A new look at your paper may reveal that it is too long, because, as we mentioned early in this chapter, of the inclusion of irrelevant warmup paragraphs, too many illustrations, or digressions from your thesis. The writing itself may be repetitive or wordy. This is fine in a first draft, but you have to be willing to cut drastically the second time around, eliminating the dead wood, the duplications, the false starts and irrelevant digressions.

Or you may find that the paper is too short, that it's unclear or unconvincing because its thesis or subordinate points need to be developed more fully. If you can't understand—or paraphrase—what you've said, chances are that your audience won't be able to either. Again, the chapters preceding this one provide some suggestions on what to do, not only to solve problems of development but also problems regarding organization, paragraphing, and word choice.

Writing the second draft is also the time to correct the mechanics of spelling, grammar, footnote accuracy, and format. At this point, you may want to consult a thesaurus or a dictionary to vary a monotonous vocabulary or spice up too bland a tone.

REVISIONS: CHANGES FOR THE BETTER

The following examples from first and later drafts of student papers illustrate some of the most common sorts of writing problems beginning writers are confronted with and show how revisions have dealt with them. Throughout the chapters in Part I, you will have also seen how revision can function in improving a paper's outline and organization (Chapter 4), paragraphs (Chapter 5), sentences (Chapter 6), and words (Chapter 7). You will want to bear these in mind as you apply individual suggestions to an entire paper.

Revising an Introduction

Introductions, often difficult to write because you're warming up to your subject as well as focusing on it, often need to be revised to remove evidence of such difficulties—to sharpen the focus and eliminate the wordiness that results from false starts (see the Checklist, I; III, A).

Stephanie Darnell's introduction to "The Effects of the Teapot Dome Scandal" went through three versions, each becoming more focused on the topic. Here, as in other papers quoted in this chapter, the grammar, spelling, and punctuation remain as they were in the original, errors and all. (Note that parenthetical references in the discussion below are to pertinent sections of this chapter's Checklist.)

FIRST VERSION:

Teapot Dome was a petroleum scandal during the Harding Administration in which the Secretary of the Interior, Albert B. Fall, secretly leased naval oilfields to oil companies that practically depleted the fields. Secretary Fall accepted bribes of over a $100,000 in return for leasing the fields to two friends, Harry Sinclair and
5 E. L. Doheny. When the Government realized these illicit dealings, Senate investigations were initiated to uncover the details and convict the participants. Eventually the oil leases were voided.

The immediate effect of Teapot Dome was an immediate scrupulous investigation of every governmental department. Much to everyone's dismay practical every
10 scrutinized bureau was found to be scandal ridden to some degree. [The author abandoned the first version at this point.]

The first version is essentially a warmup. Stephanie is writing about the general topic area but hasn't yet arrived at a clear statement of her thesis or the main supporting points her essay will discuss. She is already in possession of the information on which to base her essay (and which would, in every version, require footnotes or some other acknowledgment of sources), but she hasn't decided exactly what to do with it. In this draft, she puts it all down to see how it looks, breaking off when she realizes that this attempt places the definition of the Teapot Dome scandal before the potential thesis and that she's getting even further from the mark when she becomes sidetracked in the investigations of the various government departments.

SECOND VERSION:

Teapot Dome, a petroleum scandal during the Harding administration had three immediate effects on national policy. The first was a total breakdown of administrative efficiency as corruption was discovered in many bureaus besides the Department of the Interior. Senate investigations were initiated to scrutinize many
5   governmental agencies, the Veteran's Department and Attorney General's office being only two. Secondly, Teapot Dome was a significant factor in determining the outcome of the presidential election of 1924. Ex-Secretary of the Treasury McAddoo's name was so besmirched with scandal that eventually he had to withdraw from the race. Finally, Calvin Coolidge's oil policy during the first year of his
10   administration was marked by an effort to reverse the trend set by Teapot Dome. He adopted a conservative stance aimed at preserving our natural resources and restoring confidence in a government pockmarked by corruption.
Teapot Dome was a naval oilfield in Wyoming and the name given to a petroleum scandal in the early 1920's, during the Harding administration. Albert Fall,
15   Secretary of the Interior, secretly leased naval oil fields to two of his oil magnate friends, who proceeded to defraud the government. . . .

The second version is much clearer. Here Stephanie has decided to emphasize the three immediate effects of the Teapot Dome scandal (III, A) and to establish the pattern (III, B) for what's to come later in the paper by explicitly identifying them, "First . . . ," "Second . . . ," "Finally. . . ." She has written an essentially new first paragraph, bringing the three main points to the foreground and deferring background information (which defines the Teapot Dome scandal) until the second paragraph. However, she has included in the second draft the idea explored in the second paragraph of the first version—investigations of scandals in various government departments—and designated this topic as one of the major points to be discussed at greater length in the body of the paper.

THIRD (AND FINAL) VERSION:

Teapot Dome, a petroleum scandal during the Harding Administration, had three immediate effects on national policy. The first was that the discovery of the oil infamy served to initiate Senate investigations of many other departments, such as the Veteran's Bureau and the Attorney General's office.[1] Second, Teapot
5   Dome was a determining factor in the outcome of the 1924 presidential election.

Cabinet member William McAdoo's name was so besmirched with calumny that his White House aspirations were crushed.[2] Finally, Calvin Coolidge's domestic oil policy, during the first year of his administration, was marked by an effort to reverse the trend set by Teapot Dome. He adopted a conservative stance aimed at
10 both preserving natural resources and restoring confidence in a national government pockmarked by corruption.[3]

Teapot Dome, a naval oil reserve in Wyoming, was the name given to a petroleum scandal in the early 1920's originating when Albert Fall, Secretary of the Interior, secretly leased naval oilfields, including Teapot Dome, to oil magnates
15 E. L. Doheny and Harry Sinclair. . . .

The revisions in the third version are primarily stylistic. The most conspicuous change is the stylistic economy in the second sentence (IV, B). Two sentences totalling forty-one words in the second draft are here combined into a single sentence of twenty-nine words, without loss of meaning. Other changes substitute more specific phrases or words for the vaguer terms used in the second version (IV, F, 3). For example, in line 8, *domestic* is added to identify Coolidge's oil policy; in line 13 the more precise *oil reserve* is substituted for *naval oilfield* (second version), though, had it been used, *naval oil reserve* would have been the most precise of all. However, the more specific identification of McAdoo in the second draft as *Ex-Secretary of the Treasury* is here generalized to *Cabinet member* for reasons that are not apparent until the fourth paragraph, where he is identified again, more specifically, as *President Wilson's son-in-law and a former Secretary of the Treasury*. The initial identification is shorter and in keeping with the conscieness of the opening paragraph; the additional information is provided where it's needed.

Revising to Moderate a Biased Tone

It is not only appropriate but desirable to express a point of view in your writing; this will be natural and inevitable if you have an opinion about your subject. Yet in most instances you will want to write from a reasoned and reasonable perspective rather than from one that is immoderate and loaded with highly biased language (IV, F, 4).

Stephanie Darnell, author of the previous paper, wrote another essay identifying the causes leading to the Teapot Dome scandal. Although the assignment called for the expression of a particular attitude toward her material, the first paragraph of the first version came out sounding too partisan (italics supplied here to indicate bias and/or overstatement):

Teapot Dome, one of the *most scandalous episodes* in American governmental history, was *inevitable*. The *bureaucracy's lack of foresight* and *incompetency* in handling crucial business affairs created *ideal* circumstances for an *effusion of corruption*. Thus the administration should not have been surprised or dismayed at the *burgeoning debauchery* in their midst, for Teapot Dome was the *natural result of their stupidity*.

On being advised by an objective reader that she was "overkilling the reader with bias" and that she should "be more subtle," she revised the paragraph as follows:

> Teapot Dome, an oil *scandal* in the 1920's, was *inevitable* due to the government's *lack of foresight*. President Harding's transfer of control of the naval oil reserves to Secretary of the Interior Fall set up an *ideal* situation for exploitation. Fall was subsequently bribed to lease the oilfields to two influential oilmen. The government, unaware of these illegal transactions, lost not only hundreds of millions of dollars but valuable oil resources as well.

In the revision Stephanie still makes her opinion very clear. She has, however, substituted objective information (III, B) about Fall's bribery and the government's lack of awareness of the illegal activities (sentences 2, 3, and 4 above) for the opinions expressed in sentences 2 and 3 of the original paragraph (III, B). And she has eliminated most of the biased language and overstatement (IV, F, 4); what little remains is in italics above. Its presence helps to convey her opinion, but it now seems much more reasonable and subdued, because such words as *scandal, inevitable,* and *lack of foresight* are expressed in a more moderate context.

Revising for Clearer Focus and Emphasis

If you write the way you speak—which is a reasonable way to get started—your first draft will probably reflect the natural wordiness and repetitiveness of speech. But what works in conversation can be boring or distracting in a written context. Too many words or repetitious phrasing will clog up your writing and slow it down.

Angela Bowman's first draft of "Freddie the Fox and My Fifth Christmas" clearly reveals these problems.

> I am fond of my collection of stuffed animals. I received one of my first stuffed animals for Christmas when I was five years old. Stuffed animals did not mean very much to me then. My first stuffed animal was a red and white fox. I named him Freddie. He was just another toy under the Christmas tree. There was some-
> 5   thing different about my fifth Christmas. It was a confusing time. The night before Christmas my father had told me about the legend of Saint Nicholas and tried to explain who Santa Claus really was. I did not understand what he was talking about. It was confusing for me. Freddie helps me to remember that event. As time went by I realized what my father was trying to explain to me. Freddie also helps
> 10 me to remember when the realization of who Santa was was not clear to me and the fact that it did become clearer.
>   When I look at Freddie now I remember that Christmas. I also remember some of the thoughts and feelings that I felt when I woke up on Christmas morning and saw the tree. The first toy under the tree that I noticed was a doll. I hated the doll

¹⁵ because she was black, and I was angry about it. I could not understand why Santa had left me that ugly doll. When I look at Freddie now, I remember that exact moment and I am ashamed. Freddie represents the fact that now I realize that at that age I had been brain-washed to think that only white dolls were pretty.

Freddie helps me to remember the ideas and feelings that I experienced on my ²⁰ fifth Christmas morning. Yet the day and the items involved are not what are important. What is important is that I remember it as a confusing time which caused me to think and question what was going on around me. This can perhaps be seen in the instance when my father told me about Santa. Even though I did not understand what he was explaining I did not accept it either. I just listened to him ²⁵ politely and thought about it later. I still do not accept half truths and must research everything for myself.

Although Freddie is old, torn and perhaps worthless to most people who see him, he means a lot to me. He has grown up with me. He was with me in the past when certain ideas were confusing to me. Since those confusing ideas have become ³⁰ clearer to me, Freddie represents my ability to search for answers that will satisfy my curiosities.

When Angela reread her first draft, she could easily see that some of the phrasing was repetitious and that some of the ideas were not as clearly expressed as they might have been. As a first step in revising what is essentially a good paper, she made a paragraph-by-paragraph outline of what she had written. Such an outline can be very helpful in highlighting instances of redundancy. It will also help you as an author to recognize omissions—explanations, definitions, or steps in reasoning that must be added if your writing is to be as clear and convincing as it can be.

In composing her outline, Angela did not try to keep a strict heading format or to keep the grammar parallel, as she might have done in an outline written in advance of composing a paper. So sentences, fragments, and single words are intermingled:

I. I am fond of my collection of stuffed animals.
   A. One received for Christmas at 5
      1. Didn't mean much then
      2. A fox
      3. Named Freddie
      4. Just another toy

Original   II. Fifth Christmas different
Paragraph 1   A. Confusing
      1. Father explained Santa Claus legend
        a. I didn't understand
        b. Confusing
   B. Freddie reminds of this event
      1. I gradually understood what Father meant
      2. Freddie helps me remember
        a. The confusion
        b. The later clarity

Original   III. Freddie reminds me of my fifth Christmas

Paragraph 2	A. I remember my thoughts and feelings on that Christmas morning
	B. The black doll
	1. Angry at receiving it
	a. Ugly doll
	b. Didn't understand
	2. Now ashamed at my childhood reaction
Original	IV. Why should my fifth Christmas seem so important?
Paragraph 3	A. Freddie helps me remember ideas and feelings then
	B. Day itself and material items not the most important
	C. Most important
	1. Confusing time
	2. Caused me to think and question
	3. A beginning of my life pattern of questioning
	4. Stopped simply accepting and taking things for granted
Original	V. Freddie's significance to me
Paragraph 4	A. We've grown up together
	B. He links past and present
	C. He represents my ability to search independently for satisfying answers.

The outline revealed to Angela a number of things that weren't apparent to her when she wrote the first draft. She could now see that her first paragraph really consisted of two different main topics (I, A, B; II, A, B, D; III, A—parenthetical notations refer to sections of the Checklist, pp. 182–186, not to the outline directly above.): the significance of Freddie, a toy fox she received on her fifth Christmas (IV, G); and the confusion Angela experienced when her father tried to explain the symbolism of Santa Claus (IV, G) on that same Christmas. This dual-topic paragraph is hard to follow.

The second paragraph (III, B) focuses on Angela's receipt of a black doll and how her more mature understanding has caused her to be ashamed of her initial anger and perception that the doll was ugly. Freddie triggers memories of the event and symbolizes Angela's new recognition of her former lack of understanding.

Paragraph three (II, B) identifies the main reason why Angela considers her fifth Christmas so significant: it was the time when she "started questioning everything" and stopped accepting what she was told without examining it. The fourth paragraph (III, B) tries to summarize Freddie's significance to Angela as a symbol of her maturation—the progression from early confusion to the adult habit of questioning and independently searching for answers.

Read in this way, the main points Angela wanted to make became clear. She realized that in her paper she wanted to show how over the years Freddie has come to symbolize a cluster of events, ideas, and understandings that were triggered by her fifth Christmas (IV, G). With this in mind, Angela wrote a new outline, based on the first outline, that presented her major points much more clearly.

TITLE: "FREDDIE THE FOX AND MY FIFTH CHRISTMAS"

Thesis: Freddie, a stuffed toy fox that I received on my fifth Christmas, has come to symbolize several important phenomena of that day: my having to cope with Santa Claus as a symbol rather than as a person; my initial rejection and later acceptance of a black doll; and the beginning of my growing independence of mind.

I. Introduction: Freddie, a stuffed toy fox, is an important symbol of my fifth Christmas.
   A. A gift then
   B. Assumed symbolic meaning later as significance of unusual, confusing fifth Christmas became apparent
II. Father identified Santa Claus as legend, not real person
   A. My initial reaction
      1. Confusion
      2. Disbelief
   B. My later reaction
      1. Understanding
      2. Acceptance
III. Present of a black doll
   A. My initial reaction
      1. Thought it ugly
      2. Anger
   B. My later reaction
      1. Pride in blackness, symbolized by doll
      2. Shame at initial reaction
IV. Began my life pattern of independence of mind
   A. Stopped simply taking things for granted
   B. Stopped accepting everything I was told
   C. Started questioning
   D. Began life pattern of investigating and exploring to make important decisions and discoveries for myself
V. Freddie's current significance to me
   A. We've grown up together
   B. His presence symbolizes these major events and my reactions to them
   C. He links past and present

The new outline enabled Angela to eliminate repeated statements (IV, B) of how confused she was by various events. It also helped her to frame the paper by discussing Freddie at the beginning and end without referring to him continually in every paragraph. The new outline also showed Angela that she had to develop her discussion of the three points obscured by repetition in her earlier version: her father's explanation of Santa Claus; her present of a black doll; and the beginning of her life pattern of independence of mind. She recognized also that her attitudes toward Santa as Christmas spirit (II, D, 1) and toward her own blackness had changed considerably over time, and she decided to emphasize these changes from past to present (II, B, 2) in her revision.

In revising the essay, Angela also employed a number of the sentence-combining techniques (see Chapter 6; V, B, 2). So even with the addition of new material, the revised version, below, is about the same length as the original, although it says a great deal more.

FREDDIE THE FOX AND MY FIFTH CHRISTMAS: PAST AND PRESENT

On my fifth Christmas I was given Freddie, a stuffed toy fox that has since come to symbolize several important phenomena of that day: my having to cope with Santa Claus as a symbol rather than as a person; my initial rejection and later acceptance of a black doll—and pride in my race; and the beginning of my grow-
5   ing independence of mind.

On Christmas Eve my father told me about the legend of St. Nicholas and tried to explain that Santa represented the spirit of Christmas but was not a real person. I became confused and rejected his explanation, though secretly I felt that my father was right. He had never lied to me. I was so upset that I jumped down from
10   his lap, stomped off, and hid in my room. Later I understood what I hadn't wanted to admit at the time. I had felt that if there wasn't a flesh-and-blood Santa I might not get any presents, but I couldn't tell my father this because that would have ignored his explanation of the true spirit of Christmas, generous and loving. Only when I was older and could express the genuine Christmas spirit myself was I
15   able to fully understand what my father had meant.

The next morning I tiptoed to the Christmas tree, fearful that I'd find nothing after what my father had said the day before. What I saw was worse than nothing —an ugly black doll. I hated the doll because she was black. At that age I had been brainwashed to think that only white dolls were pretty. Maybe I'd been given the
20   doll as punishment for rebelling against my father's explanation of Santa Claus. Now when I remember that moment I feel ashamed. With plenty of encouragement from my parents and others I have grown to be very proud of my blackness, symbolized by the doll. It's painful to think that I could ever have hated that doll.

Both events caused me to question ideas that I had previously taken for granted.
25   I stopped accepting everything I was told, though the realization that white skin wasn't prettier than black didn't come overnight. I started finding out things for myself, investigating and questioning. I must have driven my parents, teachers, and the local librarian wild because I never stopped asking questions. I still haven't, because I like to make important discoveries and decisions for myself.
30   Freddie the fox has been my mascot during the whole time. We've grown up together. His presence symbolizes not only my fifth Christmas but the changes I've experienced since then. He links past and present.

Revising to Improve Verbal Expression

In a number of respects revision to improve verbal expression is the easiest to perform, because it is the least dramatic. The focus here is on the way you express whatever it is you want to say.

Revision to improve verbal expression involves a close look at word choice (IV, F), vocabulary level (IV, F), figurative language (IV, G), grammar (V), and mechanics (VI, A, B). It may also require thoughtful attention to sentence and paragraph structure and development (II; IV, D). When you revise with these aspects in mind, you must listen to the sounds as well as the sense of your *whether it was poverty, suffering, or despair,*

From this lowest rung,/ the Tramp always made his entrance into the

films. For example, in "City Lights" he is homeless, ~~out of a job~~ *jobless*, and lacks

a place to sleep; in "The Circus" he has been left alone in a littered field

when the circus as moved on. ~~This, in essence is~~ *Then, in one of his worst situations* and in "The Gold Rush"

(5) he is so hungry that he boils one of his old shoes for dinner. Despite all

→ somehow conquered these

this misery though, ~~he Charlie Chaplin~~ the Tramp (struggled with) universal human

humorous but ~~comical~~ *sympathetic*   *refusing—pretending ignoring the*

problems in a ~~comical~~ manner, ~~pretending to admit that everything was out of the~~

~~fact~~   *with intention of*   ~~For instance~~ Looking again at

~~way, he attempted to~~/maintaining his dignity. ~~As such~~

one notices that

"The Gold Rush",/he ~~eats~~ *ate* the boiled shoe as if was the most delicious meal

(10) ever prepared. From ~~this~~ such/ *a case* ~~an incident~~, it was apparent that he was a

character who refused under any circumstances to take anything seriously, no

how life was determined to knock him about.

matter ~~what obstacles the universe set infront of him~~. With this attitude

he gave a little ~~light~~ hope to ~~the~~ even the lowlyest of the low , ...

Chaplin captivated his audiences through such comic inventions, but ~~the~~

main influence   ~~of the Tramp~~ *of his style*

(15) ~~one aspect characteristic which wasn't studied premeditated~~ was an aspect

the profoundly *bitter*

released from somewhere deep within Charlie Chaplin himself: It was the/

~~bitter~~   *It emerged*

memory of his ~~thwarted~~ childhood. ~~that surrounded the Tramp. to act as a~~

who transmuted the

with the creation of the Tramp

~~symbol of his first identification hand experience you cry as well as laugh~~

joyous and sorrowful aspects of his past   ~~sadness~~

~~and generating tears as well as laughs at the sweet and bitter melancholy of~~

of   *into bittersweet humor for all times*

~~not only his past but our times.~~

(20) ~~our times present times.~~

words. At this stage, it's helpful to read your draft aloud, or have someone read it to you.

A look at two paragraphs of freshman Karen Cathey's resource paper on "Charlie Chaplin and His Struggle for Freedom" (reproduced in its entirety in Chapter 14) indicates the nature and extent of some typical changes.

Many of Karen's revisions substitute more precise words or phrases for more general or abstract terms: "humorous but sympathetic" for "comical" (line 7); "hope" for "light" (line 13); "the main influence" for "the one aspect/characteristic" (line 15). Some of her additions of words or phrases also provide greater specificity, as in the addition of "whether it was poverty, suffering, or despair" to line 1.

Other changes are grammatical. Sometimes they make the construction grammatically parallel: "jobless" (line 2) parallels "homeless," which immediately precedes it. At other times the revisions maintain consistency in verb tenses (for example, the substitution of "ate" for "eats," line 9) or correct punctuation (for example, underlining the movie titles and deleting the original quotation marks around them).

Occasionally, in keeping with her subject, Karen substitutes more conversational language for the more elevated: "case" for "incident" (line 10); "how life was determined to knock him about" for "what obstacles the universe set in front of him" (line 12). Although she uses unpretentious language, Karen is also aiming for stylistic distinction. She achieves this through a sophisticated use of two pairs of opposites, stated and implied, in the last sentence. At first she wrote "his ability for making you laugh. . . ." She changed this to "for the purpose of generating tears as well as laughs at the sweet and bitter melancholy not only of his past but our times." The three pairs, *tears and laughs, sweet and bitter, his past* and *our times* are not quite parallel, and they stretch out an already long sentence. Karen tightened it further in the final, much more concise version: "transmuted the joyous and sorrowful aspects of his past into bittersweet humor for all times." She maintains the opposites of joy and sorrow, bitter and sweet, and captures the time element in *Chaplin's past* and *all times.* Karen's writing is interesting, precise, and flows smoothly, with sufficient variety in sentence pattern and rhythm to maintain the reader's interest.

TITLES

Giving a paper a title helps both the author and the readers to know what to expect. If you select a paper's title after you've completed the first draft, you will be sure that it fits the intention of what you've written. If you need to, you can always remodel it later after you revise the paper.

The best titles are short (except for some specialized technical papers), attractive, and informative. Titles should be easy to pronounce; not "A Dissertation on Integration in the Nation." They should have connotations favorable to your point of view. If your title involves some witty word play so much the better, as long as it's in keeping with the tone of your paper. You might want to think of several titles, and then choose the most appealing one. Here are some possible sources of titles.

1. *A pertinent phrase from the paper itself.*
   Premarital Counseling as Premarital Communication
2. *An adaptable quotation from another source.*
   Everything You Always Wanted to Know About One Another . . . : Premarital Counseling Can Find the Answers

Do not use quotation marks around your title unless you're quoting directly from another source. Paraphrases of other material, such as Everything You Always Wanted to Know About One Another . . . , are not direct quotations and so do not warrant quotation marks.

3. *A variation on your thesis.*
   One Plus One Makes Number One: The Usefulness of Premarital Counseling

Without the subtitle the title wouldn't make sense, though the subtitle itself could stand alone.

4. *A relevant question.*
   To Marry or Not to Marry? Premarital Counseling Asks the Question

Once you've decided on a title, center it at the top of the first page of your text. For short papers it is usually unnecessarily elaborate (and ecologically wasteful) to prepare a separate title page, unless your instructor so specifies. If you do use a title page, it should contain the title, your name, your instructor's name, course name, course number, section number, and date:

THE IMPORTANCE OF BEING IN EARNEST:
PREMARITAL COUNSELING CAN HELP YOU DECIDE

by
Oscar Wilder

Prof. A. B. Eardsley
Freshman Composition
English 102, sect. 7
March 31, 1982

If you don't use a title page, it is customary to put all the information except the title in the upper left-hand corner of the first page of the text.

PREPARING THE FINAL COPY

It's always better to lose some sleep to revise a paper than to turn in a first draft as the final copy. And when you are finally ready to submit the revised paper, there are a number of conventions to observe (your instructor may specify alternatives or your field may have special requirements). Like washing and polishing a car, these may not make it run any better, but they certainly make it look more impressive.

1. Use white, standard size paper, 8½″ x 11″.
2. If possible, type your paper with a black ribbon, double spaced, on one side of the paper. Typed papers are easier to read. (Incidentally, studies have shown that typed papers earn higher grades than papers written in longhand.)
    If you do write in longhand, use conservative colored (black or blue) ink, and leave enough space between the lines for the reader's written comments.
3. Identify your paper by title and author as indicated above. Triple space between the title and the first line of the text.
4. Use standard margins: 1½″ at the left and top, 1″ at the right and bottom. The left-hand margin should be even; the right-hand margin can be more variable.
    Indent each new paragraph five typewritten spaces, or about an inch.
5. Number each page in Arabic numerals (1,2, 3) in the upper right-hand corner. It's advisable to put your name on each page, as well, to avoid mix-ups: B. Kostanecki, p. 3.
6. Proofread for typing errors; even if someone else types your paper you're still responsible for its accuracy. Check also for misspellings, missing words or lines, and misquotations (compare your version with the original source). White correction liquid or tape makes it easy to paint out mistakes and to write again in the space. If you find you're "whiting out" whole lines, or that the page is messy and unclear, retype it.
7. Clip the pages together to keep them intact.
8. Make a carbon or photocopy of your paper, in case the original goes astray. Keep the marked originals after they have been returned; editorial comments should help you in your subsequent writing.
9. Make sure that you personally deliver the paper to its intended recipient, unless you're mailing it (if so, send it first class with sufficient postage).

Now, relax! You've earned a rest, the satisfaction of having written the best paper you possibly could and, we hope, a favorable reception for it.

SUGGESTIONS FOR REVISING ALOUD OR ON PAPER

1. Use the Checklist (pp. 182–186) when writing and revising each of your papers.
2. The following three paragraphs were composed in response to an assignment asking students to "describe a three-dimensional object small enough to be held with one hand. Description should be detailed enough so that the reader could distinguish the object from several similar objects."
    Which of these three paragraphs is the initial draft of the opening paragraph? Which is the second draft? Which is the final version? On what evidence do you base your conclusion?
a. The lemon yellow alarm clock explodes with sound, CL-ANG! CLANG! CLLANG!, convoking the sleeping people in the room to report for the day's action. The resounding reverberation causes the timepiece to vibrate on the table-top. One envisions immediately a fat cook banging on an iron skillet with a serving spoon in an attempt to summon a household to dinner, however the actual sight is much different.

b. The triangular, lemon yellow alarm clock is a bomb in disguise as it explodes with sound—CLANG, CLANG, CLANG—mustering sleeping bodies to report for the day's action. The violent cacophony causes the timepiece to vibrate on the formica tabletop. Instantly the image of a harsh, muscle bound army cook banging an iron skillet with a large serving spoon in a vain attempt to summon recalcitrant stragglers to dinner comes to mind. However, the actual sight is much different.

c. The lemon yellow alarm clock explodes with sound, CL-ANG, CL-ANG- CLANG, awakening everyone in the room to report for action. The resounding reverberation causes the timepiece to vibrate on the table top. One expects the sound to issue from a corpulent cook banging her iron skillet with a serving spoon as a summons to dinner instead of a portable alarm clock that is only a little larger and heavier than a lady's powder compact.

3. Here are two versions of the second paragraph of the same essay. Which is the revision? How can you tell?

a. It is difficult to believe that such a harsh noise emanates from such an innocent looking piece. Not much bigger or heavier than a lady's powder compact, the clock appears at first glance to be cheerful and bright, with little ability to jar a sleeping person back into reality. Its half-inch numbers which are black and about a half inch high, stare complacently through a 2 by 2 inch clear plastic face, marred by small scratches. The odd numbers are designated by mere dots the size of tack heads. The dots, however, are not as nondescript as previously thought, for they, as well as the long slender clock hands, glow in the dark like a cat's eyes. From the side of the clock's face, which is edged in gold, as is the whole clock, protrudes the red lever, like the flattened end of a toothpick, which controls the alarm. The lever itself slides vertically quite simply, the trick is finding it once the alarm goes off.

b. It is difficult to believe that this harsh, tinny sound emanates from such a small inconsequential object. A travelling alarm clock not much bigger or heavier than a lady's powder compact, it appears to be an innocent device with little ability to shock a corpse back to life. The black, even numbers, which stand about an inch and a half high on a bright yellow background, stare boldly through a two inch square clear plastic face marred by small scratches. The odd numbers are designated by mere black dots with white centers the size of pinheads. Upon turning out the lights though, one finds that these dots are not as nondescript as previously thought, for they, as well as the long slender clock hands, gleam in the dark like a firefly in the black of night.

4. The following essays or excerpts from student essays represent a number of the problems discussed in this chapter. Revise one or more of these passages as necessary to improve its comprehensiveness, development, organization, paragraph or sentence structure, clarity, coherence, word choice, grammar, and spelling. Eliminate wordiness and redundancy.

a.

MY FAVORITE PLACE

Like Kipling I have my one place on earth beloved above all others. South of Monrovia Indiana is a one-hundred-thirty acre farm of densely wooded rolling hills and hollows.

During the late afternoon when the sun is hidden behind the trees, the fields are

⁵ suffused with an irridescent, rosy glow. It lends a spell of super-reality to the fields
which would somehow be broken if you walked up and touched one of the trees.
The only sounds are the gurgling strem, the chirring crickets, and the echo of a
morning dove up from the woods.

   As the twilight deepends it blends all the individual tree shadows together under
¹⁰ a mantle of black. Venus stands out in the sky like a beacon tourch. Slowly the
stars wink into place, and, before long, the entire night, sky is covered by the starry
light. No bright headlights or glaring street lamps here. The contrast of the bright
night sky over the dark earth is inspiring. You seem to become a part of this silent
world.

¹⁵   Slowly and majestically, like a great ship, the moon rises and sheds her benevo-
lent radiance over the earth below as she strides along her trackless path, the stars
no less dimmed for her brilliance. For some reason this gives me a sense of security
and makes me fell that I am not a stranger to the natural world. This is a silent
drama of life. Perhaps the more dramatic because it is silent.

b.
MILITARY NON VERBAL COMMUNICATION

   The typical examples are the uniform with the many symbols, badges and rank
insignias that the in group instantly know the meaning of. The uniform of a com-
missioned officer can bring about some reactions that communicate non-verbally
recognition by enlisted men that the man in that uniform is in a position of com-
⁵ mand. The most common reaction is a hand salute. The man who does not have a
hat on will not salute. The man without a hat will instead come to the position of
attention and probably nod his head. The man on guard duty will execute a rifle,
salute.

   The aviation group have taxi signals one of which is the engine cut off hand
¹⁰ signal. The signal has been adopted into non-verbal slang for a no response to a
specific request made or a way of telling someone to stop what they are presently
doing. The wheel chock pull signal has been adopted to mean your work is done
you are free to go.

   The military formation is to communicate at a glance three basic things. The
¹⁵ first is the presense of order and organization. The second belonging to a particular
group such as a squad and a department within the total formation. Most important
the chain of command is unquestionably stated to whoever knows the usual format
of the system. In the military context knowing just where you stand comes from
the formation idea.

²⁰   These and other forms of communication are subtle but invaluable to the smooth
operation of a military command. With all of this information available at a glance
the job at hand can be started without the verbal preliminaries getting in the way.

c.
A FRIGHTENING EXPERIENCE

   It frightens me to know that he was so close and I didn't even know. I simply
closed and locked the door against the shouting not against a gun. And he just
walked in. Pulled the gun and entered the building. Heaven only knows what he

wanted to do with it. Who he wanted to use it on. Thank heavens I just innocently
locked the door.

Tammy had presence of mind. Tammy called the police when she saw the gun. Thank heavens she had presence of mind. What would I have done? screamed? Run? But she was behind him and he didn't know it so she called the police.

Six police cars came silently then and Dragnet style surrounded the building. Covered the exits. Careful he has a gun. Hardly anyone in the dorm—they're all at the football game. Just a few girls left studying, writing, washing their clothes.

Almost shot him. After all he's got a gun. Tear gas. A tear gas gun. A not-deadly weapon masquerading as a lethal instrument—holding the threat of death. The power wielded by it without the power to perpetuate it. He didn't even use it.

Only sixteen at that. Two young for such a weapon. Released custody of his parents. Bad, bad. Hope he isn't angry at us now. Hope he doesn't come back to carry out his threat. He could have put the gun to me and I wouldn't have known it wouldn't kill. And what wouldn't you do in the face of death?

5. Which of the following titles from student papers are interesting and sufficiently appealing to you to make you want to take a look at the paper to which they are attached? Why?
   a. The Lady in the Locker Room
   b. You, the Divorced Father, and Your Adolescent Children
   c. The Automobile, Symbol of Sex, Status, and Speed
   d. An Apple a Day Keeps the Devil Away
   e. Man's Destruction of Natural Recreation Areas
   f. Country-Western: Lyrics of Loneliness, Betrayal, Death
   g. Don't Choose Chickens by Their Cackle
   h. Autobiography of an Autumn
   i. Those Sunday-Night, Paper-Due-Tomorrow Blues
   j. Alcohol: A Social Necessity or America's Curse?
6. As a class, play "The Essay Game." It resembles "The Paragraph Game" (see p. 98), except that the scrambled items are paragraphs of whole essays rather than sentences. Each group of players is given several paragraphs, each one typed or pasted on a separate card, and a thesis sentence to use as the focus. With other groups they trade paragraphs irrelevant to their thesis for paragraphs pertinent to their thesis. As the paragraphs are obtained, the group tries to arrange them in their original (or some other reasonable) order. Each group should supply a title for the essay after the paragraphs are arranged, and should be prepared to identify and defend the methods of organization of the paragraphs.

NOTES

[1] For a discussion of these concepts see Linda Flower, "Writer-Based Prose: A Cognitive Basis for Problems in Writing." (Working paper developed at Graduate School of Industrial Administration, Carnegie-Mellon University, 1978.)

[2] Adapted from Lynn Z. Bloom and Rebecca S. Wild, "A Checklist for Improvement in Theme Writing," *Exercise Exchange*, XI: (May 1964), 15–17. Rpt. as "A Checklist to Improve Writing Papers," in *Writing Exercises from Exercise Exchange*, ed. Littleton Long. Urbana, Ill.: NCTE, 1976, pp. 13–15. The version included here is considerably expanded and modified.

[3] Lynn Z. Bloom, "An Interview with John Nichols." *Webster Review*, III:4 (Winter 1978), 38–43.

9
STRATEGIES
FOR
DESCRIPTION

14
A RESOURCE
PAPER

2
THE WRITING PROCESS IN PRACTICE

The purpose of Part 1 of *Strategic Writing*, "The Writing Process," is to help you develop an effective process—or processes—sufficiently flexible and versatile to enable you to write with ease, eloquence, and efficiency.

Yet you won't know how well (or badly) a particular process works until you've tried it on a

13
USING RESOURCES:
TOOLS FOR
STRATEGIES

10
STRATEGIES
OF EXPLANATION:
EXPOSITORY WRITING

variety of types of writing, such as an essay examination answer, a laboratory or other kind of scientific report, a description, or an analysis (Chapters 9 and 10). That's the purpose of Part 2, "The Writing Process in Practice." It can help you put the parts of the process together as you write whole essays, using the special strategies and techniques especially suited to a particular type of writing. Strategies of writing argumentation (Chapters 11 and 12) and resource papers (Chapters 13 and 14) receive particular emphasis because they are such common types of writing—in college and outside it. The Reference Handbook (the appendix) provides specific information on parts of speech, the fundamentals of grammar, usage, spelling, punctuation and mechanics; consult it for the fine tuning many papers need before they meet an audience.

11
PERSUASION:
WRITING
REASONABLY

12
TYPES
OF
ARGUMENTS

CHAPTER NINE
STRATEGIES FOR DESCRIPTION

The artist does not draw what he sees but what he must make others see.

—Edgar Degas

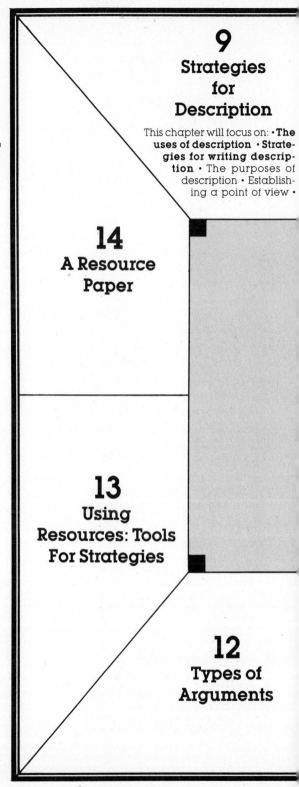

9
Strategies for Description

This chapter will focus on: • **The uses of description** • **Strategies for writing description** • The purposes of description • Establishing a point of view •

14
A Resource Paper

13
Using Resources: Tools For Strategies

12
Types of Arguments

10
Strategies of Explanation: Expository Writing

11
Persuasion: Writing Reasonably

THE USES OF DESCRIPTION

Description may be used in many ways. It can identify the size, shape, and characteristics of the Galapagos tortoise and of the Galapagos Islands themselves. It can explain the technical differences between Beethoven, Bachrach, and the Beatles, or the differences in clothing and manners of their audiences. A description can argue—against the ludicrous self-importance of the overdressed and overstuffed, whether furniture or people. Or it can re-create a mood—the langorous boredom of a too-long summer vacation in a too-small southern town.

Essays consisting exclusively of description are a vanishing species. But description is alive and of vital necessity in many other types of writing, including narratives, definitions, reports, explanations, and arguments. In this chapter, we will be discussing strategies for writing description. These can be used independently or in combination with other literary modes.

When you set out to describe something, you must ask the essential question, "What are the distinguishing characteristics of *x*?" In answering this, you will find yourself focusing on what is distinctive about *x*, what isolates it from other entities that it may resemble in some ways. You will also respond to and attempt to answer the related question, "What does *x* look like?" This will be literal if *x* is visible or tangible (say, a favorite place, person, or car), more figurative if x is an intangible quality (mercy, democracy, love) or a fictional construct (such as a character or setting in a novel).

STRATEGIES FOR WRITING DESCRIPTION

There are several major factors to consider in writing descriptions: your purpose in providing the description; your point of view in relation to what you're describing; and the criteria according to which you select and arrange the materials in your description. Although these are interrelated, we will separate them here for purposes of analysis.

The Purposes of Descriptions

Descriptions can range from the highly objective, thorough, and detached to the extremely subjective, partial, and impressionistic. Although you could describe the same subject in either of these extreme fashions, in practice you are likely to use a mode of description suited to your particular purpose and so probably will write a description that falls somewhere on a continuum between the two.

Scientific or Technical Description: In a scientific or technical description, you will be demonstrating the existence, operation, or essential features of something unfamiliar to most readers. Here you will emphasize the observable, verifiable, measurable characteristics either of an object (such as a digital calculator) and its processes or functions (what the calculator does, how it works); or of the operations of a force or phenomenon whose effects can be measured (electricity, gravity) but that itself cannot be seen.

For example, the *Random House Encyclopedia* defines "liquid" by describing its properities:

> A liquid occupies a definite volume and yet it can flow. The first property is evidence that a liquid's molecules are attracted to each other, whereas the second shows that they have greater freedom than those locked in the lattice of a solid. In a liquid, the molecules vibrate continually (at a rate of a million million times a second) and they change places with each other at nearly the same rate.
>
> A stationary liquid cannot support any stress trying to shear it (as can a solid), which is why the pressure at any point is the same in all directions. The actual value of the pressure is the product of the depth, the density of the liquid, and the acceleration caused by gravity. For this reason, solid objects can float in a liquid and even a submerged object is acted on by a buoyant force equal to the weight of the liquid displaced (Archimedes' principle).[1]

The description continues with additional explanation of the structure of liquids, the way liquids evaporate and boil, and their surface tension and viscosity.

This scientific description is, characteristically, objective, fair, and matter-of-fact. The information it contains is identified precisely and is verifiable by external means.

Exploratory Description: An exploratory description, on the other hand, tries to identify attributes of configurations that may or may not exist (such as the structure of a molecule, real or hypothetical) and to provide the basis for interpreting them. If you seek medical treatment for a stiff neck, the doctor will ask for a more complete description of your symptoms before making a diagnosis. Can you move your head at all [describe muscle functions]? Do you have headaches [describe neurological functions]? Is your neck stiff all the time or intermittently [describe continuity of functions]? Is motion impeded in any other related parts of your body, such as your shoulders, back, or arms [describe functioning of systems]? Descriptions of all these phenomena, and perhaps more, are necessary in the medical exploration that precedes the diagnosis.

If, for instance, you were writing to a manufacturer to explain why you were returning your calculator for repair you might say:

> I am returning my XBSS-154 calculator for repair. The numerals light up when it is *on,* so I am assuming that the batteries are still good and that the recharger is working properly. However, the machine is unreliable. Sometimes it gives the right answers—at least, answers that are the same when the same operations are performed. At other times the machine appears to go haywire. About every other time the *add* key is pressed briefly, instead of the number being added once it is added more than once, from twice to ten times. If the *add* key is held down for more than two seconds, the machine won't stop adding until it is turned off. The divide, square root, and percentage operations appear to be satisfactory, judging from the accuracy of the answers.

This explanation involves a certain amount of technical description, though in not-very-technical language, first to identify the machine (by model number) and then to explore the calculator's performance. The description (which in this case is also a simple analysis) tries particularly to distinguish between *what works* and *what doesn't work* in order to assist the repair person in making a diagnosis: the batteries, charger, and divide, square root, and percentage operations function well; the add operation does not.

Persuasive Description: A persuasive description functions as an *argument,* implicit or overt, concerning the subject of the description; or as an *interpretive commentary* on an object, event, or phenomenon. In persuasive description you itemize specific features and sometimes accompany these with explicit reasons as to why they are significant, desirable, or objectionable. At other times you leave the interpretation to the reader, whom you expect will agree with your implicit but conspicuous point of view, convinced by your selection and arrangement of details, as well as by the force and tone of your language.

Advertisements often include persuasive descriptions in which the details, either implicitly or accompanied by interpretation, argue that the reader should buy the advertised product or service. This International Harvester ad, for instance, extols the virtues of International Cadet lawn tractors in the process of describing them:

> We build 8 different models of Cadet lawn and garden tractors, from 8 to 16 horsepower, 36" to 50" mower widths, with two basic transmissions. Hydrostatic drive, *which eliminates clutching and shifting.* And gear drive, *which gives you more command over the speed-to-power ratio.* Each model rides atop a heavy welded steel channel automotive-type frame, *rather than bolted stamped sections. As a result, you get extra durability.* Heavy cast iron front axles are used *instead of light tubular ones.* Rack and pinion steering *gives you maximum control, responsiveness, reliability* (italics added).[2]

Here the italicized portions involve comparisons with alternative constructions of other machinery. The comparisons themselves are interpretive: "As a result [of the heavy automotive-type frame] you get extra strength and rigidity, for extra durability." Although these comparisons imply that they are supported by factual evidence, none is offered. The language becomes relativistic and subjective: "more command," "maximum control." We might ask how much is "more"? What does "maximum" control really mean? The argument, a combination of objective facts and interpretation, is reinforced by the direct commands of the conclusion: "Take a look at the whole Cadet line at your IH dealer. When you find the one that's right, take it home and put it to work for a few years."

Description that may or may not be accompanied by overt analysis often functions as interpretive commentary in works of fiction or in nonfiction essays that employ fictional techniques. Such descriptions often include many elaborate details about people, such as indications of their

1. body size, shape, and condition
2. attractiveness or unattractiveness, grooming
3. characteristic mannerisms, gestures, or posture
4. various other clues to or manifestations of their occupational, social, or economic status

Likewise, descriptions of settings often consider

1. topographical and man-made features of the landscape—lakes, mountains, highways, residential or commercial areas, specific buildings
2. number, varieties, and sizes of vegetation and animals
3. style, cost, decoration, and condition of cars and other machinery, furniture, and artifacts

The New Journalists, as identified by Tom Wolfe, one of the best-known practitioners of the art, are writers who make exuberant use of the techniques of fiction, including characterization, dialogue, and setting, in their nonfiction essays and other works. They are particularly fond of elaborate descriptions that serve as satiric or ironic commentaries on people's manners or mores. Thus in "Some Dreamers of the Golden Dream" Joan Didion describes the San Bernardino Valley as:

> . . . in certain ways an alien place: not the coastal California of the subtropic twilights and the soft westerlies off the Pacific but a harsher California, haunted by the Mojave just beyond the mountains, devastated by the hot dry Santa Ana wind that comes down through the passes at 100 miles an hour and whines through the eucalyptus windbreaks and works on the nerves. October is the bad month for the wind, the month when breathing is difficult and the hills blaze up spontaneously. There has been no rain since April. Every voice seems a scream. It is the season of suicide and divorce and prickly dread, wherever the wind blows.[3]

Didion's interpretive commentary—the beginning phrase and the two concluding sentences—reinforces the emphasis of her devastating description.

Expressive or Evocative Description: When you write *expressive or evocative description* you are trying to capture your immediate, sometimes impulsive, emotional or psychological reactions to a scene, person, event, confrontation, or other phenomenon. Your responses to what you're describing will probably provide some interpretation, perhaps even a great deal. Nevertheless, you will not necessarily be arguing a point, except insofar as your tone, structure, and details are chosen to convince your readers to see the matter from your perspective.

Student Bill Hopkins begins his description of Ontonagon, Michigan, this way:

> Industry blasted the ore out of the earth and Ontonagon developed under the settling dirt. The ore held out for ten years, then the blasting stopped. Production stopped and big industry moved on, leaving behind a loading platform and four empty "Northern Iron" freight cars. The townspeople stayed on; they had nowhere to go or couldn't summon up the interest to leave. They opened five & dime stores, hardware and "live" bait shops. Some worked in the paper mill by the tracks, others joined the logging crews.
>
> Ontonagon was an ugly weather-beaten town. It pushed into the southern tip of Lake Superior and suffered for having hacked away all the trees. In winter the wind blew snow off the ice-chunked lake into the sealed-up town. In summer it blew smut from the pulp factory into the screen doors of the diners.

Bill finds the town dirty ("Ontonagon developed under the settling dirt"), "ugly," and depressing: "The townspeople stayed on; they had nowhere to go or couldn't summon up the interest to leave." Yet he isn't arguing that the town be cleaned up or reformed, or even that the people move out or rectify their ecological disasters. He is simply sad to see Ontonagon as it is, at the mercy of the ravages created by its own greed—because people have "hacked away all the trees," the fierce wind abuses the town, blowing unneeded snow onto it in winter and smut into it in summer.

Establishing a Point of View

The way in which you see something is your *point of view*—and your point of view will limit the boundaries of your description. As an analogy, consider how a mountain would look to a climber at its foot and how it would look once she had reached the peak, or how it would look to that climber as she inched over its sheer face compared to an airplane pilot's view from his plane. Your description will vary as your point of view varies—as your vantage point shifts, as your involvement with the subject or activity varies, or as a change in focus reveals new features and details to you while deemphasizing others.

An Objective Point of View: Choosing a point of view will help to make your writing your own. This is true whether your description is subjective or objective. Even if the point of view you adopt is *objective*—let's say you are writing a scientific report—and you carefully omit overt statements of your beliefs or values, still the choice of details you include will enable the reader to detect it. In an *objective description* such as is required in many scientific discussions, detail must be restricted to what can be objectively seen or felt or to what can be measured or corroborated by such scientific instruments as thermometers, microscopes, telescopes, or altimeters. Nevertheless, in your reporting, as you select those pieces of information you wish to convey to your readers and interpret them, your particular perspective and point of view will be established. For example, in describing the flight of a hot air balloon, there are a number of ways to identify its altitude. You could specify its average distance from the ground and give its minimum and maximum height—an *absolute description*. Or you could state its altitude in relation to other balloon flights under comparable conditions. Such a *relative description* would be helpful in supplementing the meaning of the absolute description. Comparable figures would provide a sense of the significance of the particular figures applying to the flight you're discussing; by extension, they would convey a sense of the importance of the flight itself.

In describing the balloon flight, you could employ an alternative perspective, a *stationary point of view*, in which you as the observer maintain a fixed position in relation to what you are looking at and commenting on. Thus you might describe the balloon flight from a fixed point on the ground or a fixed point in the air. Or you could write from the vantage point of yourself as the interpreter of the charts and graphs that plot the balloon's flight pattern. This kind of description is the easiest to write, because it helps you maintain a clear and consistent focus on your subject, and it is a perspective favored in many textbooks and in much scientific and report writing.

A Subjective Point of View: Sometimes, however, you may prefer a *moving point of view*, in which you as the observer move from one place to another over time in order to view the object or situation from various vantage points. So, for example, you could literally follow the hot air balloon along its flight path and report on its actions. Or several observers can look at the same phenomenon, each from an individual perspective, at the same or at different times, and in combination provide a multiple perspective. This is a technique often employed by television and newspaper reporters in their eyewitness accounts of battles and natural or political disasters. Journalists sometimes employ a shifting point of view, observing—frequently satirizing—a situation from the vantage point of first one then another of the participants in the story they're reporting. In order to present their own perspective, they sometimes pose as characters in the ongoing action. This technique gives the description a narrative quality, for much narrative depends on movement from place to place. Thus, in the first two paragraphs of this article in the *New York Times*, "38 Who Saw Murder Didn't Call the Police," reporter Martin Gansberg moves among three points of view: the reporter's, the citizens', and the killer's:

> For more than half an hour 38 respectable law-abiding citizens in Queens *watched a killer stalk and stab a woman in three separate attacks in Kew Gardens.*
> *Twice their chatter and the sudden glow of their bedroom lights interrupted him and frightened him off. Each time he returned, sought her out, and stabbed her again.* Not one person telephoned the police during the assault; one witness called after the woman was dead [italics supplied].[4]

The shifts in point of view from reporter to citizens to killer to citizens and back again to reporter are so subtle as to be unobtrusive. Yet it is clearly the citizens who are watching the "killer stalk and stab a woman" and return twice more to stab her again. It is the killer who hears their chatter, sees the "sudden glow of their bedroom lights," and is frightened off. And it is the reporter whose *omniscient point of view* enables him to write as if he knew everything that went on that fatal night in Kew Gardens, even though he wasn't actually there. His psychological distance from the citizens, and his moral sense of outrage at their inaction, enables him to comment ironically that they were "respectable, law-abiding," and to show his indignation by juxtaposing that interpretation with the stated fact that "not one person telephoned the police during the assault."

The moving point of view enhances subjectivity. It is hard to shift from one person's perspective to another's without encountering their personal opinions and hard to select among available interpretations without favoring your own. In writing from a *subjective point of view*, whether stationary or moving, you are revealing your emotions, attitude, or psychological reactions to a scene, person, event, or other phenomenon in an attempt to move your readers. Your aim is to get them to respond to the matter as you do, whether you want to convince them of a point or simply encourage them to share your reactions to a picturesque, unusual, or moving scene or character.

Student writer Kristin King offers such encouragement in her interpretive description of the Crown kids, who

> lived in a three hundred thousand dollar house that looked like a sty . . . , went barefoot in November and left their ripped shirt tails hanging. Their games were full of dares and double dares ending in broken arms and taped joints. Every week brought trips to the emergency room and triumphant returns with plaster tro-

phies. The thrill of a new cast seldom lasted a day; then the victor sawed it off with a kitchen knife. The Crown kids had a driving urge to destroy. They smashed go carts in grade school, motor bikes in high school, and Porsches in college. They dressed from the Good Will and wore their tennis shoes long after the soles were gone—to swim in the pond, to school, even to church. Ten years from now they'll be wearing those same shoes with three piece suits when they sit on the board of directors of Pittsburgh Plate Glass.

It is clear that Kristin does not share the Crown kids' values or their way of dressing; her interpretive comments, such as "They lived in a three hundred thousand dollar house that looked like a sty" and "[They] had a driving urge to destroy" are subjective and negative. She can count on the readers' common sense to reinforce her own implicit interpretation that the Crown kids' behavior is self-destructive; not only do they smash up cars and themselves, they saw off the casts that are the results of such capers. Yet despite Kristin's ironic piling up of devastating details, she is not implying that the children should reform or change. Her knowledge of their status in life (which she conveys through mention of the costliness of their house and the Porsches they smash) predicts their future as corporation executives, accompanied by their incongruous artifacts of the present, their tattered tennis shoes.

Selecting and Organizing Details

It's impossible to describe anything completely. You'd have to include too many details, seen from too many perspectives in space and time. What began as an attempt at clarity would end in murk.

In selecting details, as in weeding a garden, *you remove the extraneous and the weak, so that those that remain can gain in strength and stature and give shape and focus to the whole.* Which details you select will depend on which portion of reality you want to emphasize. Your vision of reality is in turn affected by your point of view and by your purpose. Is New York City the Big Apple of your eye or is it rotten to the core? Which borough do you wish to focus on—Manhattan, Queens, the Bronx? Will you emphasize a particular segment of the population or focus on industry or entertainment? Are you interested in the modern New York City or how it was at the turn of the century?

If you are writing to provide information or to explore an issue, you will want to *select details that are representative of the whole* in kind and in number. A description of New Mexico's population will have to devote ample space to its major constituents, Anglo, Hispanic (both of Mexican and Spanish origin), and Native American, perhaps subdivided to represent the prominence of various tribes in the state. Whether you discuss less numerous minorities, such as blacks and orientals, depends on how detailed you can afford to be.

When you are writing to persuade or to express your own attitude, your *selection of details may be less representative* than when you are describing something objectively for informational purposes. Indeed, your selection of details is likely to be partial and skewed to suit your purposes. To demonstrate the thesis that "Baltimore is America's Renaissance city, undergoing a magnificent physical and cultural rehabilitation," you might describe in detail the portions of the waterfront and downtown areas that illustrate your point and play down the rest.

However, even in the most subjective description, as a responsible writer you are obliged to *accommodate information that works against your thesis.* Try to interpret it to your advantage and your opponent's satisfaction; if you don't acknowledge it, your opponent can—rightfully—accuse you of deliberately suppressing relevant material. Perhaps you can minimize its significance or offer a more favorable view of its causes, operations, or effects than your antagonist is likely to allow. For instance, a realistic description of many cities would have to acknowledge their run-down areas as well as their attractions. You can present such information in a positive rather than a negative manner, if that suits your purpose: "Baltimore's ethnic neighborhoods are now among its strongest assets. After years of blight and civic neglect, today the Victorian row houses are being refurbished and rehabilitated. . . ."

In selecting details you detach them from their larger whole; *in description you have to reassemble them in a new construct.* How you arrange the details in a description is as important as your selection of them; both should work together to reinforce the interpretation that you are aiming for. Throughout this book (see index) we have discussed various patterns of organization and the principles for determining which will best suit your presentation. It is, however, appropriate here to specifically identify those that will be most useful to you in the writing of descriptions. Careful attention to the list below should help you to organize details in the clearest and most effective way. In practice you will probably combine several of the following organizational patterns within one description.

Relationships of parts to the whole:
* parts related because of common characteristics (identity, unity, or compatibility would be emphasized, as among members of the human race, or of a family or social group)
* parts pitted against their opposites (contrast, diversity, or incompatibility would be emphasized, as in a description of political forces in the Senate or House of Commons)
* parts included, added, multiplied (new drugs or medical procedures to treat a common problem; higher taxes)
* parts excluded, subtracted, divided (the loss of an influential member of a family or organization; an income loss)
* parts symmetrical (the components of a balanced diet, orchestra, or budget)
* parts asymmetrical (many literary structures with short introductions and long developmental sections)

Relationships of order:
* causal sequence (A causes B causes C . . .)
* sequence of effects (the effect of X is Y, which in turn produces Z)

* conventional format or formal pattern
    organization of a lab report
    pattern of a sonnet
    structure of a symphony or fugue
    organization of a meeting, according to *Robert's Rules of Order*
* time sequence
    first to last
    last to first
    flashback
* developmental sequence
    simplest to most complex
    youngest to oldest
    historically, farthest back to most recent
    beginning to completion of a process
* hierarchical structures
    lowest to highest—superordination, as in military ranks, from private to general
    highest to lowest—subordination, as in a corporate structure, from the president to the office boy
    coordination, as in the establishment of equivalence among jobs of the same status, or values of the same importance
    "tree"—as in family tree, family of languages
* spatial proximity
    the order in which the eye would see it:
        far off to close up
        close up to far off
        broad focus to narrow focus
        narrow focus to broad focus
        most dominant impression (due to bulk, loudness, bright color, psychological intensity) to least significant impression
        least significant impression to most dominant impression
    psychological impression—the order in which the mind perceives or remembers something
* psychological dependence/independence from the perceiver
    most loved, appreciated, respected to most hated, unappreciated, despised
    most hated, unappreciated, despised to most loved, appreciated, admired
    most involved to least involved
    least involved to most involved

To get a better understanding of how this actually works, let us examine a description of a typical teenage Saturday night pastime in the Washington, D.C. area by student Rani Pinch, which illustrates a number of the bases of selecting and arranging details that we have just listed:

(1) At Loehmann's Plaza the neon lights drone high above the Chevy vans gathered together on the beer bottle decorated parking lot. Inside the vans, long-haired boys wearing tank tops and low cut jeans chug their beer daringly, listen to the acid rock on the radio, and discuss smoking a good joint tonight.

(2) Three girls watch the vans from the sidewalk outside a Seven Eleven food store. Their hair is perfectly sculpted and heavily sprayed, their faces are con-

cealed under foundation in hopes of layering on the years. Their eyes are dully innocent, and disguised with a lustrous blue shadow. On their hands the vivid red polish starts out at you from under the neon lights. Their young bodies are squeezed into sleeveless dark tops, and tight flared blue jeans. They strut and slouch in six inch heel "Candies" and draw deep inhalations from their cigarettes, narrowing their eyes into black slits.

(3) On the radio from the vans Donna Summer is pleading for "hot stuff, baby," "hot stuff, baby," "hot stuff, baby" and "love," "love," "love tonight."

(4) The girls move a little closer to the light. The four boys have noticed the three girls at the Seven Eleven food store. The boys laugh louder and louder as if they are having a great time, and drink their beer faster, sloshing it down their throats. They turn the music up and start to stroke their steering wheels and van tops to show their young strong muscles. They do all this without looking at the girls on the sidewalk who are wondering whether or not it's going to be a worthwhile pick-up. After fifteen minutes the girls give up and start to move away. The boys, their anticipation growing, realize their prey is wiggling off. One gets desperate and whistles. There is a still silence. The three girls turn around. The boy who whistled says, with his upper lip trembling faintly, "Where are you three foxy ladies going?"

(5) "What's here to stick around for?"

(6) "Why don't you come over here and find out?"

(7) The three girls strut across the parking lot, their wooden heels clacking enticingly in the neon lit air.

The overall organization of the details in this description follows a *time sequence*, from the beginning of a fifteen-minute period to the end. It also describes a *process*, the pickup, from beginning to end. Because both time sequence and process are techniques common to narrative, as well as description, this essay could be called a narrative description (or descriptive narrative). The *psychological movement* here is from the initially casual observations the boys and girls make of each other to their later involvement of somewhat greater intensity, and with a promise of even greater intimacy by the end of the essay. They also *move closer together* throughout the scene. The time sequence, process, and psychological movement speed up as the description proceeds; actions and reactions intensify until by the end, the girls are heading rapidly toward the van.

The organization of details within each paragraph reinforces the overall effects. The first paragraph focuses on the *sight* of the Chevy vans and their male occupants in general. Paragraph 2 shifts to the appearance of the three girls, again determined by *sight*. Paragraph 3 moves back to the van, this time describing the *sound* emanating from it. After a brief look at the girls (who "move a little closer to the light"), paragraph 4 returns to the boys, who are again identified by *sound* (louder and louder laughter and music) and now also by *action* (drinking and flexing their muscles). During this time the girls are behaving just the opposite; they are *motionless* and *silent*. Only when they begin to *move away* ("wiggling off") do the boys respond with *sound* directed specifically toward the girls—a whistle. The response is *silence*, but also *action*, which is directed toward the boys rather than away from them. This action provokes the only *dialogue* in the description, which in turn provokes more *action*, toward the boys and at greater speed.

The description of the girls in paragraph 2 proceeds from *top* (their "perfectly sculpted" hair) to *bottom* ("six inch heel 'Candies' "), *in anatomical order*. And in paragraph 3 the single song selected for *repetitive description* manifests what both the boys and the girls are thinking.

Does Rani have a thesis? Is she simply describing this common phenomenon of American culture? or is she making a statement about it? Certainly her understated description of the exaggerated actions of both boys and girls (Rani never calls them "men" and "women"—for their behavior is immature) is ironic, but there is no particular indication that she thinks they ought to change. Even though they're ridiculous, that's the way they are.

Another way of arranging details common in ironic or indirectly argumentative description is to juxtapose two details, whether or not they are technically or logically related. Their proximity will cause readers to try to make some connection between them. Either the two will be seen to reflect on each other, or the second may be interpreted as an ironic commentary on the first. Thus Joan Didion, in her description of the San Bernardino Valley, writes:

> This is the California where it is possible to live and die without ever eating an artichoke, without ever meeting a Catholic or a Jew. This is the California where it is easy to Dial-a-Devotion, but hard to buy a book. This is the country in which a belief in the literal interpretation of Genesis has slipped imperceptibly into a belief in the literal interpretation of Double Indemnity. . . .[5]

There is no necessary connection between the items in the first part of each sentence and those in the second part; whether one has eaten an artichoke or not has no particular bearing on whether one will meet a Catholic or a Jew—or does it? The proximity of the two makes the reader hypothesize a connection, particularly when this sentence is followed by other sentences of the same pattern. Does the easily accessible, but prepackaged, piety symbolized by "Dial-a-Devotion" preclude the reading of books? Their juxtaposition in the same sentence makes it seem so, whether or not it is really true. Through this careful arrangement of descriptive details, Didion indicts the values of the people who live in the arid, sinister land she is describing.

DESCRIPTIVE STYLES

A description's purpose, its point of view, and the selection and arrangement of details contribute emphatically to its style. So do the conventions of the genre in which it is written, and whether or not the writer chooses to adhere to these conventions and the cultural context. And so, of course, does the language chosen—its formality or informality, the abundance or sparseness of the modifiers and metaphors used, the emphasis and variety of its sentence patterns.

Conventions of Context and Genre

The style of your description will be influenced by the conventions of the literary genre, or mode in which you are writing, and the cultural context in which it appears. For instance, if you are writing a want ad (a genre that is almost purely descriptive), you will probably follow the conventions of overall organization, language, abbreviations, and punctuation appropriate to the culture and region of the country in which the want ad will appear. A typical American ad reads:

McLEAN TOWNHOUSE

2 yrs. new Split Level w/tuck under gar. 3 br, 2½ ba. liv. rm. w/fpl. & French doors to rear patio. Lge. din. rm. & effic. kit. All G.E. appls. w/lots stor. space. W/D CAC, heat pump. combination storms. Walk to bus, shopg. & schs. Will consider contract for favorable interest rate. 364-2533.[6]

This ad follows the conventional American format of identifying the general location first. Upon recognizing that the townhouse is in McLean, local readers would be able to supply additional information about the community's social, economic, and racial compositions as well as its amenities and liabilities. They would know that McLean is an upper-middle-class, mostly white, Virginia suburb of Washington, D.C. It has pleasant homes, attractive natural settings, some of the best public schools and city services in the area, easy access to Washington, good shopping—and very high real estate prices.

The ad itself first identifies the age ("2 yrs. *new*," not old) and style of the house (split level) and its unusual exterior feature of a tuck under garage. It then states the number of bedrooms (3) and bathrooms (2½) and the significant features of the living room (fireplace and French doors), dining room (large), and kitchen (efficiency, with General Electric appliances). Then it specifies other notable aspects of the house: lots of storage space, washer and dryer (W/D), central air conditioning (CAC), heat pump, combination storm windows. The ad concludes, as many do, with details of location and financing and how to reach the seller (the phone number).

An American reader familiar with the terminology and format can learn from this ad in less than fifty words what it takes three ample paragraphs to translate and interpret. For instance, the ad's readers are expected to be sufficiently familiar with real estate terminology to know the meanings, without explanation, of *townhouse, split level, tuck under garage, full bath, half bath, French doors, efficiency kitchen*; they should know that *appliances* means *stove and refrigerator* (but may or may not include garbage disposal and dishwasher, indicated in some ads as D/W/D), and that *combination storms* means *combination self-storing storm windows with window screens*. Readers also need prior knowledge of common real estate abbreviations: br., ba., w/fpl., W/D, CAC. They must be prepared to accept the conventions of real estate advertising punctuation (such as yrs. for years and & for and) and syntax. Such ads are written mostly in sentence fragments; grammatical subjects are missing and the real subjects must be inferred from the context. In this context these practices are appropriate, even though many are not acceptable in standard English.

Readers familiar with real estate terminology also know to beware of euphemistic descriptions: a *"tuck under"* garage, presumably located under part of the townhouse, may be small, cramped, and dangerous, if the exhaust fumes from a car warming up could seep into the rest of the house; the size of the *large* dining room is not specified, and it may be *large* only in relation to the *efficiency* (which means *small and compactly arranged*) kitchen. *Walk to bus, shopping* is ambiguous; does it imply that the townhouse is on a busy (and therefore noisy and possibly polluted) street? To get this necessary information, readers will have to go beyond the ad.

Whenever you are writing in a new mode or genre, or experimenting with a familiar one, ask yourself the following questions. They'll help make you aware of the conventions that will influence how you express yourself in your descriptions:

What is the customary point of view in this mode? For instance, scientific reports are usually objective, third person, with either a fixed or, less often, moving point of view.

Does this mode have a customary structural pattern? as classical arguments, technical reports, and sonnets do.

Does this mode customarily permit abundant description? the use of many adjectives? adverbs? colorful figures of speech?

Does this mode customarily encourage stylistic departures from standard English? If so, what are they?

If you have at hand an example of the genre you're writing in, you can use it as a model to refer to as you're writing. Try to pick one with descriptive techniques similar to those you'll be using.

Descriptive Language

The language of description is highly illustrative. Although we commonly associate description with fiction, particularly with novels, as we have seen, it is also pervasive in nonfiction, from scientific reports and informative accounts to evocations of scenery or states of mind. Descriptive language is characterized by a high proportion of *sensory details and images* appealing to the writer's and readers' senses of *sight, touch, taste, smell,* or *hearing.*

This short section of Mark Twain's *Autobiography* is particularly evocative in its description of the joys of eating watermelon, especially one stolen from the fields:

I know how a prize watermelon looks when it is sunning its fat rotundity [*sight*] among pumpkin vines and "simblins"; I know how to tell when it is ripe without "plugging" it [*sound* implied, to readers who know the way to do this]. I know how inviting it looks [*sight*] when it is cooling itself [*touch*] in a tub of water [*sight, touch*] under the bed, waiting; I know how it looks when it lies on the table [*sight*] . . . and the children gathered for the sacrifice [*sight*] and their mouths watering [*taste, touch*]. I know the crackling sound it makes [*sound*] when the carving knife enters its end [*sight, sound*] and I can see the split fly along in front of the blade [*sight*]. . . . I know the taste of the watermelon which has been honestly come by [*taste*] and I know the taste of the watermelon which has been acquired by art [*taste*]. Both taste good but the experienced know which tastes best [*taste*—though the last three references to taste leave the details to the readers' imaginations].[7]

Twentieth-century values dictate stylistic economy even in description—not every noun must be accompanied by an adjective, nor every verb by an adverb. Be particularly careful to avoid redundancies; there is no need to use the adverb in "He clenched his teeth tightly" because *tightly* is implicit in *clenched*. Only if he were clenching his teeth in some unusual or unexpected way would a modifier be necessary: "He clenched his teeth at a bizarre angle because his lower plate had come loose." Nevertheless, your individual preference, along with the conventions of the mode in which you're writing, and how much (or how little) your audience knows about what you're describing, will ultimately determine how much and what kind of descriptive language you will actually use. *Stylistic Features of Description:* The stylistic features that enhance description usually substitute the specific for the general, the concrete for the abstract. Providing illustrations, either through language or graphics, will clarify what might otherwise be murky or ambiguous. For example, in "Because of the weather, she pulled her car over to the shoulder and rested awhile," *weather* needs a modifier. The reader can already infer that the weather is bad; good weather would not cause drivers to stop, unless the sun created a blinding glare. But an indication of the specific weather conditions—foggy, hazy, increasingly snowy, or rainy—would help us to better understand the writer's intentions. A single word or two of modification will usually be sufficient; restraint is preferable to excess.

The most common stylistic features in description include extensive use of proper and concrete nouns, adjectives and adverbs, slogans, and comparisons, overt and implied.

proper nouns: Instead of tracing her route in numbers of miles, which would be bland and abstract, Joan Didion specifies: "Past Fontana Drag City and the Fontana Church of the Nazarene and the Pit Stop A Go-Go; past Kaiser Steel, through Cucamonga, out to the Kapu Kai Restaurant-Bar and Coffee Shop, at the corner of Route 66 and Carnelian Avenue."[8]

concrete nouns: To illustrate that a house was neglected to the point of abuse, student Kristin King doesn't simply label it *messy* or *abused*. She says: "On one wall of the living room was a dart board with no darts and the wall behind pocked with holes. The lining had been torn from the bottom of a yellow Chippendale sofa and stuffing poked through where the buttons had been ripped off."

adjectives and adverbs: "The girl has *solid sunburned* legs and her *worn* cut-offs are stretched <u>too tightly across the back</u>. The guy is what we termed "a grease-ball" in high school [[with the *same short dirty* hair and *aviator* glasses [that go with *jacked up* Mavericks and CB radios].]]" (student Janice Waymack)

The adjectives and adjectival phrases are italicized; the adverbial phrase is underlined. The two adjectival clauses, one inside the other, are indicated by single and double brackets.

slogans: Waymack continues, "The bumper sticker on the trailer says that the West wasn't won with a registered gun." The slogan itself, which could have been quoted directly if the writer had simply enclosed it in quotation marks, not only identifies the trailer, but describes the mentality of its owners, the girl with the "solid sunburned legs" and the fellow with the "dirty hair" and "aviator glasses." The couple's opposition to gun control is meant to connote a particular social and economic status, and it reinforces other details given in the description.

similes and other overt comparisons: "In Virginia the mountains run in ridges, fairly parallel and uniform: a ridge, a river valley, another ridge. At the West Virginia border, the landscape suddenly becomes *as crumpled as a paper wad*, and Virginia, by comparison, seems tame and domestic." (student Alan Seaman)

The simile, signaled by *as* (or *like*), is italicized. The rest of the description is direct comparison.

metaphors and symbols, implied comparisons: "I sat in the crowded auditorium covered by a bell jar. The chatter of intermission penetrated the glass in a locust-like buzz, but there were no specific voices. The isolation was a comfort, really. There was great security in being separated by my shield of anonymity and solitude. Suddenly a friend appeared, looked right at me, and I felt the vacuum beneath the bell jar start to go as it lifted slightly. . . ."

The writer, student Tara White, was inspired by the title of Sylvia Plath's *The Bell Jar* and pondered its figurative connotations. She then decided to try her own metaphorical interpretation of this symbol of both insulation and isolation as it described her state of mind on a particular occasion.

This chapter has not discussed description as ornament, the glitter and sequins to be pasted on to the completed but otherwise drab fabric of a given form of writing, because that view of description is both naive and irrelevant. By now it should be clear that description is essential to good writing in many modes, many voices, and for many purposes. Put simply, description can help us see. In seeing vividly we can visualize; in seeing clearly we can understand.

SUGGESTIONS FOR DISCUSSION AND WRITING

1. Analyze one or more of the following descriptions. Although each pertains to a specific place that can be located geographically, they differ considerably in approach. First identify the purpose and type of each description. Then show how these influence the selection of details, their number, and arrangement, the author's point of view, the tone, and the language chosen.

a.

My furniture, part of which I made myself, and the rest cost me nothing of which I have not rendered an account, consisted of a bed, a table, a desk, three chairs, a looking-glass three inches in diameter, a pair of tongs and andirons, a kettle, a skillet, and a frying-pan, a dipper, a wash-bowl, two knives and forks, three plates, one cup, one spoon, a jug for oil, a jug for molasses, and a japanned lamp. None is so poor that he need sit on a pumpkin. That is shiftlessness. There is a plenty of such chairs as I like best in the village garrets to be had for taking them away. Furniture! Thank God, I can sit and I can stand without the aid of a furniture warehouse. What man but a philosopher would not be ashamed to see his furniture packed in a cart and going up country exposed to the light of heaven and the eyes of men, a beggarly account of empty boxes? That is Spaulding's furniture. I could never tell from inspecting such a load whether it belonged to a so-called rich man or a poor one; the owner always seemed poverty-stricken. Indeed, the more you have of such things the poorer you are. Each load looks as if it contained the contents of a dozen shanties; and if one shanty is poor, this is a dozen times as poor. Pray, for what do we *move* ever but to get rid of our furniture, our *exuviae* [cast-offs]; at last to go from this world to another newly furnished, and leave this to be burned?

—Henry David Thoreau[9]

b.

[The "you" addressed below is Henry David Thoreau.]

Your front yard is marked by a bronze tablet set in a stone. Four small granite posts a few feet away show where the house was. On top of the tablet was a pair of faded blue bathing trunks with a white stripe. Back of it is a pile of stones, a sort of cairn, left by your visitors as a tribute I suppose. It is a rather ugly little heap of stones, Henry. In fact the hillside itself seems faded, browbeaten; a few tall skinny pines, bare of lower limbs, a smattering of young maples in suitable green, some birches and oaks, and a number of trees felled by the last big wind. . . .

I sat down for a while on one of the posts of your house to listen to the blue-bottles and the dragonflies. The invaded glade sprawled shabby and mean at my feet, but the flies were tuned to the old vibration. There were the remains of a fire in your ruins, but I doubt that it was yours; also two beer bottles trodden into the soil and become part of the earth. A young oak had taken root in your house, and two or three ferns, unrolling like the ticklers at a banquet. The only other furnishings were a Dubarry pattern sheet, a page torn from a picture magazine, and some crusts in waxed paper.

—E. B. White[10]

c.

POTOMAC-RIVER-FALLS

Stunningly beau. Colonial home on gorgeous professionally planted lot w/deck & patio overlooking pvt. treed yd! 5 oversized bedrms. & 3 full baths up (master bedrm. has joint dressing rm), loads of storage & closets! 1st flr. has lge. liv. rm. w/fpl., formal din. rm., bright kit. w/finest updated appls. adjoined by huge breakfast area, study w/full bath & exceptionally lovely fam. rm. w/firepl! Lower area has lg. rec. rm., w/firepl., wet bar & full bath. Gas heat & CAC, 2 car garage! $249,900. Eves. 365-2141.

—Washington *Post,* 12 Oct. 1979, C 32.

d. They had a three hundred thousand dollar house that looked like a sty. I remember walking into the living room once and seeing the abuse. On one wall was a dart board with no darts and the wall behind pocked with holes. The lining had been torn from the bottom of a yellow Chippendale sofa and stuffing poked through where the buttons had been ripped off. In front of the sofa was a cherry table with a half-finished model spread out and a tube of glue dripping. There were several high backed chairs in the room, one Windsor without an arm, another with a torn velvet cover. On the carpet in front of the chair was a bowl of milk with Cheerios floating. An empty pop bottle lay on the brick hearth. Someone had tossed a crumpled McDonald's bag on the ashes of last winter's fires. A Steinway stretched underneath a broad picture window. Water rings spoiled the finish and a tinker toy was wedged between two keys. The piano bench, loaded with *Sports Illustrated,* was pushed against the wall. A china bureau, filled with Wedgwood and Lenox, stood in the corner next to the door. A la crosse stick was propped against one of its broken panes. I looked for a cat's litter box but didn't see one. A black woman in a blue housecoat pushed a vacuum back and forth over the stained carpet.

—student KRISTIN KING

2. Write a description of a place familiar to you in the manner of one of the descriptions in *1*. If you describe a house (perhaps your own) in the format of a real estate ad, accompany the description with another in a different mode.

3. The details in Kristin King's description of the millionaires' house (*1, d*) appear to be organized in the order in which she observed the room. Are there other patterns of organization that would convey both the sense of the room and Kristin's attitude toward it with equal or greater effectiveness?

   Rewrite Kristin's paragraph, using one of these alternative patterns of organization.

4. The following definitions are descriptions. What common characteristics do they share? How do they differ: in selection and number of details and their arrangement, point of view, tone, and use of descriptive language? For what purposes and contexts is each appropriate? less than fully appropriate?

a.
SWAP MEET

A swap meet is a variation on the flea market, or a kind of mestastasized garage sale. Two or three times a week, usually on weekends, the parking lots of drive-in theaters are turned over to the smallest of small-businessmen, freelance peddlers, vagrant artists, trinket salesmen, crafts people. For a nominal fee, ranging from $5 to $10 a day, anyone who wants to can rent a patch of asphalt, build a booth or pitch a tent, and hawk his wares.

The emphasis is on the handmade items. They are as various (beads, blankets, belts, blouses, toys, cozies, flower pots, wine racks, sculptured driftwood, decorated tiles, gimcrackeries that seem to have been wrenched from some libidinal distress) as their salesmen (gaunt, giggly, spaced-out, weather-beaten, messianic, hobbyistic). The clientele is standard California Motley, refugees from catastrophes of family life or the imagination, nomads hopping out of sports cars or station wagons, with or without sunglasses, wearing platform heels or Earth Shoes, polyester hiphuggers or Albanian fatigue jackets, looking as if at any moment their license might be revoked.

—JOHN LEONARD[11]

b.

KU KLUX KLAN

1. **1.** A secret organization in the southern U.S., active for several years after the Civil War, which aimed to suppress the newly acquired rights of the Negroes. **2.** a secret organization inspired by the former, founded in Georgia, in 1915 and professing Americanism as its object.

—*Random House College Dictionary*[12]

2. **1.** A post–Civil War secret society advocating white supremacy **2.** a 20th-century secret fraternal group held to confine its membership to American-born Protestant whites.

—*Webster's New Collegiate Dictionary*[13]

3. **1.** A secret society organized in the South after the Civil War to reassert white supremacy with terroristic methods. **2.** full name, Knights of the Ku Klux Klan. A secret organization founded in Georgia in 1915 and modeled upon the earlier society.

—*American Heritage Dictionary*[14]

4. **1.** A secret society of white men founded in the S[outhern] States after the Civil War to reestablish and maintain white supremacy. **2.** a secret society organized in Atlanta, Georgia, in 1915 as "the invisible Empire, Knights of the Ku Klux Klan": it is anti-Negro, anti-Semitic, anti-Catholic, etc., and uses terrorist methods.

—*Webster's New World Dictionary*[15]

c.

PRETTY FAR-OUT LITTLE DUDE

Balyogeshwar Shri Sant Ji Maharaj is a 13-year-old Indian guru-saint with 3 million disciples, a dime-store Frankenstein mask, the certainty he can put you face to face with God, a fondness for zapping people with a water pistol, a boundless love for all mankind and automobiles, except for one disciple's van in Los Angeles that had sheepskins on the seats, a stack of telegrams and letters addressed to Supreme Commander and Sweet Lord with Salutations at His Lotus Feet and so on, plus a set of walkie talkies. . . .

—HENRY ALLEN[16]

5. Write a descriptive definition, adapting the amount of information offered, point of view, tone, organization and level of language to a specific purpose and a specific audience.

6. Write an argument in which the force comes primarily from the evidence in your description, or perhaps from descriptions of two different but related things or phenomena juxtaposed, such as Didion provides in the description from "Marrying Absurd" quoted below:

> Las Vegas is the most extreme and allegorical of American settlements, bizarre and beautiful in its venality and in its devotion to immediate gratification, a place the tone of which is set by mobsters and call girls and ladies' room attendants with amyl nitrite poppers in their uniform pockets. Almost everyone notes that there is no "time" in Las Vegas, no night and no day and no past and no future (no Las Vegas casino, however, has taken the obliteration of the ordinary time sense quite so far as Harold's Club in Reno, which for a while issued, at odd intervals in the day and night, mimeographed "bulletins" carrying news from the world outside); neither is there any logical sense of where one is. One is standing on a highway in the middle of a vast hostile desert looking at an eighty-foot sign which blinks "STAR-DUST" OR "CAESARS PALACE." Yes, but what does that explain? This geographical implausibility reinforces the sense that what happens there has no connection with "real" life; Nevada cities like Reno and Carson are ranch towns, Western towns, places behind which there is some historical imperative. But Las Vegas seems to exist only in the eye of the beholder.
>
> —JOAN DIDION
> "Marrying Absurd," in *Slouching Towards Bethlehem*
> (1968; rpt. New York: Delta, 1968), pp. 80–81.

7. Write an essay in which you:
   Pick an object, person, or setting and describe it from a stationary point of view in order to fulfill a particular purpose.

   Then, do the same from a moving point of view, perhaps one that looks at your subject at disparate points in time, or in space.

   Now, view the same subject as it might be seen by different people looking at it from the same or different vantage points.

   You might, for instance, view your college (or your particular curriculum) from your current point of view, the perspective of a prospective applicant to your college, the viewpoint of a graduate of ten, twenty, or thirty years ago, the standpoint of a faculty member, an administrator, the parents of a student, and others.

NOTES

[1] Eds. James Mitchell and Jess Stein (New York: Random House, 1977), p. 1504.

[2] © International Harvester, *Popular Mechanics*, 151:5 (May 1979).

[3] In *Slouching Towards Bethlehem* (1968; rpt. New York: Delta, 1968), p. 3.

[4] The *New York Times*, March 17, 1964, B 1.

[5] In *Slouching Towards Bethlehem*, p. 4.

[6] The *Washington Post*, October 13, 1979, C 29.

[7] *The Autobiography of Mark Twain, Including Chapters Now Published for the First Time*, ed. Charles Neider (New York: Harper & Row, 1959), p. 13.

[8] "Some Dreamers of the Golden Dream," in *Slouching Towards Bethlehem*, p. 5.

[9] From *Walden, or Life in the Woods*, ed. Brooks Atkinson (1854; rpt. New York: Modern Library, 1950), pp. 58–59.

[10] "Walden" [1939], in *One Man's Meat* (1942; rpt., Harper & Row, 1966) p. 76.

[11] "Handcraft Swapping at Drive Ins: A Bit of California Dreaming," the *New York Times*, January 17, 1977, B 30.

[12] Ed. Jess Stein, rev. ed. (New York: Random House, 1975), p. 745.

[13] (Springfield, Mass.: G. C. Merriam Co., 1973), p. 640.

[14] Ed. William Morris, new college ed. (Boston: Houghton Mifflin, 1975), p. 278.

[15] Ed. David B. Guralnik (Cleveland: World, 1974), p. 783.

[16] " 'Pretty Far-Out Little Dude,' " *Writing in Style*, ed. Laura Longley Babb (Boston: Houghton Mifflin, 1975), p. 107.

CHAPTER TEN
STRATEGIES OF EXPLANATION: EXPOSITORY WRITING

The contemplation of things as they are without error or confusion, without substitution or imposture, is in itself a nobler thing than a whole harvest of invention.

—FRANCIS BACON

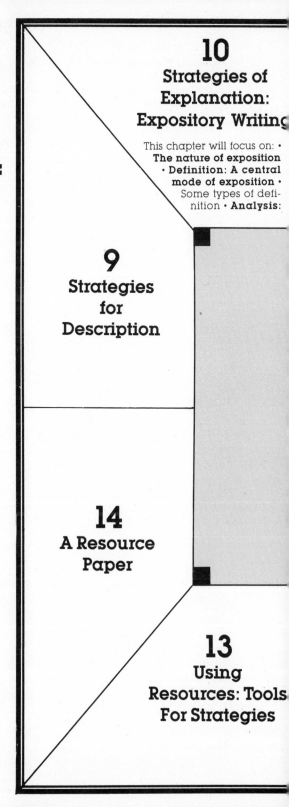

10
Strategies of Explanation: Expository Writing

This chapter will focus on: • **The nature of exposition** • **Definition: A central mode of exposition** • Some types of definition • **Analysis:**

9
Strategies for Description

14
A Resource Paper

13
Using Resources: Tools For Strategies

11
Persuasion: Writing Reasonably

12
Types of Arguments

THE NATURE OF EXPOSITION

Book, play, or movie reviews. How-to-do-it articles. Extended definitions or illustrations. Interpretations or analyses. Essay examination answers. Reports. All of these are *expositions* if their primary purpose is to inform or explain, to help readers understand. In some expository writing, you may simply want to present the facts or the evidence in a logical arrangement to make them clear to the reader, as in a recipe or definition. At other times, you may offer not only the facts but an interpretation of them, as writers often do in book reviews, political commentaries, or analyses of events.

Expository prose is to the realm of writing what the Ford car has been historically to the automotive world—useful, versatile, accessible to the average person, and ubiquitous. Expository prose carries much of the freight of the academic world. Without it, there would be no research reports, critical analyses, essay examinations, case histories, or term papers. And it is equally serviceable in the worlds of work and everyday affairs. Most letters, reports, recommendations, memorandums, newsletters, articles for trade or professional journals or organizational newsletters make use of exposition.

You will be likely to use exposition to discuss matters of explanation and interpretation. You can answer questions such as the following:

What is X?

How may X be classified? What does it resemble? In what ways is it unique?

What are its purposes?

How does X work, function?

What are its component parts?

What steps are necessary, and in what sequence, to create X? to transform X into Y?

What are the causes of X? What is its background, history?

What are its implications? its short- and long-term effects, actual or projected?

What are its good qualities? deficiencies?

What does X mean? to you, the writer, as interpreter? to others, past, present, or future, who may encounter it or whom it may affect?

Expository writing has a great many functions and is very versatile; unlike the early Ford cars, all expository models are not of the same stodgy design and uniform color. Indeed, to fulfill its numerous functions exposition, like any other writing, has to be flexible as well as versatile. And, like other writing, exposition is sometimes more effective with help from other modes, such as description, narrative, or even dialogue.

In much of your expository writing you will be explaining matters to readers unfamiliar with your subject or your point of view. As you write the exposition, you should consider the following questions. If you can answer them to your satisfaction, you will probably also satisfy your reader's need for information and understanding. Ask yourself:

Are the main points conspicuous? emphatic?

Is my language clear? Have I defined key terms that my readers may not be familiar with?

Are the main points organized in an appropriate sequence (such as logical, chronological, spatial, etc.) that will enhance my explanation? (see pp. 213–214)

Have I provided enough evidence and supporting details to illustrate my points?

If I'm analyzing or interpreting the material I'm presenting, have I provided sufficient evidence or information to convince my readers of the truth and accuracy of my views?

The rest of this chapter will examine several of the most common types of expository writing—definition, analysis, scientific explanation, and essay examination answer—and will discuss the strategies for composing each.

DEFINITION: A CENTRAL MODE OF EXPOSITION

A definition can set limits or expand them. An objective definition may settle an argument; a subjective definition can provoke one. But no matter what its point of view, a good definition can forestall pages and pages of later explanation or debate. It is the writer's ounce of prevention.

Definition itself needs to be defined. The definer's fundamental question is, What is X? In explaining what something is—or is not—the definer may use illustration, description, analysis, comparison and contrast, or analogy, either singly or in combination. A definition may specify the purpose of something, its distinctive characteristics, boundaries, extent, causes, or mode of functioning. You have probably been accustomed to including in your essays brief definitions of unfamiliar concepts ("quark," for example) or new or specialized meanings of words (a definition of "stratification" as used in meteorology, sociology, or geology, and so on). The same principles governing short definitions can be used to develop definitions of essay length, as we shall see below.

Some Types of Definition

The more common types of definition may be grouped under the general headings of (1) definition according to purpose; (2) descriptive definitions; (3) logical definitions; and (4) process definitions. Each category or subcategory may be considered as asking one or more questions that the definition is meant to answer. If you use more than one category or subcategory in an extended definition, you will be answering more than one question.

Definition According to Purpose: A definition according to purpose specifies the qualities an object, principle or policy, role, or literary or artistic work has—or should have—in order to fulfill its potential. Thus such a definition might explicitly answer such questions as What is the purpose of X? ("A fable is a simple story designed to teach a moral truth.") What is X for? ("Horror movies exist to scare the spectators.") What does X do? ("A thermometer is an instrument used to measure temperature."), or What is the role of X? ("A watchdog should protect its owner.")

Definitions of purpose are often used in evaluation, to determine how well an object, performer, or work of literature or art has fulfilled the ideal implied in the definition. ("Fang is a failure as a watchdog; he befriends every stranger he sees.")

Descriptive Definitions: A descriptive definition identifies the distinctive characteristics of an individual or group that set it apart from others. Thus a descriptive definition may begin by *naming* something, answering the question What is X called? A possible answer might be Tallulah Bankhead (unique among all other women); a walnut (as opposed to all other species of nuts); or *The Sound and the Fury* (and no other novel by William Faulkner).

A descriptive definition may also *specify the relationship among the parts of a unit or group*, responding to the questions What is the structure of X? How is X organized? How is X put together? Thus such a definition might identify the structure of a chemical compound, or the administrative organization of a university ("Siwash U. is governed by the board of trustees. Under them is the president, assisted by the vice-president for financial affairs, the vice-president for academic affairs . . ."). A descriptive definition may also define something by *identifying its environment*, answering such questions as Where is X located? ("Williamsburg is located in Tidewater, Virginia, fifty miles southeast of Richmond."), or In what company or milieu is X ordinarily found? ("Groupies cluster around rock music stars.") Lastly, a descriptive definition may *identify or describe the obvious traits of something:* What does X look like? ("The lost ark is 5' x 3' x 2', and is covered with gold.") What is X's personality? ("Laird, thoughtful and sympathetic, brings out the best in others.") What are the customary duties of this job? ("Waitresses at Alice's Restaurant have to set the tables, serve the customers, and comfort the lost souls.") Some descriptive definitions may answer more than one of these questions, perhaps identifying the location, appearance, and other obvious traits. ("Williamsburg, located in Tidewater, Virginia, fifty miles southeast of Richmond, is an upper-middle-class, picturebook-pretty, restored Colonial village of 10,500.")

Logical Definitions. Logical definitions (sometimes called *Aristotelian definitions,* after their originator) are concerned with (1) deciding in what category a given item or concept fits, according to the common characteristics of all its members—*establishing the genus;* and (2) differentiating that item or concept from others commonly associated with it in the same category—*identifying the differentia.* Thus logical definitions answer two related questions: Into what general category does X fall?, and How does it differ from all other members of that category? ("A porpoise is a marine mammal but differs from whales, seals, dolphins, and the others in its. . . .") Logical definitions are often used in scientific writing.

If you follow the five rules below, your definitions will satisfy the criteria of scientific writing, as well as of logic.

☐ A Checklist for Writing Logical Definitions

☐ *Use the most specific category to which the item to be defined belongs, rather than broader categories.* This is the most economical way to proceed. For example, it would take too much time and effort to categorize porpoises by starting with the *animal kingdom,* or even *vertebrates; marine mammals* is a much more specific category.

☐ *Any division of a class must include all members of that class.*[1] A division of the class *marine mammals* into porpoises, dolphins, and whales is not comprehensive. It omits, among others, manatees, sea lions, and seals. However, a division of undergraduate students into freshmen, sophomores, juniors, seniors, and unclassified students is comprehensive; all undergraduates belong to one or another of these subdivisions.

Negative definitions also result from classification, explaining what is excluded from a given classification, what something is not: "A Moslem is not a Christian." They answer the questions What is X not?, and How does X differ from Y? This mode of definition, which proceeds by the process of elimination ("Unlike many sects of Christians, Moslems do not believe in a trinitarian God. . . ."), is not in itself usually adequate to provide a comprehensive definition. Positive characteristics are needed to supplement the negative: "Allah, for Moslems, is. . . ." Such definitions may involve extensive comparison and contrast.

☐ *Subdivisions must be smaller than the class divided.* Appropriate subcategories for the class *housing* are apartment buildings, condominiums, single-family dwellings, houseboats. To try to subcategorize *housing* into *living units* and *rental units* would be inappropriate; all housing, by definition, consists of living units. The accurate subcategorization would be *owner-occupied units* and *rental units.*

☐ *Categories should be mutually exclusive;* they should not overlap. To divide clothing into formal wear, informal wear, and sports clothes is inappropriate; the categories of sports clothes and informal wear overlap. Indeed, without additional definition, the distinction between formal and informal wear is blurred. Is a long skirt or an embroidered shirt formal or informal?

☐ *The basis for subdividing categories must be consistent throughout each stage of subdivision.* A division of clothing into summer clothes, winter clothes, wool clothes, cotton clothes, mass-produced clothes, and designer clothes is inconsistent; it uses three different bases for classification, season of use, material of manufacture, and quantity produced. Any one of these categories would be consistent and satisfactory.

Process Definitions.   Three other types of definitions may be termed *process definitions,* for they classify their subject according to various processes that either cause or produce it, or in which it participates. For instance, *operational definitions,* answering the question How is X produced? specify the process(es) —operations—performed to produce the phenomenon. They often define things in terms of quantitative measurements that result from readings on instruments: *mean temperature,* for example, is the average of readings on a thermometer (at a given time of day, in a given location, during a given period of time). Operational definitions often refer to volume, height, weight, velocity, voltage, or other quantifiable physical characteristics. They are very valuable in the physical sciences but sometimes are used in other fields (such as psychology) as well. *Genetic definitions,* concerned with What causes X? identify categories by their causes: synthetic rubber, woven bedspread, metamorphic rock. *Distinctive definitions,* concerned with What are the effects of change on X? explain how a substance or individual acts or reacts when affected by different processes of change. Victims of Parkinson's disease, for instance, may be characterized by shaking hands, loss of facial elasticity, drooling, and fits of irrational anger.

Distinctive definitions are often used in sociological, psychological, or chemical analyses; medical diagnoses; and essay examinations.

Many expositions, short or long, use more than one type of definition, of which the most common have been discussed here. Even a single entry in a dictionary may employ several types. Writers commonly define by more than one method, using examples, descriptions, analyses, comparisons and contrasts, analogies, metaphors. There is no single best way to combine multiple types and modes of definition, but considering the following questions will help you decide how to go about it:

1. What questions do you want your definition to answer about the subject? (This will help you anticipate the questions your readers will want answers to.) Knowing what you want your definition to do will enable you to decide what type or types of definitions to use; as we've seen, certain types answer certain questions.
2. What mode or modes of presentation—analysis, comparison and contrast, analogy, and so on—are likely to provide the clearest, most accurate answers to these questions?
3. In what order do you wish to answer these questions? Some patterns of organization are clearer, more logical, or better suited to the subject than are others.

An Extended Definition

In the following essay of extended definition, student John Reilly has used a variety of types and modes of definition as he grapples with what it means to be "human." Let us see whether he has answered the above three questions to his own and our satisfaction.

WHAT'S IN A HUMAN?

1   What is meant by the term "human?" At first, the definition seems simple enough; at least most of us can distinguish humans from nonhumans. Certainly the writer of this paper is human and presumably, all the readers are. However, one need not earn an "A" in a college writing course to be considered human. In fact, one need not be able to read or write at all. This suggests that being human is an innate rather than an acquired state and that a biological basis exists for the distinction between human and nonhuman. For example, humans walk upright, and they lack a tail and long, floppy ears. Furthermore, most are capable of rational thought, of recalling the past and projecting themselves into the future, and of using language to effectively communicate with each other. Using such characteristics, scientists conveniently label us *Homo sapiens.*

2   The classification is complicated somewhat by feral man and by individuals who have lived in extreme social isolation. Dramatic historical cases illustrate that such persons often lack the distinguishing characteristics of "humans." As a way of dealing with this problem, Linnaeus proposed in the 1758 edition of *Systemae Naturae* the designation of *Homo ferus* (L. wild man) as a subdivision of the genus

Homo sapiens. According to Linnaeus, *Homo ferus* was mute, excessively hairy, and walked on all fours. Even in our more sophisticated, modern age, interest in feral man continues, and real-life proof exists that stories of "wolf children" are not mere remnants of medieval myth.

3   For example, in India in 1920, two small girls (ages eight years and eighteen months) were found along with two wolf cubs being nurtured by an adult wolf. . . . They had adapted amazingly well to the wolf society. They had sharp-edged teeth, and calluses on their knees and palms as a result of moving on all fours; in addition, they prowled and howled at night and on one occasion killed and promptly devoured a whole chicken. Clearly their behavior was inconsistent with the "sugar and spice" image associated with little human girls. The attempt to integrate the girls into human society met with only moderate success. One of them learned to walk erect and speak a few words, but her early death left many questions unanswered. However, from this case we see that *Homo sapiens* acquire many of their "human" characteristics only through imitation and continual reinforcement from the environment.

[A paragraph has been omitted that contrasts the "wolf children" with the "smart," laboratory-raised chimpanzee Sarah, who is said to communicate in abstract and symbolic language.]

4   For many people the term "human" carries associations beyond the mere ability to use language or walk upright. One is human if he is "civilized," if he adheres to a certain standard of conduct and value system. In the past, explorers often failed to acknowledge the humanity of primitive people because tribal customs differed radically from familiar European ones. Also, an admission that the howling, dancing jungle-dweller was human implied a kinship and raised the disturbing question of equality. Even today, we find it difficult to accept that a man who departs significantly from our value system and violates our moral sense can still be human. We feel outrage at Nazi war crimes, at the induced suicides at Guyana, or at the assault of an elderly woman on a city street. Coupled with our anger at the atrocities is an undeniable element of bewilderment. "How can human beings do such things?" we ask. The deviant behavior is "brutal" or "bestial"; it is not human even if it is exhibited by *Homo sapiens.* Therefore, the classification "human" implies such qualities as honor, loyalty, compassion, friendliness, and a respectful attitude toward the lives and property of others. The term is also related to a concept of moderation; a man with excessive sexual drive is an "animal." The title of the movie *Animal House* reflects the notion that many of the Deltas' exploits would not satisfactorily meet standards of human conduct.

5   The term "human" also carries association with culture, with man's lofty ideas and ideals. Art, music, and literature are among the humanities because they emerge from something thought to be unique to man—the creative impulse. The humanities appeal to man's subtle emotions, to the wide range of feelings which distinguish him from machines. Something in us (the "human" part) responds to something in a beautiful piece of music (the "human" aspect put in by the composer), and thus we are assured that we are more than robots commuting daily to a meaningless task in a factory or an office.

6   Clearly, the term "human" may be attached to the virtues and ideals of *Homo sapiens,* but it can also be used as a defense against defects. Shortcomings, mistakes, and weaknesses are considered part of being human. Thus the dieter who succumbs to temptation and eats a chocolate bar or the student who mysteriously fails to accumulate a 4.0 G.P.A. forgives himself by saying, "I'm only human." This state-

ment acknowledges human imperfection. We are not supermen or deities, and therefore we can only expect so much of ourselves. When a surgical procedure fails and a patient dies, one frequently hears the remark, "the doctor tried, but he's only human." He, too, is subject to errors in judgment and as a mere *Homo sapiens* cannot perform miracles.

7   The definition of "human" is necessarily broad because of the complexity of the behavior of *Homo sapiens*. The number of our strengths and weaknesses and the nuances of our emotions seem almost limitless. All of these contribute to making us human and must be accounted for in a realistic definition of the term. Perhaps this points to the most fundamental characteristic of being human—we have a capacity for endless variety.

Extended Definition: An Analysis   John's essay begins somewhat obliquely, calling upon the reader's own experience and common sense (often used as frames of reference in definition) to provide an implicit definition of *human:* "At least most of us can distinguish humans from nonhumans." He eliminates literacy as a necessary qualification for *humanness,* a form of negative definition, and then, in the middle of paragraph 1, begins a descriptive definition by identifying several characteristic traits, among them thinking rationally and using language, that distinguish humans.

In the second paragraph he elaborates on a negative definition of feral man, who lives in "extreme social isolation" and whose characteristics he specifies as "mute, excessively hairy, and walk[ing] on all fours." In so doing, he uses Linnaeus's identification of the genus, *Homo sapiens,* and the botanist's differentiation, *Homo ferus.* John implicitly and explicitly contrasts feral man with *humans,* and in paragraph 3 he illustrates the distinction with an extended description of the Indian "wolf girls."

The fourth paragraph continues the descriptive definition of *human* as *civilized,* and categorizes *animals* as separate from *humans,* whose characteristics of honor, loyalty, and so on are further identified. He also defines *human* through a number of brief negative examples, which include the antisocial behavior of Nazi war criminals and the slobs of *Animal House.* Paragraph 5 furnishes additional, positive characteristic traits of *human* as derived from the humanities—the creation of art, music, and literature and the subtle emotional responses to these of which we as *humans* are capable.

Paragraph 6 changes the frame of reference, offering, via an implicit comparison with God, a negative definition of *human* as being imperfect and subject to errors of judgment. The final, summary paragraph employs no new techniques of definition, but concludes by identifying yet another distinctive *human* characteristic—the "capacity for endless variety."

Now we can try to determine how well John has defined *human,* how adequately he has fulfilled the potential of his subject in a short essay about a subject on which others have written volumes. His definition is not meant to be comprehensive generally, nor does it adopt the perspective of any particular discipline, such as linguistics, psychology, anthropology, sociology, or zoology. Rather, it is intentionally impressionistic, identifying some obvious characteristics and others less familiar that constitute what for the author it means to be *human*.

The essay is interesting, lively, and uses apt examples. However, its impressionistic technique and lack of clear organization do present problems. For instance, John spends more space on discriminating between human and nonhuman behavior (paragraphs 2, 3, and 4, plus an omitted paragraph) than on any other aspect of the subject. He spends one paragraph discussing the *humanness of "humanities"* and another discriminating between human and divine qualities. Given the small amount of space devoted to *humanities*, in general, John might have eliminated this discussion and concentrated entirely on the comparisons and contrasts that he has begun to make between human, nonhuman, and divine. This emphasis would have enabled him to focus his paper immediately, instead of offering us random thoughts haphazardly as he does in the first paragraph. It would have permitted the presentation of a coherent thesis, a concrete and precise definition of *human* (missing here) and a more consistent and logical pattern of organization (which is broken in paragraph 5). Finally, the new emphasis would have encouraged a more precise and focused conclusion. At present, the concluding paragraph is too broad and too vague to be either meaningful or emphatic. John should also have indicated, throughout, the sources of his information.

SUGGESTIONS FOR DISCUSSION AND WRITING

1. The following expository writing about reptiles, from Charles Darwin's *The Voyage of the Beagle*, contains classification, description, analysis, comparison and contrast, and interpretation—which combine to define the species Darwin is describing. Analyze the passage to determine what function(s) each of its sentences or groups of sentences perform and how they work together to produce two paragraphs of definition.

Amongst the Batrachian reptiles, I found only one little toad (Phrynsicus nigricans), which was most singular from its colour. If we imagine, first, that it had been steeped in the blackest ink, and then, when dry, allowed to crawl over a board, freshly painted with the brightest vermilion, so as to colour the soles of its feet and parts of its stomach, a good idea of its appearance will be gained. If it had been an unnamed species, surely it ought to have been called *Diabolicus*, for it is fit toad to preach in the ear of Eve. Instead of being nocturnal in its habits, as other toads are, and living in damp obscure recesses, it crawls during the heat of the day about the dry sand-hillocks and arid plains, where not a single drop of water can be found. It must necessarily depend on the dew for its moisture; and this probably absorbed by the skin, for it is known that these reptiles possess great powers of cutaneous absorption. At Maldonado, I found one in a situation nearly as dry as at Bahia Blanca, and thinking to give it a great treat, carried it to a pool of water; not only was the little animal unable to swim, but, I think without help it would soon have been drowned.

Of lizards there were many kinds, but only one (Proctotretus multimaculatus) remarkable from its habits. It lives on the bare sand near the sea coast, and from its mottled colour, the brownish scales being speckled with white, yellowish red, and dirty blue, can hardly be distinguished from the surrounding surface. When frightened, it attempts to avoid discovery by feigning death, with outstretched legs, depressed body, and closed eyes: if further molested, it buries itself with great quickness in the loose sand. This lizard, from its flattened body and short legs, cannot run quickly.[2]

2. Write a short definition of a word or phrase commonly used but not clearly defined (such as "good personality," "well-rounded education"). Provide both the meanings you think general users of the term would intend and also the particular meanings the term connotes for you.

   What type of definition are you constructing? What questions have you answered in writing this definition?

3. Use the definition you wrote in 2 in another paper you're writing either as the basis for an entire paper on the subject or as an adjunct to your general topic (you could perhaps use it by way of preliminary explanation).

TRY THIS

Whenever you come upon an unfamiliar term, or a common one used in an unfamiliar way, write a short definition of it. Try to incorporate these definitions at appropriate places in your longer writings.

ANALYSIS: EXAMINATION FOR UNDERSTANDING

Analysis provides the basis for examination, interpretation, and understanding. A doctor analyzes a patient's symptoms in order to diagnose the state of his health or the nature of his illness. The findings will determine the prescribed course of treatment. A social scientist may do the same with some aspect of society, for instance, poverty or alcoholism. Similarly, a critic examines the significant features of a novel, play, film, or poem in order to understand it better and to explain, to herself or her readers, its artistry and meaning and whether it is successful as a work of art, social criticism, or human understanding. Sometimes this commentary is an end in itself; at other times, the analysis provides the basis for suggestions for revision.

Analytic writing always involves:

1. Division and subdivision of the whole into its component parts;
2. Examination of these parts individually to determine what they are and what purposes or functions they serve, and how they work together in relation to the whole; and
3. Interpretation or diagnosis.

Analytic writing may also include: suggestions, recommendations, or prescriptions, based on what the analyst has previously determined.

When you write an analysis, as you will often do in examination essay questions and in essay papers in a variety of courses, you will find that its utility depends on how accurately and thoroughly you have subdivided your material, how comprehensive and specific your supporting evidence is, and how appropriately you have organized it.

There are many ways to analyze. Chapter 4, Designing Your Writing, discusses some of these: the sequential (step-by-step) organization that can analyze a process; the various ways to consider cause-and-effect relationships; and the comparison and contrast that emphasizes the similarities and distinctions between two or more things or qualities. Other types of analyses include extended definitions, examples, and analogies.

Beginning to Analyze: Asking the Right Questions

Asking questions adapted to your subject—and answering them—can help you subdivide it appropriately. Such questions can also provide the basis for analyzing the subject under consideration and can furnish the supporting evidence for your interpretation. Journalists frequently ask of their subjects Who? What? When? Where? Why? How? In a brief writing, the relevant questions (not all will fit every subject) will be answered succinctly, perhaps even in a single sentence or paragraph. Even in this context, however, you would discuss some aspects of the analysis in more detail than others. For instance, a newspaper article written to inform readers of a major disaster might begin, "Hurricane Diabolo [who] struck [what] the Florida coast from Miami Beach to Fort Lauderdale [where] on September 21, 1984 [when], at a walloping 99 miles per hour [how], destroying over $6 million worth of property" [what].

The article could then proceed to elaborate on Diablo's manifestations [how it happened, what its effects were], for these would probably be more diverse and unusual than the information that could be presented succinctly, such as the date [when] and place [where] of the occurrence. Not only would its manifestations and effects require greater elaboration for the analysis to be clear and comprehensive; these aspects would also be of greatest potential interest to the readers. In an account of a specific hurricane, an answer to the question of why [do hurricanes exist] is not necessary; the causes of hurricanes in general, if not known to the readers already, could be discussed in a separate writing that focused on the subject.

Each of these key questions can be made more specific, when necessary, and thereby subdivided further. The resulting answers are likely to provide more elaboration of the point(s) they make, and consequently will give more emphasis to these in the total analysis. Here, for instance, are some of the questions you might ask in connection with *who, what, when, where, why,* and *how.* Not all of them would apply to every subject, nor would they always be answered in the same sequence. Indeed, some of the questions in each of the six categories below may fit other categories as well. So use them wherever they fit your analysis best, in whatever order.

Who

> Who is/are the main participant(s) in the event? Who are the subordinates?
>
> Who are the principal characters in the novel, play?
>
> Who controls the central situation(s)? Who holds the power? over whom or what?
>
> Who did, does, or may do what to whom?
>
> What are the significant traits of the principal actors?
>
> What are their principal motives? beliefs? values? accomplishments? deficiencies?

What

> What happened?
>
> What are the main events/phenomena/incidents? What is their nature? What do they mean? to whom?
>
> Are there significant subordinate events?
>
> In what ways, if any, do the events/phenomena manifest the values, strengths, weaknesses, or other characteristics of the participants?
>
> What is the relationship, hierarchy among events, phenomena, incidents? What is their sequence?
>
> What was the inciting incident? Did it start a demonstrable chain of events?
>
> What was/is the climax of the action? its turning point?
>
> In what ways, if any, do the events/phenomena present problems for the people affected by them?
>
> What is/has been the resolution of the problem? Is this satisfactory? to whom? according to what terms?
>
> What are its immediate and long range effects? What are its consequences, actual or potential?

When

> When did the event(s) happen? at what time of the day, month, year? in what time relation to other relevant events?
>
> In what state(s) of mind were the participants when these event(s) occurred?
>
> What is the significance of the timing of the events? If they were timed differently, would this have affected the people involved differently? the consequences?
>
> Do the events occur repeatedly? at regular, predictable intervals? at erratic times?
>
> Or is the event/phenomenon a one-time occurrence?

Where

> Where did the events take place? Are they real? mythical? Or did they take place in the character's mind?
>
> What are the major characteristics of the setting?
>
> Did the setting influence the participants of/events in any significant ways? for better or for worse?

Could the events have happened in the same way anywhere else?

Is a particular person or character ordinarily associated with the milieu in which she or he is presented?

Why

Why did the event(s)/phenomena occur? Why did the participants behave as they did?

What are its ultimate, intermediate, or immediate causes?

Are these causes human? susceptible to human influence or control? or beyond human control?

What, if any, human strengths, weaknesses, values contribute to the causes of this event? to its consequences?

Could the participants have behaved differently and changed the course of events? the aftermath? the operation of procedures?

How

By what techniques, methods, processes, mechanisms is a given event, characteristic, phenomenon produced? influenced? altered? stopped?

How does it work?

How does it affect its environment? era? climate of opinion? other people? its audience?

In what language and tone is the information, work, character presented?

Through what actions, imagery, symbols is the character phenomenon manifested?

Analyzing an Analysis

In "The Rock Fantasy" (the outline of which appears in Chapter 4), student Jennifer McBride analyzed the appeal of rock concerts, and in the process answered a number of the questions on which the preceding commentary has focused. Let's first see what she said, and then analyze her analysis.

THE ROCK FANTASY

1   If a Mecca exists for today's youth, it must take the form of a rock concert. Such a colossal event draws people from surprisingly distant places and from oddly diverging lifestyles. The sophisticated college student may be seated next to the wide-eyed junior high cheerleader, the latter showing fright at the approach of a wild-eyed freak. How do these incompatible character types find a mutual appeal in rock concerts? What induces young people to exchange the few dollars earned through babysitting or car washing for a concert ticket?

2   To many, the answer is immediately obvious—the music is the source of appeal at a concert. The quality of the sound produced, however, frequently casts doubt on this explanation. Unquestionably, rock concerts are loud; the decibel level at some reportedly exceeds that attained by a jet plane on take-off. In addition, this aural

assault is often intensified by an out-of-tune guitar, by the faltering voice of the performer, or by the bad acoustics in the concert hall. Rock groups generally correct these problems in a studio; their recordings may even boast pleasing harmonies with intelligible lyrics. So why do we battle crowds to secure choice seating at a concert? Why endure the stench of beer spilled in our lap? Somehow an evening spent at home listening to a $100 speaker system and staring wistfully at the rock star's poster on the wall constitutes an inadequate substitute for the real thing. The atmosphere is just not the same.

3   A concert creates a magical, otherworldly atmosphere, reminiscent of a childhood never-never land. An eerie darkness shrouds the hall, and then, just as in our favorite fairy tale, the supernatural being (otherwise identified by the vulgar term, "rock star") appears in a burst of light. In another context he would have been known as a "god out of the machine." Bizarre lighting schemes and gimmicks such as mock hangings or fire-breathing contribute to the atmosphere of otherworldliness in some acts. The fans are permitted only a brief glimpse of the star before he vanishes once more in the darkness, only to materialize the following evening in a concert hall hundreds of miles away. The stage becomes the rock star's only natural habitat; for us, he can have no existence apart from it. We can scarcely conceive of our idols performing such mundane activities as going to the dentist, shopping for tuna fish, or changing the baby. Perhaps we have a need to believe in an illusory creature of the night, somehow different from ourselves. Who fits this description better than a rock star?

4   Many rock musicians consciously work to maintain the aura of mystery surrounding themselves. Typically, they walk on stage and proceed to sneer at or completely ignore the audience. If a star is especially articulate, he may yell, "A-a-all ri-i-ight! Gonna rock to-o- ni-i-ight!" He cannot use the vocabulary of the common man, for fear of being mistakenly identified as such. Besides, a few well-timed thrusts of the hips communicate the message just as well. The audience responds wildly to this invitation, and the concert is off to a good start. The performer has successfully gauged the mood of the spectators; now his task is to manipulate it, through his choice of material and through such actions as dancing, prancing, foot-stomping, and unearthly screaming. His movements, gestures, and often, his bizarre clothing, high heels, and make-up deliberately violate accepted standards of conduct and appearance. He can afford to take chances and to risk offending people; after all, as every good student of mythology knows, deities are not bound by the same restrictions as mere mortals. The Dionysus figure on the stage tempts us to follow him into the never-never land where inhibitions are nonexistent.

5   Initially, the audience may be content to allow the performer alone to defy civilized constraints. We rebel vicariously; the smashing of instruments onstage perhaps serves as a catharsis for our own destructive impulses. As the intensity and excitement of the concern mount, however, the audience is drawn into the act. People begin to sing along, clap, yell, dance, or shake their fists. This is a particularly favorable setting for the release of tensions by the timid. No one can hear their screams (the music is too loud) and no one can see the peculiar movements of their bodies (the hall is dark, and the strange smoke reduces visibility—everyone's eyes are glued to the stage anyhow). The rock god has successfully asserted his power over our bodies, and now all that remains is for him to master our minds and our imaginations.

6   Since inhibitions have been jarred loose by the pulsating rhythm, our thoughts can at last run free. Like children, we return to the world of fantasy (with a few

adult modifications). The bright young star in front of us flashes overt sexuality and personifies D. H. Lawrence's Phallic Force. The spectators begin to wonder about his sex life, which must be infinitely more fulfilling than their own. The college girl concludes that the rock star would be a much more exciting lover than that bespectacled "preppie" in biology lab. Her younger sister can safely dream of a tender first experience with the rock star. Objectively, she knows that it will never really happen and thus, she need not even have guilt feelings about this fantasy. The males in the audience recognize the star's appeal and fancy themselves enjoying the most interesting fringe benefit of his job—obliging the "groupies."

7   Obviously, young people project their fantasies onto the rock star, endowing him with the powers, attractions, and beliefs that they wish to see in themselves or in those close to them. They can create his personality at will because in one sense, he is just a figment of their imaginations. Thus some may choose to regard him as a sex symbol; for others, he may represent nonconformity and the youthful search for individuality. Unquestionably, in the past, a major appeal of rock music was the shock effect it produced on parents. This attraction may diminish now that the early rock and roll "rebels" are parents themselves and the age of the young devotees is steadily decreasing. At present, however, many young teens still attend rock concerts, believing that they are asserting independence and maturity. Ironically, they conform perfectly—to the expectations and pressures of their peer group.

8   For young people, familiarity with rock music is a status symbol, a sign of sophistication. Everyone eagerly awaits the great rite of passage—driving the car (unescorted by adults) to a concert; such a feat elevates the teenager to the rank of homeroom hero for a day. A concert gives the teen a change to brag about how many albums he owns or about his knowledge of the star's personal life. In this manner, he may join the ranks of the enlightened, sophisticated crowd at school. He finds security in identifying with this group, and profiteers at concerts successfully capitalize on this need to fit in. How else do we explain the fact that teenagers (and even older people) spend ten dollars for a rock star t-shirt which invariably shrinks four sizes the first time that it is washed?

9   The idealistic, socially conscious members of the audience may see the rock star as a messiah or guru, a proponent of truth, love, and peace. They project their own attitudes regarding justice, materialism, and other social issues onto the performer. Apparently, they see no inconsistency in the rock star lamenting greed in our culture; maybe they forget that he escapes from the stage into a limousine which whisks him quickly to the airport and his waiting jet.

10   This idealistic group has become smaller in recent years, with the absence of a burning social issue uniting youthful consciousnesses and with the tendency toward introspection and self-absorption. The new breed of concert-goer seeks no message or hidden meanings in the lyrics as a way of justifying his musical preferences. Rock music is thus no great social force; what is of importance is his specific personal reaction to it. Perhaps this idea is best expressed in a popular song from a few years ago in which the singer simply asserts that although the music is "only" rock and roll, he likes it simply because he likes it. For such a person, this whole analysis of the reasons why he likes it would be beside the point.

In "The Rock Fantasy" Jennifer analyzes rock concerts to demonstrate the thesis: "Rock concerts attract young people because of their magical, otherworldly atmosphere, in which the performing idols manipulate the audience into defying convention, sexual fantasies, and hero worship of the stars." The analysis makes intermittent use of the metaphor or implicit analogy of the rock star to a god (5—numbers throughout refer to paragraphs), messiah (9), or guru (9). It also makes a number of comparisons and contrasts—between the pleasing music of rock recordings and the "aural assault" of the concerts (2); and between freaky, uninhibited rock stars and their more conventional audiences (3, 4, 6). However, throughout most of the essay Jennifer concentrates on providing and interpreting evidence that pertains to various implications of four of the six key questions: who, what, how, and why. The matters of *when*— in the evening (3), any evening during the fans' teenage years (7)—and *where*—in concert halls with bad acoustics (2)—are evident and need no further discussion.

Who   The main participants in the event are the teenage and college age audiences "from distant places and oddly diverging lifestyles" (1, 2, 3, 4, 5, 6, 7, 8, 9, 10), and the godlike rock stars (3, 4, 5, 6, 7, 9). Subordinate and offstage, but implicit in the analysis, are the parents against whom the teenagers are rebelling by going to rock concerts (6, 7) and the profiteers who sell records and sleazy t-shirts (8).

What   Jennifer identifies several of the major components of rock concerts. The music, loud and out of tune (2). The concert atmosphere—dark, eerie, otherworldly (3), and full of "strange smoke" (5). The rock stars, mysterious (4), bizarre (4), and sexual (6). And the audience, which is drawn into the act (5) and projects childlike (5) fantasies (7) and social values (9) onto the rock star.

How   For one-third of the essay Jennifer analyzes the stars' techniques of audience manipulation. They ignore the spectators (4), express contempt for them (4), and holler unintelligibly (4). They make sexual gestures, with "well-timed thrusts of the hips" (4, 6). Through these and their other actions—"dancing, prancing, foot-stomping, high heels, and make-up" (4)—these Dionysian figures encourage the audience to lose their inhibitions and to respond in kind (5).

Why   In the first two-thirds of the essay, Jennifer has analyzed the main elements of rock concerts (who, what, where, when) and the ways in which the performers arouse the audience (how). This analysis, informative and interesting in its own right, also provides the necessary background for the last third of the essay, an interpretation of the audience's reactions. Jennifer explains that the spectators can now sing and gyrate along with the performer (5), having had their inhibitions loosened (6). They can begin to "rebel vicariously" against civilized constraints (5), by defying and shocking their parents (7). One manifestation of defiance is their sexual fantasies (6), but this rebellion is essentially imaginary. Objectively, the audience knows that their conjectured sexual liaisons with rock stars or groupies "will never really happen" (6).

Rock concerts, says the author, provide the context for further pseudosophistication: for instance, the teenage spectators can drive to the concert "unescorted by adults" (8), brag about owning record albums (8) and "knowledge of the star's personal life" (8), and thereby identify with the "enlightened, sophisticated" but conformist (7) crowd. Furthermore, the spectators erroneously endow the performers with their own attitudes concerning justice, materialism, love, and peace, while ignoring the stars' materialism and other behavior that undermine these projections (9).

In concession and conclusion Jennifer, still probing the *why*, acknowledges a change in the audience. In recent years, the idealistic spectators have been replaced by "a new breed of concert-goer [who] seeks no message or hidden meanings in the lyrics" (10), but simply likes the music (10). In "The Rock Fantasy" Jennifer's main concerns have been with the first three steps of the analytic process—to identify, explain, and interpret the main aspects of her subject. She did not perform step 4; she has no suggestions or recommendations to offer. Jennifer wrote an excellent analysis of rock concerts; it is logical, precise, thorough, and lively.

SUGGESTIONS FOR DISCUSSION AND WRITING

1. Reviews of books, plays, films, concerts, and art shows are usually expository writings that analyze and interpret the work or performance in question and offer some judgment of it accompanied by a recommendation (overt or implicit) to partake of or avoid that work.

    Below is a review of a book. Analyze it according to the criteria identified in 2, below. Or, compare and contrast it with "The Rock Fantasy."

LETTERS FROM THE FIELD 1925–1975
By Margaret Mead, 343 Pages
Harper & Row, $12.95

Collections of letters can be as fascinating or as mundane as the minds and lives of the people who write them, and as lively or dull as the language they are written in. By these standards, Margaret Mead's "Letters from the Field" is a valuable and beautiful book.

Mead's lively, witty, warm letters were written over a 50-year span of intensively studying the peoples and cultures in Samoa, Manus, the Admiralty Islands, New Guinea, Bali—with a brief excursion to the Omaha Indian reservation in the summer of 1930. In all of these Mead shares with her correspondents—family members, friends, fellow anthropologists—"a very personal record of what it has meant to be a practicing anthropologist over the last 50 years. . . . and the unique, but also cumulative, experience of immersing oneself in the ongoing life of another people, suspending for the time both one's beliefs and disbeliefs, and simultaneously attempting to understand mentally and physically this other version of reality."

Mead has an anthropologist's eye for the small, significant details that reveal the larger cultural pattern: the feelings of the half-caste woman "are raw and bleeding under insults from white people and with shame for the commercialization which has overtaken her own people."

Mead observes and accommodates the local customs in the process of studying and recording them. In Bali, "Anyone who visits a house where there is a new baby under 12 days old (if a later child) or under 42 days (if a first child) becomes ceremonially unclean for a day. What is a day? The rest of the time after seeing the child until one has slept a full night in one's own house. *Note:* Visit a new baby near the end of the day. Can one go from one taboo house to another? Yes. (Note: Visit new babies in bunches.)"

Always her letters reflect not a scientific coldness but the warmth and sympathy that permeate Mead's work and make it glow with incandescent humanness. Thus she mulls over how to prevent the suicide of "the most promising and crucial young man in the village," and decides to tell him, "You remember the old genealogies, and you best understand the new, (you) who write better than anyone else in the village and have had the energy to organize and keep a school going without any help or materials from anyone. You are the link which will bind the past and the future together; without you the hopes of this village will lie scattered and broken." Mead's letters, like her anthropological field methods, exhibit the virtues of a good guest as well as those of a good scientist; she is patient, not patronizing; curious, not condescending; exploring, not exploiting.

These letters transport us to far-off lands—exotic, enriched, occasionally barren, but always interesting. Through Mead's vision, amplified by more than 100 photographs, we become more than armchair anthropologists, imaginary voyagers; we are on every page, in every paragraph, reminded of our common humanity. We are bound together by our approaches and solutions to the fundamentals of life—providing food, clothing and shelter; coping with forces natural and supernatural; living in groups; maintaining health, welfare and an economy. Not one of us, as Mead's letters so clearly let us see, reader or tribesman or anthropologist, is or can ever be an island.

—LYNN Z. BLOOM, St. Louis *Post-Dispatch*[3]

2. Write an interpretive review of a book, play, film, or concert that you have read, seen, or heard. This is *not* to be a plot summary. Instead your review should:
   a. Inform the readers about the basic nature of the work/production/performing group or star(s).
   b. Give the readers enough information, through an overview supplemented with specific details, so they can decide whether to read or see it for themselves.
   c. Indicate, either overtly or implicitly, your opinion of the work and your reasons for it.

   You will have to judge, in advance, the extent of your readers' knowledge of the work or performers, so you can determine how much background information to supply.

   If you're reviewing a play, book, or film, you will want to consider the relevant aspects of the following: theme(s), plot, characterization (mostly of major characters, unless the minor roles are conspicuous), setting(s), symbols, language, costumes, sound and lighting effects, audience reaction to a live performance, relation of this work or performance to the author's/artist's other work.

   If you're reviewing a musical performance, you will consider the selection of pieces performed, musical arrangements/interpretations, artist's technique and technical mastery, artist's originality and virtuosity, audience reaction, and the relation of this performance to the artist's other performances. If an ensemble is performing, you will also indicate how the different participants contribute to or detract from the whole.

3. Using techniques similar to those for reviewing a book or concert, write an interpretive review of, or analytic commentary on, a political campaign, an issue of

public or college policy or common concern, or the behavior of a public or college official. You might put this in the form of an editorial that will set forth the issue, analyze it, and offer some conclusions or recommendations about what should be done.

SCIENTIFIC EXPLANATIONS: THE SCIENTIFIC PAPER OR RESEARCH REPORT

Scientific and technical reports, whether written for college, business, or industry, usually focus on a specific, limited problem or issue. They identify the issue and its dimensions, and explain its background or review the preceding research on the subject. Then the authors describe their own research methodology, specify the results of the research, and analyze these. As a rule, they conclude by showing the implications of their work and by making suggestions for future research. Reports intended for an audience of specialists may eliminate definitions of common terms and basic explanations that would be necessary in reports for general readers, or be required in student papers.

Scientific reports customarily have six sections:

1. Statement of the problem
2. Review of the relevant research on the subject
3. Step-by-step description of the research design and method
4. Statement of research results ⎱ often combined
5. Analysis of the results ⎰
6. Conclusion and suggestions for further research.

We will examine each in detail, illustrating our discussion by reference to social psychologist Donald Pelz's report of his research on driver education for male teenagers, "Driving 'Immunization' in Alienated Young Men."[4]

Statement of the Problem

This is a statement of a large issue or topic from which the writer will eventually produce one or more *hypotheses*, propositions stated in a form that can be tested and thereby proved correct or incorrect. In many instances, you can generate a hypothesis by asking who, what, how, or why questions, as we discussed above. Before you write the report, you will have investigated the hypotheses that most nearly cover the phenomena with which you are concerned and that exclude irrelevant matters.

In the introduction to "Driving 'Immunization' . . ." Pelz briefly describes his research problem. Experienced male drivers aged eighteen to twenty have more accidents than less experienced male drivers aged sixteen to eighteen. In exploring why this should be so, Pelz offers three hypotheses that appear to fit the facts and that his research will attempt to accommodate.

What might account for the high danger at these ages? One hypothesis is that the young driver at age 18 is overconfident. After two years of experience he has gained considerably in driving skill, and he knows it. He begins to take chances for which he is not fully prepared, and the result is a crash or a ticket for reckless driving. . . .

Another hypothesis concerns the emotional pressures which intensify at this period of transition from adolescence to adulthood. . . .

Yet another hypothesis relates heavy drinking to the worsening driving records. . . .

Review of the Relevant Professional Research on the Topic

Researchers rarely operate in a vacuum; a knowledge of what has gone on before in the field can provide background, direction, and perspective for new investigations. A review of the literature is not a series of book reviews but rather a survey of the major issues and problems relevant to the area you're focusing on. Thus a literature review would touch briefly on the major research articles and books pertinent to your topic (see Chapter 13 for how to select relevant materials), showing their importance to your own research. Researchers identify the sources of every idea or cluster of ideas that the research of others contributes to their own. This is called *documentation*.

In Pelz's brief review of the literature he establishes sources for some of the background information, such as the fact that "young men under the age of 25 have excessive rates of crashes and traffic violations compared to men in their forties. . . ." He cites "a series of research studies in southeastern Michigan beginning in 1966" (Pelz and Schuman, 1968; 1971a; 1973; Schuman, Pelz, Ehrlich, and Selzer, 1967) as the sources of the "countermeasure program" that his current research and article will focus on and identifies relevant findings from his own and others' previous research: "In these data driving danger was found greatest not when the young man began to drive around age 16, but after he had gained two or three years of highway experience. . . . Similar trends have appeared in other studies (Lauer, 1952). . . ." Backing your own hypothesis with such references will offer support for specific propositions as they arise about the nature of your research data.

How long and how detailed your review of the literature will be may depend on how much your readers already know about the subject, how much each book or article requires, and how significant any given item is in relation to your work. If the focus of your report is on your own research methodology and findings, you will not want these to be dominated by the literature background. Furthermore, if you are a student and simply repeating other people's research, or performing well-known experiments, then it may not be necessary to supply an exhaustive review of the literature. Your professor can tell you whether this is necessary and can suggest sources to consult. It may simply be sufficient to cite the articles or books that report on the research that you are replicating.

Innovative research, however, might require a more extensive survey to show the context into which your contribution fits.

Step-by-Step Description of the Research Design and Methodology

In writing a scientific paper, you must next provide a step-by-step description of your research design and a clear statement of the procedures and devices used in conducting the research. In many research reports, you will probably need to answer the relevant questions that appear in the *what, how, where,* and *when* categories in the section Beginning to Analyze, pp. 237–239. If the research involves people, the *who* category will also be appropriate, along with an acknowledgment of why you chose to study that particular person or group.

The main purpose of a precise description of the method is to help people understand how you derived the evidence on which you based your conclusions and interpretations. A precise description of your design will also enable subsequent researchers to follow your procedure exactly in order to repeat your research and test it to determine whether your results were accurate.

In designing his research, Pelz first examined the facts and then developed several concepts and propositions (hypotheses) that would explain them. Finally, he devised a method to test these hypotheses. He was looking for a method that would examine the following question: "If the excessive danger at eighteen or nineteen does arise from a combination of overconfidence, emotional pressure, and drinking, what kind of countermeasure program might help young men to surmount this hazardous period?" Pelz and his colleague, Schuman, then "formulated the concept of *driving development*" on which to focus their investigation. They define "the notion that responsible driving develops gradually over a half-dozen years as a result of highway experience." During this time the youthful driver learns "the limits of his skill" and how alcohol and his emotions affect his driving. He learns how to compensate for these, and how to "anticipate the mistakes of other drivers" (p. 466). Pelz then identifies the specific focus of his research: to test the hypothesis that it is possible to speed up "this normal kind of learning" in order to prevent accidents.

Pelz continues with a detailed description of the study. It involved a pilot program of a fourteen-session "driving workshop" for a random cross-section of suburban high school seniors in the spring of 1968. They participated in group discussions of their own driving experiences, focusing on "the many things that can go wrong, and how to avoid these hazards." They also watched a series of one- to three-minute "trigger films" that show young drivers facing crises—but which leave the solutions to group discussion (p. 466).

The pilot study followed the driving records of the workshop seniors and a matched control group for two years; the workshop group had half as many accidents as the control group.

These encouraging results, though with small numbers, led to the Main Workshop Experiment, five hundred senior men and women participating in six driving workshops that emphasized trigger films and group discussions. Through five mailings in the subsequent year they were asked "to report their driving experiences" (p. 467).

A second matched sample did not attend the workshops, but received the same five mailings as the first group. A third matched sample of 250 men "received no treatment and constituted the 'internal control' group" (p. 467) ["internal" here refers to male students from the same high school]. Pelz also describes how an "external control" sample of 1,900 men from high schools other than the one studied was selected for the research project.

Statement of Research Results

Ideally, the statement of research results is an objective, unadorned presentation of the data or other information obtained in the study. It will answer such questions as What happened? Under what conditions? In what sequence? What did I find out? and other questions identified under *what* in the section Beginning to Analyze, above. To avoid misinterpretation, you will want to offer the evidence in as simple, clear, and unambiguous a manner as possible. Diagrams, charts, graphs, or other illustrations may accompany your written explanation (Pelz uses many), and are particularly helpful if your evidence includes extensive numerical data. Remember that such illustrations are not necessarily self-evident; they usually require some written interpretation, too.

Pelz's explanation of his data begins by saying that the data apply to young men only, because the young women had low rates of crashes and violations and "showed no benefit from the driving workshops" (p. 467). He then presents a graph showing "Total Accidents for Young Men in the Main Workshop Experiment, Adjusted to 12-Month Rates" and a table showing "Significance Tests for Annual Accidents per 100 Young Male Drivers" for data plotted in the graph. He interprets the graph and table: The men who attended the workshops had more accidents in the first twelve months afterward than they had had before enrolling in the workshops. During the second twelve months, the rate dropped and remained low. Yet accident rates remained consistently high among the men who had not attended the workshops. Pelz also identifies the statistical tests that were used in analyzing the data, and discusses the statistical significance of the results.

Analysis of the Results

This is your interpretation of the meaning of the data presented in the statement of research results and a statement of how they relate to the hypotheses tested. This section should answer the appropriate *why* questions identified in the Beginning to Analyze section, above, such as Why did the events/phenomena occur? Why did the participants behave as they did? Here you will also answer such questions as What is the meaning of this deviation from the expected pattern or behavior?

If your hypotheses are supported, your answers to such questions should explain why. If your hypotheses are not suported, then your analysis should try to account for the factors that might be responsible for the unexpected or disappointing results. Among possible explanations are:

The hypotheses involved testing concepts inappropriate to the issue you were trying to get at.

The research design or methods were inappropriate or inadequate to the task.

The data were incomplete.

If you've made mistakes, admit them but put them in perspective. Have errors made all your data suspect? or only a small portion of it? Could the problems you encountered this time be corrected in subsequent research?

In analyzing his data Pelz notes that after the initial year of "mildly worse" driving after the workshops, in the last six months of the two-year follow-up the young men in the experimental workshops "had crash and citation rates as low as those of any other subgroup":

One is tempted by the analogy of a fever chart. The driving workshops appeared to produce a mild "infection" which lasted up to nine months and gave way to a healthy trend in the second year. It appeared as though the "infection" had partially "immunized" the workshop groups to highway hazards (p. 469).

Pelz also reports that in the more extensive project, men did not seem to benefit as much from the accident prevention workshops as men did in the preliminary study. He attributes these findings to significant differences in the ways the workshops were taught. The researchers were the instructors in the "more successful pilot program" of fourteen class periods; regular teachers were instructors in the main experiment, which took only six class periods. Moreover, the workshops were scheduled very close to the time when participants would reach the dangerous ages of eighteen or nineteen; Pelz claims that the spring of the senior year may be too late (p. 474).

Conclusion and Suggestions for Further Research

Science is cumulative, so in the conclusion to your scientific paper you will want to summarize what you have learned and to connect what you have done with the theory or the larger body of knowledge of which it is a part. If your hypotheses are supported by your results, in your conclusion you might consider such matters as:

1. How does my research illustrate or validate the larger issue?
2. What does my hypothesis add to previous theory?

3. How do my research results contribute to previous knowledge? surpass what was previously known?
4. What are the implications of my research for future investigation?
5. How could my research be improved on?
6. What, in the interests of expediency, limited funds, or time, have I had to omit from this study that warrants additional investigation? What relation does this have to the research at hand?

In his conclusion, Pelz discusses and shows some implications of his research. He found that driving workshops for young men appear to be feasible alternatives to two standard approaches, "the *protective* approach of driver education and the *corrective* approach of remedial training." The present *developmental* approach uses young drivers' on-the-road experience to make them better able to cope with the emotions and situations involved in driving.

Pelz's research led him to conclude that if the "immunizing" concept is valid, the workshops should be held in the middle of the junior year, after the participants have been driving for several months. This would give the "immunization" a chance to take effect before the onset of the epidemic in the senior year. Young men alienated from school, he discovered, such as those who have poor grades or are older than average, are likely to benefit the most from this program. Therefore, "immunizing" classes should contain a large proportion of such students (pp. 475–476).

Pelz also offers a thoughtful suggestion for how his research might be improved. In addition to group discussion stimulated by trigger films and accident diagnoses, the participants should have more opportunity to examine and analyze their own driving styles (p. 476).

This study, like much scientific research, is not the final answer. Can the exact methods of the successful pilot study be applied to other groups and produce a significant improvement in driving safety? Additional research might tell, says Pelz.

SUGGESTIONS FOR ANALYSIS AND WRITING

1. Although a complete scientific report is too long for inclusion here, if you have one available, identify its parts, and the amount of space (and emphasis) the report gives to each of the required sections: statement of the problem; review of the relevant professional literature on the topic; step-by-step description of the research design and methodology; statement of research results; analysis of the results; conclusion and suggestions for further research.

    Why is the report you are analyzing proportioned as it is? How much prior knowledge of the subject does the author expect of the readers? How has this influenced the degree of technicality and the emphases of the report?

2. Write a scientific or technical report of your own investigations, either according to the suggestions provided in this chapter or according to the directions of the instructor or researcher for whom you are preparing the report. Using a model may help. If the report is not for a course but for your own interest, be sure to keep its intended readers in mind and consider how you will accommodate the breadth and depth of their prior knowledge.

ESSAY EXAMINATION ANSWERS

A college joke says that the examination questions remain the same from year to year but the answers change. Indeed the answers do, just as they vary from student to student. And, just as in many instances there is no single right answer to a question but many, so there are many methods of answering essay examination questions.

An essay examination question may be thought of as an abbreviated essay that defines, explains, analyzes, and argues for or against a point or an interpretation of evidence. It may also identify the steps in a process, compare and contrast two phenomena or ways of viewing an issue, or summarize and analyze a case history or a research study to make a point.

Faced with the necessity of answering an exam question, you will find it useful to consult the checklist below before the exam. It will help you tackle the problem and frame an answer in the most effective way.

☐ A Checklist for Answering Essay Questions

☐ Make sure you understand the question. If you don't, or if you find the question ambiguous, ask the instructor.

☐ Frame a thesis that will answer the question. The thesis should (a) cover all the points you wish to make in the allotted time; (b) restrict the topic to an answer you can manage on the basis of your knowledge and the available time; and (c) give you the chance to demonstrate what you know, including material from extra reading or research, without straying from the central point. (If your own knowledge is weak in some areas, consider whether you can frame a thesis to emphasize your greatest knowledge and minimize your weak spots.)

[You may reverse the order of steps 2 and 3.]

☐ Jot down ideas in a scratch outline, using key words or sentence fragments as the basis for it. Feel free to keep adding brief supplements to this as you're writing the answer. Organize these according to a pattern (such as cause and effect, or classical argument) that fits the material and your approach. Since you won't want to spend time recopying scratch notes, simply number the word clusters in the order you'll use them.

It's probably a good idea to discuss your strongest point first, in case you run out of time. Be realistic, however, and spend the most space on the most important parts of your answer and only a little space on the minor aspects.

☐ State your thesis early in your answer. It's important to make your focus and emphasis apparent at the outset so readers won't have to guess what you're talking about.

☐ Following your outline, specify each point with sufficient completeness so your readers won't have to guess what you mean—they might guess wrong. Illustrate each point with enough specific information or other details to present a clear and informed answer without being redundant. You don't have time to waste on repetition. Paragraph to emphasize each separate point that warrants more than one sentence of development.

☐ Write a brief conclusion, not more than a sentence or two. You may want to incorporate this into the last paragraph of development.

☐ If you have time when you're studying for the exam, frame a sample question and write an answer in the time that will be allotted on the test. This will help you become accustomed to how much you can say in the designated time and will help you gauge your writing pace.

Because a sample may provide an informative model, a typical question, outline, and answer are included here. Note, as you read, the excellence of the essay answer. It speaks directly to the question, without digressing. It is well-organized. The thesis comes early; it is particularly helpful to tell exam readers immediately what the writer will address. The subsequent paragraphs discuss each of the points in the thesis and illustrate them with specific evidence. There is a brief concluding paragraph that summarizes the answer's main points.

QUESTION: Benjamin Franklin, as characterized in his *Autobiography* and other works, has been considered the quintessential representative of the American character. Do you agree or disagree? Explain your answer. (30 minutes)

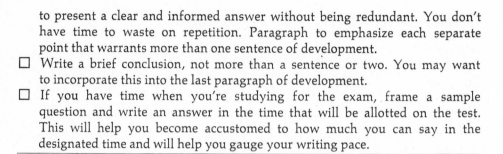

Scratch outline:

1. business
   - printing
   - hard work
   - good quality
   - retired at 42

   Note: these items are memory-joggers. The essay includes more comparable details.

2. science
   - inventions—electricity
   - Franklin stove

3. civic improvements
   - street paving
   - hospital

   education
   - academy
   - American Philosophical Society

4. statesman
   - Pennsylvania legislature
   - 2nd Continental Congress
   - Minister to France
   - Declaration of Independence
   - Constitutional Convention

Key to essay below:
italics = specific details
boldface = specific references to the question being answered

Essay answer:

HESIS
Benjamin Franklin is the quintessential representative of the American character because he was a practical, resourceful, hardworking man who through his own efforts rose from poverty to become an affluent printer, renowned scientist, and respected statesman and patriot.

Typical of his time (*1706–1790*) and *humble social class*, Franklin *started work at ten*, and *became a printer's apprentice at seventeen*. Through *extreme hard work, frugality* (**American virtues** he extolled in *Poor Richard's Almanack*), and *enterprise* he soon became the *co-owner of a printing business in Philadelphia*, known for *high quality work, efficiently performed*. So *successful was he financially* that he could *retire at forty-two*, the **rags-to-riches American dream fulfilled.**

But there was more to Franklin's—and **America's dream**—as he **devoted the rest of his long life to science, civic betterment, and politics.** Franklin's *resourcefulness* and *practicality*, **typical American characteristics**, led him to the famous *discovery of electricity* (which *ensured his election to the Royal Society*), and to the *invention of such useful things as bifocal glasses and the Franklin stove*. His **American concern for civic betterment** led to the *very practical plans for paving and cleaning the Philadelphia streets* and *for organizing a hospital and a fire protection company*.

Franklin's **concern with education, a phenomenon more important in America than anywhere else in the world,** led him to *found an academy that later became the University of Pennsylvania*. He also *established the American Philosophical Society*.

Franklin's **typically American patriotism led to his extraordinary public service,** from *clerk of the Pennsylvania legislature* (*1736*) to becoming the *leading American spokesman in London against harsh legislation* (*including the Stamp Act*), to becoming a *member of the Second Continental Congress*. He was a *framer of the Declaration of Independence* (**what could be more American than that?**), *Minister to France during the Revolution, and a drafter of the United States Constitution*. Although he *vowed to "imitate Jesus and Socrates,"* his interests were more secular than sacred, **as they tend to be for most Americans.**

ON –
CLUSION
Franklin indeed embodied American character through his virtues (industry, temperance, practicality), values (education, civic betterment, patriotism), and work (as a printer, scientist, and statesman).

By now, you will probably have had experience in writing several types of expositions—perhaps essay examination answers, lab reports, and book reviews. The Checklists in this chapter can help you remember what you have learned about exposition as you write other expository essays, or incorporate definitions, explanations, and analyses into the types of writing discussed in the following chapters.

SUGGESTION FOR ANALYSIS

Students were expected to answer the following examination question in thirty to forty minutes, by writing a short, concise, well-organized, specifically illustrated essay.

Question: Write an essay in which you agree or disagree with the following statement, taking into account all of the features of language identified below, and any others you think are relevant.

The essence of a living language is change. It is no more possible for humans to stop or even to regulate the changes in language over time than it is possible to stop the ebb and flow of the tides.

Illustrate your answer with reference to (among other things):

phonology [the sounds of the language]

morphology [the meaning units of the language]

linguistic relations of one language to other parent and sister languages

the influence of the mass media

specialized words (such as jargon and slang)

social influences (such as political or human rights movements)

movement of speakers, either geographically or from one social or occupational class to another

governmental laws (such as those concerning bilingual education)

"standard" dictionaries

What conservative (if any) influences does the written language exercise over the spoken language?

Answers: Which of the three short essays that follow best answers the question? Why? Which is the least satisfactory? Why? What grade would you assign to each?

a. The essence of a living language *is* change. As new concepts introduced through the achievements of science or other brands of "higher" learning occur, necessary changes occur in the language to accommodate them. This is one example of where changes are likely to originate.

It is not really completely possible for humans to stop changes in language, yet I do believe it is possible to regulate these changes to a certain degree. It is possible to provide a standard (flexible) grammatical framework in which changes are allowable. For example, on the issue of subject-verb agreement. Of course they have to agree, but how they go about agreeing is subject to change and revision as time marches on.

Specialized words, slang, jargon, et al., all possess a changing influence upon the language. As single words come to express entire concepts or acronyms come to stand as the concept they represent, the language is changed. The mass media play a significant role in shaping our usage and understanding of language. They often shape our understanding of how language is used.

All these factors plus many more possess influential elements that shape our usage of language. When one goes for an interview, one is very careful as to how one speaks for fear of the impression one will make. Furthermore, the groups you associate with all influence how you use the language. The written language stands over the whole mess as sort of the "standard" you appeal to as a last resort. It plays the role of enabling generations and separate groups to communicate with one another despite differences in the spoken language.

Language is bound to change whether we like it or not.

b. I agree that the essence of a living language is change. Phonology, in its broadest sense, does not change: every human is capable of making the sounds necessary for every language. (He may not acquire the ability to pronounce certain ones not in his speech community during the language acquisition period.) Yet the introduction of foreign phrases may precipitate the introduction of foreign pronunciations (at least until the word has been anglicized, in the case of English—as in *laissez faire*).

Morphology constantly changes: people coin new words (*O.K.*), borrow foreign words (*mutton, arroyo*), and adapt old words to new meanings. The latter is especially true of slang. The contemporary words for *to be drunk* are, today: *bombed, trashed, wasted*. These would convey an illogical meaning in the standard sense. Additionally, the slang of yesterday seems silly to us: *the cat's pajamas, the bee's knees*. Other specialized words, such as many of those in technical jargon of a particular kind, are coined; the ideas or objects they represent are new and need a new word to express them (*Sputnik, astronaut, penicillin*).

The natural tendency is for dialects to form in each speech community. Thus speakers from Maine talk slightly differently from those in Massachusetts who in turn differ from speakers in Connecticut and those in New York City and so on. . . . Once dialects become far enough differentiated in pronunciation, vocabulary, and perhaps in grammar so as to be mutually unintelligible, they form their own barrier of noncommunication which accelerates the breaking of former linguistic ties—such as those that originally existed among the Romance languages.

The mass media of today's technology help in breaking dialectal barriers, causing changes in each speech community that make the dialects more mutually intelligible. Additionally, changes in morphology will be more widespread and less "pocketed" because of the mass exposure of the changes, as when Mork introduced *nanew-nanew*. Through standard English spoken by television and radio announcers, these media help eliminate variations of pronunciation among speech communities.

Human rights movements help eliminate words with offensive connotations, such as *boy* for a forty-year-old black man, *broad, gook*. The changing political situation also causes changes in the language: during WW II *Krauts* and *Nips* were the enemy. Now that we're friends these words are frowned upon.

Geographical movement of the speakers introduces regional words and pronunciations into different speech communities, as among the Appalachian speakers in Detroit. Movement among social classes exposes people to different slang and jargon and modifies their speech so they can communicate with people now surrounding them.

If the government passes legislation authorizing bilingual education, then the second language will gain acceptability. The speakers of the first language will find themselves exposed to the second and will invariably pick up a smattering of it. Their linguistic horizons will be broadened.

Standard dictionaries are outdated by the time they reach the press, due to the long compilation and editorial time. Their influence varies depending on the manner in which people view them: (1) as *prescriptive*, requiring only the meanings specified in the entries and outlawing any meaning not stated within; or (2) as *descriptive*, merely stating what people were using the words to mean when the dictionary was compiled from citations of actual usage.

The written language is far more immune to change than the spoken language. Speech disappears as soon as the words are uttered. The deep structure will remain in the memory, but if called forth again will probably be rephrased into the latest mode of speaking. The printed word, however, endures at least as long as the paper and ink—longer if the work is recopied. Any literate person can refer back to the written speech of generations and generations ago. Yet since people learn to speak years before they learn to write (if ever), the influence of the written word is not as great as it might be if people were to write first. That, however, is impossible.

c. I agree. Language is organic the way human beings are organic. Humans grow and change, the languages they speak grow and change with them. People move, and take their language with them. They see and do and encounter and experience new things, and their language changes accordingly. The people who didn't move also start doing some things differently; they also start seeing some things differently. One thing that changes with time, as well as with place, is language.

Pronunciations change. Life is generally more laid back in the South and the West, so the speech of the people there is more relaxed, too, than in the Midwest and up North. In different areas and at different times the morphology is different.

⊖ is a pail in some places, a bucket in others, or both or either in other places.

Objects, concepts, and situations common or peculiar to one place or time are foreign to another place or time.

Languages keep certain things from the parent language, drop others, or create new ones from parts of the old (example: the word *television*, from Greek and Latin). Languages borrow from sister languages and completely unrelated languages all the time, sometimes to name new things, sometimes to give something a certain air or flair.

The mass media is very influential. It standardizes many aspects of language, such as vocabulary and pronunciation, but it also shows people of different areas— and/or different decades—the linguistic differences of others. Many new terms are introduced through the mass media (TV, radio, newspapers, periodicals).

Different professions, trades, social groups, political groups, and age groups create, use, and introduce new words—slang, the jargon of a trade or of a way of living (hippies, or thieves, for example). Many of these words enter the language of the main culture and *stay*.

Occupations have certain terms they use. They may be highly technical, as in a doctor's jargon, or less so. This summer I was a waitress and a bus driver. These two jobs had jargon I had to pick up and use. As a bus driver I had to learn some CB lingo.

Different speech communities have different words and pronunciations, and these change, too.

The written language, such as dictionaries, is important in that it standardizes much. But sometimes it can be too conservative and restrictive. As an author in our text said, language changes easily and quickly, but opinion is very difficult to change. Often the written language tends to be prescriptive, ethnocentric, and snobby. The written language, especially when we're writing something, often makes us aware of grammar, etc., and since, in English, it's been fairly prescriptive since Dr. Samuel Johnson and his dictionary came along in 1755, we get nervous and unsure of ourselves, because we've been raised with the idea that our speech is often ungrammatical, too informal for writing, etc.

NOTES

[1] The headings in categories 2–5 are quoted or adapted from James L. Kinneavy, John Q. Cope, and J. W. Campbell, *Writing—Basic Modes of Organization* (Dubuque, Iowa: Kendall/Hunt, 1976), p. 72.

[2] Ed. Leonard Engel (1860; rpt. New York: Doubleday 1962), p. 98.

[3] *St. Louis Post-Dispatch*, February 17, 1977, D3.

[4] *Human Factors*, 18:5 (1976), 465–476. Names and dates in parentheses refer to authors of articles and publication dates of references cited in the article's bibliography.

CHAPTER ELEVEN
PERSUASION: WRITING REASONABLY

Say and do everything according to the soundest reason.

—MARCUS AURELIUS

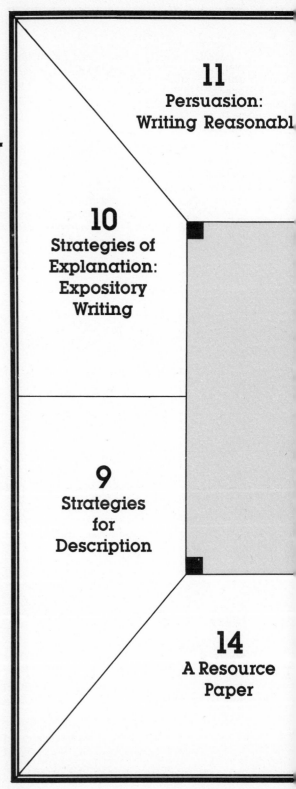

11
Persuasion:
Writing Reasonabl

10
Strategies of
Explanation:
Expository
Writing

9
Strategies
for
Description

14
A Resource
Paper

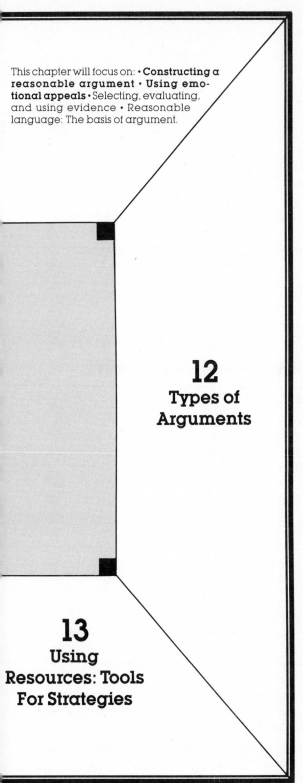

12
Types of Arguments

13
Using Resources: Tools For Strategies

Persuasion is a significant aspect of our lives. We spend considerable time and effort trying to persuade others to believe or do what we want, and dealing with others' attempts to persuade us. Much writing you do in college is argumentative, particularly in papers or exam answers that try to prove a point or change an attitude. So is much of the writing you will do or encounter out of college: letters to newspapers or colleagues in which you try to establish a debatable point; organizational or corporate memorandums or reports that attempt to persuade; sales pitches, speeches, sermons, campaign platforms. It is useful, therefore, to know both how to construct a reasonable and persuasive argument and how to analyze the reasoning of ourselves and others to make sure that it is sound and not fallacious.

An argument, as the term is used here, does not mean a heated, knock-down confrontation over an issue: "Chicago is the most wonderful in the world to live!" "No it's not. It's too cold in the winter and too hot in the summer!" Nor is an argument hard-sell brainwashing that admits of no alternatives: "America— love it or leave it!" An *argument* is, rather, the reasoned attempt of a reasonable writer to convince his or her readers—through logic, evidence, and at times, emotion— of the merits of a particular viewpoint. In writing an argument you try to get your readers to adopt your perspective, to move them to act favorably on behalf of your views or to enable them at least to recognize the merits of your side whether or not they agree with you.

You might consider the various ways of conducting an argument as existing on a continuum. This ranges from, at one end, the most objective-sounding arguments, backed up by extensive and explicit evidence, to, at the other end, the most emotional arguments, made without direct evidence. This chapter and the next will concentrate on the first three-quarters of the continuum—on various types of reasoned attempts to persuade that appeal to readers' intellect, interests, and emotions. Arguments on the most extreme, most highly emotional end of the continuum will not be discussed here, because they are often too subjective and too personal to permit generally useful suggestions. Chapter 11 will focus on several aspects of argument in general: how to establish an arguable proposition; how to establish that you are a credible and reasonable arguer; and how to assess your audience and adapt your argument to it. Chapter 12 will carry on the discussion and focus on developing and organizing specific types of arguments. Keep in mind that most of the same considerations apply to oral arguments as well as to written ones.

CONSTRUCTING A REASONABLE ARGUMENT
Select an Arguable Issue

An arguable issue is a proposition that is objectively definable and uncertain. An issue that is too vague to be defined is too vague to be debated convincingly. "The government needs money" needs more definition. What government? in what country? national, regional, or local? Does more money mean more revenue from taxes? more disposable money resulting from budget cuts? or from fewer expenditures? more money for what? officials' salaries? military spending? parks and recreation? The proposition would be arguable if it were made more specific: "The federal government should guarantee every adult American a minimum income," and you might want to add, "by means of a negative income tax."

A proposition that is certain, either according to absolute standards or the values of the culture that's discussing it, isn't debatable. In Judeo-Christian cultures "Sin is evil" is not arguable. However, what constitutes "sin" may vary from one culture to another. Margaret Mead's anthropological study *Coming of Age in Samoa* indicates that in non-Christian Samoa casual sex among unmarried teenagers was appropriate behavior. Consequently, it was neither sinful nor a debatable issue there. But in more puritanical cultures, whether permissive or not, this is a controversial matter subject to argument.

Other issues are unarguable because they can be resolved by presenting and accurately interpreting up-to-date information. Your state's requirements for getting a driver's license or adopting a child are on the statute books. Statistics on income, population, immigration, the Gross National Product, or gas mileage can be obtained from encyclopedias, government reports, or other reference works. Assuming that this information has been accurately collected and reported, it is beyond debate, and it would be ridiculous to try to do so. You can simply look up the information.

For similar reasons **it is also futile to debate topics by applying self-serving standards in opposition to the requirements of a profession, an institution, or the law.** If you don't have enough credits to graduate according to the regulations of your high school or college, then you won't get a diploma. Arguing with your teachers or the administration won't change either your performance or the regulations. This issue, and those similar to it, are not suitable for debate.

By questioning the basis on which such rules or laws are established or interpreted, or the basis on which some of the statistics are determined, however, you could construct a debatable issue: "My college, East Overshoe, should reduce its graduation requirement of 160 hours for a B.S. in Chemistry to the 120 hours that Utopia State U. mandates for the same degree." or, "The U.S. census figures for 1980 ought to be reassessed because they may underrepresent blacks, due to alleged inaccuracies in the collection of data."

Other topics are unarguable because they are subjective and admit of no objective conclusions. Often these are matters of *personal taste or opinion.* Daughter: "Sammy's wonderful. He's a straight-A student and captain of the football team." Father: "He's a jerk. He neglects his widowed mother shamefully." Sometimes they *can't be supported by evidence.* Ann: "Chicken livers are so delicious that everyone should like them as much as I do." Betty: "Ugh."

Or else the evidence is **inconclusive and highly subjective.** For example, you might argue that women have a higher tolerance of pain than men do and that they need this tolerance in order to endure childbirth. But your opponent might reply that men are tougher and more resistant to pain, because historically they have been the hunters, explorers, adventurers, and soldiers. Would citations of the quantities of painkillers sold to men and women resolve the matter? Probably not; definitions of pain are subjective, and in Western culture men have been taught not to admit they're in pain. You would probably want to table an unresolvable discussion of this sort, rather than try to write an inconclusive paper about it.

However, **you will have an arguable issue if you can transform a subjective proposition into an objective one.** If you can reinforce your taste or personal convictions wtih reasons based on external, generally agreed-upon or definable standards, you can supply evidence worthy of serious discussion. This is often the strategy of critics of film, art, architecture, TV, or literature. Saying "I like Faulkner better than Hemingway" is a matter of personal opinion and unarguable. But saying "Faulkner is a better writer than Hemingway because of his evocative vocabulary, complicated and varied sentence structure, and encompassing view of humanity" transforms a matter of taste into an issue debatable according to more objective criteria.

Define Your Terms

At the outset of an argument, make certain that you and your readers—including potential opponents—have a common understanding of the key terms you're using in your thesis. Throughout your writing, supply definitions of words or phrases that might be unfamiliar or ambiguous to your readers, or that you're using in special senses. So, for example, if you wanted to argue that "The public schools in our community do not adequately meet the needs of exceptional children," you had better define your understanding of *exceptional* before proceeding. Do you mean *intellectually accelerated? intellectually retarded? emotionally disturbed? physically handicapped?*

As a side benefit you will probably discover that establishing clear definitions will eliminate many of the objections to your arguments that your readers might otherwise raise. That in itself will simplify the task of constructing a convincing argument. For instance, in a newspaper article "Policing the Gene Splicers," the author argues that Congress needs more time to construct sensible impartial guidelines and enforcement procedures for "possibly hazardous genetic research." Since the article is an editorial in a newspaper with a wide range of readers, many unfamiliar with the topic, let alone the controversy surrounding it, the author begins by defining "recombinant DNA research, a new laboratory technique for splicing genes." This is followed immediately by a brief identification of its advantages and disadvantages, which provides additional definition and prefaces the argument itself:

> [It] was both a blessing and a curse. The technique held great promise for yielding new knowledge and better ways to produce drugs and vaccines, grow crops and treat disease [*advantages*]. But concerned scientists warned that the research might inadvertently create disease agents that could cause devastating epidemics or produce new organisms that could disrupt the evolution of life [*disadvantages*].[1]

Most of your papers will probably require fairly brief and nontechnical definitions similar to those in "Policing the Gene Splicers." Yet longer, more complex, and more specialized papers, such as research essays and term papers, often demand longer, more complex, and more specialized definitions of terms. Thus Family Medicine professor Betty E. Cogswell begins her review of research literature in an essay "Variant Family Forms and Life Styles: Rejection of the Traditional Nuclear Family" by indicating several definitions of the term "variant family form":

> Some authors use the term to refer exclusively to experimental forms such as communes, group marriage, cohabiting couples, homosexual unions, and open marriages. Cogswell and Sussman (1972) . . . use the term "variant" to include all deviations from the traditional nuclear family, "which is characterized by households of husband, wife, and children living apart from both sets of parents with male as the breadwinner and female as homemaker" (Sussman, 1971). Our definition of variant thus includes such forms as dual work, single parent, and three generation families . . . as well as experimental forms which are predom-

inately middle class in membership. We arrived at this definition of variant in the attempt to avoid negative connotations toward any existing family form. . . .[2]

This collection of definitions of variant family forms in turn requires a definition of "traditional nuclear family," which Cogswell includes—you can't define a variant unless you define the norm. The author also makes clear her attempt to arrive at an objective definition of variant family form by avoiding bias and negative connotations in the terms that compose the definition, a very sound practice.

Present Reasonable Propositions that You Can Defend

The more outrageous, novel, or general your central idea is, the more difficulty you will have in convincing an audience of its truth. Even the most liberal of audiences will tend to become conservative if accosted with a proposition they haven't contemplated before, no matter how sensible it might seem to you because you're familiar with it. "Day-care centers can raise children better than their own parents can" are fighting words to many. And a proposition like "Ninety percent of private automobiles should be abandoned in favor of public transportation" is guaranteed to strike terror or anger into the hearts of concerned motorists. Or they might simply dismiss the idea, saying, "It'll never happen here," and stop reading.

A more moderate alternative to the first sentence would be: "Day-care centers offer the advantages of thoughtful care, hot meals, supervised group play, and rest periods to the young children of working parents." The second sentence would be less likely to ruffle feathers if it were recast in this more reasonable tone: "As energy sources and raw materials become progressively more costly and more depleted, public transportation will again become a necessary alternative to private automobiles."

Qualify Your Generalizations

You will construct a much more convincing argument if you stick to a limited thesis that you can illustrate and defend adequately rather than if you try to cover too broad a topic. " 'All people are equal under the law' is a myth" is too broad and vague to set the direction for a limited paper. A more specifically focused alternative would be: "That 'all people are equal under the law' is a myth is proved by the fact that wealthy people of high status who are convicted of crimes receive much lighter sentences and fines than poor people of lower status who commit similar offenses."

The generalizations that we make orally are appropriately interpreted more as matters of emphasis than as matters of fact. If you remark to a friend, "All the nuts live in Southern California," you're not likely to be taken literally or expected to prove it. In writing, however, different standards apply. You are expected to be a responsible and reliable author and therefore to be as accurate as possible. This means that, among other things, you must moderate your language (substitute "eccentrics" for "nuts" in the above example) and qualify your generalizations to avoid making claims that you can't fulfill. Don't say *all* if you mean *most* or *some, never* if you mean *seldom* or even *sometimes.* A qualified statement such as "A number of eccentric groups flourish in Southern California" is safer than the categorical generalization "All the nuts live in Southern California." It's easier for you to prove, and it's more difficult for your opponents to find exceptions to the exceptions you've already allowed for. Such moderation should also help convince your opponents that you're treating their views fairly.

Don't Oversimplify Your Argument

Provide Sufficient Options.   Many arguments are complex. There are often more than two—even three or four—sides to a question. Consider, for instance, some of the possible positions on abortion: "Abortion on demand should be available to all females of childbearing age." "Abortion is murder and should be prohibited." "Abortion should be permitted only to save the life of the mother." "Abortion should be permitted if the mother's mental or physical health is endangered, or in cases of rape or incest." "Abortion should be permitted to all women of legal age but to underage women only with their parents' consent."

If you arbitrarily restrict arguments to two contradictory alternatives, you're likely to greatly oversimplify the issues and solutions involved: "Marry me or you'll end up an old maid." "Your money or your life." You are also treating your readers unfairly if you try to trick or force them into thinking that the alternatives you suggest are the only ones—and that they have to choose between the two.

Oversimplified arguments imply an ultimatum: either you agree with my side (whatever it is) or disaster will strike. Once they've caught on to your manipulation, readers can easily evade the trap by thinking of other alternatives (even one will do) to whatever issue you raise in this *either/or* fashion. If you said "Either we send massive foreign aid to Japan, or it will turn Communist," the reader could counter with: "If we can't send foreign aid to Japan, some other non-Communist country may do so." or, "Japan is such a capitalistic country that it's not likely to turn Communist under most circumstances, with or without foreign aid."

Don't Beg the Question.   In *begging the question* you treat a debatable proposition as if it had already been resolved and use that as the basis on which to build a subsequent step of the argument. You are assuming what you ought to be proving.

To write "Rapists and murderers awaiting trial shouldn't be let out on bail" is to beg the question, because until such people have been judged in court, it is prejudicial to label them with the crimes they have been accused of. They could be referred to as *suspects* or *alleged rapists and murderers*, but they must be assumed for both legal and argumentative purposes to be innocent until proved guilty.

"Everybody knows that legalized gambling will attract the Mafia." "It's a fact that sexual promiscuity results in VD." When you see such airy assumptions about matters that *everybody* supposedly knows or that are *obvious* facts, be on the lookout for the unproved assumptions that characterize question-begging arguments. Such statements need to be demonstrated before they are acceptable; they belong properly in conclusions rather than as thesis sentences or early points in an argumentative sequence.

Avoid Hasty Generalizations. The easiest way to demonstrate the merits of a position or to illustrate a case is to use an example from your personal belief or experience and to generalize from it. Although a personal example can become a fascinating and vivid anecdote, it can also be a dangerous basis for argumentation. Since many of us are the center of our own universe, it's easy to think that what is true of our own experience must of course be typical of everyone else's, as well—though it may not be so. If you lost your job and a recent immigrant was hired in your place, it might be tempting to claim that "Immigration should be stopped because foreigners are taking away the jobs that rightfully belong to Americans." However, it would be a dangerous and inaccurate assertion. A general claim derived from one person's single experience is particularly suspect.

It is also easy to generalize on the basis of other types of limited and selective evidence: the experiences of friends, an incident or two reported in the newspapers, information or misinformation partially remembered. But such generalizations might not be accurate either and are to be carefully examined. If three Girl Scouts were abducted from their tents in widely separated camps, does that mean that girls shouldn't be allowed to go to Scout camp? or to sleep in tents? If Cadillacs are observed parked in front of some slum tenements, does that mean that the welfare rolls are full of people living extravagantly at public expense?

The answer is, in both cases, *not necessarily.* Such generalizations would not be convincing support for an argument unless you could demonstrate that they were derived from a sufficiently representative sample of evidence.

Establish Yourself as Credible and Reasonable

When you are writing for an audience that is personally familiar with you, say your teacher and your classmates or your employer and associates, you can probably assume they have formed some opinion about your credibility and reasonableness just from your presence on the scene, even if they don't know you very well. Because your audience has to believe you if you're going to be convincing, if you have seemed truthful and thoughtful in person, a familiar audience will expect you to write in the same way. So they will probably be predisposed to believe what you say—even if they don't agree with it.

However, if you're writing for an audience that doesn't know you either in person or by reputation, as may be so if you're writing for a professor or students in a large or impersonal class, or for the student newspaper or other publication with a wider circulation, you will need to establish yourself as a thoughtful arguer. You can do this both by using *reasonable language* (see Chapter 12) and by scrupulously identifying *the sources of your information and opinions*, whether they are your own or belonged originally to others (see Chapter 13).

Obviously, if you're an expert on the subject under discussion, it's appropriate to identify your expertise. But don't break your arm patting yourself on the back; your readers are more likely to be irritated than impressed by boastfulness. So instead of saying, "I'm the world's greatest authority on skin diving (or oysters or Tolkien)," and flaunting your credentials to prove it, it would be better to refer to your five years' experience in undersea exploration (or with oyster culture or your familiarity with *The Lord of the Rings*).

But if your concern for the subject stems more from interest than expertise, you can always draw on the experience and authority of others to back you up. Then one of your tasks will be to establish the expertise of your sources, by citing briefly their relevant background and experience when you identify them. This can often be done easily by briefly mentioning the person's:

Title: "Senator Ted Kennedy, long an advocate of health insurance reform . . ."

Job: "My academic counselor says . . ."

Professional contribution: "In *Guernica*, Picasso expresses his hatred of fascism through . . ."

Human experience: "My little brother knows what it's like to be a scapegoat because for a month when he was ten . . ."

You will also want your readers to believe that you are an ethical person morally worthy to argue your case. An overt statement of your benign motives or good reputation may arouse suspicions that you are not what you're professing to be. Don't say, "I am not a crook" unless your honesty has been questioned. Any audience, favorably disposed or not, is likely to treat you with respect if you and your sources speak with authority. Their receptiveness will be enhanced if you speak in moderate language, avoiding emotional excesses, especially those directed against your opponents, and if you examine and acknowledge with fairness points of view and arguments that differ from your own (see Chapter 12). These techniques, buttressed by your audience's presumed sense of fair play, will probably be sufficient to establish a climate of understanding between you and your readers if they're either neutral or inclined to agree with your thesis.

The next chapter will discuss how to deal with readers who disagree with your thesis. However, if other readers are prejudiced against you personally, or against what they think you represent (*teenagers, labor unions, the wrong political party*), you may want to anticipate their imagined charges against you and speak to these at the outset. This will enhance your credibility and that of your argument. To determine how much to say in discussing or refuting any prejudicial charges against you, you will want to ask yourself the following questions:

1. How serious is the charge?
2. How essential to my reputation is a discussion of the charge?
3. How relevant to my thesis is a discussion of the charge? Would it detract from my thesis?

If you decide the charge is worth pursuing (and you may discover it is *not*), you can deal with it in a number of ways. If the charge is false, you can deny it: "I am not a Republican, as my voting record shows." If the charge is true, you can show why it's irrelevant: "I can still recognize a good restaurant, even though I'm not a gourmet cook"; less serious than alleged: "Because I don't speak computer language, my mathematics professor, C. R. Ford, has interpreted the following data"; or an asset rather than a liability: "The fact that I'm from the South makes me more, not less, sympathetic to minority civil rights." Or you might prove that the allegation is the result of an honest or unintentional mistake: "I'm from Hawaii, where people of various cultures and backgrounds get along well. So I had mistakenly expected the same cultural harmony between the French and English in Montreal"; or you could contend that the disputed issue or action was caused by a motive different from the one alleged: "I come to bury Caesar, not to praise him."

Whether or not the prejudicial charge is true, it is not usually recommended that you succumb to the desire to discredit your attacker. When a citizen criticized her congressman's voting record by writing, "I wouldn't vote for you if you were Saint Peter," the official snapped back, "If I were Saint Peter you wouldn't be in my constituency." This tactic is dangerous because you run the risk of name calling and *ad hominem* arguments (see below), both of which are irrelevant and unfair. However, in an extreme situation when the stakes of winning are high and your opponents are arguing from innocence, ignorance, or evil motives, it might be more expedient at the outset to demonstrate their incompetence, and thereby demolish their arguments, than it would be to refute them point by point. Nevertheless, if your audience is generally hostile to your perspective, you may wish to confine your argument strictly to the issues, or to wait until late in your essay to discredit your antagonists, after your arguments have been established on their own merits.

USING EMOTIONAL APPEALS

But what if you feel passionately about an issue? Can't you ever let your emotions show? Or do you always have to sound calm and thoughtful and write in reasoned, measured tones? Isn't it hypocritical to appear to be more moderate than you really are?

The answers to these questions depend in part on your relation to your audience and on what you're trying to accomplish in your argument. If your readers are on your side, you can probably share similar emotions with them. Freedom can be an emotionally compelling cause, as the Declaration of Independence so fervently states. If, however, the audience is indifferent or hostile to your views, you may wish to begin your essay with moderate language to win them over. After you've attracted your readers, you can become more emotional as you build toward an emphatic conclusion. Lincoln did this in the "Gettysburg Address" which, though short, starts in a low key and ends emotionally: "that this nation, under God, shall have a new birth of freedom; and that government of the people, by the people, for the people, shall not perish from the earth."

If you want to move your readers to act on an issue rather than merely to think about it, you may wish to state your reasons in emotional language: "Stop child abuse! Every year more than 50,000 innocent, virtually helpless children under fifteen are discovered with horrible bruises, painful burns, and disfiguring scars inflicted by hostile or callous adults, usually their own parents. But the psychological scars that don't show are even worse. . . ." If you want to compel your readers' complete emotional conviction about a matter on which they might otherwise be lukewarm, you may want to subdue the counterarguments while you magnify your own points: "Drug abuse is suicide!" "Communists are evil!" And so you may try to appeal to the readers' emotions, sympathies, and prejudices by evoking their sense of justice, freedom, patriotism, outrage, pathos, or humor—or any other possible reaction. Thus General Douglas MacArthur, after being fired by President Truman for insubordination, publicly lamented, "Old soldiers never die, they just fade away." And Franklin D. Roosevelt's First Inaugural Address sought to inspire the American people, suffering in the depths of the Depression, with this by now famous statement, "The only thing we have to fear is fear itself."

. Emotional appeals can be successful, but they are hard to control; once you get caught up in the passion of your own rhetoric it's difficult to know when to stop. The liberty to use emotional appeals is not license to be dishonest, to substitute passion for rationality, or to abandon logic and authoritative information as support for your points. As a responsible writer, you must supplement your emotional appeal for action with a clear statement of the goals of that action and a realistic plan for accomplishing these. In a political platform speech, "Throw the rascals out!" would have to be accompanied by ideas on how to campaign for the candidate of your choice.

SELECTING, EVALUATING, AND USING EVIDENCE

After you have determined your thesis and generated supporting ideas (the next chapter will discuss how to do this in relation to different types of arguments), you will need to find evidence to prove your case and to help refute opposing views. Essentially, you can draw on either your own knowledge and experience or that of other people, either firsthand or through documents and printed sources.

The following questions will help you decide whether the evidence (of whatever sort) you're considering will serve your purposes. Ask yourself:

> Does the evidence support my thesis rather than an opposing point of view? Am I interpreting it to my best advantage?
>
> Does it demonstrate what I say it does?
>
> Could my opponents interpret the evidence differently and use it to their advantage?
>
> Is my evidence sufficiently representative of its type so that I can generalize about it?
>
> Is my evidence important enough to include in my argument? Which evidence is most important? Which is least important?
>
> Is my evidence central to my argument? or peripheral?
>
> Is my evidence true? authoritative? believable?
>
> Does the total of my evidence cover all my major points?
>
> Am I making any points for which the evidence is either scanty or nonexistent?

Evidence that fulfills these criteria can strengthen your case enormously, for it should be very hard to refute.

Arguing from Personal Experience, Knowledge, and Opinion

In many instances you'll be writing arguments that are based largely on your personal experience and opinions rather than on extensive evidence from outside sources. You will want to make such an argument as impressive and convincing as you can by making sure your personal evidence meets as many of the criteria listed above as possible.

In author John Oliver Killens's essay "Negroes Have a Right to Fight Back," the author begins by illustrating his thesis, which is also his title, with the following personal anecdote:

> I remember as a child on Virgin Street in Macon, Georgia, there was this boy who took delight in punching me, and one of his favorite sports was twisting my arm. Onlookers would try to prevail upon him: "Shame! Shame! The Lord is not going to bless you!" Which admonitions seemed to spur my adversary on and on.
>
> One day I put two "alley apples" (pieces of brick) in my trousers' pockets and ventured forth. I was hardly out in the sun-washed streets before Bully-boy playfully accosted me. He immediately began his game of punching me in the stomach, laughing all the while. He was almost a foot taller than I, but I reached into my pockets and leaped up at both sides of his head with the alley apples.

Bully-boy ran off. We later became great friends. We never could have become friends on the basis of him kicking my backside, and my counter-attack consisting solely of "Peace, brother!"[3]

Killens has chosen well. His anecdote supports his thesis, clearly demonstrates what he says it does, and could not be interpreted to his opponents' advantage. It is important, central to his argument, true, and believable. Killens has chosen carefully; his evidence is representative of its type, and it is not extreme. If he had illustrated his point with a shoot-out by armed assailants instead of a painful but not deadly fight between two children, the evidence might have worked against him. And it might have backfired if the big kid had won. But here the underdog—with whom the readers' sympathies lie—is victorious, justice triumphs, and peace and friendship are the result.

Part of the reason that the argument succeeds is, of course, because Killens, using the authority of personal experience, has employed the evidence that would best suit his purpose and the interpretations he wants readers to derive from it. That is an author's prerogative in using personal materials—to select evidence that most convincingly makes the case and to eliminate experiences that would weaken the argument. As long as Killens himself seems credible, fair-minded readers will be inclined to accept what he says at face value.

Arguing from the Experience, Knowledge, and Opinion of Others

Unless you're an expert on the subject you're arguing about, you will probably find that arguing from personal experience is helpful in supporting your thesis but that in an extended or a complicated argument you will need to provide evidence from additional sources. To expand his argument, Killens himself draws on a variety of other sources, including *history,* for information about master-slave relationships; the *authority* and *moral example* of Dr. Martin Luther King, Jr.; and the then *current events* of race riots in Watts, Bedford-Stuyvestant, and Harlem (the piece was written in 1966).

To help judge the authoritativeness of your sources, whether they are people you know personally or published works you consult, you should ask yourself the following questions:

Does the person's (or author's) background, human experience, profession, or current activity give him/her sufficient expertise to be an authority on the subject at hand?

Does the person or work have a well-known and respected reputation? (That is, what do other authorities in the same field say about the author or the work? Can your teacher or your textbooks tell you?)

Is the source reasonable? responsive to alternative evidence? fairly objective? Or, if it's biased, are the biases apparent so you can recognize and allow for them?

Is the source accurate? up-to-date? Does it take into account recent events and new knowledge (see Chapter 13)?

Even if a source uses fancy language or appears in print, it is not authoritative unless it meets the above criteria.

How Much and What Kind of Evidence Do You Need?

When you're beginning an argumentative essay, it's tempting to assume that since your cause is right and just, the truth of your side will be obvious to the reader if you merely state your position. If you believe firmly in the merits of a case, especially if the people with whom you've discussed it share your view, it may be hard to imagine an opposition. How could anyone be against the preservation of America's natural wilderness areas? saving the whales? or mass transit? If you're not convinced that these and a host of other issues are highly controversial, a quick random sampling of opinions should convince you otherwise. In fact, you are most likely to be writing an argument to an audience that needs to be convinced and that may disagree with your thesis. After all, there's no point in debating an issue to convince an already eager supporter. Keeping this audience in mind will be of great help in deciding just how much and what kind of evidence you must include to back up your argument.

Don't provide evidence for what is common knowledge or self-evident. Most arguments depend partly on information that most people already know: it's a waste of effort to rediscover fire each time you write a paper. But how do you decide what's common knowledge? You don't want to belabor the obvious, but you don't want to overestimate your readers' sophistication either. If, for example, you were writing about federal regulation of drugs, you could probably assume that your readers would know what the federal government and the Food and Drug Administration are but would not know all of the significant duties of the FDA that relate to the issue at hand.

Generally speaking, if you're writing for an audience similar to yourself in age, background, and education, you can assume their fund of information to be about on a par with yours before you began to investigate the specific topic of your paper. If you're writing for an audience quite different from yourself, try out a sample draft of your argument on a typical prospective reader to determine how much she or he already knows about the subject, as well as to learn first-hand of some possible objections to your line of reasoning.

Provide representative evidence. Make sure that the information you provide represents *all* major sides of an issue, not just the one that you favor. (Is a greater use of coal the only alternative to the world's oil crisis? What about using more wood? nuclear power? solar energy?) If you're drawing upon partisan sources, try to balance the relevant factors: the conservative with the liberal, the historical with the contemporary, the scientific with the humanitarian. Of course, you can still come out in favor of your side. But if you have examined the major appropriate points of view in arriving at your conclusions, you will be more likely to convince your audience that you are being fair.

However, don't overlook the interesting exceptions and extremes. Even if the bizarre or unusual is not representative of the norm of your evidence, it can be illuminating to include a case history or other reference to atypical examples and tell what makes them so memorable, *as long as you indicate that they are exceptional.*

Probably the typical students at most colleges are between eighteen and twenty-four, with smaller percentages ranging through the twenties and thirties into their early forties. But suppose that also in attendance are a prodigy of thirteen and an octogenarian. If your argument concerns the student population, the very fact of their uniqueness would be worthy of note. Nevertheless, you would still have to remember that *you cannot generalize from the unusual or leave the impression that it is typical.*

Provide evidence for what is not commonly known or self-evident in direct proportion to its signifiance in your argument. The arguable points that you have determined are the most important warrant the most evidence, because these arguments are to carry the most weight and to generate subordinate points. If you're demonstrating that "It's appropriate for the FDA to test drugs, but the choice of whether to use them should be left to the consumer," you might discuss the controversial banning of saccharin or laetrile to illustrate your larger point, but you wouldn't devote the whole paper to either substance.

The more controversial or ambiguous your subject is, the more evidence you will need to supply. As an argument becomes more controversial or ambiguous, both you and your readers can take less and less for granted. You will, therefore, have more explaining and convincing to do, which will consequently take more evidence. In such cases, you must also:

Diversify your evidence. It is wise to use varied illustrations that support new issues or different facets of your topic, or that speak to objections your opponents may raise. But don't multiply examples that pertain to the same point. One or two illustrations of a given aspect of your topic are usually sufficient, if they typify the available evidence. Illustrations can quickly reach a saturation point; like eating chocolate ice cream cones, the first one may be memorably delicious, the second satisfying, but by the fifth you've had enough, no matter how intrinsically appealing any individual cone might be.

For instance, in arguing that the FDA should leave the choice of chemical and drug use to the consumer, you might support your point by citing such relatively safe, nonprescription substances as aspirin or iron tablets. You could also list several others to indicate that those selected were typical of a class, but you wouldn't need to analyze your reasons for each additional citation. However, to let your readers know that you are considering a representative sample of drugs, which includes the problem substances as well as the safe ones, you would want to include in your discussion one or two drugs that are controversial, such as laetrile—does it cure cancer or not? or thalidomide, banned in the United States by the FDA after it had caused grotesque birth defects in Europe, where it had first been introduced.

Anticipate and accommodate contradictory evidence or other points opposing your own. Suppose you have thought of an issue that opponents of your viewpoint could use to their advantage. Wouldn't it be better just to ignore that aspect of the evidence or topic and hope that your readers won't think of it either? Perhaps a discussion of thalidomide would weaken your thesis about the FDA.

Letting sleeping contradictions lie is actually more detrimental to your cause than an open discussion would be. Just because you back away from an issue doesn't mean that your readers will—especially if they oppose your thesis. If your readers think of fairly obvious points of disagreement that you fail to examine, they may conclude that you are ignorant—which won't help your credibility. Or they may believe you're unable to cope with the controversy for fear you'll lose—which won't help your argument. So in effect, they will have already conceded the unspoken point to the other side.

You have more to gain than to lose by introducing evidence that seems to favor the opposition. In fact, to do this is strategically sound, because it implies you're so thoroughly in command of the evidence that you believe you can make a strong case for your side by meeting objections directly. You can do this by raising objections to your argument and then either conceding them, refuting them, or both.

In *concession* you introduce an objection and/or evidence that contradicts your point and admit its truth. You then try to reduce its strength by showing why, though true, it's fairly weak and doesn't do particular harm to your thesis. For instance, you might argue that as long as the FDA publicized the bad effects of thalidomide, it wouldn't be necessary to ban the drug. Doctors, informed of its harm to fetuses, wouldn't prescribe it to pregnant women (and perhaps others), and so compliance with the FDA's aims and maintenance of public safety would be accomplished by desirable voluntary means rather than by undesirable governmental coercion.

In *refutation*, you cite the contradictory point or evidence and then attempt to negate it by rebuttal with counter-evidence intended to prove the opposition false, ineffective, or worthless. Remember, *you can't refute one opinion with another; you need demonstrable evidence.*

In developing the FDA argument you could produce data to demonstrate that ever since saccharin came into use as an artificial sweetener, no one ever died or became ill from using it. You could cite additional evidence to show the positive benefits to people who are trying to lose weight and to diabetics who are dependent on saccharin and harmed by sugar. Then you could project, using statistical data, the detrimental effect that a saccharin ban would have on these groups. You could also point out that once informed that consumption of enormous amounts of saccharin causes some laboratory rats to develop cancer, consumers could decide for themselves whether they wanted to assume that minimal risk. You might add that failure to heed the FDA warning could harm the individual consumer but not society as a whole, and conclude that the federal government should not regulate private citizens' private acts, which have no broader social consequences.

Do not push your refutation beyond what you need to say to make a solid case for your side. If your opponent is wrong on three major points and seventeen minor ones confine your rebuttal to the major cases, with allusions to the minor ones. If your opponent is wrong on seventeen *major* points, then confine your criticism to the three or four issues most central to your thesis.

REASONABLE LANGUAGE: THE BASIS OF ARGUMENT

For most arguments, no matter who you're trying to convince, it's a good idea to use reasonable language—language that says what you mean without equivocating, but language that is *moderate in expression.* Arguing in language that is exaggerated and heavily connotative—especially the use of negatives—can seem particularly powerful, especially if you and your readers happen to be in agreement beforehand. However, what may seem "punishing and repressive measures" in one opinion may be "mild restraints" in the opinion of another. Although consistently loaded language may enable you to vent your emotions, it is more likely to offend the uncommitted than to persuade them. You'll be wise to tone it down.

Take a Definite Stand

To be moderate in your language, to qualify your generalizations, does not mean to abdicate a point of view. In your attempt to be reasonable, don't be wishy-washy; after all, you're arguing to prove the thesis of your choice, so neither your language nor your argument should be evasive or ambiguous. Say what you mean, but say it tactfully. It is better to say, " 'Law and order' measures restrict people's civil liberties without producing a decrease in the crimes they were intended to curtail," rather than " 'Law and order' measures are repressive, anti-civil-libertarian, and unconstitutional restrictions that cause horrendous injustice."

Face the Issue Directly

Equivocation through avoidance of a definite stand on an issue is usually deliberate. Politicians are known for fence straddling in their attempts to avoid giving offense and to appeal to as many diverse voters as possible: "Everyone is entitled to a full exercise of civil liberties as guaranteed in the Bill of Rights, but the sale of pornographic materials should be stopped immediately."

Fence staddlers often fall off— or are pushed. You will be writing responsibly if you make an explicit, unambiguous statement of your position and defend it in equally explicit, unambiguous terms: "Because freedom of the press is such an important Constitutional guarantee, our country must allow the unhampered distribution and sale of pornographic materials to adults. To restrict this would be the first step in eroding the freedom of expression that has maintained our country's liberty for two centuries."

Stick to the Subject

Suppose that instead of confining your discussion to pornography, as your thesis promised, you got carried away with the subject of the freedom of the press and ended up defending the right of newspapers to criticize our elected officials. If you spent most of your essay on this, and illustrated it with an elaborate discussion of the uninhibited (though careful) reporting of the *Washington Post* as it discovered and pursued the Watergate scandal, you'd be equivocating (whether intentionally or not) by evading the issue. In fact, you would have shifted topics completely.

Your readers are entitled to a discussion of what your thesis promises. If you don't provide it they're perfectly justified in ignoring your essay.

Attack the issue itself, rather than your opponents. Don't shift from debating an issue to attacking the person(s) who disagrees with your stand. Three common, and inappropriate, ways of focusing on your opponent rather than on the real issues are: (1) name calling; (2) *ad hominem* arguments; and (3) *tu quoque* arguments.

Name Calling. Here the writer attacks individuals or groups unfairly by calling them biased names with stereotypical, negative connotations (*fascist, nigger, Canuk, atheist*). Such labels are intended not only to arouse hostility in hearers but to play on their prejudices, so they will blame the persons labeled, the scapegoats, for the problems under discussion ("Kike businessmen caused the Depression") and ignore the real causes.

Ad Hominem *Arguments.* Conducting an *ad hominem* argument, an appeal "to the man," emphasizes irrelevant aspects of a person's character, physical qualities, private life, or background rather than his or her stand on an issue, for better or for worse. "Napoleon was too short; how could he command the respect of other nations?" Napoleon's height was irrelevant to his military and diplomatic powers, which depended much more heavily on the size of his army, his military strategy, and success (or defeat) in battle.

Tu Quoque *Arguments.* In conducting a *tu quoque,* "you're another," argument, the person charged with a particular view or offense accuses the opponent of similar behavior rather than meeting the charges directly. "How can you criticize me for smoking cigarettes," says the angry asthmatic patient to the doctor, "when you're puffing on a cigar?" Although the accusation that the doctor smokes may be true (or false), it is irrelevant to the issue of whether cigarette smoking will harm the asthmatic.

Focusing on the issues instead of on your opponents' personal characteristics can help you concentrate on relevant points of your argument and strengthen them with appropriate evidence. Furthermore, attacking the opposition unfairly may arouse the reader's sympathy for your victims, and antagonism toward you as a writer who would try to take unfair advantage of people not able to reply immediately, if at all.

If you've followed the suggestions in this chapter, by now you should have focused on an arguable idea and determined some of the dimensions and evidence for your argument; established yourself as a credible and reasonable arguer; and begun to assess your audience in order to adapt your argument to them. The next chapter will help you to build on what you have accomplished by this point, to develop additional ideas, and to organize them into arguments of various types.

SUGGESTIONS FOR DISCUSSION, ANALYSIS, AND WRITING

1. Analyze the following argument (or another of your choice) to show whether it is a reasonable treatment of the subject. How does it accommodate opponents' anticipated objections? What techniques does the author use to convince readers rather than to antagonize them?

THE HOMOSEXUAL IN THE CLASSROOM

Should homosexuals be permitted to teach? Not in the opinion of 65 percent of Americans, many of whom approve of equal job rights for homosexuals in other professions. The fear that a homosexual teacher may become a "role model" for an impressionable adolescent evidently worries most parents more than the injustice of barring an entire category of people from a major profession on insufficient evidence of danger.

One of these people, James Gaylord, was fired from a Tacoma high school in 1972, after school officials learned that he was a homosexual. He had been teaching social studies for almost 13 years, apparently with a good record. Mr. Gaylord lost his appeal in a state court, and now the Supreme Court has declined to review that decision. It has also refused to review a case involving a homosexual teacher in New Jersey who was ordered by the Paramus board of education to undergo a psychiatric examination after he became president of the state's Gay Activist Alliance. So in the state of Washington homosexual teachers may now be dismissed, while in New Jersey they become fair subjects for psychiatry.

Homosexuals have taught in America's schools for years but few parents or children have been aware of it. Now, as homosexuals emerge from the closet, they are encountering the kind of fear and hostility which led a few months ago to the successful crusade against an antidiscrimination ordinance in Miami. In some places experienced teachers are finding that they cannot be honest about themselves—outside the classroom—without jeopardizing their careers.

The desire of parents for reassurance that their children will not somehow be "converted" to homosexuality at school is understandable. Unfortunately, society's understanding of the causes of homosexuality is not sufficient to provide total reassurance. But the consensus among psychiatrists is that the propensity begins early, before school age, and that some "constitutional" or physiological factors may be at work. It seems unrealistic to speak of homosexuality as a mere "preference," but it is no more realistic to think of it as a contagious disease; the fear that a "normal" child may be infected simply by the presence of a homosexual teacher seems naive. For the most part, professional teachers can be trusted to behave responsibly in the classroom. If a child were wooed or proselytized by a teacher, homosexual or heterosexual, that would be a violation of professional responsibility and cause for instant dismissal.

Present knowledge, then, does not justify barring homosexuals from teaching—though they may not be the best instructors for sex education—and despite the setbacks in states such as Washington and New Jersey, the trend elsewhere appears to be in the direction of candor and fairness. In upholding the rights of homosexuals to teach, the courts in California, Maryland, Oregon and Delaware are keeping pace with psychiatric opinion.

Since 1973, the American Psychiatric Association has held to the position that homosexuality as such implies no impairment of judgment, stability, reliability or vocational capacity. The organization's president stated in 1975, "There are many homosexuals in our school systems now, but they are forced to live in fear of being found out—at considerable psychological cost to themselves and in turn to society. . . . A teacher should be judged only on the basis of professional competence." Unless, and until, compelling evidence to the contrary is presented, homosexuals should not be disqualified as teachers.[4]

2. Here are several thesis sentences that are difficult to defend in their present form. Revise each statement so it could serve as the basis for an appropriate argumentative essay. Explain why you revised each sentence as you did.
   a. Sweden has the lowest number of convicts per capita in the world; this proves that socialism fulfills people's wants and keeps them from stealing.
   b. Exercise is good for everybody.
   c. Minority children consistently do more poorly in school than whites; they must be dumber.
   d. Homosexuals should be allowed to teach school.
   e. Americans should work for what they get; we don't want a nation of welfare chiselers.
   f. The rise in rape rates since the advent of women's lib proves that women are better off at home.
3. On the basis of criteria given in this chapter, evaluate the adequacy of the reasoning and evidence provided in one or more of these letters to the newspaper. Or choose a letter from your own local or campus newspaper for your analysis.

a.

Mr. Mojdehi's Oct. 14 letter, "Pure Punishment," on alternatives to capital punishment presents some rather incredible lines of reasoning, both in regard to the justification for state execution, and in regard to his idea of "pure punishment."

"Punishment is necessary in a society for two basic reasons: to restrict or eliminate undesirable elements and to serve as a deterrent for potential violators of laws," Mr. Mojdehi writes.

How many times in the history of human society has the definition of a class, race or group of believers as "undesirable elements" led to campaigns of terror, abuse and even extermination? The story of our own nation has not been free of such tragedies.

Mr. Mojdehi admits that the "deterrence" argument has not been substantiated—he goes so far as to say that it "probably cannot" be. But interestingly enough, he is willing to err in the direction of . . . can we call it caution? This is a strange brand of caution; it tells us that it is better to sacrifice human lives now than to react with reason and patience while we continue the struggle to understand the roots of crime.

Finally, Mr. Mojdehi offers his "alternative." He takes a peculiarly American approach—things will turn out fine if we can just refine the technology. We won't feel so bad about taking men's and women's lives if we can do so without hurting them. It is an amazing, cruel absurdity, and surely cannot be called an alternative.

Capital punishment is a short-range, technological, cost-benefit analysis solution to a long-lived, intensely tragic, deeply human problem that is both individual and social in nature. The question is not whether we can provide ourselves with a painless, "humane" form of "elimination" for undesirable elements. It is, rather, whether we have the right, or even the need, to end the lives of men and women, no matter how angry or outraged we may be at their actions. For criminals are, finally, men and women, not "elements" or "violators" or "capital offenders" or "jail bait." Capital punishment is no less than the state-sanctioned delivery of death, the arbitrary ending of whatever we or those men and women themselves might have hoped for their lives to become. With the stakes so incredibly high, the question of pain is sadly irrelevant.

—Tim Manion[5]

b.

DEAR ANN LANDERS: In 1975 you advised a lonesome girl who had trouble meeting nice men to take a few adult education courses at the local university and join organizations so she could meet people whose interests were similar to hers. Then you added, "Church groups have a lot to offer."

My 28-year-old daughter, Tillie, joined a church group on your say and that's where she met Albert. She devoted her whole life to him for 22 months. We had him to dinner twice a week and they even took a little trip together.

Last week, Albert's wife showed up at our door with three little kids. She asked Tillie to please leave her husband alone. We almost died of the shock. He seemed so respectable and decent.

So please, Ann, don't recommend church groups as a place to meet nice men. It's a perfect front for scoundrels.

—Columbus, O.[6]

c.

To the Editor:

Jane Doe [Op-Ed Sept. 23] has described the impenetrable eyes and mask-like faces of her son and the woman with whom he lives as they tell her she "wouldn't understand" their decision not to marry legally, even though they have recently had a child. She proceeds to focus what appears to be her much deeper, personal feeling of alienation from her son and his generation with its different attitudes, on the particular issue of marriage. It is a subject that raises questions which can only faintly be heard through all her nagging and scolding.

Isn't the central issue whether or not marriage continues to be a supportive institution to those who enter into it? Shouldn't we attempt, among other things, to examine those societal changes which have affected our attitudes to traditional marriage; question the practice of penalizing couples who are not married by depriving them of economic benefits enjoyed by married couples; reappraise the strengths that marriage can bring to a relationship and attempt to deal with its shortcomings?

One thing we can be sure of: There is no perfect arrangement. A relationship between a man and a woman is not "legitimized" by a marriage ceremony, and parental responsibility is not legislated by a marriage contract.

Surely it is hypocritical to suggest, as Jane Doe does, that marriage is a necessary convenience, and that "open marriage" and the promise of easy divorce should somehow allay fears and sidetrack concerns. Jane Doe's son and his mate have made certain choices. Those of us who grew up at a time when stricter limits governed our behavior can still be sensitive to the extra burden placed on those faced with so many more acceptable alternatives.

Personally, I hope that my children will be thoughtful and realistic when, as adults, they choose for themselves a satisfactory way of living this life.

—Kate Roosevelt[7]

d.

In her letter about marriage and its alternatives, Kate Roosevelt says, "One thing we can be sure of—there is no perfect arrangement" (Oct. 7).

It is not the arrangement of marriage that is imperfect, but the parties to it. Many couples lack the maturity, unselfishness and good humor required in marriage. We need to change ourselves, and not our arrangements, if we are to find a satisfactory way of living this life.

—Nancy Allen[8]

e.

Kate Roosevelt's Oct. 7 letter on marriage says: "Isn't the central issue whether or not marriage continues to be a supportive institution to those who enter into it?"

The answer is "no." Marriage is a social institution. It was devised to further the stability of society. Children need to follow good examples. The first examples they see, and the most important, are those set by parents. Loyalty, in good times and bad, in sickness and health—that is the example loyal partners in a marriage set. In the casual, self-centered style of life advocated by Kate Roosevelt loyalty takes a back seat. Society suffers.

—Richard L. Day, M.D.[9]

f.

For Haldeman, Ehrlichman and Mitchell, apparently, freedom means only having to say you're sorry.

—Edna Toney[10]

4. Write an argument representing three points of view on a controversial issue, such as the debate over the nature of marriage carried on in the letters above (*c, d,* and *e*). Each argument should be of equal length, perhaps a page, and should accommodate the major views of the other arguments. Each argument should sound sincere and be as strong and convincing as you can make it.

5. Select one of the following theses, or another of your own choice, and construct an argument pertinent to it based on accurately representative evidence.
   a. College juniors do/do not study harder than seniors/freshmen and do/do not get better grades.
   b. Women are/are not better students than men.
   c. People over thirty are/are not better students than people under thirty.
   d. People who participate on athletic teams are better/worse students than people who don't.

6. Following the suggestions on evaluating information, read and evaluate the following pairs of statements. What problems does each pair raise? What do you need to know to interpret each statement or pair accurately? How would you decide which alternative in each pair to use in an essay on the topic? Or could you use some modified combination of both?
   a. My great grandmother said all rural doctors at the turn of the century were quacks.
      Infant mortality in rural areas at the turn of the century was three times higher than it is today.
   b. The American family is disintegrating; last year there were over a million teenage runaways across state lines.
      The American family is expanding; last year 1,700,000 new single-family homes and condominiums were built.
   c. Blacks are worse off in America than ever before; in 1979 39 percent of black youths were unemployed.
      Blacks are better off in America than ever before; in 1980 15 percent of the total college enrollment was black—five times higher than in 1940.
   d. Americans are growing more and more affluent; in 1980 per capita income was four times the per capita income in 1945.
      Americans are growing poorer and poorer; income taxes in 1980 take eight times the average worker's paycheck than they did in 1945.
   e. Ceramic cooktop stoves have various disadvantages. They waste energy, cook slowly, require elaborate care, and are a potential burn hazard.
      Ceramic cooktop stoves have a number of advantages. They cost only pennies a day to operate; provide a large, even cooking surface; wipe clean with nonabrasive cleansers; and generate less waste heat than conventional stove tops.

NOTES

[1] The *New York Times*, October 10, 1977, A, p. 26.
[2] *The Family Coordinator*, October 1975, 391–392.
[3] *Saturday Evening Post*, July 2, 1966.
[4] The *New York Times*, October 24, 1977, A, p. 26.
[5] St. Louis *Post-Dispatch*, October 26, 1977, G, p. 2.
[6] St. Louis *Post-Dispatch*, October 26, 1977, H, p. 2.
[7] The *New York Times*, October 7, 1977, A, p. 30.
[8] The *New York Times*, October 14, 1977, A, p. 26.
[9] The *New York Times*, October 22, 1977, A, p. 20.
[10] The *New York Times*, October 22, 1977, A, p. 20.

CHAPTER TWELVE
TYPES OF ARGUMENTS

Form follows function; argumentative form enhances argumentative function.

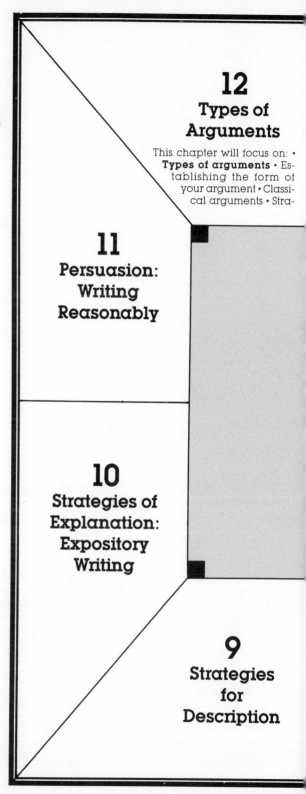

12
Types of Arguments
This chapter will focus on: • **Types of arguments** • Establishing the form of your argument • Classical arguments • Stra-

11
Persuasion: Writing Reasonably

10
Strategies of Explanation: Expository Writing

9
Strategies for Description

13
Using Resources: Tools For Strategies

14
A Resource Paper

ESTABLISHING THE FORM OF YOUR ARGUMENT

Suppose you wanted to argue on behalf of the controversial proposition, "In spite of the philosophy that every student has the right to communicate in his or her own language, it is essential for American college students to write in standard English." As with many other debatable topics, there are a number of ways to approach this subject and defend it successfully, following the principles of argumentation that were established in the preceding chapter and the specific strategies that will be discussed in this chapter.

You might debate the above proposition using as your primary material the *analysis of a single case,* treated as representative of all similar cases. From this you would derive most of the evidence for your argument. Thus if you speak in one or more languages or nonstandard dialects, you could draw inferences about the experiences of comparable speakers from the *single case* of yourself. You would use your own experiences as a speaker of, say, Spanish, Southern dialect, or Black English, and generalize from these to make your points.

Or you could argue by *analogy,* exploring points of similarity between the linguistic skills of contemporary speakers of nonstandard English and those of immigrants of the last century. In tracing the history of an immigrant group, say Germans, Chinese, or Russian Jews, you might point out that as they learned standard English they were able to become better educated, to get better jobs, and to adapt more easily to life in America. These advantages will also be possible, you could argue, for today's immigrants from the Far East, Mexico, or Cuba, if they learn to use standard English fluently.

You might also argue the issue in terms of *cause and effect*. First you'd specify the *cause* (or *causes*): "If writers use a nonstandard dialect" and then the *effect:* "their readers may decide that they are uneducated or incompetent." You could discuss *additional effects* of such judgments (or misjudgments): "This might lead readers to refuse to take such writers seriously, to treat them without respect, or to refuse to hire them for jobs that require verbal communication."

Your argument could be a *classical* one, offering a series of logical steps in favor of your point and in rebuttal to the opposition. Thus you might demonstrate, step by step, that proficiency in standard English is essential in providing American college students with access to careers in many fields, such as law, journalism, broadcasting, teaching, and public administration. Your rebuttal would have to account for the exceptions.

Or your argument could be an *assertive* variation on the classical format, in which before presenting your main point the argument devoted considerable space to demonstrating a thorough knowledge of the opposing view, that encouraging people to speak and write in their own dialect shows respect for their origins and culture, enhances their ethnic or regional pride, and so on.

Or you might *combine forms,* perhaps buttressing a classical argument with cause and effect, analogy, case illustration, or all three. The form(s) your argument takes, what kinds of and how much evidence you use, and how you arrange these will be determined not only by your view of the subject but by your understanding of the view of intended audience and the circumstances under which you're arguing.

All of these forms of argumentation have some elements in common. Most arguments begin by specifying the topic, if not the thesis, to be argued. All seek to establish the author's credibility and competence to argue the case. Effective arguments are (or appear to be) logical, with each succeeding step built on those that come before. Using strong representative evidence, the authors incorporate the opinions of their supporters and seek to appeal to the uncommitted. But they must also speak to the views, vested interests, and prejudices of opponents and try to counter their points (accurate and otherwise) with powerful representative evidence that will support their proposition. The conclusion of an effective argument aims to be the inevitable or highly plausible result of everything that has come before. Many of these aspects of argumentation have been discussed in detail in the preceding chapter. After providing a checklist for developing argumentative propositions, this chapter will focus on how to present the various types of arguments, with suggestions on how to develop and organize each.

☐ A Checklist for Developing Argumentative Propositions

In order to conduct any kind of argument you need to construct a proposition, a statement of the issue you will debate throughout your essay. Because this statement, the thesis sentence of your argument, is the focal point of everything else that you'll be saying, it needs to be clear, unequivocal, and forceful. You can follow the suggestions for writing an arguable proposition in Chapter 11 to help make it so. Such a statement is likely to appear overtly near the beginning of a classical or cause-and-effect argument, but may sometimes be implied rather than stated openly in some other forms of arguments, such as arguments by analogy or single case.

Once you have constructed a proposition that concisely states your case, you should find it helpful to ask some of the following questions to help develop and strengthen your argument, whatever its form.[1]

☐ What do its key words mean? What definitions, if any, do I need to supply in order to make the argument understood?

☐ Does it contain or imply subpoints that I need to deal with in order to establish the main point?

☐ What points do I have to establish so my readers will believe my proposition?

☐ Is it true or false? How do I know?

☐ What evidence (political, moral, ethical, legal, personal experience, and so on) will I use in making my points? What are my strongest points? What are my points of medium weight (those I will use with caution)? What points will I discard or downplay because the evidence is weak?

☐ What illustrations do I need?

☐ What would opponents say about this? What arguments can I use to counter their opposition?

☐ If this proposition is accepted or rejected, what will the consequences be?

☐ Is my proposition a prediction? Does past experience or knowledge warrant this? How likely is it to occur?

☐ Does the proposition require that some action be taken? If so, what? Is the action feasible? Is it likely to work? At what costs—social, economic, or other? and to whom?

See how you can answer these as you argue specific issues in one or another of the forms discussed below.

CLASSICAL ARGUMENTS
The Format

Classical arguments attempt, through a series of logical steps, to persuade the audience to accept the writer's proposition on rational or emotional grounds, through respect for the writer's character or credentials, or some combination of these. A classical argument usually consists of an introduction, explanation of the issue being discussed, proof of the case, and a refutation of opposing arguments—all of which culminate in the conclusion. This format, widely used today as it has been throughout the centuries, is derived from the organizational pattern for a persuasive speech or essay as it was developed in classical Greece; its survival testifies to its utility. You will find this format, presented below, both general and flexible. It can be particularly helpful in debating ideas or in analyzing literary (or other) works when you are trying to argue a thesis that can be demonstrated by a series of logical steps, illustrated by evidence.

Introduction.   In the introduction, which may occupy one or more paragraphs, you will want to state your thesis, attract your readers' attention, and establish your credibility and suitability to argue your case.

Explanation of the Issue Being Discussed.   This part of the argument is essentially expository. Here you provide readers with information (beyond what they can already be assumed to know) sufficient to enable them to understand as many aspects of the issue as are relevant to the argument. You define terms and you may break a larger, complex issue into its smaller components for ease of later discussion. If your audience is likely to be unreceptive to your thesis or to the facts you need to present in order to argue it, you may consider using the format for an assertive argument instead (see the discussion later in this chapter).

Outline of the Points or Steps in the Argument.   Although classical orators informed their audience of the direction their speech would take so listeners could follow it more easily, you may or may not find it to your advantage to do so. If your argument will be long or complicated and if you expect your audience to be at least moderately receptive to it, you may wish to tell them in capsule form what to expect. However, if your argument is short and simple, don't bother with the anticipatory outline; your readers can remember each point well enough as it comes along. Also, if your audience is likely to be hostile to major points that you intend to present near the end of the argument, you probably won't want to antagonize them by tipping your hand too early.

Proof of the Case.   In presenting the proof of the case, you will probably find it best to present the points of your argument in logical order. Each point should be appropriately explained, illustrated, and supported with evidence, as indicated in the preceding chapter. This will be the main and longest portion of your essay.

Refutation of Opposing Arguments.   In this section, you must try to confront and answer anticipated objections to your thesis in order to weaken or demolish the opposition's case and remove readers' doubts about your own. Refutation does not invariably *follow* the proof. If your audience favors your opponents or is receptive to their case, you may want to prepare the ground for your views by putting the refutation before the proof. Or you may decide to interweave them, refuting each opposing point in turn and following it with a counterargument of your own, in sequence throughout the argument.

Conclusion. A conclusion presents the logical—and emotional—outcome of what has preceded it. A conclusion to a long argument often summarizes its essence, drawing all its diverse themes into a coherent whole before making the final point. Or a conclusion can aim to inspire readers to go out and act on what has just been proved.

However, short, straightforward arguments may not need elaborate conclusions if the major points are easily remembered. A single statement or even a phrase will often suffice.

Analyzing a Classical Argument

The following essay, "Standardized Tests: They Don't Measure Learning," by Edwin P. Taylor and Mitchell Lazarus, uses the format of the classical argument.

1   The controversy over achievement testing starts from a simple fact: Achievement tests reward test-taking skills as much as they reward achievement. Different children who know a subject equally well can still receive very different scores on a multiple-choice achievement test.

2   Some children work fast, not taking time to think deeply: they may make quick conventional guesses on some questions, be tidy and accurate in shading boxes on answer sheets and have suburban, middle-class backgrounds—useful for quickly grasping the words and pictures on most tests. These children get credit, perhaps, for what they know about the subject matter.

3   Other children may work slowly, think through too many possibilities, be too insecure to guess fast or be sloppy with the answer sheet. Children come from a variety of cultural and linguistic backgrounds. Thus many children's test scores will probably not reflect their grasp of the subject, even if they know the subject well.

4   And nearly every achievement test is a reading test first, before it is a test of anything else.

5   Neatness, accuracy, speed and good reading are useful skills, worth encouraging in children. But as long as test scores depend so much on skills that supposedly are not being tested, the results are bound to be inaccurate.

6   All questions on standardized achievement tests are multiple choice. The child must (1) read the question and (2) think of the answer—but not write it down! Instead, he or she must (3) try to find this answer among those given; (4) and when it is not there, pick one that is; (5) keep track of its number or letter, and (6) shade in the correct little box on the answer sheet. Only two of these six steps concern the subject being tested. The other four help the computer grade the test.

7   Multiple-choice questions distort the purposes of education. Picking one answer

among four is very different from thinking a question through to an answer of one's own, and far less useful in life. Recognition of vocabulary and isolated facts makes the best kind of multiple-choice questions, so these dominate the tests, rather than questions that test the use of knowledge. Because schools want their children to perform well, they are often tempted to teach the limited sorts of knowledge most useful on the tests.

8   Questions are often badly worded, confusing, or downright wrong. For many questions, the thoughtful or imaginative student can see several acceptable answers among those given. . . .

9   Aside from the content of the tests, there is the fact that some children are intimidated by the testing procedures—vastly different from ordinary classroom activity—and perform poorly.

10   "Keep quiet. Sit with an empty row of desks between you and your neighbor. Listen hard to the instructions. Don't mind the teacher stalking up and down between the rows during the test. Remember how much your future depends on your score—but don't be nervous. Imagine what your folks will say if you land in a low percentile. If you tighten up under pressure, you are in real trouble. Hurry. Stay calm. Hurry. Stay calm."

11   There are many stories of children breaking down during a test or being physically ill the night before. But life is full of trials and fears; why should we protect children? Because they are children; because we want to find out, for example, how well they are learning rather than how well they stand stress, and because those children already hobbled by insecurity, past failure or discrimination will be the most vulnerable in a vicious cycle.

12   Once the tests are administered and scored, the purpose to which the results are put—comparing children using numbers—is of no use.

13   Every person is complicated, everyone has unique skills and difficulties. But each test score reduces the pattern of a child's strengths and weaknesses to a single number. Why? To compare the child with others around the country. Why? To tell if the schools are doing their job. But the single numbers and averages carry no hints about how to improve either the schools or individual children.

14   Healthy competition encourages excellence. But competition in standardized tests encourages intellectual narrowness and triviality.

15   Society does need to measure people's achievement and school performance, and could do so in much better ways. Imagine school tests set up like the test for a driver's license, each test matched to the skills under test and each child doing "well enough" or not, with a chance for those who did not to try again later. In judging a school, attention would focus on the fractions of its children who passed various tests at various ages. . . .

16   In the past we developed an unjustified faith in numbers, and then in computers. Objectivity and statistical analysis became major virtues; automatic data analysis often replaced thoughtful evaluation. Now we are learning that numbers can misrepresent children and can lead to wrong decisions about their lives. There can be no true objectivity in a heterogeneous society and all data analysis is subject to the GIGO principle: garbage in, garbage out.

17   The task is to find out how well children are learning. The present standardized multiple-choice achievement tests are doing it badly, sometimes destructively. There are better ways to find out, without compressing children into uniform molds that misrepresent their accomplishments.[2]

The first paragraph states part of the thesis: "Achievement tests reward test-taking skills as much as they reward achievement." The rest of the essay implies the rest of the thesis: "and therefore other means [unspecified] should be found to measure children's achievement."

The next four paragraphs (2–5) explain the case being discussed: middle-class children who work rapidly may be tested on what they know; other children may work slowly or sloppily and their test scores will probably not reveal their knowledge. Paragraphs 2–5 explain that achievement tests measure "neatness, accuracy, speed and good reading"—all "skills that supposedly are not being tested"—and thereby favor middle-class children.

This essay, being relatively short, does not outline the steps of the argument, but devotes most of its remaining space (about two-thirds of the total) to alternating proof of the authors' points with refutation of actual or hypothetical points the opposition might raise. Thus they demonstrate that in multiple-choice questions "only two of the six steps concern the subject being tested" (paragraph 6), and in paragraph 7 provide evidence that multiple-choice tests seem to concentrate on "recognition of vocabulary and isolated facts" rather than on knowledge. Paragraph 11 says that testing causes children too much stress and refutes arguments to the contrary. Paragraphs 12 and 13 demonstrate that test scores reduce the "pattern of a child's strengths and weaknesses to a single number" that enables comparison with other numbers but tells nothing about the child. In the process, the authors ask rhetorical questions, "Why? . . . Why?" which they answer to refute the opposition. And paragraphs 14 and 15 develop the point that "competition in standardized tests encourages intellectual narrowness and triviality," and propose an alternative.

The last two paragraphs (16 and 17) provide a conclusion in the form of a summary and two restatements of the thesis: "Numbers can misrepresent children and can lead to wrong decisions about their lives"; "The present standardized multiple-choice achievement tests are testing children's learning badly, sometimes destructively." According to the authors, the essential task is "to find out how well children are learning" and there are better ways to do this than through multiple-choice testing. What these better ways are is not specified; that would require another essay.

The language in this essay reinforces the strategy of beginning in a fairly objective manner and enhancing the logical argument by emotional appeals as the reasoning proceeds. Thus the first six paragraphs are neutral in language, but by paragraph 8 test questions are identified as "badly worded . . . downright wrong." The emotional climax is reached in the next-to-last paragraph with use of derogatory language well known among computer users: "garbage in, garbage out."

Likewise, the children, who the authors claim are victimized by poor tests and who are initially labeled in paragraph 3 as possibly "insecure," have become by paragraph 11 "hobbled by insecurity." This escalation of the emotional pitch has, in part, been emphasized by the hypothetical example in paragraph 10, of the anxiety-producing test-giver "stalking up and down between the rows during the test" barking high-pressure contradictory instructions to the children.

It is clear from the argumentative structure, language, and examples that the authors have made their point through a combination of logical argument and emotional appeals that intensify as the argument proceeds. The argument is convincing, particularly if readers can think of instances they know about personally, in which creative or otherwise able children did not perform well on standardized tests. But there is still room for debate, as the next section indicates.

SUGGESTIONS FOR DISCUSSION AND WRITING

1. The following is an example of a classical argument. Analyze its reasoning, choice of examples, argumentative techniques, and organization. Then, comment on its effectiveness.

   If you prefer, find another example of a classical argument and analyze that.

HOW NOT TO EASE THE TUITION SQUEEZE

It is called the Tuition Tax Credit Plan and at first glance it looks socially just and politically irresistible. Steadily mounting school bills now face millions of middle-income taxpayers who lack the means of the rich and the access to scholarship aid of the poor. Private education is hard-pressed and needs financial help. What, then, could be more welcome than the new proposal to give tuition-paying taxpayers a tax credit of up to $500 per student? That approach, say its advocates, Oregon's Republican Senator Packwood and New York's Democratic Senator Moynihan, would not only help families; it would permit consumers to choose freely from "the supermarket" of educational institutions. It would apply to every full or part-time student who pays tuition in an accredited elementary or high school, college, university, trade or vocational school.

The Senators' analysis is sound. Galloping tuition inflation has indeed begun to squeeze middle-income families. But despite the clear evidence of trouble, the tax credit seems to us the wrong route to a worthy goal. Yet more tampering with the tax system is ill-timed; it flies in the face of current efforts to simplify the system. But an analysis of the tuition tax credit suggests even more fundamental flaws in the plan as it affects higher, let alone secondary, education.

One is practical. Even present high tuition fails to meet the operating costs of reputable schools and colleges. Hence, merely providing more students will not solve—and may even intensify—their long-term financial problems. Many schools and colleges would view tax credits for students merely as an opportunity to raise tuition even further to close their budget gaps. Unless tax credits also were to escalate, the students' relief would prove short-lived. A tax credit, more likely, would produce a windfall for low-quality institutions that profit from enrollees by using a bargain-basement approach.

A second flaw is more fundamental. Senators Moynihan and Packwood have won the support of 41 Senate colleagues with the tantalizing argument that it is unfair to ask those who choose private schools and colleges to pay tuition as well as taxes to support public institutions. This reimbursement of people who do not use public services is a dangerous idea. Should there be a tax break for the citizen who prefers to ride in a taxi or limousine rather than on public transportation? Should people with spacious backyards be reimbursed for their support of the public parks they do not frequent?

Fortunately, the Packwood-Moynihan approach is not the only alternative to the educational disenfranchisement of the middle class. There is an existing system of basic opportunity grants, entitling students to subsidies based on family income, and it need only be raised to bring instant relief to middle-income families whose plight rightly worries the Senators. At the same time, the institutions' budgetary dilemma could be eased by paying them the "cost-of-education" grants which originally were to accompany every federally subsidized student. The Higher Education Act of 1972 authorized such payments, but Congress, short-sightedly, has never funded them although they seem well designed to halt the tuition spiral by shoring up institutional budgets.

The annual cost of the tax credit plan is estimated at $4.7 billion. That is a figure sufficient to inspire finding alternatives to the flawed Senate proposal.

—The *New York Times*[3]

2. Pick a controversial issue on which you feel strongly and construct a classical argument for or against it.

STRATEGIES OF ASSERTIVE ARGUMENTATION

An *assertive argument* differs from a classical argument not so much in kind as in emphasis. Whereas the audience for a conventional classical argument may be favorable, neutral, or opposed to the arguer's thesis, an assertive argument presupposes an antagonistic opponent. This assumption means that the writer will need to establish considerable rapport with the opposition before the points of the controversy are discussed.

But creating a climate of conciliation at the beginning of your argument does not mean that you must back down completely—to do so would be nonassertive and ineffective. Nor is it any more useful to take an overaggressive stance and subject your readers to a barrage of information and opinions that support only your side without taking the opposition into account. People who hold strong, emotional views often argue aggressively in the belief that if they present their opinions often enough, or loudly enough, or supported by enough good reasons, their audience will be compelled to recognize the truth of their assertions and be converted on the spot. You have only to try this tactic on a firm opponent of your views to recognize the antagonism and rigid resistance it can provoke, as in the following exchange:

A: Some portions of the Bible, like the Creation, are meant to be interpreted figuratively.

B: No, they're not. The literal interpretation is the only true one. And that's final!

As an assertive writer, you will try to promote an understanding of your opinions and present your point of view without making your readers angry.

To do this you should show your readers that you understand their perspective and encourage them to do the same for you. The goal is to create both a climate of understanding and a strong, logical case that will win the audience to your side, or at least make them receptive to a compromise. Remember, a good assertive argument, like assertiveness in other kinds of behavior, is the golden mean between nonassertive capitulation—no argument at all—on the one hand, and the extreme of aggressive argument, on the other.[4]

The strategies of assertive argumentation discussed here should enable you not only to communicate your points effectively but to improve your relations with your opponents. They should appreciate the thoughtful attention to their views, even while you are arguing with them. Likewise, you can apply what you have learned as an assertive writer in self-defense when you're the target of the techniques of the hard (or soft) sell, whether in the written or spoken pitches of the salesperson, the advertiser, the politician, or others with a mission.

The Format for an Assertive Argument

Below is a checklist that provides a model for assertive argumentative writing. Before you begin, ask yourself the same questions that you asked in developing the conventional classical argument (see above). Pay particular attention to number 3, "What do I have to establish so my readers will believe my points?" and to number 7, "What would opponents say about this? What arguments and what evidence can I use to counter their opposition?" You'll also want to consider an additional question, "What concessions to my opponents' views should I make?" (You may find that you want to acknowledge the facts your opponents cite but to disagree with their interpretations of them.) To strengthen your rapport with the audience, remember that you must include your concessions near the beginning of your argument.

☐ A Checklist for Writing an Assertive Argument

☐ *Specify the topic of your discussion at the outset.* However, if your thesis is controversial, or possibly objectionable to your intended readers, you may wish to defer a direct expression of it until later when you have prepared your audience.

☐ *Demonstrate at or near the beginning of the essay that you understand the opposing position(s), and show what you find of value in these views.* Acknowledge your readers' opinions on the issues, their preferences and prejudices, by summarizing the principal points they would be likely to make in opposition to yours, even if these would appear to contradict or undermine your own arguments. Let readers know that you recognize the basis of their reasoning, whether it be commitment to a particular philosophy or tradition, or a concern for morals, ethics, values, or laws.

☐ *Show where you and the opposition agree, and why.* Include the points of agreement early in the discussion. You may even intermingle these with your acknowledgment of the merits of contradictory views. Certainly you will want to maintain, as far as possible, the meeting of the minds that you have tried to establish from the outset. As much as the first third of the essay may concentrate on acknowledging matters of common concern and in conceding some points to the opposition.

☐ *Then specify your own opinion. Show why it differs from the opposition in significant ways and demonstrate that it merits serious consideration.* State your own opinions, accommodating, as far as possible, the objections of prospective readers and information contrary to your views. Specify on your own behalf, as you did for your opponents earlier, the moral, ethical, legal, or other bases for your views. Support your points with relevant facts and illustrations. Your attack, if any, should be directed against ideas and issues rather than against your opponents personally. This is a block format (see pp. 82–85); you could also use point-by-point organization, as Ebel does in the essay that follows.

You may want, in this assertive format, to begin your own argument with a fairly nonthreatening point or an objection of low intensity and build toward more controversial points as your argument gains momentum. An easy way to tell which are the least controversial points and which are the most debatable is to see which points require the most development. The more evidence it takes to make a point, the more likely it is either to be unfamiliar to readers, or to be uncongenial, or both. This is especially true if strangeness provokes resistance—and it often does. Remember how people laughed—for a while—at Henry Ford's Model T. So the most highly debatable points will be the most fully developed and will probably come last.

☐ *Finally, provide the conclusion, which will be a statement of the best solution to the problem, some other indication of what ought to be done, or a resolution of the issue under debate.* If you can sincerely reconcile opposing viewpoints, so much the better. If you can't, simply express your conclusion forthrightly.

Analyzing an Assertive Argument

In "Standardized Tests: They Reflect the Real World" Professor Robert Ebel (for six years vice-president of the Educational Testing Service) refutes the arguments offered by Taylor and Lazarus in "Standardized Tests: They Don't Measure Learning" (quoted above as an example of a classical argument). Ebel uses an assertive format, with some variations.

1   Are standardized tests headed for extinction? To judge from news reports, magazine articles and some popular books the answer might seem to be yes. A variety of charges have been laid against them, and there is substance to some. But the

effects are neither so overpowering nor so harmful as the critics imply. On balance the case for standardized tests is persuasive.

2   A common accusation is that some pupils have, and others lack, a special talent for taking tests and that tests end up measuring this ability rather than academic achievements. Only on a carelessly or ineptly constructed test, though, can a pupil inflate his score by special test savvy. Most widely used standardized tests have been constructed carefully by experts. Unfamiliarity with the item types or response modes employed in a standardized test can indeed handicap a naïve examinee. But that kind of naïveté can be removed quite easily by careful instructions and practice exercises.

3   Bear in mind that the test score reports only the level of knowledge the pupil possesses, not how frequently or how effectively he makes use of it. It reports what the pupil can do, not what he typically does. What a pupil does and how well he does it, depends not on his knowledge alone. It depends also on his energy, ambition, determination, adroitness, likableness and luck among other things. A pupil's knowledge as measured by a standardized or any other test is one ingredient—but only one—of his potential success in life.

4   The simplicity with which answers to multiple-choice questions can be recorded on an answer sheet, and the objectivity and speed with which correct answers can be detected and counted by modern scoring machines, offends some devotees of the other common type of examination, the written essay. They confuse the simplicity of the process of recording an answer with the complexity of the process of figuring it out. Some of them charge that multiple-choice questions test only rote learning, or superficial factual information. That is clearly not true. Consider this question [complex example omitted] : . . .

5   Multiple-choice questions can be trivial or irrelevant. They need not be.

6   Critics of tests and testing sometimes provide examples of questions that seem to be ridiculously trivial or impossibly ambiguous. In some cases their criticisms are justified. Bad questions have been written and published. But few of these come from professionally constructed standardized tests of achievement. In other cases the criticism is not justified. The objection is based on a possible but unlikely interpretation different from the clearly intended sense of the question. One who sets out to discover how a question might conceivably be misconstrued is likely to find some way to misconstrue it. Language, after all, is not a flawless means for the precise communication of thought.

7   Another charge is that standardized testing harms children. It is said that the tests threaten and upset pupils, that if a pupil gets a low score he will be seriously damaged and that standardized testing is incompatible with educational procedures designed to support the child.

8   There is, no doubt, anecdotal evidence to support some of these claims. However, common sense suggests that the majority of pupils are not harmed by testing, and as far as I know there is no substantial survey data that would contradict common sense on this matter. The teachers I talk with seem much more often to be concerned with pupils who don't care enough how well or how poorly they do on such tests, than with the relatively rare instances of pupils who care too much.

9   It is normal and biologically helpful to be somewhat anxious when facing any real test, regardless of one's age. But it is also a necessary part of growing up to learn to cope with the tests that life inevitably brings. Of the many challenges to a child's peace of mind, caused by such things as angry parents, playground bullies,

bad dogs and shots from the doctor, standardized tests must surely be among the least fearsome. . . .

10   It is sometimes charged that tests distort school curriculums by causing schools to teach to the tests and by thus hampering curricular innovation.

11   A school that is teaching what the tests test will surely teach many other things besides. Even in the basic areas that the test does sample, there will be time and cause to venture into areas of learning not covered by the standardized tests. Standardized tests can dominate local curriculums only to the extent that school administrators and school teachers allow them to.

12   There are, of course, some programs of open education that are satisfied merely with maximum pupil freedom, trusting nature alone to do what others employ the art and science of teaching to help nature do. To say that standardized tests of achievement are inappropriate for such programs may imply more criticism of the programs than of the tests.

13   Standardized tests are also charged with encouraging harmful comparisons of one pupil with another. Let a pupil measure his achievements against his potential, or against his own past performance, say the critics, not against his classmates.

14   I believe they are wrong. What they should criticize is unwise reactions to comparison, not comparison itself. For those who are interested in excellent education find it difficult to believe that comparisons of educational achievement are irrelevant or unnecessary. No proud parent believes it. No capable teacher believes it. It simply is not true.

15   The only basis for judging a human performance excellent, acceptable, or inferior is in comparison with other human performances. The only basis for setting reasonably attainable objectives for pupil learning is knowledge of what similar pupils have been able to learn. Of course it is good for a pupil to compare his present performance with his own past performance. But that is no substitute for comparing his present performance with the present performances of his classmates. Surely it is cold comfort to a pupil when his arithmetic teacher says, "For you, five out of ten is quite good."

16   Only in some eyes have tests lost favor. Quite clearly they are not headed for extinction. They are much too useful to the competent, concerned educator. They are much too essential to the pursuit of excellence in education.[5]

Whether or not Ebel is replying directly to "Standardized Tests: They Don't Measure Learning," his essay *demonstrates a thorough familiarity with the opposing arguments*. Indeed, Ebel's first paragraph concedes that "there is substance" to some of the charges "laid against the tests" before stating his thesis: "On balance the case for standardized tests is persuasive."

Ebel then devotes the next six paragraphs (2–7)—about two-fifths of the argument—to identifying the opposition's specific objections to standardized testing. Essentially, these are the main arguments of Taylor and Lazarus (compare the article quoted above). *As he specifies each objection he offers an alternative explanation* for the problem; this in every case shifts the blame or responsibility for performance away from the good, standardized tests and onto other factors. For instance, to the argument in paragraph 2 that tests measure the pupil's ability to take tests "rather than academic achievements" Ebel makes a *partial concession*. This is true but "only on a carelessly or ineptly constructed test." Ebel counters that naive test takers can "quite easily" learn to take the high quality standardized tests constructed carefully by experts—an *argument from authority*, both the test makers' and the author's.

In paragraph 6 Ebel, continuing assertively, agrees with the opposition that some of the criticisms of "ridiculously trivial or impossibly ambiguous" test questions are justified. He then condemns the sorts of tests on which such questions appear—again siding with his opponents. Then he tries to refute another of the critics' objections, that some test questions can be misinterpreted, with the *generalization* that "Language, after all, is not a flawless means for the precise communication of thought." Because the generalization is true, however, does not excuse test makers from the obligation to write clear, unambiguous questions, he says.

By paragraph 8, halfway through the essay, *Ebel shifts to presenting a higher proportion of his own opinions, with supporting evidence.* The opposition, though still acknowledged, receives less emphasis than it did in the earlier part of the essay. In paragraph 8, for example, Ebel replies to the charge in paragraph 7 that "tests threaten and upset pupils" by conceding that there is "anecdotal evidence to support some of these claims." He *counters these anecdotes* (deliberately left imprecise and unspecified) with an explanation that combines *"common sense,"* an *allusion to research evidence* (also not specified here, perhaps because the essay is written for a nontechnical audience), and *first-hand reports from teachers,* who much more often encounter indifferent pupils than pupils who care too much.

He follows a similar method of arguing in paragraphs 9 to 15, ending his line of reasoning with *two strong generalizations and an assertion of a certainty:* "For those who are interested in excellent education find it difficult to believe that comparisons of educational achievement are irrelevant or unnecessary. *No proud parent believes it. No capable teacher believes it. It simply is not true"* [italics added]. The carefully chosen adjectives of praise *"proud* parent," *"capable* teacher" damn by implication those parents and teachers who do oppose comparisons of pupils by test scores—they are neither proud nor competent.

Ebel concludes with a defense of his philosophy that "The only basis for judging a human performance . . . is in comparison with other human performances." Even here Ebel is careful to accommodate the opposition's view: "Only in some eyes have tests lost favor," before again asserting his claim that "Quite clearly standardized tests are not headed for extinction." His concluding remarks strongly imply the solution to the controversy: standardized tests ought to be retained because "They are much too essential for the pursuit of excellence in education."

SUGGESTIONS FOR DISCUSSION AND WRITING

1. Although the Bakke case itself has been resolved by the Supreme Court, similar cases continue to appear on the court dockets, and the issues Bakke raised remain relevant. Analyze Jake McCarthy's " 'White Rights' Case" as an example of an assertive argument. Where does he acknowledge the merits of the opposition? How

much space/emphasis does he devote to this? Where does he make his own views apparent? How much space and what kinds of evidence does he devote to his viewpoint? Which side is most convincing on the basis of the arguments presented here?

"WHITE RIGHTS" CASE

The "white rights" case argued before the United States Supreme Court last week finds a lot of liberals on the fence, trying to keep their balance, because, of course, a liberal can't be against white rights either, can he?

So the Allan Bakke case has become the most delicate to face the Supreme Court since abortion and the death penalty. Its ruling could affect the course of what we call minority opportunity in America for the rest of the Republic's history.

Basically, if all the furor has become boring to you, the case involves the claim by a white man that he was denied admission to the University of California at Davis medical school because the school had reserved a certain number of spaces for minority people who, he alleged, were less qualified than he. So he thought he was unfairly discriminated against, and the California Supreme Court agreed with him. The U.S. Supreme Court agreed to try to resolve the question.

One of the side issues turns on the notion of "quotas," a hated word in discriminatory history, since the concept was used for decades to keep so-called minorities in their place. That explains why some liberal groups, as they once were known, are on the side of Bakke. Others are pleading that it is not a matter of quotas but of "affirmative action" in hiring or admitting minorities to privileged things like jobs, schools and professions.

I know some non-discriminatory people who are tortured by the Bakke case, and it isn't an easy question within our tradition, I'll grant. For one thing, I can feel for white, middle-aged males who can't find work in their expected occupations any more because managers and administrators have to do a better job of letting blacks and other racial groups into the economic and professional mainstream. Oh yes, and women.

For the Bakke case is not about "white rights" but about "white male rights." More specifically, the rights of upper- and middle-class white males. And since America's founding, those were traditionally the only rights enshrined in law and custom, despite the Constitution.

So we came to a point in time where conscience and consciousness—prodded by movements—said we ought to have redress of past wrongs. The phrase, "affirmative action," in hiring and admission policies became the euphemism for opening the opportunity doors to those oppressed by the exclusions of the past. Its use was meant to avert the concept of the hated and once-oppressive "quota" notion, and it was meant to correct a blatantly unconstitutional condition (and for ethicians, an immoral one) by "catching up."

After all, we had given lip service for so long to so many hallowed phrases. All men are created equal. Liberty and justice for all. Equal justice under the law. Equal opportunity. God-given rights. But nearly everybody knew the words were as hollow as they were hallowed.

It is a hard notion for some that a present generation of white men should have their traditional privileges circumscribed by a national repentance. But sons must sometimes pay for the sins of their fathers. And if we are truly to reach the constitutional dream of a pluralistic and egalitarian society in America, it seems to me that white males are the ones who owe restitution.

The irony is that white males are themselves, in fact, a minority of the whole population—although likely a majority of the voters and certainly of lawmakers. This suggests that all along we have not been talking about minority rights but about the power and privilege of an elite racial gender in our society. Women and non-white males were only expected to serve them.

How else can we be true to our constitutional ideals—if we really believe them—than to reverse this historic injustice and go on with the business of opening more and more doors to the servant class? If the white male minority some day were to be thus oppressed, it would be time enough for a future Bakke to seek his own redress. But I doubt we will ever get to that place.

—St. Louis *Post-Dispatch*[6]

2. Pick a controversial issue on which you and many other people feel strongly. Construct an assertive argument for it that fully accommodates your opponents' views and attempts to mitigate the force of their opposition.

CAUSE-AND-EFFECT ARGUMENTS

Many types of arguments, classical and assertive included, incorporate a discussion of causes and effects. Indeed, the Taylor and Lazarus argument against standardized testing discusses the allegedly bad effects of such tests, while Ebel's argument in part explains the bad effects by demonstrating bad causes. However, arguments that concentrate heavily on cause and effect often proceed somewhat differently from the conventional classical argument, because they are less concerned with directly refuting an opponent than they are with demonstrating either the causes or the effects (or both) of a phenomenon.

The three most common relationships (and consequently the three most common organizational patterns) demonstrated in cause-and-effect arguments are discussed in Chapter 4. One common pattern is to demonstrate an event or chain of events initiated by the first cause: cause A produces effect B, which in turn causes effect C, which leads to effect D, and so on. Another cause-and-effect pattern shows that a single cause (H) produces multiple, possibly concurrent, effects (I, J, K, L, M), which may, if the argument is extremely drawn out, produce still other effects. Still another pattern explores the multiple causes of a single effect: Q, R, S, T, and U produce V.

These patterns are deceptively simple. Cause-and-effect arguments are particularly difficult to deal with because of the complexity of causes and effects and the problems in sorting out which are related to which, and which are related to other factors not considered in the original hypothesis. For instance, just because two events always appear in sequence doesn't mean that the first necessarily causes the second. The observable fact that the late evening news on TV is always followed by five hours of test patterns doesn't mean that the news program causes or even influences the test patterns. In fact, each has independent causes not related to their sequence.

The more complicated the issue, the more tempting it is to oversimplify cause-and-effect relationships. However, it is dangerous to do so. The most obvious cause is often not the only cause or even the direct cause. Also, in oversimplifying the analysis of a phenomenon that has multiple causes, it is easy to leave out a step or two in the cause-and-effect sequence by considering some causes but not others that might be equally important. For instance, if you were trying to demonstrate that "Watching violent TV programs causes children to behave violently," it would be difficult to identify all the causes—and equally difficult to explain all the effects. Even if you could show that a given group—or random sample—of children behaved more violently after watching violence on television than before, it would be hard to determine whether TV watching and *only* TV watching influenced their behavior significantly. Maybe the violent children were incited by other causes that your argument hadn't accounted for—the behavior of their parents or other children; the reading of violent literature; pressure from a violent peer group. And what about the children exposed to the same TV programs who remained peaceable afterward? Might they be temperamentally more placid? or pacifistic because of religious views? influenced by their nonviolent parents, peers, or community? And so it goes. How broad do you make your search for causes, and where do you stop?

Developing, Organizing, and Evaluating a Cause-and-Effect Argument

Despite the difficulties inherent in constructing a clear, accurate, and reasonably complete cause-and-effect argument, it can be done. Consideration of the following questions will help you develop your materials, provide a pattern of organization, and reveal where the problems in your argument lie. Once the argument is underway, you will be able to decide whether you need to supply more evidence, restructure your argument to make it more accurate, or, as a last resort, abandon it, if you should discover you are trying to argue an impossible case.

1. When the alleged cause (C) is present, is the effect (E) always present?
2. When the alleged cause is absent, is the effect always absent?
3. When the alleged cause increases (or decreases), does the effect always increase (or decrease)?
   a. How strong is the association between cause and effect?
   b. How consistent is the association between cause and effect?
   c. Does the alleged cause always (or regularly) precede the effect?
   d. How specific (and exclusive) is the association between the alleged cause and the effect?
   e. Is the available information concerning the alleged cause and effect congruent with other existing knowledge of the issue?
4. Could an alternative hypothesis explain the presumed cause-and-effect relationship more satisfactorily than does the hypothesis under consideration?

Ideally, you would like emphatic "yes" answers to the first three questions and a firm "no" to the fourth. However, in real life, issues are rarely that clear-cut. You'll still have a good argument even if you answer, "No, not always, but more often than would be expected by chance" to the first two questions; "yes" to the third; and "no," even if somewhat qualified, to the fourth.

Imagine, for instance, that you are trying to argue that "cigarette smoking causes lung cancer," and you develop your argument according to the above questions.

The first consideration might be, When cigarette smoking (Cause) is present, is lung cancer (Effect) always present? No, some cigarette smokers don't develop lung cancer. But lung cancer occurs in a significantly higher proportion of cigarette smokers than among nonsmokers, well beyond what chance would allow. The death rates from lung cancer are three times higher for smokers than for nonsmokers.[7]

Next, you could raise the question, When cigarette smoking (C) is absent, is lung cancer (E) always absent? No, some nonsmokers develop lung cancer, but in a significantly lower proportion than do smokers, well beyond what chance would allow. The converse of the figures cited in point 1 would apply here.

An equally significant issue is, When the amount of cigarette smoking (C) increases, does lung cancer (E) increase? Yes—and here's the important point—it *always* does, according to the following criteria.

How strong is the association? The stronger the presumed cause, the greater the effect should be. In three major studies evaluated by biomedical experts in the Surgeon General's Report on Smoking and Health (1964), the death rates from lung cancer increased with each successive increase in the amount smoked. Two of the studies showed the mortality rate for heavy smokers to be twenty times that of nonsmokers; the third showed it to be forty times higher.

How consistent is the association? The more consistently the presumed cause produces the effect, the more likely the cause is to be genuine. Diverse studies in several countries verify the United States data cited above.

In studies that examined past evidence, people with and without lung cancer were identified, matched on various factors (age, sex, etc.), and their smoking histories compared. In studies that examined phenomena occurring while the research was in progress, large numbers of comparable groups were "classified with respect to their smoking habits and then followed over time to observe the occurrence of lung cancer and other diseases."[8] All of this research corroborated the findings cited above.

Does the alleged cause always (or regularly) precede the effect? The answer to this should always be positive, and in the case of the causal relationship between smoking and lung cancer, the various aspects of the cause regularly precede the effect. Carcinogens take a long time to cause cancer. Young smokers have a much lower rate of lung cancer than do older smokers. Light smokers (less than a pack a day) who quit develop cancer less often than do heavy smokers who quit. There are high death rates from lung cancer among the latter for years after they've quit smoking, but their death rate is nevertheless lower than that for heavy smokers who never quit.[9]

How specific (and exclusive) is the association between the alleged cause and the effect? The more specific and exclusive, the stronger the likelihood of a causal relationship. Tobacco smoke contains a variety of carcinogens, as well as carbon monoxide and other toxic ingredients; could these different components produce different diseases in addition to lung cancer? Although smoking is in fact associated with a variety of diseases, the difference in the death rate from lung cancer in smokers and nonsmokers far exceeds that for any other condition. For instance, the ratio in lung cancer is 10:1, whereas smokers die of coronary heart disease only 1.7 times more frequently than do nonsmokers.[10] It is true that some nonsmokers also develop lung cancer (presumably from inhaling other airborne carcinogens, including the "borrowed" smoke of smokers), but at a rate far below that of smokers.

Is the available information concerning the alleged cause and effect congruent with other existing knowledge of the issue? Again, the answer should be a consistent "yes." This is true with cigarette smoking. Cigarette smoke contains various carcinogens; inhalation brings these into intimate contact with the lung tissues, which undergo many more bizarre cell changes than do the lung tissues of nonsmokers. Furthermore, a marked increase in cigarette smoking among men was followed thirty years later by proportionately more lung cancer deaths. As women's smoking has increased, so their death rate from lung cancer has risen proportionately."[11]

Another significant question is whether an alternative hypothesis could explain the relationship between cigarette smoking and lung cancer more satisfactorily than the causal relationship postulated between the two. The answer to this is a strong "no," with one qualifier. Opponents of the cigarette hypothesis suggest that there might be constitutional differences between smokers and nonsmokers that would explain the apparent effects of cigarette smoking. The only indisputable way to test the alternative hypothesis is to experiment with human beings. Since such experimentation could cause disease or death, it is unethical and would not be performed. Nevertheless, the constitutional hypothesis is contradicted, though not absolutely disproved, by massive research evidence from major studies over extended periods. This consistently supports the original hypothesis strongly enough to warrant the firm conclusion that cigarette smoking causes lung cancer.[12]

When the total authoritative evidence you can find enables you to answer the four questions in the ways suggested here, you may be reasonably assured that you have constructed an argument that will satisfy and convince your readers. Of course, this is not a 100 percent guarantee that the cause under consideration produces the effect you hypothesize, but it's as close as you can be expected to come.

SUGGESTIONS FOR DISCUSSION AND WRITING

1. Analyze the *Declaration of Independence* (you should be able to find a copy in a history or literature textbook) as an argument, in terms of assertions, evidence presented, organization, and tone. What was its intended effect on the American colonists? Did Jefferson assess their mood and their desires accurately? What was its intended effect on the King of England and royal officials? Are these people Jefferson's intended audience?
2. Find a cause-and-effect argument. Evaluate it according to the questions on p. 299 and according to the generalizations about effective argumentation made in the preceding chapter. If you find the reasoning of your chosen argument deficient, rewrite the problem portions to improve them.
3. Write a cause-and-effect argument following the criteria identified in this chapter. Or write a scientific report (see pp. 245–250), making sure that you thoroughly account for the alleged causes of the effects you've discovered.

ARGUMENT BY ANALOGY

An analogy (see below) may be used either as the basis of an argument or as reinforcement for one. An argument by analogy, direct or indirect, says or implies that because A and B share qualities Q, R, and S, they probably also share quality T. We can deduce that because a given phenomenon applies to A, it will also apply to B. (Or, because A produces certain effects, so will B. And so on.)

The more closely that A in fact resembles B in *significant* and *relevant* ways, the more likely is the analogy to be a logical and convincing argument. The most appropriate circumstances in which to argue by analogy are when your readers can already be expected to know—and accept—your interpretation of one half of the comparison. They, therefore, can be assumed to be predisposed to accept your viewpoint of the other half of the analogy.

Formulating an argument by analogy will be made easier if you try to answer the following questions first:

1. What qualities does A have in common with B?
2. As a consequence of these similarities, what other qualities are A and B likely to share? If A produces a given effect, is B likely to do so, too?
3. How significant are these points of comparison?
4. How relevant are these points of comparison to what I'm trying to demonstrate?
5. Are there any significant dissimilarities between A and B that have to be accounted for? or that would discredit my argument?
6. At what point must I stop the comparison before it goes astray?
7. How familiar can my readers be assumed to be with one or both halves of the analogy? How much or how little background information do I need to supply to enable them to follow and accept the analogy?
8. To what extent can I count on my readers to be predisposed to favor the half of the argument they already know about?
9. What information and evidence do I need to provide to encourage my readers to accept each half of the comparison?

An argument by analogy can be organized point-by-point, comparing A_1 with B_1, A_2 with B_2, and so on until the valid points of comparison are exhausted and no more inferences can be drawn. Or you can describe part A in a block before describing part B and then compare them (see below). The following analysis provides an example of how to apply the above considerations.

Analyzing an Argument by Analogy

Arguments by analogy can constitute whole essays in themselves, or brief arguments by analogy can be inserted into other types of arguments. A single essay may employ several different analogies during the course of an extended argument. Consider, for example, columnist Russell Baker's uses of analogy in "Nobody Sues About a Fullback," where a number of analogies become arguments for his thesis that because "a college is a community with needs that cannot be met if membership is granted solely on grounds of academic performance," flexible admissions policies should promote diversity—racial, intellectual, and otherwise.

1   Even the fanciest colleges employ some sort of quota system when deciding who shall be admitted and who turned away. The admission office usually recognizes, for example, that the college needs some heavily muscled young men who can play football and a few extremely tall young men who can play basketball.

If the band's tuba player has just been graduated, the admissions office will be sensitive to the need for a replacement. If the campus has become dense with bookish drones, the admissions people may sense a need to take on a leavening detachment of not-too-bookish hell-raisers; and if the student body is heavily populated with Eastern city youths, the college may choose to take an infusion of youngsters from Midwestern farms.

2   It makes for little boiling of the blood when an applicant with straight A's in high school is passed over for a promising fullback who will obviously have to settle for the gentleman's C. At least nobody has yet gone to law claiming he has been discriminated against because a college for which he was academically qualified rejected him in favor of a football player with lower grades.

The assumption at the admissions office is that the college is a community with needs that cannot be met if membership is granted solely on grounds of academic performance. The health of the community is assumed to require a diversity unobtainable if ability to achieve high grades is the only requirement for membership.

3   This is the principle underlying the controversial programs of "affirmative action," or "reverse discrimination" as they are called by their detractors. As a healthy college community requires diversity, so does a healthy national community. If blacks are excluded because every available opening has an applicant white with better grades, the result is not diversity but an ailing community divided by color.

4   The celebrated Bakke case now before the Supreme Court poses an unfortunate attempt to deal with this extremely subtle issue by using the blunt instrument of law. Mr. Bakke, a white, argues that he was the victim of unconstitutional racial discrimination when a California medical school denied him admission because

school policy reserved 16 places for blacks, without regard to the possibility that their academic records might be inferior to his.

5   It is a delicate affair only because of the race issue. Had Mr. Bakke failed of admission to undergraduate school because the admission office chose to admit 16 academically inferior football players, there would be very little ado in the courts. The right of the college to look after its communal health by creating a diversified student body is generally presumed to transcend any injustice to students who do not get in.

6   The obligation of professional schools to look to the health of the national community they serve is also acknowledged and, indeed, insisted upon by those who argue that the best doctors are most likely to develop from the best qualified applicants to medical schools.

This view, of course, clashes with the proposition that the professional school's obligation to the health of the national community extends to enlarging the diversity of people participating in it. In fact, because of the highly limited number of places in medical schools and because of the generally superior educational facilities available to young whites, medicine tends to be perpetuated as a segregated white profession.

7   Most arguments on both sides of this issue make the error of meeting the question head-on. Proponents of greater diversity insist on the troublesome argument that blacks are entitled to preference in compensation for past discrimination at the hands of whites, an argument whose defect is that it assumes the innocent should suffer for the crimes of their fathers.

Those opposed to "affirmative action" contend that it requires repugnant racial quotas of the very sort the civil rights movement fought for decades to destroy and, so, violates the dictum that the Constitution be color blind. This is a persuasive legal argument, but it ignores the question whether the Constitution must be so color blind that it cannot see racial inequities that erode the nation's health.

Finally, the administrators of "affirmative action" have endangered their own programs with an excessive zeal for inflexible quotas. To fix constant percentages of "disadvantaged blacks" which must be admitted annually to, say, medical schools is to invite legal disaster and even absurdities, such as—in a grotesque reversal of the old Dixie dispute—whether a white-toned man with a black great-grandmother can qualify for medical school as a black.

The sensible course would seem to be abandonment of fixed, unenforceable quotas and substitution of admissions policies aimed at promoting racial diversity but adjustable from year to year at the discretion of the individual school, much as undergraduate admission policies fluctuate for football players, trumpeters and bookworms.

Nobody will fault the argument that the country needs more black doctors. Too narrow a view of the Constitution may keep us from getting them. It is up to the schools to show the ingenuity necessary to produce them without a legal shipwreck.[13]

Baker's analogy proceeds in this manner. Colleges have quota systems for admissions in order to fill their specialized needs and to ensure diversity among students. For these reasons colleges may at times give preference to football players, basketball players, tuba players, "not-too-bookish hell-raisers," or "Midwestern farm youngsters" instead of prospective students with outstanding academic records. Yet when a straight-A applicant is passed over for a promising fullback with lower grades, nobody gets upset or sues the college.

Therefore, the same principles should apply to the colleges' quest for racial diversity among students, and people shouldn't complain: "The right of the college to look after its communal health by creating a diversified student body is generally presumed to transcend any injustice to students who do not get in." Admissions policies promoting racial diversity should be accommodating and flexible, "much as undergraduate admission policies fluctuate for football players, trumpeters and bookworms."

Note that although Baker's argument includes several analogies of implied or stated similarities between athletes, musicians, Midwesterners, blacks, and other groups that contribute to student diversity, analogies do not constitute his entire argument. Throughout the second half of the essay in particular, he supplements the argument by analogy with straightforward, logical interpretations of and commentary on the reasoning of the defenders of each side of the case in which Bakke, a white man, claimed that a medical school's establishment of a quota for black applicants was a form of "reverse discrimination" against him.

Baker's departure from analogy is sensible because most arguments by analogy cannot be carried to their ultimate limit. At some point, the dissimilarities between the two entities being compared will interfere with the likenesses. If this occurs too early in the argument, the matters under consideration may really be so unlike that the analogy will be rendered invalid. For instance, one writer said, "I want to raise my children like cooked eggs—not scrambled, not hard boiled, not fried—but sunny side up." This analogy innocently overlooks the eggs' ultimate fate—to be eaten, however prepared. Since the dissimilarities between child rearing and preparing eggs far outnumber the single point of comparison the author wants to make, the analogy is ineffective and inappropriate and should be dropped.

SUGGESTIONS FOR DISCUSSION AND WRITING

1. Evaluate the accuracy and appropriateness of the following arguments by analogy. If they include cause and effect, comment on that, too.
   a. We certainly don't need the ERA. Just look at what happened when women got the vote—they started smoking cigarettes, and the divorce rate went way up.
   b. No wonder Suzie's a whiz at math. So was her brother—and after all, her mother works for IBM.
   c. You'd love it here in Tucson. Ever since we moved here our family's allergies have disappeared.
   d. Emerging nations should be protectorates of larger, well-established countries. You wouldn't send an infant out into the world until she'd grown up and learned to be self-supporting, would you?
   e. The California Sequoia Redwoods are very much like the American Indians. Like the Indians, their numbers are now countable where once they were vast. Like the Indians, they were cut down to be used for white men's self-serving purposes. Like the Indians, the Sequoias are somehow viewed by the general populace as freaks of American wildlife, tourist sights, just as what is Indian is

now marketable and popularized by the mass media. But now these native trees are protected by law so they will not become extinct. The United States Government should do the same for these Native Americans.

2. Examine the evidence in the two essays on the Bakke case by Baker and McCarthy (see pp. 297–298 and 303–304), and determine which argument is stronger on the basis of the evidence. Is the argumentative strategy in either (Baker argues partly by analogy, McCarthy by assertive format) preferable to that in the other? If so, why? If not, why not?

3. Write an argument that includes one or more analogies as part of its method. Where did you put the analogies? Why? At what point did you stop them? Why?

ARGUMENT BY A SINGLE CASE

To construct an argument by using a single case as the central—or entire—example is implicitly to argue by analogy. In offering a single case, a single example or a group is treated as a unit to represent all other cases of its kind, though you talk only about the case at hand. Arguments in advertisements for charities do this when they tell the case history of an appealing waif (often accompanied by a photograph of the pathetically pretty—never ugly—child), concluding with an indication of how much the child was helped by donations to the charity in question. Another argument by analogy is implied in the same ads when the funds appear to have been contributed by someone just like—you guessed it— yourself, the intended reader. The appeals here are more likely to be emotional than logical, though in deciding whether or not to respond to them you can subject them to the same scrutiny that you would use in examining any argument.

In writing about a single case, you can *narrate* an incident in which the central character, perhaps yourself, learns something significant about himself or the way of the world and generalizes about it, implicitly or explicitly. This is the technique of various personal essayists, such as E. B. White and George Orwell. It is the technique, also, of fables or other stories with morals. "Don't count your chickens before they hatch" is intended to apply not only to other instances of eggs and chickens, but to all situations in which one's expectations have been disappointed—no matter how certain they may have seemed.

In similar fashion, an argument by single case can *describe* a typical day in the life of a notable individual or a representative of a group (a weaver, a poor person, a black, or a white South African, and so on), and use this description as the basis for generalizing about the group ("Blacks live unbearably restricted lives under apartheid in South Africa."). The generalization may in turn be used as the basis for an argument ("This is intolerable and ought to be stopped.").

Another way to make an argument by single case is through *analysis*, by presenting the results of a single case study or experiment in scientific research and drawing general conclusions from it. In all of these instances, the single case will usually be treated as a *symbol* of all others like it—even while you deal with it individually.

A single case may be memorable, interesting, and intrinsically significant, and therefore able to carry the thesis through its own strength or importance. However, there are dangers in arguing on the basis of a single case that should be obvious to you. Asking yourself the following questions of the case in point should help you avoid them and construct a successful argument:

1. Is the case sufficiently typical or representative to warrant the heavy load of generalization that I'm placing on it? Does it allow for exceptions? alternatives?
2. If it's atypical, will this be clear to the reader? If the case is atypical, can I generalize about it at all? to what extent?
3. Is the case presented in sufficient detail so the readers can understand its significance? its implications?
4. Are all the aspects of the case at hand relevant to the points I wish to make? If not, is the case suitable for my argument?
5. Can I demonstrate the truth of my argument convincingly on the basis of only a single example, or do I need to go beyond it?
6. Will my generalization (and thesis) be explicit? implicit? If the latter, have I made it clear?
7. Are my readers likely to agree with my generalizations? Even if they are, do I need to use additional representative evidence to make my case stronger? If they are not, what must I use to be convincing?

As a result of asking such questions you may conclude, as many authors do, that a single case is useful to introduce or to illustrate an argument, but that generalizing from it is likely to be too risky without additional supporting evidence. In these instances, you would be wise to incorporate the case into one of the other argumentative forms we have discussed in this chapter.

SUGGESTIONS FOR DISCUSSION AND WRITING

1. Here is a sample résumé of personal and professional qualifications that could be submitted to accompany an application for employment. Is it organized in a manner that adequately explains the relevant aspects of Mr. Budd's life to a prospective employer? Does it present Mr. Budd in a favorable light calculated to appeal to a particular sort of prospective employer? Does it contain anything that should be omitted? Is more information or detail needed in any of the categories?
2. Write a cover letter to accompany and interpret the above résumé. In this letter present the most convincing argument possible in favor of Mr. Budd as a prospective employee of the firm of your choice.
3. Construct a résumé for yourself along the principles and organizational pattern of of William Budd's résumé in *1*. Omit irrelevancies, such as short-term jobs that don't pertain to your preferred work or study (such as babysitting or pet-sitting, for example), hobbies, or your tastes in cultural activities and sports. Include bona fide materials that present you in favorable light, such as particular references to employers who knew and liked your work.
4. Write a cover letter to accompany your résumé, in order to present the most convincing argument possible in favor of yourself as a prospective employee of the firm of your choice. If you're actually looking for a job, mail your letter and résumé, once you've turned them in for an assignment and received comments from your instructor.

Qualifications (or Résumé) of William M. Budd

Home address:

72 Ocean Drive
New Bedford, MA 02118
tel. 617-422-5348

School address:

Halsey Barracks, Box 1776
U. S. Naval Academy
Annapolis, MD 21404

tel. 301-664-7279, ext. 4272

Date of Birth: July 4, 1962   Place of Birth: Hyannisport, MA, U. S. A.

Marital Status: Single   Health: Excellent; slight stutter when excited

Height: 5' 10"   Leisure interests: sailing, scuba diving, reading

Weight: 160 lb.

Education:

New Bedford High School, New Bedford, MA, 1976–1980 (diploma 6/80)

Webb Institute of Naval Architecture, 9/81–5/82 (freshman year)

U. S. Naval Academy, Sept. 1982–to present
(Enrolled in a B. S. program with emphasis on navigation, naval engineering,
computer mathematics, B. S. expected 6/85)

Experience

Experience related to professional objectives

June–Sept. 1979, Sailor, S. S. Bellipotent, berthed in Providence, RI,
    Captain S. T. Vere

June–Sept. 1980, Draftsman's assistant, Seven Seas Naval Architects, Boston, MA,
    Supervisor, F. L. Wright

Sept. 1980–Aug. 1981, Electronics system technician, Portsmouth Naval Shipyard,
    Kittery, ME, Supervisor, H. M. Melville
    Duties: To install and repair electronics equipment; to instruct new technicians
    and supervise their work

Experience–general:

Paperboy, New Bedford Courier, 1973–1976

Attendant, Revere's Midnite Riders Gas Station, 1976–1977

Busboy, waiter, House of Seven Gables, Salem, MA, prop. N. Hawthorne,
    Summer, 1977

References available from Vere, Wright, Melville, Hawthorne, at above establishments,
or from Student Employment Bureau
        U. S. Naval Academy
        Annapolis, MD 21404

NOTES

[1] Adapted from Richard L. Larson, "Discovery Through Questioning: A Plan for Teaching Rhetorical Invention," *College English* 30 (November 1968), 126–134.

[2] The *New York Times*, May 1, 1977, 12, pp. 1ff.

[3] The *New York Times*, October 11, 1977, A 18.

[4] See Lynn Z. Bloom, Karen Coburn, and Joan Pearlman, *The New Assertive Woman* (1975; rpt. New York: Dell, 1976).

[5] The *New York Times*, May 1, 1977, 12, pp. 1ff.

[6] The *New York Times*, October 17, 1977, A 3.

[7] Judith S. Mausher and Anita K. Bahn, "The Search for Causal Relations," *Epidemiology* (Philadelphia, Pa.: Saunders, 1974), pp. 103–108.

[8] Mausher and Bahn, p. 104.

[9] Mausher and Bahn, pp. 104–105.

[10] Mausher and Bahn, p. 105.

[11] Mausher and Bahn, pp. 106–107.

[12] Mausher and Bahn, pp. 107–108.

[13] The *New York Times*, October 15, 1977, A 23.

CHAPTER THIRTEEN
USING RESOURCES: TOOLS FOR STRATEGIES

And you shall know the truth, and the truth shall make you free.

—John 8:32

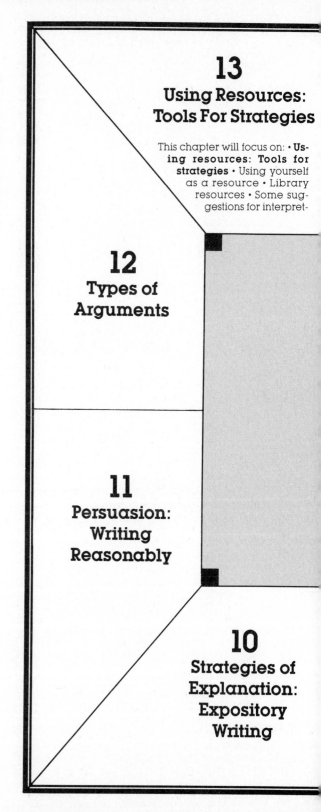

13
Using Resources: Tools For Strategies

This chapter will focus on: • **Using resources: Tools for strategies** • Using yourself as a resource • Library resources • Some suggestions for interpret-

12
Types of Arguments

11
Persuasion: Writing Reasonably

10
Strategies of Explanation: Expository Writing

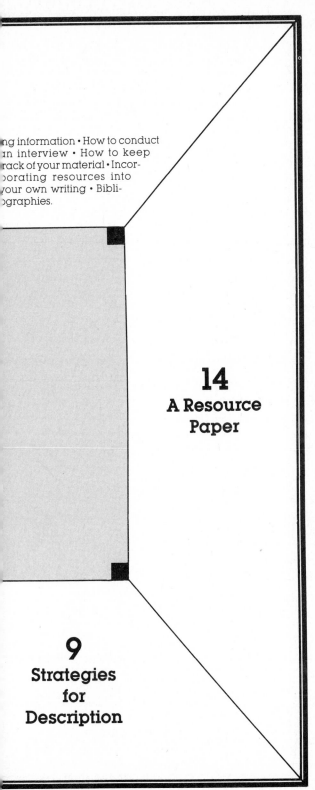

14

**A Resource
Paper**

9

**Strategies
for
Description**

USING YOURSELF
AS A RESOURCE

On many of the topics you write
about, you're your own best resource. If you're discussing a
personal experience, whether it's
being scared—or scarred—in an
automobile accident or falling in
or out of love or lingering over a
luscious piece of chocolate cake,
you know more about your own
experience than anyone else does.
You know what you thought, how
you reacted, how you felt, what
it meant at the time, and what
significance it has for you now.
Although other people may have
had comparable experiences (and
that's the basis for much of our
communication), you're the authority about your own.

Given the vast world of resources in which we live, it's
sometimes hard to know which to
choose to find information. Once
you have identified the issue
you're trying to address in your
writing, or the problem you're
trying to solve, you can think of
the possible range of resources
available on your subject. You can
choose them from among the following categories:

a. Yourself (you know more than you think you do!)
b. Your library
c. Your community—geographic, social, political, religious, intellectual, or other
d. Other people—with particular occupations, skills, interests, experiences, points of view
e. Any other category—the universe is infinite

Within each category is a range of many alternatives. Your general level of knowledge and what you're trying to write will help to determine whether you need to start with resources that are general and elementary or more sophisticated and complex. Remember that a good resource is seldom a dead end; one leads to another to another to a network.

As the problems change, so do the solutions; the resources that are suitable for one paper may not be appropriate for another. This chapter is intended to introduce you to some of the most common and generally useful resources among a universe of possibilities. Your instructor or employer or friends or your own curiosity can lead you to others.

You are also the source of much other information. You are, after all, the sum total of what you've learned, observed, and thought about throughout your entire lifetime. You've mastered various physical skills, from shoe tying to high diving; you've learned processes—how to make bread, how to solve quadratic equations; you know a multitude of facts useful (the chemical composition of salt) and perhaps useless (who acted King Kong). You know how to respond to various signs (the rising sun indicates daybreak), symbols (Red Cross), and gestures (a wink—and you know that the wink's meaning depends on the context—who's winking at whom under what circumstances). You know how to interpret a multitude of clues—indicating the condition of the weather, your health, your car, the stock market. In addition to what you've learned formally, in school or from reading, you're a genius of common sense—as you must be simply to survive in this complicated world.

What you already know, that bulging inventory of personal resources, will always help you in your writing. Often that will be all you'll need to write an interesting, memorable paper. But sooner or later you'll need to consult additional sources of information, particularly if you have a resource or reference paper to write. You will probably be consulting key resources or references from among the types discussed below.

LIBRARY RESOURCES

So much information is available from so many different sources that it's hard to know where to start looking or, for that matter, when to stop.

The most logical place to look is the library, and your best friends in the search for whatever materials you need will be librarians. Don't hesitate to ask them for help. Most libraries have introductory tours and pamphlets that explain their services. College and larger public libraries often have special librarians in charge of reference materials, periodicals, rare books, government documents, and other particular collections. Reference librarians can be particularly useful, for they know the resources of your library, your community, and the nation—and if material is not available locally they can help you get it elsewhere.

The Card Catalog

The card catalog is an alphabetical index to the printed materials in your library —books, periodicals, booklets, microfilms. Each item is usually cross-indexed in three ways: that is, it's listed on three separate cards, by author, by title, and by subject. The card catalogs of some libraries are now on microfiche (see p. 320), but the same information is available there.

Here are the cards for a representative item in a library that uses the Library

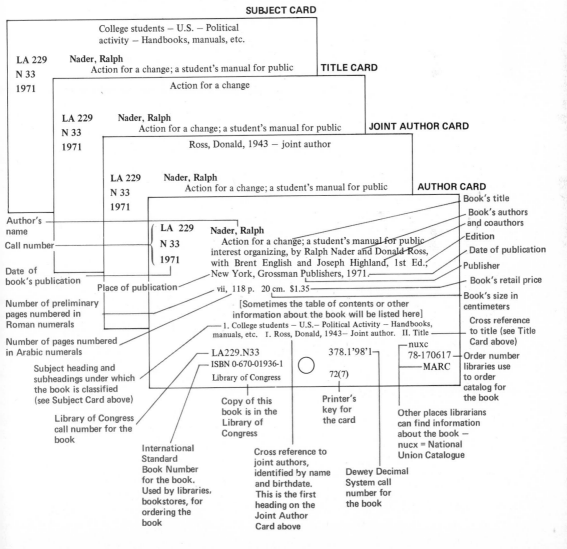

of Congress classification system. (All the material concealed by the overlapping cards in the illustration is identical.)

Various points of information on the card can help to tell you whether you'll actually want to look at the book.

1. *Author.* Is he or she known or unknown? an authority on the topic or not? Sometimes, organizations are listed as authors, such as "American Psychological Association," "Western Reserve Historical Society."
2. *Date of publication.* Is the book recent and therefore presumably up-to-date? old and of historic interest? outmoded? (Beware of reprint dates; they may make the information seem much more recent than it really is.)
3. *Edition.* First? most recent?
4. *Publisher.* University press (they usually publish authoritative, scholarly books)? reputable commercial publisher? private press? vanity press (which will publish anything the author pays for)?
5. *Length.* Too short to tell you enough? longer than you can manage?
6. *Table of contents* (if indicated). Does the book cover the topics on which you need information?
7. *Bibliography* (if indicated). If you can find two or three recent books with up-to-date annotated bibliographies on your subject, you're in luck. The annotations will help to tell you which additional sources are reliable. Books that appear on two or more bibliographies may be key works that you should consult.

If you know a book's author or title, you can go immediately to that card in the catalog. However, if you're exploring available materials on a topic, you'll want to consult *Library of Congress Subject Headings*, 2 vols. (Washington, D.C.: Library of Congress, 1975), before you look at the subject heading cards themselves. This lists most of the cross-reference headings under various key words and will give you some ideas on what subject headings to look for. Don't confine yourself to a single topic heading; it probably won't lead to all the available material central to that topic. For instance, if you're looking for references on *Utopias*, you'll find other subject headings listed under *Utopias: Exoticism in literature; Messianism; Paradise; Political Science; Socialism; Voyages, Imaginary; Utopias—Religious aspects.* If the key words you have in mind aren't listed, you'll have to think of alternatives. A librarian can help.

As you explore the card catalog, write the call number of each book you're looking for, its author, and a short version of the title on a slip of paper. Group them by call number. Then, before you head for the stacks (if your library has open stacks), you might want to stop at the circulation desk to find out whether the books you're seeking are actually on the shelves. Some books may be currently checked out, in a reference area or special collection, on reserve for a course, or if this information isn't on the card in the card catalog, the librarian can tell you where such books are.

How to Choose Reference Works

When you're looking for reference materials, either in bibliographies or on the library shelves, you will want to examine them for the features listed below that are relevant to your topic and your focus.

1. *How up-to-date is it?* The copyright date is one clue; that's usually listed on the back of the title page and preceded by a ©: "© 1982 by the Modern Language Association of America." The edition number (second, third, etc.) may also help to identify the age of the work. You will usually want to begin your quest with recent materials.

   However, old is not necessarily bad. Some senior citizens among reference works, like the Eleventh Edition of the *Encyclopaedia Britannica* (1910) may be valuable for their historical perspective, literary caliber, illustrations, or the author's or editor's point of view, even though some of their information may be outmoded. Other rare or antique volumes are simply interesting in their own right.

2. *How general or how specialized is the book—and what degree of specialization do you want?* For instance, does it discuss the history of world literature, or of British and American literature from Beowulf to modern times? Or does it discuss only twentieth-century British literature, or only modern Irish poetry, or just the poetry of William Butler Yeats, or only Yeats's poetry written 1914–1918? Is the coverage thorough or skimpy?

   It is often useful to seek an overview first from some general references. These can help you decide whether to consult more specialized works.

3. *How technical or nontechnical is the book—and what degree of technicality are you looking for?* One way to determine its technicality is to compare what it says on a given subject with your knowledge of the same topic. If you're an expert, and the book is still informative, then it may be quite technical.

   If you don't know much about the subject, does the reference begin with your level of knowledge—that is, does it explain the fundamentals before building on them for more advanced concepts? Does it use language a layperson can understand, or does it require a specialized, technical vocabulary?

4. *Is the volume accurate, as far as you can tell?* Does the author document the evidence with sources that seem reliable and that readers can check? If not, do the authors use suitable evidence and interpret it fairly?

5. *How easy is it to use?* Is it organized clearly, with conspicuous subject headings or other divisions? Does it have a comprehensive index? Does it have an introduction that identifies the book's scope and the principles according to which the materials are chosen, collected, and organized? Does the introduction identify the book's special features (such as maps, tables, graphs) and tell how to use them?

6. *Is the volume biased,* in the sense that it emphasizes one nationality, part of the world, race, sex, religion, or profession over equivalent alternatives? Bias in this sense of particular emphasis may be more an indication of point of view than a manifestation of prejudice. American histories of the world tend to point out accomplishments of American political and military leaders, and to see world events as they relate to the United States. British histories of the world focus on Britain, and so on. These emphases are appropriate for their

respective readers, who, nevertheless, need to recognize how such biases influence the selection and presentation of material. Many recent reference works are making special efforts to acknowledge women, blacks, Native Americans, Hispanics, and other minorities, neglected (perhaps unintentionally) in earlier volumes.

Each of the categories below includes a sampling of the standard reference works.

College or Desk Dictionaries

If you purchase only one reference book during your lifetime, it should be the latest edition of a good, comprehensive college dictionary. All of the volumes listed below are authoritative; they describe (not prescribe) and illustrate current usage. All have clear, accurate definitions, though they don't always agree with one another. They provide useful etymologies, synonyms, antonyms, charts and tables, illustrations, and various appendixes.

Random House College Dictionary, ed. Jess Stein, rev. ed. New York: Random House, 1975. Definitions are given in order of frequency. 170,000 entries (Based on The *Random House Dictionary of the English Language,* The Unabridged Edition, 1966, 1981).

American Heritage Dictionary of the English Language, ed. William Morris. Boston: Houghton Mifflin, 1980. Definitions list central meanings first. 155,000 entries. "Usage notes" on controversial locutions (*ain't, lie/lay*) indicate the opinions (including disagreements) of a panel of 100 experts. Abundant illustrations, including photographs.

Webster's New Collegiate Dictionary, ed. Henry Bosley Woolf, rev. ed., Springfield, Mass.: G. & C. Merriam, 1980. Based on *Webster's Third International Dictionary* (unabridged, see below). 150,000 entries, with an emphasis on "standard language." Has fewer slang words and informal usages then the *Random House* or *American Heritage Dictionaries.* Entries organized chronologically, with etymologies first, followed by oldest meanings. Biographical and geographical names are in separate appendixes.

Webster's New World Dictionary of the American Language, ed. David B. Guralnik, 2nd college ed. New York: World, 1975. Definitions arranged in chronological order, earliest meanings first. 158,000 entries.

Unabridged Dictionaries

Webster's Third New International Dictionary of the English Language, ed. Philip B. Gove. Springfield, Mass.: Merriam-Webster, 1961, 1976. The most extensive (400,000 words) and highly authoritative current dictionary of the American language; organized chronologically. Extensive etymologies. Abundant illustrations of words in context reflect the dictionary's controversial concept that current usage is preferable to an arbitrary standard of "correct" usage. Provides cultivated conversational pronunciations and regional pronunciations; omits biographical and geographical listings and other proper nouns.

Webster's New International Dictionary of the English Language, ed. William A. Neilson, 2nd ed. Springfield, Mass.: Merriam-Webster, 1934–1961. *Webster's II* is a necessary supplement to *Webster's III,* containing 600,000 words, including 150,000 obsolete, archaic, and rare words omitted in the third edition. Unlike *Webster's III*, the main text contains foreign words and phrases and fictional and other proper names, except those in the biographical and geographical appendixes. Favors educated standard English usage.

The Oxford English Dictionary, ed. James A. H. Murray et al. 10 vols. and supplements. Oxford: Clarendon Press, 1884–1928. Supplements, 1933, 1972, 1976. Usually known as the *OED*, "the greatest dictionary ever compiled for any language."[1] The *OED* shows the history of 415,000 words in the English language throughout the last 800 years, each described by variant spellings, etymology, pronunciation, and all of its meanings, including much slang. Extensive illustrative quotations (over 1,827,000) identified by date, author, and source. The *OED* is particularly useful in showing how and when the meanings of words have changed.

Specialized Dictionaries

Acronyms, Initialisms, and Abbreviations Dictionary, ed. Ellen T. Crowley, 5th ed. Detroit: Gale Research, 1976. Supplements in 1978, 1979.

Dictionary of Slang and Unconventional English, ed. Eric Partridge, 7th ed. New York: Macmillan, 1970.

McGraw-Hill Dictionary of Scientific and Technical Terms, ed. Daniel N. Lapedes, 2nd ed. New York: McGraw-Hill, 1976.

Oxford Classical Dictionary, ed. N. G. L. Hammond and H. H. Scullard, 2nd ed. Oxford: Oxford University Press, 1970.

There are hundreds of other specialized dictionaries.

General Encyclopedias

Encyclopedia Americana (International Edition), 30 vols. Danbury, Conn.: Grolier, 1978. Supplement: *Americana Annual*. Comprehensive range, mostly short articles.

Encyclopaedia Britannica, 15th ed., 30 vols. Chicago: Encyclopaedia Britannica, 1980. Supplement: *Britannica Book of the Year*. A mixture of long, authoritative articles in the *Macropaedia* (vols. 1–10), and short articles with bibliographies in the *Micropaedia* (vols. 11–19).

Chambers's Encyclopaedia, New revised (5th) ed., 15 vols. London: International Learning Systems, 1973. Supplement: *Encyclopaedia World Survey*. Short, scholarly articles for "the educated layman."

Biographical Directories

Biographical Dictionaries Master Index, ed. Dennis LaBeau and Gary Tarbett. 3 vols. Detroit: Gale Research, 1975. *First Supplement, 1979*. Start here to find out who's who and who's where. This identifies more than 800,000 prominent living persons (especially Americans) by name and birthdate and tells what other biographical directories to find their complete listings in.

Who's Who in America, 1899 to present date. Chicago: Marquis, 1899—present date. Brief entries about prominent living Americans. See also *Who's Who of American Women*, 1958—present date; and regional, national, and occupational volumes, such as *Who's Who in the Midwest*, *Who's Who in Modern China*, *Who's Who in Finance and Industry*.

Who's Who, 1849—present date. London: Black, 1849—present date. Brief data on prominent living British people.

Dictionary of American Biography [*DAB*], 22 vols. New York: Scribner's, 1928–1958. Rev. ed. 10 vols. and supplements, 1974. Long, scholarly articles about distinguished deceased Americans; bibliographies. The British equivalent is the multivolume *Dictionary of National Biography* [*DNB*].

There are also various reputable biographical directories organized according to profession, including *American Men and Women of Science, The Directory of American Scholars, Contemporary Authors,* and *Directory of Medical Specialists.*

Yearbooks and Almanacs

Published each year, these volumes contain relatively current collections of statistics and a wide variety of information, usually in abbreviated form.

Facts on File Yearbooks. Annual volumes. New York: Facts on File, 1941—present date. An American-oriented news digest, organized topically.

New York Times Encyclopedic Almanac. New York: The New York Times, 1970—present date. Comprehensive; based on the *New York Times* research materials.

Statistical Abstract of the United States. Washington, D.C.: U.S. Bureau of the Census, 1878—present date. An enormous compilation, and the basic source of American vital statistics: population figures; statistics on immigration, employment, industry, economics; and other aspects of U.S. political, social, and financial institutions.

Atlases and Gazeteers (Geographical Dictionaries)

Atlas of World Population History, by Colin McEvedy and Richard Jones. New York: Facts on File, 1978.

National Geographic Atlas of the World, 4th ed. Washington, D.C.: National Geographic Society, 1975.

Oxford Bible Atlas, ed. Herbert G. May and G. H. Hunt, 2nd ed. London: Oxford University Press, 1974.

Rand McNally Road Atlas of Europe. Chicago: Rand McNally, 1979.

Books of Quotations

These books of quotations make it possible to find multiple quotations on varied topics and subtopics, and also to identify the authors and sources of quotations.

Bartlett's Familiar Quotations, by John Bartlett, ed. Emily Morison Beck, 15th ed. rev. Boston: Little, Brown, 1980. Standard collection, arranged chronologically by author.

The Oxford Dictionary of English Proverbs, ed. William G. Smith and F. P. Wilson, 3rd ed. Oxford: Oxford University Press, 1970.

Guides to Reference Works

General Bibliographies

Accompanying the current explosion of information in every specialized field imaginable (from aardvarks to zoology) is an explosion of related reference materials—special encyclopedias, indexes, dictionaries, and others. We need bibliographies to organize these systematically, and to tell us of the scope, orientation, and potential usefulness of each work.

There are several particularly useful master bibliographies.

Sheehy, Eugene P. *Guide to Reference Books*, 9th ed. Chicago: American Library Association, 1976, and supplements. Arranged by subject; indicates the scope and significance of 10,000 reference works, general and specialized. American bias.

Besterman, Theodore. *A World Bibliography of Bibliographies*. 4th ed. 5 vols. Totowa, N.J.: Rowman-Littlefield, 1963. 117,000 independent bibliographical volumes, arranged by subject. *1964–1974*, compiled by Alice F. Toomey, 1977.

Subject Guide to Books in Print: An Index to the Publisher's Trade List Annual. New York: R. R. Bowker, 1957—present date. Companions: *Books in Print* (separate volumes arranged by author and title), 1948—present date; and *Paperbound Books in Print*, 1955—present date. These indicate what books are in print, the price, edition, year of publication, whether they're available in paperback.

Periodical Indexes

Periodical indexes are current listings of articles, reviews, news stories, and other writings published in periodicals. They are particularly useful for finding recent information.

Readers' Guide to Periodical Literature. New York: H. W. Wilson, 1900—present date. Annual and semimonthly index to 160 periodicals of general interest, arranged by subjects, authors; cross-referenced.

Related indexes that follow the *Readers' Guide* format but that cover more scholarly and specialized periodicals are:

International Index, 1920–65.

Social Science and Humanities Index, 1965–74; since then divided into *Humanities Index*, 1974—present date: includes archaeology, folklore, history, philosophy, theology; and *Social Science Index*, 1974—present date: includes anthropology, economics, geography, law, medical science, psychology, public administration.

New York Times Index. New York: New York Times, 1913—present date. Subject index to *New York Times* articles, identified by date, page, and column. Ample cross-references to names of people and organizations. Includes brief synopses of many news articles.

Book Review Digest. New York: H. W. Wilson, 1905—present date. Alphabetized by author of book reviewed. Summarizes reviews of current American books derived from 75 general British and American periodicals. Indicates whether the reviews are favorable or not.

Specialized Reference Works

There are many reference works in special fields, such as art, business, economics, education, engineering, folklore, history, literature, music, religion, technology, and the sciences.

Among these are collections of abstracts, which are concentrated summaries of articles or other works. They can help you decide, with a minimum of reading, whether you will find the entire article relevant to your particular topic. A general collection is *Dissertation Abstracts International* (Ann Arbor: University

Microfilms), a compilation of abstracts of doctoral dissertations from 240 American, Canadian, and European universities, issued monthly since 1938. There are hundreds of specialized abstracts in various fields, *International Aerospace Abstracts, Chemical Abstracts, Statistical Theory and Method Abstracts,* and *Women Studies Abstracts.*

A good general bibliography, such as Sheehy's *Guide to Reference Books,* can help you locate specialized encyclopedias, abstracts, indexes, dictionaries, histories, bibliographies, and other surveys of particular fields. The following are typical of more specialized works.

Government Publications

The U.S. Government publishes an abundance of materials, enough to stock some libraries from cellar to attic. Among the best known are the *Congressional Record,* a daily account of the proceedings of the U.S. House and Senate; transcripts of Congressional and commission hearings; and bestselling pamphlets on subjects such as *Infant Care* and *Oral Contraceptives.*

In addition, the Government publishes hundreds of thousands of catalogs, manuals, yearbooks, newsletters, research documents, and films. In many libraries these are catalogued separately as "Government Publications" or "Government Documents." The reference librarian can help you find and use these. The Government Printing Office publishes catalogs and price lists of some of the more popular publications; many are free.

Microfilm and Microfiche

Microfilm is a film that reproduces greatly reduced photographs of newspapers, books, letters, or other documents. Microfiche (pronounced "micro-feesh") is a sheet of microfilm the size of a 4″ x 6″ filing card, on which books (about 98 pages per card) or other materials are reproduced. Both allow bulky items to be greatly compressed; one microfilm reel can hold two weeks' issues of the *New York Times.* Microfilm and microfiche also permit access to rare or fragile documents, which could be damaged if people actually handled the originals. They have two disadvantages for the user, however. They require a viewing machine, which usually means that they must be read in the library. And, because they're tiny frames of film, they can't be photocopied or written on; you have to copy the information you want from the viewer and make your notations on the copy.

Computerized Information Retrieval Systems

Computers may turn out to be the researcher's best friends. With floods of information cascading from the presses each month, it's impossible for specialists, let alone undergraduates, to keep up with a fraction of the new knowledge in even a very narrow field. Much of this information is stored as annotated bibliographies in computer data banks. They cover six major areas, to date: business and marketing, engineering and technology, government documents, life sciences, physical sciences, and social sciences. More materials are being added continually, sometimes thousands of items each month.

To use these computerized services, request from the librarian an annotated computer printout bibliography of twenty (or so) central resources on your topic. Suppose you were writing on the topic "Should high school students be allowed to earn credit by substituting proficiency tests for course work?" Possible key words might be *high schools, students, academic credit, proficiency tests,* and *course work*. But you'd reject *students* and *high schools* as topics for the computer search; the concepts are too broad and your information wouldn't be specific enough. However, you might request a combination of *high school students, academic credit,* and *proficiency tes's*, which together would be focused on your topic.

Of all the library's reference services, automated information retrieval is one of the few for which there may be a charge. It is often worth the money to consult such a retrieval service, however, because of the scope of the data bank and the fact that it is up to date and can provide information with great speed.

Instructional Media

Many college libraries and/or learning resource centers have a variety of other materials, *hardware* (such as tape recorders, computer terminals, and film projectors), and *software* (such as audio and video tapes and films) to assist you in your research.

Many libraries have collections of records, both musical and spoken. You can investigate different interpretations of the same work by listening to its performance by various artists and conductors, its rendition from classical to jazz. You can gain a better understanding of theater from hearing recorded plays and of poetry from listening to modern poets reading their own works.

You can view your library's collections of slides—of a given movement, period, or artist's works; of historic sites; of notable art collections; of memorable architecture. Many libraries also have collections of art prints, engravings, cartoons, photographs, maps, or other graphics. Some schools have film libraries and can supply projectors and projectionists.

Instructional media centers often provide closed-circuit TV, which can be connected to a campus-wide network. On this can be shown films, videotaped reruns of professional programs, and course lectures, either live or taped.

SOME SUGGESTIONS ON INTERPRETING INFORMATION

Once you have found the material you're looking for, you will need to know how to interpret it. The following suggestions should help you to interpret evidence and information in your source materials, especially if they are facts or figures that seem susceptible to manipulation or misinterpretation. You might also enjoy reading Darrell Huff and Irving Geis, *How to Lie with Statistics* (New York: Norton, 1954), a witty exposé of abuses of statistics.

☐ A Checklist for Interpreting Sources

☐ *Use your common sense; when you come to a new fact or figure, see how well it fits with what you already know to be true.* If you're told that the average per capita income in your home town is $20,000 a year and you're aware that many people are on welfare, you might question how that figure was determined. If the income of a millionaire is lumped with that of several hundred paupers, the average of the incomes might be $20,000, but the median (the figure at which half the incomes were above and half below) might be closer to $4000. So $4000 would indicate the town's economic figure more accurately than $20,000 would.

☐ *If you're trying to interpret conflicting information, pick the least biased (most objective) source.* This should be the most accurate because those who produce or release the information have little or no vested interest in its use. Using this criterion, how would you determine the relative merits of statistics on Volkswagen safety released by the manufacturer, the Ford Motor Company, Ralph Nader, the federal government, or the independent Consumer's Union?

☐ *If you're trying to interpret conflicting information from sources with equal bias, pick the source with the most authoritative reputation.*

Suppose you're writing a paper on the protests against U.S. involvement in the Vietnam war, and you want to tell how many people attended the Spring Mobilization rally in Sheep Meadow, Central Park, in April 1967. One New York newspaper puts attendance at 250,000; another estimates that it was 500,000. You might account for the discrepancy in terms of the respective papers' political biases. The conservative paper probably chose the smaller number to imply lack of support for the protest; the liberal used the larger number to signify an important political action.

Although both papers are biased, in this and in comparable instances (since even if you'd been present at the rally you couldn't have counted the crowd), you'll have to rely on each paper's overall reputation for accuracy. If both papers are equally reputable, then give the two figures as the range for estimated attendance: "Between a quarter million and a half million people attended the rally." If one paper is known for greater accuracy than the other, choose its figure.

☐ *Absence of information is preferable to misinformation; don't use unreliable sources.* If both papers in the above illustration are notoriously inaccurate, disregard them entirely and seek more accurate alternatives.

Resources for the Handicapped

Among the library resources for the handicapped are books with enlarged type, Braille volumes, and books and magazines recorded on discs and cassettes. Some libraries have teletypewriters to enable patrons with impaired sight or speech to write out requests.

Community Resources

The whole world can be a vast treasure of resources for your research. Some projects may depend primarily on materials not available in libraries, and can be particularly satisfying because of the original research they involve. For instance, interviewing people either about themselves or on a topic they know about can be a pleasant and relatively simple way to find out information or to supplement other types of investigation.

HOW TO CONDUCT AN INTERVIEW

The best way to gain information from living people in order to write about it is to interview them. It's not sufficient simply to go out and interview without any advance preparation. However, the interview should go smoothly if you follow this procedure.

1. *Have the purpose of the interview clearly in mind.* Why do you want to talk with the person you've chosen? What do you want to find out?
2. *Set up the interview in advance.* Write or call the person you want to interview. Tell him/her briefly who you are and why you want to see him or her.
3. *Before the interview, make a list of specific questions to ask, both about the main issues and related matters.* Try to keep values and judgments out of the questions. Say "What do you think about waitressing as a job?" rather than "Don't you hate the way your customers flirt with you?"
4. *When you're interviewing, talk as little as possible.* An interview is not a conversation. Keep the focus on the subject. Nonverbal gestures—smiles, nods, leaning slightly toward the speaker—can indicate your attention and appreciation. If in response to an appropriate question the speaker pauses . . . and the pause gets longer and longer, *wait!* Even after a very long pause the speaker will usually start in again. At the end of the interview you can ask your subject to verify the spellings and proper names of unfamiliar people and places.

Because interviews are likely to be repetitive and disorganized, you will need to reorganize the information you have collected according to whatever plan of arrangement you have determined for your paper—logical, chronological, topical, or otherwise.

OTHER COMMUNITY RESOURCES

People can also lead you to other sources—perhaps to *other people*, perhaps to *family memorabilia*—scrapbooks, *photograph albums*, family *Bibles* with *genealogical information* inserted, *school records, college catalogs*, or *yearbooks*. People often keep *diaries* or *letters*. These can tell you a great deal about the lives and times of the writers and the recipients, about their world and their concerns, large and small. Margaret Mead's *Letters from the Field*,[2] for example, records what it meant to be a practicing and pioneering anthropologist.

Financial records of current or bygone years—*account books, ledgers, canceled checks, prices in mail order catalogs*—can also reveal people's priorities and how they spent their money, as well as prices of goods and services.

What private citizens can't or won't provide, local or state *historical* or *genealogical societies* often can. These organizations often have fascinating collections of unpublished *diaries, letters, manuscripts, financial records,* and *legal documents.* So do some *businesses, church groups, clubs, unions, political parties,* and *civic organizations. Newspaper offices* often have all the *back issues of their papers,* and abundant reference files on many subjects.

Hobbies and *collections* might reveal considerable information. Stamps, coins, postcards, cars, glass, weapons, campaign buttons, comic books . . . you name it, there's probably a collection of everything you can imagine—and many things you can't. And collectors are notoriously eager to discuss their treasures.

A visit to someone's *home town* or *house* may provide you with more information than you or your host would expect. The *size, style, decor,* and *condition of a house and surroundings* may tell you not just about the values, social and economic status of your informants, but about their neighbors, as well. So can *furnishings* and *artifacts,* if you observe them as an anthropologist might. Is the house neat or messy? Is it full of knickknacks or other objects? What kinds? costly or inexpensive? tasteful (in your opinion) or garish? You can make comparable observations of people's *clothing, food preferences, expenditure of leisure time,* or other aspects of their lives.

Moving farther afield, you can learn about cities and towns by *driving around, walking the streets,* and *investigating the public services, shops,* and *businesses.* Many city officials, business people, and workers—white and blue collar—will be pleased to tell you about their work. You can learn about organizations, both their explicit functions and their ambience, by *attending meetings* and talking with officers and members—of labor unions, political organizations, consciousness raising groups, or Overeaters Anonymous. A *visit to an institution* can also be revealing, whether it's to a day-care center, school, hospital, Salvation Army hotel, shelter for runaways, or jail.

If you're talking with someone or touring a house, factory, or institution, take brief notes at the site. Within twelve hours of your visit *expand on them,* filling in very *specific details* of who, what, when, why, and how. Be as thorough as possible. If you find when you're writing a draft of your paper that your information is incomplete or uncertain, you can supplement it or clarify it by checking with the people you asked originally (be sure to get their names, addresses, and phone numbers).

HOW TO KEEP TRACK OF YOUR MATERIALS

Whenever you're investigating a subject, through printed sources or firsthand exploration, it's essential to keep careful track of *what* you've discovered, *where* it's located, *who* wrote or told it to you, and *when.*

BIBLIOGRAPHY CARD

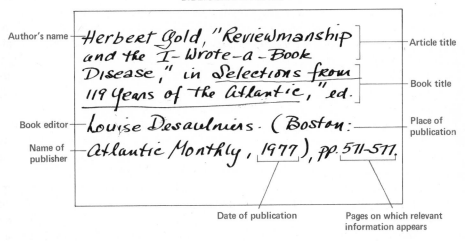

Author's name — *Herbert Gold, "Reviewmanship* — Article title
and the I-Wrote-a-Book
Disease," in Selections from — Book title
119 Years of the Atlantic," ed.
Book editor — *Louise Desaulniers. (Boston:* — Place of publication
Name of publisher — *Atlantic Monthly, 1977), pp. 571-577.*

Date of publication | Pages on which relevant information appears

The following suggestions can help you to take notes that are accurate, appropriate, and capable of being organized easily.

Establish a topic area or question involving a number of specific attributes (For instance, "What is the relationship between alcoholism and child abuse?"). Use the key words to help locate the relevant information.

Survey by skimming several major sources to get an overall impression of your topic area. You will probably begin with the more general references, such as almanacs or encyclopedias, before proceeding to the more specific ones.

Don't take notes indiscriminately or too soon, or you'll waste time copying a great deal of material that you'll never use. At the early stages of gathering in-

NOTECARD: DIRECT QUOTATION

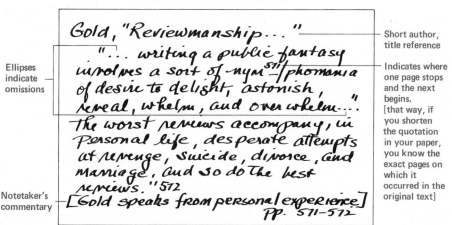

Gold, "Reviewmanship . . ." — Short author, title reference
Ellipses indicate omissions — *". . . writing a public fantasy involves a sort of nym-*[571]*/phomania of desire to delight, astonish, reveal, whelm, and overwhelm . . ."* — Indicates where one page stops and the next begins. [that way, if you shorten the quotation in your paper, you know the exact pages on which it occurred in the original text]
The worst reviews accompany, in personal life, desperate attempts at revenge, suicide, divorce, and marriage, and so do the best reviews." [572]
Notetaker's commentary — *[Gold speaks from personal experience]*
pp. 571-572

NOTECARD: PARAPHRASE

Gold, "Reviewmanship..."
A good book reviewer
provides a guide to the book,
even if he's wrongheaded.
(pp. 573-74)

formation from written materials, the only notes you might take would be bibliographic references to other sources.

On an index card or small piece of notepaper, keep a bibliographic reference for every reference you consult. If you're using a library book, include the call number as well, so you can easily find it again if you need to.

To keep track of materials, use a separate card for each work, and write bibliographic references and all notes on only *one* side of the paper.

After you've finished your preliminary survey, return to the more promising sources and read them more carefully; take notes this time. Because you already have the full bibliographic reference on one card, you can use a short reference to it on subsequent cards. However, be sure to identify *each* card. *Always* cite page numbers, whether for direct quotations, paraphrases, or summaries.

It's easier and more economical to paraphrase and summarize in your own words, unless the language of the original source is so memorable that you wish to retain the exact words. This helps to avoid the chance of plagiarism later, for you're more likely to use your own words to expand on the ideas in later versions.

If a printed source is very complicated or highly detailed and crucial to your paper, photocopy the relevant portions instead of spending long hours copying it by hand.

Don't get so absorbed in the process of taking notes that you become buried by your references. The notes are a means to an end, not an end in themselves.

INCORPORATING RESOURCES INTO YOUR OWN WRITING

There are several different ways to incorporate source material into your own writing. The simplest is *direct quotation:*

Do not provide extra indentations unless the quotation begins with the beginning of a paragraph.

Indent quotations of five lines or more by **five** extra spaces in margin. Do not put quotation marks around block quotations.

Indent to indicate paragraphs in source

As an analyst of human development, at M.I.T., Kenneth Keniston observes in *All Our Children:*

> The prosperity of the whole [eighteenth-century American] family depended on how well husband, wife, and children could manage and cultivate the land. . . . Boys were necessary to the hard work of cultivating the land and harvesting the crops, while girls were essential to the "homework" of storing and cooking food, caring for domestic animals, spinning, weaving, and sewing.
>
> Children were, in short, economic assets. Early in life, most children began to pay their own way by working with and for their families. Many years later, when the parents were elderly, children paid another economic dividend: in a time when there was no government old-age assistance or social security, grown children were often the chief source of their parents' support.[6]

Introduce quotation with a colon

use [ ] to insert explanatory material in your own words

ellipses indicate omission from source; three spaced periods signify part of a sentence; add another period if sentence ends in the quotation, i.e. . . . .

quotation marks indicate quotation marks in original

The footnote comes at the end of the quoted material unless the complete reference has been given earlier. In that case, page references in parentheses will suffice (pp. 13–14).

The main advantage of using direct quotations is the completeness and accuracy you gain from quoting the information in the context in which it occurs. You may find yourself tempted to quote too many words, as one worthwhile observation of the author leads to another and yet another. Your readers will be puzzled if you insert quotations without relating them clearly to your own text. You must make the significance of your quotations apparent to your readers through analyses of your own. Avoid inserting blocks of unanalyzed quotations.

To shorten the amount of quoted material but retain its essence, you can use short, memorable phrases from the source and put the rest into your own words:

As long as the source is acknowledged in the footnote, it is optional in the text. To give the source in the text is to give it prominence.

use single quotations inside double quotations

According to Kenneth Keniston, M.I.T. analyst of human development, children were essential to the economic functioning of eighteenth century American families. Even as youngsters they worked for their families: "boys were necessary to the hard work of cultivating the land and harvesting the crops, while girls were essential to the 'housework' of storing and cooking food, caring for domestic animals . . . and sewing."[6] Later on, as grownups, children "paid another economic dividend" by supporting their elderly parents.[†]

This footnote number covers the short direct quotation in the same sentence and also the paraphrased information immediately preceding the number.

By using more of your own words, you are likely to provide more of the necessary interpretation and analysis of your sources.

This is particularly likely to occur if you paraphrase the entire passage from the source:

Kenneth Keniston, an analyst of human development at M.I.T., has observed that children were essential to the economic survival of the eighteenth-century American family. Boys worked productively from early ages to farm the land and harvest the crops. Girls prepared food, sewed, wove, and took care of domestic animals, such as chickens and pigs. When their parents got old, grown children could be counted on to support and care for them.[6]

The footnote number comes at the end of all the material paraphrased from the same source.

The paraphrase omits the flavor of the language of the original source. This can be a disadvantage if the original is particularly savory, in which case direct quotations, short or long, will be preferable. But if the original is badly written, or if you are quoting from many sources whose styles clash, your own writing may be preferable.

Acknowledging Sources

You are responsible for everything that appears over your name, and you are assumed to be its author unless you specify otherwise. Therefore, you do not need to acknowledge what originates with you—your own ideas, experience, imagination, research results—or what is common knowledge (such as the chemical composition of water, H_2O). You *do* need to give credit, through a reference in your text or a footnote and mention in your bibliography, to others whose:

Words you quote directly.

Ideas, opinions, arguments, or point of view you adopt, summarize, or paraphrase.

Information, illustrations, or research methodology you employ.

Stimulus has inspired your own train of thought or line of investigation.

Expertise has been provided as a consultant—for instance, in checking over your completed paper for accuracy of information or spelling or mechanics.

Acknowledgments have several purposes. They give due credit to the originator of the material. They provide enough information about your sources so that anyone else who wants to can find out exactly where they came from and whether you've quoted or interpreted them correctly. And they minimize the possibility of plagiarism.

When you present other people's contributions without acknowledgment you are, in effect, encouraging your readers to think these are your own. This is *plagiarism,* a form of dishonesty that most colleges (and publishers) won't tolerate. The penalties can be severe—at best, damage to your integrity; at worst, expulsion or a lawsuit. So you must be scrupulously careful to distinguish between your ideas and words and those of others, through accurate quotations and acknowledgments. These can be made either in the text itself or in footnotes.

Acknowledgments to the people who give you good ideas are easy. A footnote at the beginning of the paper expresses the author's thanks: [1]"I (or, "The author") would like to thank Professor Ben E. Day of Boston University for suggesting in conversation [or, in American Folklore 372] March 12, 1978, the possibility that the wolf is really a manifestation of Little Red Riding Hood's *id,* and represents her unconscious hostility toward her grandmother."

You can also use this format to acknowledge consultant help, with a footnote at either the beginning or the end of the paper:

[20] My laboratory assistant, Martha Mattox, performed the statistical analyses cited on pages 10–14.

Or,

[21] My typist, H. V. Finger, corrected various mechanical and spelling errors.

If you've had help from a tutor, paid or volunteer, say so and indicate the nature and extent of the assistance.

You may occasionally use footnotes to provide supplementary comments tangential or intrusive to the paper's main line of thought. These are like extended parenthetical remarks, but should not be long enough to distract the reader from the essential flow of your paper:

[22] In addition, it is possible to examine *Little Red Riding Hood* from an entirely different perspective, the Marxian. The little girl thus clearly becomes a symbol of the proletariat, and is identified as a Communist by her red cloak. The wolf, epitome of the greedy bourgeoisie. . . .

Acknowledgment of direct quotations and paraphrases is more formal. If you are writing a paper according to the format favored in the humanities, you will need to provide complete bibliographic information about the first reference to each source—usually in a footnote (see below). In many scientific and social science fields, all references are incorporated into the text (see below).

Footnote and Bibliographic Form

There are a number of different styles of constructing footnotes and bibliographies. None is necessarily better than another; they simply reflect different conventions that have grown up in diverse fields of study. For general purposes there are two established guides:

A Manual of Style, 12th ed. Chicago: University of Chicago Press, 1969. (Some fields in the sciences and the humanities use this.)
The MLA Handbook for Writers of Research Papers, Theses, and Dissertations. New York: Modern Language Association, 1977. (Some humanities fields, including English, use this.)

However, specialists in the social, physical, and biological sciences, in mathematics, medicine, and engineering use still other formats, designated in special style manuals such as *Publication Manual of the American Psychological Association,*[4] *Manual for Authors of Mathematical Papers,*[5] and *Recommended Practice for Style of References in Engineering Publications.*[6]

In general, the footnote form in scientific and technical writing integrates numerical references within the text itself with a bibliography or reference list at the end of the paper. The entries in the bibliography are arranged in numerical sequence (1, 2, 3) according to the order in which they first appear in the text. In this format, a (1) after a quotation from or reference to a source refers to the first entry in the bibliography. A (2) refers to the second entry in the bibliography, and so on. A second number in the parentheses (4:63) refers to the page number in the source identified by the first number.

Instead of using numerical references in the text to numbered bibliographies, many of the social sciences have another simple citation format. They incorporate into the text itself citations that indicate the author's last name, date of publication—and page, if necessary—for all references:

A recent study on the effects of tickling showed that under certain conditions nobody laughed (Fields, 1982, p. 14).

If any of the foregoing information is included in the text, then only what remains is put in parentheses:

Fields's 1982 study on the effects of tickling showed that under certain conditions nobody laughed (p. 14).

Complete information goes in an alphabetically organized reference list.

The following format for footnotes is recommended by the *MLA Handbook*. The first footnote reference to any item should contain the most complete bibliographic information; susbequent references can be much briefer. The first line of each footnote is indented two spaces; the footnote number is raised. Subsequent lines of a given entry begin at the left-hand margin.

First Footnote References to Books and Pamphlets

Include the relevant items from the following list. Most of the items are followed by commas unless the next item is enclosed in parentheses, in which case the comma is omitted. The last item in the series is followed by a period.

a. Author's or authors' names in normal order: John A. Doe and Mary B. Deer,

b. Title of the chapter or named section of the book used, enclosed in quotation marks, followed by a comma inside the final quotation mark: "Celebrities Make Spectacles of Themselves,"

c. Title of the work, underlined: Going Steady,

d. Editor's or translator's name in normal order, preceded by ed. or trans.: ed. Dag Hammarskjold,

e. Edition used, if not the first, in Arabic numerals: 5th ed.,

f. Series name, separated by a comma from the Arabic numeral designating the number of the works in the series: American Women's Diary Series, No. 6,

g. Place of publication, publisher, and date of publication, all in parentheses: (New York: Random House, 1982),

h. Volume number (if there's more than one volume), in capital Roman numerals: Vol. VII,

i. Page number(s) in Arabic numerals: p. 77. Use p. or pp. to precede page number(s) unless a volume number is cited.

Examples of common footnotes

One author, first edition:

[1] Alex Haley, *Roots* (New York: Doubleday, 1976), p. 147.

One author, chapter of a book:

[2] Edward T. Hall, "The Anthropology of Space," *The Hidden Dimension* (New York: Doubleday, 1966), pp. 72–78.

Corporate author (indicated in book title)

[3] *MLA Handbook for Writers of Research Papers, Theses, and Dissertations* (New York: Modern Language Association, 1977), p. 61.

A reprint:

[4] Maxine Hong Kingston, *The Woman Warrior: Memories of a Girlhood Among Ghosts* (1976; rpt. New York: Vintage, 1977), p. 163.

Citation of more than one book:

[5] See Carolina Maria de Jesus, *Child of the Dark,* trans. David St. Clair (New York: E.P. Dutton, 1962) and Theodore Rosengarten, *All God's Dangers: The Life of Nate Shaw* (1974; rpt. New York: Avon, 1975).

First Footnote References to Articles

The punctuation is similar to the punctuation for books. Include relevant items from the following list.

a. Author's or authors' names in normal order.
b. Title of article, in quotation marks.
c. Name of periodical, underlined.
d. Volume number, in Arabic numerals.
e. Date of issue, in parentheses.
f. Page number(s), in Arabic numerals, preceded by p. or pp. unless volume number is cited. Neither p. or pp. are needed, if the volume number is cited.

Signed article in a journal with continuous pagination through the entire year's volume:

[6] Bonnie E. Carlson, "Battered Women and Their Assailants," *Social Work,* 22:6 (Nov. 1977), 455–460.

Signed article in a journal with separate pagination for each issue:

[7] Max E. Mumm, "Phototropism in the Upper Half," *Worm Runners' Digest,* No. 13 (1982), pp. 18–22.

Signed article in a weekly magazine or weekly newspaper, or monthly magazine:

[8] Robert Coles, "The Children of Affluence," *Atlantic,* Sept. 1977, pp. 52–66.

An unsigned daily or weekly newspaper or magazine article:

[9] "Cities and People in Distress," *New York Times,* 21 Nov. 1977, Sect. A, p. 30, cols. 1–2 (sometimes simplified to A 30).

Article in an edited collection:

[10] Alice Walker, "The Civil Rights Movement: What Good Was It?" *The American Scholar,* 36 (Autumn 1967), 550–554; in *The Borzoi Reader,* ed. Charles Muscatine and Marlene Griffith, 3rd ed. (New York: Alfred A. Knopf, 1976), pp. 432–438.

Encyclopedia article, unsigned:

[11] "Mining, Underground," *Great Soviet Encyclopedia,* 1979.

Footnotes for Other Types of Material

Government documents:

Congressional Record requires only the date and page number:

[12] *Cong. Rec.*, 13 Feb. 1980, pp. 1776–77.
[13] "The Foreign Assistance Program: Annual Report to Congress for Fiscal Year 1973 (Washington, D.C.: GPO, 1974), p. 44. [GPO indicates Government Printing Office]

Unpublished speech or paper:

[14] Jacques Trop, "The Impact of Women's Intercollegiate Sports on the Total College Athletic Program," Phys. Ed. 348 (Sports Management), Ohio State University, 4 April 1981.

Unpublished letter:

[15] Sophia Loren, Letter to Carlo Ponti, 4 April 1979.

Unpublished interview:

[16] Personal interview between the author and Benjamin Spock, M.D., pediatrician and antiwar activist, 11 July 1967.

Second and Subsequent References

For later references to a source already acknowledged, you can often insert into your text sufficient information to identify it without using a separate footnote. One way is to acknowledge the author:

As George Bernard Shaw once sagely observed, "He who can, does. He who cannot, teaches" (p. 230).

Or:

"He who can, does. He who cannot, teaches" (Shaw, p. 230).

Or, if more than one work by Shaw has already been cited:

"He who can, does. He who cannot, teaches" (Shaw, *Maxims*, p. 230).

In the sciences, second and subsequent references follow the same form as first references; all are incorporated into the text.

Bibliographies

A *full bibliography* is an alphabetical list of all the sources consulted in the preparation of a research paper, book, or other writing. A *selected bibliography* lists only those materials actually referred to in the text. An *annotated bibliography* provides brief comments that explain and evaluate some or all of the items.

Some scientific bibliographies are numbered; those in the humanities are not.

Some bibliographies in the sciences and all those in the humanities are arranged in alphabetical order by authors' last names. Anonymous works are incorporated into this list by the first main word of the title. Multiple works by the same author are arranged in order of publication date; a long dash (————) is substituted for the author's name after the first citation.

Basically, the bibliographic form in the humanities is like the footnote form except for:

1. Transposition of the first author's first and last names: Moore, Marianne. Second and subsequent authors remain in normal order: Moore, Marianne and Edith Sitwell.
2. A period instead of a comma following the author's name(s) and the title: Terkel, Studs. *Working.*
3. Absence of parentheses around the place and date of publication.
4. No page references for whole books, but full page references for articles, or chapters or other portions of books.
5. The first line of each bibliographic entry begins at the left-hand margin; subsequent lines are indented three spaces.

Examples of Common Bibliographic Entries

Bernstein, Theodore M. *Miss Thistlebottom's Hobgoblins: The Careful Writer's Guide to the Taboos, Bugbears, and Outmoded Rules of English Usage.* New York: Farrar, Straus & Giroux, 1971. [book; single author; subtitle optional]
Council of Biology Editors, Committee on Form and Style. *CBE Style Manual.* 3rd ed. Washington, D.C.: American Inst. of Biological Sciences, 1972. [pamphlet; collective author]
Crawford, Samuel D. and Robert H. Bentley, "An Inner-City 'IQ' Test." In *Black Language Reader.* Ed. Robert H. Bentley and Samuel D. Crawford. Glenview, Ill.: Scott, Foresman, 1973, pp. 80–83. [chapter of an edited book that contains other chapters by other authors]
Kleinfield, Sonny. "The Handicapped: Hidden No Longer." *Atlantic,* Dec. 1977, pp. 86–90, 92, 94–96. [Article from a monthly magazine. Pages containing advertising but no text of the article are omitted from the pagination sequence]
Sandburg, Carl. *Abraham Lincoln: The War Years.* 4 vols. New York: Harcourt Brace, 1939. [book, several volumes]
Sawyer, Thomas M. "Why Speech Will Not Totally Replace Writing." *College Composition and Communication,* 28 (1977), 43–48. [journal article with continuous pagination throughout the entire volume]

Some scientific bibliographies, including many in the social sciences, use the following format, in this sequence:

1. The names of all the work's authors in inverted order, with surnames followed by initials: Freud, S.; Skinner, B. F. and Harlow, H.
2. The title of the article or chapter (without quotation marks), followed by the title of the periodical or book in which it appears, underlined. In journal titles capitalize the first letter of all major words. In article, chapter, and book titles only the first letter of the first word and proper names are capitalized.

3. For journals: publication date, volume number, pages included. For books: city of publication, publisher, date of publication.

Examples of Scientific Bibliographic Entries

American Institute of Physics. *Style manual* (2nd. ed., rev.). New York: Author, 1970. [book, subsequent revised edition. Note that an institution is both author and publisher.]

Harlow, H. F. Fundamental principles for preparing psychology journal articles. *Journal of Comparative and Physiological Psychology*, 1962, 55, 893–896. [journal article]

Strunk, W., Jr. and White, E. B. The elements of style (3rd ed.). New York: Macmillan, 1979. [two authors]

The easiest way to follow the appropriate footnote and bibliographic form is to look at models, rather than to try to memorize complicated sequences of details and punctuation. So follow the illustrations here that fit your format, or consult a style manual in your field. (They are relatively inexpensive.)

SUGGESTIONS FOR DISCUSSION AND WRITING

If you follow the items below in sequence you will end up with a great deal of the work done for a resource paper.

1. Suppose you are writing an essay on one of the following topics, or on an assigned topic, or on one of your own choice. What resources would you use to develop that topic, and why? Before you answer this, narrow the topic and focus it on several of its key words or concepts.

preferred treatment of college athletes

the military draft

the impact of the 1964 Civil Rights Act on your community

the history of your favorite word

an interview with an interesting person about his/her life or occupation or eye-witness of a memorable event

a biographical portrait of a notable person

an analysis of your home town, county, or state

how to do ———

a study of the critical or popular reception of your favorite book, film, or television program

2. Find at least three cross-reference headings on the topic you have chosen in the *Library of Congress Subject Headings*. Using these subject headings, find ten references to your topic in the card catalog. Make a bibliography reference card for each.

3. Look up materials related to your topic in at least six standard reference works, one of each kind:

encyclopedia   dictionary
periodical index   government publication
newspaper index   microfilm
atlas   microfiche
specialized volume on the topic   biographical directory

Which are the most useful volumes for your purpose? Evaluate them according to the criteria discussed earlier in the chapter.

4. Using notecards, take reference notes, some direct quotations and some paraphrases, on at least six of your sources. Be sure to take down the appropriate bibliographical information.

5. Following the quotation below are several paraphrases such as you might make in a paper. Which are adequate to convey the essence of the original? Which are not? Why?

> The personal cost of alcoholism is tremendous. Alcoholics' life expectancy is shortened by 10 to 12 years. Their mortality rate is two and a half times greater than that of nonalcoholics. They have a higher rate of violent deaths. In 1968, alcoholism accounted for 7% of all deaths. Alcoholism is listed as the reason for death on 13,000 death certificates yearly. This is an amazingly high figure considering the suspected, undetected, unreported cases. Some 36 million Americans are affected by their relationships to an active alcoholic. According to the 1968 *Alcohol and Highway Safety* report, alcohol plays a role in about half the 60,000 highway deaths each year. In other words, more Americans were killed on the roads as a result of alcohol than were killed in the Vietnam War. According to Accident Facts, from the Indiana University Institute for Research in Public Safety, in 1971, out of 111 million drivers, 80 million drink, 13 million are heavy drinkers, 5 to 7 million are alcoholics. Chronic drinkers, as opposed to one-time offenders, were responsible for two thirds of the fatalities. Disabilities as a result of highway accidents are estimated at 500,000 people yearly. In accidents involving pedestrians, 40% of pedestrians in fatal accidents had been drinking; 32% of pedestrians and 53% of the drivers had blood alcohol levels of more than 0. 10%, the legal evidence for intoxication.
>
> JEAN KINNEY and GWEN LEATON, *Loosening the Grip: A Handbook of Alcohol Information* (St. Louis: C. V. Mosby, 1978), pp. 23–24.

a. Alcoholics can expect to live ten to twelve years less than nonalcoholics, but to die more violently, perhaps in automobile accidents. Alcohol is a factor in 30,000 highway deaths a year and 500,000 injuries.[7]

b. According to alcohol researchers Jean Kinney and Gwen Leaton, an enormous number of people are killed or injured in automobile accidents that result from drinking.[7]

c. Alcoholism can have violent repercussions on the lives of alcoholics and on their families, say researchers Jean Kinney and Gwen Leaton in *Loosening the Grip* (St. Louis: C. V. Mosby, 1978). Over 36 million Americans are "affected by their relationship to an active alcoholic." Chronic drinkers are responsible for two-thirds of the fatal accidents each year, which affect 60,000 people; another 500,000 people are injured annually in alcohol-related accidents (p. 23).

d. "Alcoholism is listed as the reason for death on 13,000 death certificates yearly, an amazingly high figure," say reasearchers Jean Kinney and Gwen Leaton. Furthermore, alcoholics have a much shorter life expectancy than nondrinkers.[7]

6. If you find that any of the information you have gathered conflicts with any other information you have, how will you treat the discrepancies that you find and resolve the disagreements? According to what criteria will you interpret your sources (see p. 322)?

7. Which of the following would you need to document in an essay? Why or why not? What sort(s) of documentation would be suitable? If you prefer, examine statements you have gathered for an essay of your own.
   a. In human relations, too often the Golden Rule is more a dream than a reality.
   b. The bombing of Pearl Harbor by the Japanese on Dec. 7, 1941, marked the formal entry of the United States into World War II.
   c. The hazards of the Bermuda Triangle to navigation can be explained by reference to a combination of air and water currents.
   d. Less work and more play reduces stress and enhances longevity.
   e. Shaw was right when he said, "He who can, does; he who cannot, teaches."
   f. Our foreign policy with regard to [you pick the country] is thoroughly misguided.

8. Write first footnotes or other first references in the appropriate format for your field (or for an English course for the following, or for material you have collected for an essay you are writing). Include only the information that is necessary.
   a. A book called *A Guide to Writing and Publishing in the Social and Behavioral Sciences*. It was published in 1977 by John Wiley, Inc. of New York, Interscience series, and was written by Carolyn J. Mullins.
   b. An article in the *Journal of American Indian Education,* a journal whose pagination begins anew with each issue, and which is published by the Bureau of Educational Research and Services, Arizona State University. It was written by Rosalie Wax and Murray Wax, and is titled "Cultural Deprivation as an Educational Ideology," and appeared in Volume III; number 2, January 1964, on pages 15 through 18.
   c. The third volume of *The Collected Works of Charles Dickens, Pickwick Papers,* edited by Kathleen M. Tillotson. Published in London by the Dickensian Society in 1954, it was reprinted in paperback by Penguin Books, Inc. of Baltimore, Md. in 1968.
   d. A discussion on the nature of totalitarian regimes, in your class in political theory, between you and your teacher, Prof. May O. T. Marx. It occurred on March 15, 1984, at Southwest Mississippi State Community College.
   e. A newspaper article by Ellen Goodman that appeared in the Washington *Post* on Saturday, September 27, 1980. It is titled "Alone, Sooner or Later." It appeared in the Virginia edition on page 23, Section A, column 1.

9. For the above footnotes in *8,* write two subsequent references according to the format in your field or that recommended by your instructor or supervisor.

10. Make a sample bibliography, either of the items in *8* or of the items you are using as references for your resource paper.

11. Write your resource paper, using the relevant materials you have collected and following the composing process recommended in Part I.

NOTES

[1] Edward P. J. Corbett, *Classical Rhetoric for the Modern Student*, 2nd ed. (New York: Oxford University Press, 1971), p. 189.

[2] World Perspectives Series, ed. Ruth Nanda Anshen (New York: Harper & Row, 1978).

[3] Kenneth Keniston and the Carnegie Council on Children, *All Our Children: The American Family Under Pressure* (New York: Harcourt Brace Jovanovich, 1977), pp. 13–14.

[4] American Psychological Association. 2nd ed. Washington, D.C.: American Psychological Association, 1974.

[5] American Mathematical Society. 4th ed. Providence, R.I.: American Mathematical Society, 1971.

[6] Engineers Joint Council, Committee of Engineering Society Editors. New York: Engineers Joint Council, 1966.

CHAPTER FOURTEEN
A RESOURCE PAPER

*Writing that entails a great deal
of reflection, research, organization, and revision . . . calls upon
all the inventive and stylistic resources at [one's] command. . . .
[But as] Quintilian once said,
"Write quickly and you will never
write well; write well and you will
soon write quickly."*

—EDMUND P. J. CORBETT

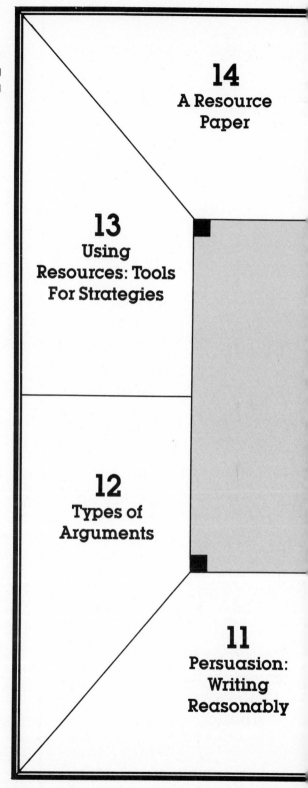

14
A Resource
Paper

13
Using
Resources: Tools
For Strategies

12
Types of
Arguments

11
Persuasion:
Writing
Reasonably

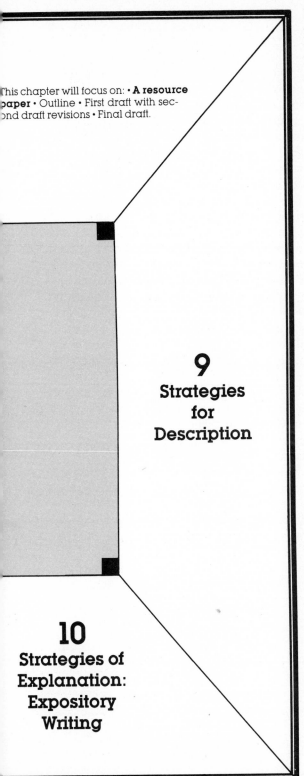

9
Strategies for Description

10
Strategies of Explanation: Expository Writing

In some ways *resource papers*—papers incorporating source material—are the safest kind to write, because you're not dependent wholly on your own thoughts, opinions, or knowledge that might be imperfectly recollected. In other ways they can be the most challenging, because the sources that you use for information or explanations can open up a universe of new vistas, each of which could contribute to the topic at hand or provide the basis for additional writing.

How much you depend on your sources will vary in relation to how much you know about the topic before you start to investigate it. If you're an expert on skydiving, for example, you may use outside sources simply to corroborate your information or views or to supplement them. But if you don't know much about your subject at the outset—the Department of Education, for instance, or the latest research in color chemistry—you will probably depend more heavily on outside information when you write about it. However, no matter what your subject is, you will want to make the essay your own rather than a collection of excerpts from others' writings stitched together with a few phrases of your own.

But what can you contribute, when people who seem to know a great deal about the subject have already written authoritatively on it? What's left for you to add? In many instances, you can supply a great deal, if you're willing to use your sources—especially those in conflict with one another—as a springboard for your own opinion on the topic. If you choose a subject in which you're genuinely interested as you explore varied aspects and interpretations of it you're likely to form your own independent opinion. As you read, try to think of ways to treat your topic with originality and conviction. At this stage, you can hold a dialogue with yourself or others or write a zero draft of your topic or one aspect of your topic to develop ideas. You will also want to aim for a high originality factor, a large ratio of your own words and thoughts to those of others. You can attain this by using short quotations instead of long ones and through brief paraphrases of longer originals. When it comes to quotation, shorter is better. The more you say in your own words, the more likely you are to develop and express your own thoughts.

Freshman Karen Cathey didn't know much about Charlie Chaplin when she decided to write a resource paper on some aspect of his life or work; in fact, she'd never even seen any of his films. But she was intrigued by the pathetic-comic image of the little tramp with baggy pants and duck-toed walk and decided to explore these in her reading. As she read, she found that although the printed sources were clear, she needed to see Chaplin in action both to understand better what the commentators were saying and to gain some first-hand knowledge of his film personality and acting style so that she could evaluate the commentary. Fortunately, she was able to view *The Gold Rush* before determining her thesis, and she found this enormously helpful—as well as entertaining. Karen could react independently to the film, a primary source, and use her own judgment of the actor and his work to evaluate her secondary sources. As a result, she was able to write "Charlie Chaplin and His Struggle for Freedom" with an appropriate mixture of dependence on her sources for information and independence from them for interpretation.

The paper is presented here as Karen wrote it (first version) and revised it (changes superimposed on the first version). She changed the organization of some portions, moving paragraphs around, crossing out some parts, adding others, rewriting some sentences to improve the emphasis and style. She added information from outside sources in several places to illustrate her points or reinforce her own opinions. She also corrected the grammar and mechanics. The final version, also included here, incorporates the revisions and corrections. Marginal comments have been inserted where necessary to call attention to various aspects of this process.

First Draft, with Revisions

Number in ( ) indicates paragraph number in final version.

~~-The Struggle~~
~~Charlie Chaplin's Final Aim in Life~~
Charlie Chaplin and his Struggle for Freedom

1(1) Charlie Chaplin, born on a bitter ~~in April, 1889~~ *spring day*, has

been referred to time and time again as the comic genius

of the entertainment world. ∧¹

Ever since ~~Charlie~~ Chaplin made his first ∧ *stage* appearance ~~on~~

stage at the age of five, his purpose was to make people

laugh by extracting as much amusement as possible from life.

Portraying a rags-to-riches clown, he ''shook the world in

as well as in laughter. ∧ ~~He also expressed~~ his understanding of those who

"exist in anonymous poverty, gracelessness and loneliness" ∧²

2(2) Chaplin stumbled on the future generator of laughter *his*

first around 1914 when he was ∧ ~~just~~ breaking into the film industry.

in an emergency, he was *to put on a skit for an* When told ∧ to dress in a comical outfit and ~~take the place of~~

at first audience, ∧ he had no idea of what to do. ~~exept at~~ He ~~finally~~

finally ~~decided~~ wanted everything to be a contradiction and ∧ ~~thought~~

decided on *a tight frock coat, with starched* *of* baggy trousers; ∧ oversized shoes *shirt and black tie* *well-worn*

an undersized derby hat *and a shuffled walk, was a touch made up at last* ∧ a cane; ~~and~~ a moustache: ~~and~~ ~~Then~~ Once ~~he was~~ dressed, "the *moment*

clothes and the make-up made me feel the person he was: I

began to know him, and by the time I walked onto the stage

the Tramp he ∧ was fully born." ∧³ It was here that Chaplin saw the

peculiar meaning for this ∧ little character and excitingly gave *a*

description ~~the description~~ ∧ of the figure which was to remain with him

The next 25 yrs of for ∧ the ~~his entire~~ film career. Moreover, ~~while~~ he tried to

ened prevent us from being disheart ~~ed~~ by the ever-present

the world *Chaplin knew* seriousness of ∧ ~~life.~~ And ~~he felt~~ that laughter was the

around us *he said remarks:* best tool ∧ to achieve this, as ∧ ~~Chaplin once remarked~~; "I laugh

because I laugh, and to laugh is sufficient reason for

existence, and there is no limit to our laughter."

Sentence moved in revision.

Sentence is out of order here; it sounds as if Chaplin played a clown and moved the world world to laughter when he was five.

The description begins paragraph 4 and is too far away from the references to it. The reader would not know this connection.

Karen's attempt to break the original quotation into two sentences is unsuccessful. This revised sentence is smoother.

Additions enhance the specificity of the writing and makes and make it clearer.

The substitution of "25" for "entire" makes the sentence more accurate.

the idea
along with ~~Tramp's~~ of self respect

3(6) Chaplin used two aspects of human nature ʌto enable the audience to identify with the T̲ramp. The following exerpt from <u>The Adventurer</u> demonstrates the result of his artistic ability.

> "I first placed myself on a balcony, eating icecream with a girl.
> On the floor directly underneath aʌ*the* balcony I put a stout, dignified,
> well-dressed woman at a table. Then, while eating the ice cream,
> I let a piece drop off my spoon, slip through my baggy trousers &
> and drop from the balcony onto this woman's neck . . . The first
> laugh came ~~when~~ at my embarrassment over my own predicament. The
> second and much greater one, came when ice cream landed onʌ*the* woman's
> neck and she shrieked and danced around."[5]

average
The first reaction of theʌaudience toward such an incident would beʌ *of*
~~the~~ *a*
delight in seeingʌwealthy ~~and~~, "too" dignified person in trouble.

recognize &
Then the tendency of the human being would be toʌidentify with the
of the characters   *the Tramp's*
various feelingsʌon the screen, such as that ofʌembarrassment.

But Chaplin wasn't satisfied in accomplishing this
(serious) effect; he wanted a more comical ending   *became*
So ~~At this point~~ ~~Chaplin~~ the Tramp, ~~in~~ his embarrassment,ʌ~~was~~ very

much in earnest about clutching his cane, straightening his derby hat,
leave &
and fixing his coat and tie, eager toʌdismiss the entire accident

from his mind.[6]

4(in 3) "You know this fellow is many-sided, a tramp, a gentleman, a
poet, a dreamer, a lonely fellow, always hopeful of romance
and adventure. He would have you believe he is a scientist, a
musician, a duke, a polo player. However, he is not above
picking up cigarette butts or robbing a baby of its candy.
And, of course, if the occasion warrants it, he will kick a
lady in the rear--but only in extreme anger!"[7]

is
The secret of ~~the~~ Chaplin's success with the Trampʌwas the surprising
features   ~~completed the Tramp~~ *made him up*
fact that all the exaggeratedʌparts which ~~made-him-up~~ʌfitted together
was to.
into the mysterious and many-sided figure whoʌsoonʌwon the hearts of
audiences around the globe,

whether it was poverty, suffering or despair
5(5) From this lowest rungʌ the Tramp always made his entrance into
the films. For example in <u>City Lights</u>, he is homeless, jobless,
and lacks a place to sleep; in <u>The Circus</u> he has been left alone in
Then in one of the his worst situations
a littered field when the circus moved on.[8]ʌ~~Then in an extreme ? ?~~

in <u>The Gold Rush</u> he is so hungry that he boils one of his old shoes

for dinner.[9] Despite all this misery though, ~~he Chaplin~~ the Tramp
somehow conquered these   *humorous but sympathetic*
ʌ~~struggled with~~ universal human problems in aʌcomic manner, ~~pretending~~
~~That is, refusing~~ *Ignoring* the ~~fact~~   *with the intention of*
~~to admit that everything was out of the way; he attempted to be~~
For instance   *one notices that*
maintaining his dignity. ~~As with~~   Looking again at <u>The Gold Rush</u>,ʌ

he ∧eats the boiled shoe as if it was the most delicious meal ever
ate

prepared. From ~~this~~ such ∧~~an incident~~, it is apparent that he was a
a case

character who refused under any circumstances to take anything seriously,

no matter ~~what obstacles the universe set in front of him~~[10] ~~In~~ W/ this
how life determined to knock him about

attitude he ∧gave a little ~~light~~ hope to ~~the~~ even the lowliest of the low.

6(4) ~~With~~ ∧the Tramp outfit ~~arose~~ the Tramp personality. ~~Although he~~
From With   *came*

~~was many-sided he~~ He represented the common man in that he was a

a combination of both ∧~~the~~ gentleman and ∧~~the~~ tramp. ∧~~The~~ hat, coat,
a   *a*   *His*

and cane ∧of an English gentleman along with ∧~~the~~ trousers and shoes
like those   *his*

∧of a street bum united the two opposite rungs of the social ladder.
like those

Logically this paragraph should precede the paragraph above. Their order was reversed in revision.

Final Draft, Revised and Corrected

Title, centered ——————————Charlie Chaplin and his Struggle for Freedom

by
Author's name ———————————Karen Cathey

Course section
and number ———————————English Composition 101-7
Instructor's name ——————————Dr. Bloom
Date submitted ——————————December 5, 1981

Charlie Chaplin and His Struggle for Freedom

1 Charlie Chaplin, born on a bitter day in spring, has been referred to for over sixty years as the comic genius of the entertaiment world. Portraying a rags-to-riches clown, he "shook the world in laughter as well as in his understanding of those who exist in anonymous poverty, gracelessness and loneliness."[1]

2 Ever since Chaplin made his first stage appearance at the age of five, his purpose was to make people laugh by extracting as much amusement as possible from life. Moreover, he tried to prevent us from being disheartened by the ever-present seriousness of the world around us. And Chaplin knew that laughter was the best tool to achieve this, as he remarks: "I laugh because I laugh, and to laugh is sufficient reason for existence, and there is no limit to our laughter."[2]

3 Charlie stumbled onto the future generator of laughter around 1914 when he was first breaking into the film industry. When, in an emergency, he was told to dress in a comical outfit and to put on a skit for an audience, at first he had no idea of what to do. He wanted everything to be a contradiction and finally decided on baggy trousers; a tight frock coat with a starched shirt and a black tie; oversized, well-worn shoes; an undersized derby hat; a cane; a moustache; and a shuffled walk, a touch made up at the last moment. Once dressed, "the clothes and the make-up made me feel the person he was. I began to know him and by the time I walked onto the stage the Tramp was fully born."[3] It was here that Chaplin saw the meaning for this peculiar little character and excitingly gave the following description of the figure which was to remain with him for the next twentyfive years of his film career:

> You know this fellow is manysided, a tramp, a gentleman, a poet, a dreamer, a lonely fellow, always hopeful of romance and adventure. He would have you believe he is a scientist, a musician, a duke, a polo player. However, he is not above picking up cigarette butts or robbing a baby of its candy. And, of course, if the occasion warrants it, he will kick a lady in the rear — but only in extreme anger![4]

4 With the Tramp outfit came the Tramp personality. He represented the common man in that he was a combination of both a gentleman and a tramp. His hat, coat, shirt, tie, and cane like those of an English gentleman, along with his trousers and shoes like those of a street bum, united the two opposite rungs of the social ladder.

5 From this lowest rung, whether it was poverty, suffering, or despair, the Tramp always made his entrance into the film. For example, in City Lights, he is homeless and jobless; in the Circus, he has been left alone in a littered field when the circus moved on.[5]

Although essays, especially long one, do not have necessarily to open with the essence of the thesis, this one does just that.

The six opening paragraphs emphasize Chaplin image as an entertainer.

The footnotes are placed consecutively at the end of the main main text. They also could have come at the bottom of the page on which the reference appears.

Indented block quotations do not require quotation marks unless they are quotations within quotations. (See paragraph 16)

Footnote 4 refers to the same reference as footnote 3, so the reference could also have been included in the text in parentheses instead of appearing at the end.

Notice the variation among short, medium, and long paragraphs throughout this essay.

This paragraph
concisely identifies
several major aspects
of three fims, suitably
and briefly illustrating
the author's point.

Then in one of his most desperate situations in <u>The Gold Rush</u>, he is so
hungry he boils one of his old shoes for dinner.[6] Despite all this misery,
though, the Tramp somehow conquered these universal human problems in
a humorous but sympathetic manner, with the intention of maintaining
his dignity. Looking again at <u>The Gold Rush</u>, one notices that he ate
the boiled shoe as if it was the most delicious meal ever prepared.
From such a case, it is apparent that he was a character who refused
under any circumstances to remain seriously depressed, no matter how life
was determine to knock him about.[7] With this attitude he gave a little
hope to even the lowliest of the low.

6   Chaplin used two aspects of human nature along with this idea of self-
respect to enable the audience to identify with the Tramp. The following
exerpt from <u>The Adventurer</u> demonstrates the result of his artistic ability:

Quotation marks
indicate that this
is a direct quotation—
in this case, of Chaplin's
own words, within a
quotation.

"I first placed myself on a balcony, eating ice cream with a girl.
On the floor directly underneath the balcony I put a stout, dignified,
well-dressed woman at a table. Then, while eating the ice cream, I let
a piece drop off my spoon, slip through my baggy trousers and drop from the
balcony onto this woman's neck... The first laugh came at my embarrassment
over my own predicament. The second and much greater one, came when ice
cream landed on the woman's neck and she shrieked and danced around."[8]

The first reaction of the average audience toward such an incident would be
of delight in seeing a wealthy, "too" dignified person in trouble. Then
the tendency of the human being would be to recognize and identify with
the various feelings of the characters on the screen, such as that of the
Tramp's embarrassment. But Chaplin was not satisfied in accomplishing this
serious effect; he wanted a more comical ending. So at this point, the
Tramp, quite aware of his embarrassment, became very much in earnest
about clutching his cane, straightening his derby hat, and fixing his coat
and tie, eager to leave and dismiss the entire incident from his mind.[9]

This is a transition
paragraph
linking the
cinematographic
image with the
the biographical
information
which follows.

7   Chaplin captivated his audiences with his comic inventions, but the
main influence of his style was the profoundly bitter memory of his
childhood. It emerged with the creation of the Tramp, who transmuted
the joyous and sorrowful aspects of his past into universal bittersweet
humor for all times.

8   Born on April 16, 1889, Charlie Chaplin was faced with a long, hard
struggle to survive the rugged childhood experiences that lay before him.
His life could best be described as a constant change. His mother and
father were theatrical performers and separated shortly after their son's
birth; Charlie and his half brother Sydney remained with their mother.
Because Mrs. Chaplin received so litlle income from her ex-husband, she
resumed her short stage career briefly to provide for the boys. When
she began losing her voice, Charlie would substitute for her on stage.

The footnote always follows the information which came from the source to which it refers. The footnote at the end of this paragraph indicates that all the information in the paragraph came from the same source.

His act included singing, dancing, talking, and doing several imitations of his mother's songs and voice cracking. The resulting cheers, laughs, and money-throwing from the audience signaled the start of Charlie's career and the end of his mother's.[10]

9   Circumstances grew worse and more wretched until Mrs. Chaplin finally sent the boys off to an orphanage outside London. After several whippings, and the shaving of his head due to ringworm, Charlie persuaded his mother to let him leave school to get a job. In addition to joining a clog dancing group called the "Eight Lancashire Lads," he tried his hand as an errand boy, a printer, a toymaker, and a news vendor, but none suited him.[11] These were the longest and saddest days of his life as his father died of alcoholism and his mother eventually went insane and was in and out of mental institutions. So during these times he lived alone, mostly in the streets, and moved from job to job. His principal aim in life was to become an actor and he decided to audition in various theatrical agencies. Successful, he received several small stage parts.[12]

Look for clues in the text that indicate how much information a given footnote pertains to. Footnote 12, for instance, although at the end of this paragraph, refers to information in the four preceding sentences — which follow footnote 11.

10   For a time he worked with Casey's Court Circus and it was here that he decided to become a comedian. As he began to develop his act he resorted to pantomime, for many people in the audiences spoke different languages. This proved highly successful and landed him a job with the Fred Karno Company.[13] Thus began his move upward toward being a successful comedian.

11   However, Chaplin was not to forget those hard times and he later used the combination of both humor and tragedy in his films. For instance in <u>The Gold Rush</u>, the Tramp and his mountaineer friend have slept through a blizzard, and awaken to find that their house is at the very edge of a cliff. As each one begins moving around within the house, the building tips back and forth, until it gets stuck at a dangerous angle. While the two men engage in a mad but cautious effort to climb out to safety, the audience is struck not only with the characters' humorous actions but also with the ever-present sense of danger. Finally, though, both the Tramp and his friend reach safety and at the same time find the long sought gold mine.[14] This scene may have a deeper meaning than just a dangerous moment in the life of

Interpretation without footnotes is the author's own.

the Tramp. Chaplin could have very well been reflecting on his earlier life. The house could represent his unsteady childhood and his constant desire to escape such an unstable life. The escape would then symbolize his entrance into a new world, as when he joined the Karno Company and a new career. Finally, the gold mine would represent his success after the many years of prosperous films that were to follow. In this manner, Chaplin continued to recall that memory of his struggle toward success.

12   In 1913, during a trip to the United States, Chaplin was seen by Mack Sennett of the Keystone Comedy Company. A year later, Sennett sought Chaplin out and offered him a job in the film industry at $150 a week, more money than he had ever seen in his life. This was the opportunity that Chaplin had been waiting for. He had now entered the career which he had longed for and he never returned to the stage.

13   Chaplin's popularity grew enormously. In 1915 he joined the Essanay Company at $1,250 a week. With this company he adopted the character of the Little Tramp and the art of pantomime. Chaplin wanted desperately to write and direct his own pictures and this was his chance. The public went wild over his films and the demand increased more and more. In 1916, he signed for twelve films with the Mutual Film Company and received $670,000. At the end of the contract, although the company wished to renew it, Chaplin preferred the greater artistic liberty offered by the First National Company and began at once to build a studio of his own at Hollywood, California. He received one million dollars for eight pictures, $15,000 for signing the contract, and half of the profits. Finally in 1919, Chaplin, with Douglas Fairbanks and Mary Pickford, formed the United Artists Corporation so that each could produce and distribute his own films indenpendently.[15] In a period of only five years, Chaplin had risen from a small comedian to his own writer, producer, director, chief designer, film cutter, and make up man, and had captured the attention of audiences in all parts of the world. Truly, " he came to conquer America and ended up conquering the world."[16]

14   Fate would not allow Chaplin to be successful in everything, however. The turbulence of his private life was manifested in a series of marriages and divorces. In 1918, he married his first wife, Mildred Harris, and two years later divorced her. In 1924, Lita Grey became his second wife, and they had two sons; however, the marriage ended in 1927. These two divorce procedings raised much public concern and disgrace, so Chaplin decided to move to New York. In 1936, he married Paulette Goddard and divorced her in in 1942, without any public fuss. Shortly before the divorce he had met Joan Barry, who charged him later with a paternity suit; although the charges were dropped later he had to support the child. The problem with these marriages was that Chaplin's work was much more important to him at the time than family ties.[17]

15   His idea of a perfect wife materialized in 1943 when he married Oona O'Neill. It proved to be a happy and lasting marriage, producing eight

A vivid quotation caps the paragraph.

Here, as throughout the paper, the author does a good job of blending her own literary style with the style of the quotations.
The paraphrases are in her own words.

children. In <u>The Gold Rush</u>, the film he wishes to be remembered by, the Tramp falls in love with Georgia, a cabaret singer, and mistakes her kindness and joking for love. A heart-breaking scene follows in which she deserts him; he leaves with his mountaineer friend and later discovers gold. Meanwhile, Georgia becomes aware of his true love for her and sees him as a true person. At the end they find each other at last and live happily ever after.[18] Payne in his book <u>Great God Pan</u> (p. 204) sees this as the one fault of the film, for it was Chaplin's tragic style not to let the Tramp win his girl.[19] However, it is possible that Chaplin wished his dream of a perfect wife to come true and at that time it was only possible through a film.

> **Oops, the author slipped up! Because this parenthetical reference is inconsistent with the other footnotes, it should be deleted and replaced by footnote 19.**

16   Chaplin also encountered another problem during the later years of his film career. He was a producer of silent films so when sound came into the industry, he simply ignored it at first. He feared that the Tramp would be destroyed, for as soon as he was made to talk he would be an entirely different person. He changed his mind when World War II started. He began to get ideas of how to ridicule the war and awaken people to the horror of dictatorship: "He [Hitler] is the madman, I am the comic, but it could be the other way around."[20] Up to this point, Chaplin had been silent about his beliefs, but in <u>The Great Dictator</u>, he put into words what for twenty-five years he had been trying to say in one way or another:

> **Quotation marks are used in block quotations to designate a quotation within a quotation, compare with paragraph 3 above.**

> "I'm sorry, but I don't want to be an emperor. That's not my business. I don't want to rule or conquer anyone. I should like to help everyone — if possible — Jew, Gentile — black men — white. We all want to help one another. Human beings are like that. We want to live by each other's happiness — not by each other's misery. We don't want to hate and despise one another. In this world there is room for everyone. And the good earth is rich and can provide for everyone."21

He goes on to tell of man's faults, those things he had so often expressed in previous films through the Tramp, on whose shoulders he placed the problems of the world.

17   This expression of feelings led to the accusation that he was a Communist sympathizer. Eventually he was denounced by the United States in 1952 and exiled until he could prove his "moral worth." Angered, Chaplin and his family spent the rest of their lives in Vevey, Switzerland. As the years went by, though, Chaplin and the United States mellowed and in 1972, Chaplin received a special Oscar from The Motion Picture Academy. However, he continued to live in Switzerland until he died on December 25, 1977.[22]

18   All his life Charlie Chaplin had lived on the edge of things, but possessed a remarkable ability not to give up. "You have to believe in yourself, that's the secret." he said. "Even when I was in the orphanage,

when I was roaming the streets trying to find enough to eat to keep alive,
even then I thought of myself as the greatest actor in the world. I had to
feel that exhuberance that comes from utter confidence in yourself. Without
it you go down in defeat."[23]   This trust in himself was sparked by his mother
when she first recognized Chaplin's special talent.   One night she told him
the story of the New Testament and Jesus' crucifixion and described "how
human He was and, like us, suffered doubt. Jesus wants you to live and
fulfill your destiny here before you join Him above."[24]   This provided
Chaplin with a direction in life, during which he in turn touched the hearts
of people in a religious manner. He exhalted those who were humble and
humbled those who were exhalted."[25]

19   This faith, which was so important to him was manifested in the endings
of several of his films. We see him walking sadly down an empty road with
a bundle on his shoulder; the sorrow is unbearable until, all of the sudden,
he does a little skip and goes off dancing into the horizon.[26] Here Chaplin
summed up the meaning of life he tried to reveal in his films. When at last
he saw the world as a series of complications — the bundle on the Tramp's
shoulder — with little or no joy and comfort, and felt as if he could go no
further, he remenbered that the promised land awaited him at the end of the
road and gave a little hop to symbolize renewed faith and kept moving
towards that day of freedom.

Twenty-six
references in a
six-page paper
seem about right—
four or five to a
page.

The author uses
supporting
quotations in
the preceding
paragraph to build
to a climax in her
own own words.

NOTES

[1]Richard L. Coe, "Remembrances of an Evening With 'The Great Dictator.'" The Washington Post, 26 December 1977, C15.

[2]Robert Payne, The Great God Pan (New York: Hermitage House, 1952), p.177.

[3]Charles Chaplin, My Autobiography (New York: Simon and Schuster, 1964), p. 144.

[4]Chaplin, p. 144

[5]Conrad Hyers, "Farewell to the Clown: A Tribute to Charlie," Christian Century, 22 February 1978, p. 190.

[6]Charlie Chaplin, director, The Gold Rush, with Charles Chaplin and Georgia Hale, United Artists, 1925.

[7]Payne, p. 170.

[8]Alden Whitman, "Charlie Chaplin Dead at 88; Made the Film an Art Form," The New York Times—Biographical Service, (New York: The New York Times), December 1977, p. 1601.

[9]Whitman, p. 1600.

[10]Chaplin, pp. 18-19.

[11]Chaplin, pp. 27-76.

[12]"Charlie Chaplin," Encyclopedia Britannica, 1970.

[13]Whitman, pp. 1604-1605.

[14]The Gold Rush.

[15]"Charles Spencer Chaplin," Chambers's Encyclopedia, 1973.

[16]Payne, p. 85.

[17]Charles Chaplin, Jr., My Father, Charlie Chaplin (New York: Random House, 1960), pp. 180-182.

[18]The Gold Rush.

[19]Payne, p. 204.

[20]Chaplin, Jr., pp. 180-192.

[21]Chaplin, p. 399.

[22]Whitman, p. 1606.

[23]Chaplin, Jr., p. 9.

[24]Chaplin, pp. 22-23.

[25]Hyers, pp. 190-191.

[26]Payne, pp. 122, 137.

BIBLIOGRAPHY

"Chaplin, Charles Spencer." Chambers's Encyclopedia. London: International Learning Systems Corporation, 1973.

"Chaplin, Charlie." Encyclopedia Britannica. Chicago: William Benton, 1970.

Chaplin, Charles, director. The Gold Rush. With Charles Chaplin and Georgia Hale. United Artists, 1925.

Chaplin, Charles. My Autobiography. New York: Simon and Schuster, 1967.

Chaplin, Charles, Jr. My Father. New York: Random House, 1960.

Coe, Richard L. "Remembrances of an Evening with 'The Great Dictator.'" The Washington Post, 26 December 1977, pp. A1, B11, C1, C15.

Hyers, Conrad. "Farewell to the Clown: A Tribute to Charlie." Christian Century, 22 February 1978, pp. 190-194.

Payne, Robert. The Great God Pan. New York: Hermitage House, 1952.

Whitman, Alden. "Charlie Chaplin Dead at 88: Made the Film an Art Form." The New York Times—Biographical Service. New York: The New York Times, December 1977, pp. 1599-1607.

A REFERENCE
HANDBOOK

The material that follows in the rest of *Strategic Writing* is intended for easy reference when you need help with grammar, usage, spelling, punctuation, and mechanics. Some of the information supplements Chapters 5 (Strategies of Paragraphs), 6 (Strategies of Sentences), and 7 (Choosing and Using Words); all of it is intended to enhance your finished papers. The index of this book can help you find specific information quickly.

GRAMMAR

All of us learn to speak long before we learn the names of the parts of speech or the formal rules about their use. In that sense, all of us *know* grammar by the time we're five or six, and we use grammar every time we communicate in speaking or in writing. As we mature we learn a great deal about grammar from reading—not grammar books but newspapers, novels, poetry, magazines, even the labels on cereal boxes.

To talk about language and how language works, however, we need to learn the terminology of grammar and some of its principles. What follows in this section is a composite of the most useful and logical explanations derived from several current systems of grammar—traditional (which is probably what you studied in elementary or high school), structural, and transformational.

Nouns

**Noun
Definition**

Nouns name—people, other living creatures, places, things, and ideas.

> people: *man*, the *tree surgeon*, *Mme. Curie*, *children*, the *Scott family*
> other living creatures: *elephant*, *butterfly*, *bacillus*, *Jumbo*
> places: *city*, *San Francisco*, the *Badlands*, the *Alamo*

Common nouns name general members of a class of things; they begin with lower-case letters. *Proper nouns* name specific members of a class (individuals), and always begin with capital letters.

common noun	proper noun		common noun	proper noun

My pet *iguana, Ignace,* always sleeps under my *bed* in *Houston.*

**Noun
Position**

Nouns can occupy any position in a sentence where the common or proper name of a person, place, thing, or idea would fit. Typically, nouns appear as *subjects, objects of verbs,* and *objects of prepositions.*

> subject　　object
of verb　object
of preposition
> The *computer* made an *error* in *addition.*

> object
of preposition　subject　object
of verb
> Because of the *mistake,* the *customers* received enormous *rebates.*

A noun usually refers to whatever is *doing the acting* or *being acted upon,* or being *described, explained,* or *referred to* in other ways.

> actor　　thing
acted upon
> The celebrated *author* decided to write *film scripts.*

> subject
being described
> *War* is devastating.

**Noun
Patterning**

Nouns are often preceded by *determiners*—articles, possessive pronouns, or demonstrative pronouns—that further restrict or specify the thing named.

> articles: *a* religion, *an* artichoke, *the* United States
> possessive pronouns: *my* grandfather, *your* idea, *their* typewriter
> demonstrative pronouns: *this* oyster, *that* Mercedes, *those* relationships

**Noun
Inflections**

Nouns can be *inflected* (changed in form) to form plurals and possessives. Nouns are usually made plural through the addition of -*s* or -*es* to the base word (*spoon* + -*s* = *spoons*) [see below, pp. 372, 388–389]. Nouns can usually become possessive through the addition of '*s* (*book* + '*s* = *book's*) [see below, pp. 379–380]. While *possession*, in this sense, may mean ownership, it may also refer to other relationships—*a long day's journey, the statue's perfection.* In most cases possessives may also be expressed in an *of* construction: *the perfection of the statue.* But the two methods are not interchangeable. *The cream of the crop* means *high quality,* but *the crop's cream* is unintelligible.

Be careful not to confuse plural and possessive forms of nouns. The plural form does *not* have an apostrophe.

noun singular	noun plural	possessive singular	possessive plural
ship	ships	ship's	ships'
life	lives	life's	lives'

Pronouns

**Pronoun
Definition**

Pronouns substitute for nouns and noun phrases.

pronoun   noun
   It [the refrigerator] clanks when it cools.

It replaces the noun, *refrigerator.*

pronoun   noun phrase
   He [the man who delivers the mail every day] is an FBI agent.

He substitutes for the noun phrase, *the man who delivers the mail every day.*

**Pronoun
Forms and
Functions**

Pronouns, unlike nouns, change their forms to show *cases* that indicate the different way(s) they function in sentences. *Personal pronouns* indicate the speaker, the person spoken to, and the person or thing spoken about. The following chart indicates the forms of the personal pronouns.

Personal Pronouns	*SUBJECTIVE (OR NOMINATIVE) CASE* [*designates speaker*]		*OBJECTIVE CASE* [*designates person spoken to*]	*POSSESSIVE CASE* [*designates person or thing spoken about*]
Singular				
first person	I		me	my, mine
second person	you		you	your, yours
third person	he, she, it		him, her, it	his, her, hers, its
Plural				
first person	we		us	our, ours
second person	you		you	your, yours
third person	they		them	their, theirs

In sentences, these pronouns appear in the following positions.

SUBJECTIVE/NOMINATIVE
   subject of the verb: *We* left fingerprints.

OBJECTIVE
   direct object of the
      verb: The secret agent spotted *them.*

   indirect object of
      the verb: The secret agent read *us* the Bill of Rights.

   object of a
      preposition: The secret agent read the law to *us.*

POSSESSIVE   The secret agent performed *his* duties
                              without violating *our* legal rights.

Reflexive and Intensive Pronouns

Reflexive and *intensive pronouns* are personal pronouns that form compounds with *-self* and *-selves: myself, oneself, yourself, himself, herself, itself, ourselves, yourselves, themselves.*

As intensives, they supplement the noun or pronoun to which they refer, to make it more emphatic.

The chef *herself* not only prepared the dinner, but ate it.
Since you refuse, I *myself* will tame the iguana.

As reflexives, these pronouns function as direct or indirect objects of the verb. (See also Chapter 6, Sentences.)

The dog scratched *itself.*
We have only *ourselves* to blame.

Relative Pronouns

Relative pronouns introduce relative clauses that relate or refer to some *antecedent,* an element appearing earlier in the sentence. *Who, whose, whom, which, that,* and *what* function as relative pronouns in such contexts.

antecedent   relative clause

      relative
      pronoun

The man *who came* to dinner drove an elderly Mercedes.

antecedent   relative clause

      relative
      pronoun

The aging car, *which* had been highly polished, was a pleasure to see.

Interrogative Pronouns

Interrogative pronouns—who, whose, whom, which, and *what* (the same words as the relative pronouns except for *that*)—ask questions.

Who was that masked man?
What needs to be done to get the car ready for inspection?

Indefinite Pronouns

Indefinite pronouns do not identify or specify what they refer to. Among the most common are:

all	both	few	nothing
another	each	many	one
any	either	most	other
anyone	everybody	neither	someone
anything	everything	none	something

Everybody loves *somebody* or *something* passionately.

Pronoun Agreement

Generally, in speaking and in writing, *pronouns should agree in number with the noun or pronoun they refer to*—singular with singular, plural with plural.

singular   singular   plural   plural
antecedent   pronoun   antecedent pronoun

The *mechanic* scratched *her* head when she saw the *birds* in *their* nest on the air filter.

Mechanic and *her* are singular; *birds* and *their* are plural. Today, however, the conventions of pronoun agreement are changing somewhat. In conversations and in casual writing many people use plural pronouns when referring to some singular indefinite pronouns *any, someone, nobody,* because these words have plural connotations.

singular   plural
antecedent   pronoun

"Did *anyone* leave *their* bird nest here?" she asked.

> singular   plural
> antecedent   pronoun
>
> In response to the question, *no one* raised *their* hand.

Conventional usage would require a singular masculine pronoun in both sentences.

> singular   singular
> antecedent   pronoun
>
> "Did *anyone* leave *his* bird nest here?" she asked.

> singular   singular
> antecedent   pronoun
>
> In response to the question, *no one* raised *his* hand.

Usage is also influenced today because *he, his,* and *him* are often interpreted as masculine, rather than having a general meaning of *person* or *humanity*. As a consequence, some usage experts are now recommending the plural pronouns (as shown in the above sentences) in formal writing. Others suggest *his or her* as a substitute for the generic masculine pronouns:

> singular   singular
> antecedent   pronouns
>
> *No one* raised *his* or *her* hand.

But to many people this sounds self-conscious or unnecessarily cumbersome. See whether your own preference agrees with that of your intended audience, including your employer or instructor. (See also p. 359.)

Adjectives

Adjective Definition

Adjectives (and adverbs) modify—that is, describe, limit, qualify, or specify—nouns, pronouns, or words functioning as nouns. They can precede or follow what they modify.

> the *happy* cooker   the house *beautiful*   *wonderful* you

And, functioning as *predicate adjectives*, they follow various verbs that often indicate states of being—*be, appear, seem, taste.*

>   predicate
> adj.   adj.   adj.   adj.   adj.
>
> The *warm apple* pie, *juicy* and *succulent*, smelled *appetizing*.

Comparison of Adjectives

Many adjectives can be compared; that is, their form can be changed to show the extent or intensity (degree) they designate. The *positive* form is the base word (*weak, pretty*). The *comparative* form designates a state greater than the base but less than the ultimate it can attain (*weaker, prettier*). The *superlative* form represents the maximum attainable (*weakest, prettiest*).

To show comparison, add *-er* or *-est* to the positive base of one-syllable adjectives and some two-syllable adjectives. If they end in *-y* change the *-y* to *-i* before making the addition.

POSITIVE ADJECTIVE BASE	COMPARATIVE ADJECTIVE FORM	SUPERLATIVE ADJECTIVE FORM
deep	deeper	deepest
happy	happier	happiest

For all other adjectives of two or more syllables, put *more* or *most*, *less* or *least* before the positive base.

POSITIVE ADJECTIVE BASE	COMPARATIVE ADJECTIVE FORM	SUPERLATIVE ADJECTIVE FORM
stubborn	more stubborn	most stubborn
understanding	more understanding	most understanding

Irregular Adjectival Forms

A few adjectives have irregular forms, which your dictionary can supply.

POSITIVE ADJECTIVE BASE	COMPARATIVE ADJECTIVE FORM	SUPERLATIVE ADJECTIVE FORM
good	better	best
bad	worse	worst
many, some, much	more	most

Adverbs

Adverb Definition

Adverbs, like adjectives, modify—that is, describe, limit, qualify, affirm or negate, or express logical relationships among—verbs, adjectives, other adverbs, prepositions, phrases, clauses, or whole sentences.

                                                verb   adverb

verb: Just when they *were beginning to dance easily* and

adverb   verb   adverb

gracefully, the music *stopped abruptly.*

                                       adverb adjective

adjective: Ann and André were a *very attractive* couple,

adverb   adjective

exceptionally well-dressed.

adverb   adverb

adverb: They danced *remarkably well.*

preposition adverb

preposition: Only after dancing did they take off their shoes.

                  phrase
      adverb

phrase: They were not nonchalant, *however* self-confident they seemed.

      adverb

sentence: Therefore, even though they were novices, their obvious talent gave them a chance to win the prize.

Adverb Meaning

In addition to what they modify, adverbs may be classified according to their meaning. Adverbs characteristically express a variety of qualities and conditions that often answer such questions as *how, where, when, why, to what degree,* and *with what frequency.*

place: "Come *here,*" the master of ceremonies said, smiling.
time: Eventually Ann and André realized he was speaking to them.
manner: Ann ran *quickly* to the platform, but André, being barefoot, walked *more slowly.*
degree: Indeed, he moved *very reluctantly.*
frequency: They had *never before* won a prize for dancing, particularly an iguana.
negation: In fact, André did *not* want an iguana.
affirmation: But Ann *certainly* did.
qualification: However, she wanted to treat her partner fairly.
logical relationship: Consequently, Ann traded her favorite album, *To Live Is to Dance,* for André's share of the prize.

Forms of Adverbs

As the above illustrations reveal, many adverbs end in *-ly* (*easily,* unexpected*ly*), but many do not (*around, down, however*). Some adverbs have forms identical to those of adjectives.

early   slow   loose   more   low

Comparisons of Adverbs

And, like adjectives, many adverbs have three degrees of comparison—positive, comparative, superlative. They usually form the latter two by putting *more* or *most, less* or *least* before the positive base.

POSITIVE ADVERB BASE	COMPARATIVE ADVERB FORM	SUPERLATIVE ADVERB FORM
vigorously	more vigorously	most vigorously
slowly*	more slowly	most slowly

But a few adverbs, usually of one syllable, do form their comparative and superlative forms by adding *-er* and *-est* to the positive base.

POSITIVE ADVERB BASE	COMPARATIVE ADVERB FORM	SUPERLATIVE ADVERB FORM
late	later	latest
low	lower	lowest
slow*	slower	slowest

* Note that slow, like some other adverbs, has alternative forms of comparative and superlative.

Verbs

Verb Definition

Verbs, essential to every sentence, either specify the subject's condition, existence, or occurrence; or tell what the subject does (that is, they indicate the subject's actions).

    action   condition
I *think;* therefore I *am.*

Although other parts of speech, such as nouns, can show action (the noun *recall,* for instance), a verb does not function in the sentence as a thing or idea, the way a noun does. Nor does it occupy a substantive (nounlike) position as the subject of a sentence or the object of a verb. Instead, a verb needs a subject—a noun, pronoun, or equivalent—to say something about.

    noun-
    sub-
    ject   verb   noun-object
Enrique *had* total recall.

    pronoun-subject   verb   noun-object
Nevertheless, he couldn't *recall* the name of his brother-in-law.

Verb Functions

Likewise, although other parts of speech, such as adjectives and adverbs, can denote existence or states of being (*sad, happy*), verbs can be distinguished because they never modify other words, as adjectives and adverbs do. Instead, they perform several functions—transitive, intransitive, and linking.
A *transitive verb* transmits an action to a direct object.

    subject   verb   direct object
I *love* you.

An *intransitive* verb specifies an action or state, but does not take an object. It is often followed by an adverb.

       verb   adverb
Hedonists *relax* frequently.

A *linking verb* links the subject with a noun, phrase, or adjective which refers directly to that subject.

   subject verb adj.   adj.   adj.
The tycoon *is* healthy, wealthy, and happy.

    subject   verb   noun
The tycoon *remains* a robber baron.

Verb Tenses

The states of being or action that verbs connote always *take place in time;* they begin or will begin at some time, they continue, they end. The *tense* of a verb is the time it expresses, which is signified by the inflections *-s, -ed, -en* or *-ed,* or *-ing* added to the base form, sometimes supplemented by auxiliary words.

   verb   verb participle
I *will* always *be thinking* of you.

The principal parts of a verb are:

base infinitive (simple present): I *love,* he *loves,* they *love*
past (base + *-ed*): I *loved,* he *loved,* they *loved*
past participle (form of the verb *to be* + base + *-ed*): I *have loved,* he *has loved,* they *have loved*
                     or
(form of the verb *to be* + base + *-en*): I *have driven* . . .
participle (base + *-ing*): *loving*

Verb Voice

Verbs are either *active,* if the subject performs the action (is active); or *passive,* if the subject receives the action (is passive to it). This designation is known as the *voice* of the verb.

active voice: Actors and actresses *enchant* audiences.
passive voice: Audiences *are enchanted* by actors and actresses.

Note that in the passive voice the recipient of the action becomes the grammatical subject of the sentence.

The chart below illustrates the first-person forms and most common tenses of regular verbs.

	ACTIVE VOICE	PASSIVE VOICE
Present (action going on now)	I love	I am loved
Present progressive (action continuing in the present)	I am loving	I am being loved
Present perfect (completed action seen from the present)	I have loved	I have been loved
Past (action completed)	I loved	I was loved
Past progressive (action continuing in the past)	I was loving	I was being loved
Past perfect (action completed in the past)	I had loved	I had been loved
Future (action to occur in the future)	I will (shall) love	I will (shall) be loved
Future perfect (action that will have been completed in the future)	I will (shall) have loved	I will (shall) have been loved

The tenses of *irregular verbs*, very common words, have to be learned separately because of the variable ways in which the past tenses and participles are formed. A dictionary will identify the irregularities.

INFINITIVE (BASE)	PAST TENSE	PAST PARTICIPLE
be	was	been
begin	began	begun
go	went	gone
lie	lay	lain

Verb Moods

Verbs have three *moods* to indicate the manner of a statement. The most common is the *indicative mood*—a statement of fact or a question.

Travel *is* exhilarating.
Should I *go* to Europe?

The *imperative mood* is used for giving commands or directions, or for making requests.

You *should go* to Spain.
Please *try* Portugal, as well. [the subject of the verb is implied here]

The *subjunctive mood*, much less common, is used to indicate a doubt, wish, uncertainty, or condition—often hypothetical. The subjunctive verb is often expressed by the verb *were* (or *be* or *had been*) and *if*.

If I *were* rich, I'd go around the world.
Had I *taken* that trip, I'd still be in orbit. [*If* preceding the *had* is implied.]

Two-Part Verbs

A *two-part verb* is a verb form followed by a particle—a short word that looks like a preposition.

drown out   fill in   look up   tune out

However, unlike prepositions, these particles can be moved around in the sentence without changing the sentence's meaning.

If Sam traveled by moped, he wouldn't have to *tune up* the car.
If Sam traveled by moped, he wouldn't have to *tune* the car *up*.

Auxiliaries

Auxiliaries, traditionally called "helping" verbs though they are uninflected, are inserted before inflected verbs to create different emphases or to imply obligation or degree of likelihood. Auxiliaries include:

can   could   will   would   shall   should   may   might
do   did   need   ought   must

Note the different implications connoted by the following auxiliaries:

You *could* wait.
You *may* wait.
You *should* wait.
You *must* wait.
You *did* wait.

Prepositions

Prepositions

Prepositions indicate relationships of time, space, or logical connection between the nouns, pronouns, or equivalents and some other word in the sentence.

               time   logical connection
Precisely *at* midnight, the princess turned *into* a pumpkin

logical
connection place
instead of into her driveway.

Some prepositions are single words, such as

at   by   above   below   in   on   for   against   of   to
(among others).

Prepositional Phrases

In a *prepositional phrase,* a preposition is followed by a noun or noun substitute (the *object of the preposition*) with or without modifiers.

> prepositional phrase
> *Except for his grandmother,* Bob's German shepherd was his best friend.

Conjunctions

Coordinating Conjunctions

Conjunctions connect words, phrases, or clauses. Like prepositions, they indicate relationships of time, space, or logical relationships. However, *conjunctions always function as connectors;* prepositions and other words (some adjectives, adverbs, and pronouns) do not.

Conjunctions are either coordinating, correlative, or subordinating. *Coordinating conjunctions (and, but, or, for, so, yet)* join comparable or equivalent grammatical elements.

> The fairytale princess had a peaches *and* cream complexion, *but* the frog had a face that only a mother could love.

In the above sentence, the *and* shows the equivalence between *peaches* and *cream;* the *but* shows the equivalence between the first and second halves of the sentence.

Correlative Conjunctions

Correlative conjunctions (both . . . and; either . . . or; neither . . . nor; not only . . . but also) relate one equivalent element to another.

> equivalent elements
> *Either* a frog *or* a prince would be acceptable, she thought.

Subordinating Conjunctions

Subordinating conjunctions (after, as, as soon as, because, since, unless, until, when, and many others) join two elements that are not equivalent; the one that cannot stand alone grammatically supports, explains, or diminishes the other and is considered *subordinate.*

> subordinate dependent clause
> subord. conj.   main clause
> *Although* she thought she had chosen a frog, she was mistaken.

subordinate dependent clause   subordinate dependent phrase
subord. conj.   subord. conj.
When a handsome prince emerged, *though* tinted slightly green,
   main clause

the princess was overjoyed.

Sentence Connectors

Sentence connectors are some adverbs that connect independent clauses; they function partly as conjunctions and partly as adverbs. They indicate the logical relationship of one grammatically independent sentence element to another (the *conjunctive* role), and they also modify the sentence element they precede (the *adverbial* role).

sent. connector
The prince was articulate; *nevertheless,* he still croaked on occasion.

Some common sentence connectors are:

also   consequently   however   indeed   likewise   then
therefore   thus

Sentence connectors are conventionally preceded by a *semicolon;* don't mistake them for coordinating conjunctions and use a comma, or you'll have a comma splice.

Right: The prince and princess lived happily ever after; *furthermore,* their offspring were known throughout the realm for their unusual skill at broadjumping.
Wrong: The prince and princess lived happily ever after, *furthermore,* their offspring. . . .

Articles

Article Definition

Articles are uninflected words that immediately precede and limit the nouns they modify. There are only three articles. *A* and *an* (generally equivalent to *any*) are *indefinite articles* and precede a general category, often expressed in the singular. *A* is used before initial consonant sounds, *an* before vowels.

A clover, *a* bee, and reverie create *a* prairie for poet Emily Dickinson.
An articulate writer needs *an* up-to-date dictionary.

The, the *definite article,* precedes specific items or their modifiers, whether singular or plural.

"*The* quality of mercy is not strained" has been transmuted into *the* punch line for *the* supreme shaggy dog story, "*The* koala tea of Mersey is not strained."

USAGE

Usage changes over time

Usage changes over time, more rapidly in speech than in writing. In Shakespeare's era *hussy* and *housewife* meant the same thing, but later *hussy* took a turn for the worse while *housewife* remained respectable. Likewise, *pot, grass, fuzz* acquired special meanings during the years of violent protests against the Vietnam War.

Usage in writing vs. speaking

We tend to choose our words more casually in speech than in writing. Slang or profanity can pass almost unnoticed in conversation; in writing, it may stick out like a hip flask at a temperance meeting. As language changes, as the context changes, the so-called "rules" of language usage change, too. Such "rules" reflect custom and individual preference more than logic or grammatical inevitability. Consequently, authorities on usage often disagree over such matters as *It's me* vs. *It is I*, and various meanings of *shall* and *will*.

Middle-of-the-road usage

When you conform to current middle-of-the-road usage you will usually avoid faddish terms that would make your writing sound out of date very quickly; today, *the cat's pajamas, groovy,* and *boss* seem strange. Conforming to the current standard is also an unobtrusive way to help convince your readers (some of whom may be sticklers for the right word) that you're an educated writer who knows what you're talking about.

The following suggestions on usage represent a moderate—and, therefore, fairly safe—middle ground between inflexible conservatives who claim that ending a sentence with a preposition is something up with which they will not put, and ultra liberals for whom anything goes, from fad usages (*interface* used either as a noun or a verb— "When the sciences and the humanities *interface* . . .") to the latest slang ("Sylvia *blew* her chance for promotion because she *let it all hang out*.").

Common difficulties with usage

Below is a list of some of the more common difficulties with usage, particularly when one member of a pair of words is mistaken for the other.

accept/except: Accept is a verb meaning *receive* or take. Although *except* may be a verb meaning *exclude*, it is more often a preposition meaning *excluding. Except* for the fact that she couldn't find a parking place at the awards ceremonies, she was delighted to *accept* the Nobel Prize.

aggravate/irritate: Aggravate means *to make worse; irritate* means *to annoy* or *stir to anger.* The buzzing mosquitoes *irritated* the picnicker; their bites *aggravated* his allergies.

all ready/already: All ready (two words) means *everything is ready* or *prepared. Already* (one word, an adverb) means *so soon, so early,* or *previously.* "Is it midnight *already?"* he asked, although he had been *all ready* to leave the party at ten.

all right (two words): In spite of its resemblance to *already* (see above), *alright* (one word) is not *all right* (two words) to use.

allusion/illusion: An allusion is a *casual or passing reference;* it's often followed by *to.* The physicist made an *allusion* to Einstein. An *illusion* deceives through creating a *false or misleading impression;* it's often followed by *of.* Although ballet costumes may convey the *illusion* of delicacy, they are actually very strong, to withstand the dancers' energetic movements.

a lot (two words)/*allot* (one word): *Alot* isnot aword. *Allot* means to *divide* or *apportion.* The philanthropist *allotted a lot* of money for research on the common cold.

among/between: Use *between* (Old English meaning *by two)* with *two items, among* (Old English meaning *in a crowd)* with *three or more. Between* flights, she frantically searched for her luggage *among* huge piles of suitcases.

amount/number: Amount is used with *total quantities* (mass nouns) not considered as individual units: a large *amount* of money. *Number* is used with *countable items* (count nouns) that can be thought of as individual units and that can be replaced by specific numbers: a *number* of dollar bills. Caution: Don't substitute *amount* for *number,* particularly where people are concerned:

> avoid: A large *amount* of fans attended the rock concert.
> use: A large *number* of fans attended the rock concert.

angry/mad: In formal writing *mad* means *insane;* in informal writing or speaking the two terms are often interchangeable. Are you *mad* [or *angry*] that you didn't get a raise?

complement/compliment: As a noun, *complement* means *something that completes or accompanies; compliment* means *an ex-*

pression of praise or respect. The gourmet *complimented* the wine steward on his choice of beverage: *Chateauneuf du Pape* was the perfect *complement* to the roast beef.

continual/continuous: Continual means *recurring at intervals; continuous* means *uninterrupted.* The sleeper's *continuous* heartbeat, though strong and steady, was much quieter than his *continual* snores.

criterion/criteria: Criterion is the *singular form.* The only *criterion* for admission is academic excellence. *Criteria* is *plural.* The *criteria* for admission are academic ability, participation in extracurricular activities, and good character.

could have/should have/would have: Use these forms in writing rather than *could of/should of/would of,* even though they may sound alike in speaking or in their contracted forms, *could've/ should've/would've.* I *would have* caught the fighting crab if I *could have* protected my hands from its pincers.

disinterested/uninterested: Disinterested does not mean *not interested,* but *impartial* or *unbiased.* The *disinterested* report on auto safety recommended air bags and rear seat belts as the most effective lifesaving devices.

effect/affect: Effect is most often used as a noun, in the sense of *result* or *consequence; affect* as a verb meaning *to influence.* The *effects* of high oil prices are now being seen, as they *affect* people's attitudes toward long-distance driving, suburban living, and carpooling. As a verb *effect* means *to bring something about* or *accomplish.* The judges *effected* a just solution to the rival claims of the Nobel Prize nominees.

few/little, fewer/less: Few and *fewer,* like *number* are used with *countable items* that can be thought of as individual units. *Little* and *less,* like *amount,* are used with *total quantities* not considered as individual units. A *few* cake recipes call for only a *little* flour; *fewer* still for even *less.* (See *amount/number,* above.)

former/latter: When used as a pair, *former* refers to the first-mentioned item of the two; *latter* refers to the second-mentioned item of two. Among Joni's exotic pets were a borzoi and a pirhana; although she pretended to love them equally, she secretly preferred the *former* to the *latter.*

good/well: Well refers to either a *state of health* or a *quality of performance; good* identifies *a pleasing appearance* or *virtuous moral qualities.* The Wolverines played *well* and looked *good* in their new maize and blue jerseys.

hanged/hung: Hanged as a past participle refers to *stringing up criminals; hung* refers to *stringing up inanimate objects*—laundry, bird feeders, Christmas stockings.

imply/infer: Imply means to *suggest* or *express indirectly; infer* means to *perceive, conclude,* or *deduce.* The speaker or writer implies; the listener or reader infers. The Beatles' lyrics *imply* many truths about life and love which careful listeners can *infer.*

in to/into: In to (two words) indicates *direction* plus *purpose;* Herkimer went *in to* study. *Into* (one word) indicates *direction* exclusively: Philomena went *into* [not in to] the library.

it's/its: It's is a contraction representing the subject, *it,* and the verb, *is: It's* raining. *Its* is a possessive pronoun (The hungry anteater devoured *its* dinner). This is sometimes confusing because unlike many possessive pronouns, *its* is written without the apostrophe—so it won't be confused with *it's.*

it is I/it is me or *it's me:* Formal writing still requires the nominative case after the verb *to be,* thus "It is *I.*" But in informal writing or speaking "*It is me*" and the contraction "*It's me*" are widely used.

lay/lie: Lay (past tense, *laid*) in the sense of *set* requires an object: "*Lay* the laundry in lavender," the Duchess commanded. Alice *laid* it down. *Lie* (past tense, *lay*) means *rest* or *repose,* and does not usually require an object. "*Lie* down, Phydeaux!" The dog *lay* down.

like/as: Current usage is divided, with *like* often used interchangeably with *as* in casual speech. She acts *like/as* if she owns the place. In formal writing, however, it's safer to use *like* before nouns and pronouns (He runs *like* a wombat), and *as* before phrases and clauses (He runs *as* a wombat runs).

lose/loose: Lose (one *o*) is a verb meaning to *misplace, give up,* or *be deprived of.* "Cheer up," Jim, newly engaged, told his mother. "You won't *lose* a son, you'll gain a daughter." *Loose* (two *o's*) is an adjective or adverb meaning *free, unrestrained, unfastened.* You'll *lose* your marbles if you let them *loose.*

one of those who is/one of those who are: Conventional advice recommends a plural verb to agree with the plural referent. She is one of those outstanding *athletes* who *qualify* for the decathlon. In practice, however, usage is divided because of the *singular* (*one*) and *plural* (*those*) indicators. So use *one of those who* with either the singular or the plural verb, depending on whether you want to emphasize *uniqueness* or *plurality.*

> Emphasis on *one* (singular): Bard is the only *one* of the dozen in his computer class who is speedy enough to make the math team. Emphasis on *many* (plural): Laird is one of those extremely thoughtful *people* who continually *anticipate* others' needs, from celebrating birthdays to watering abandoned plants.

only: Only and similar adverbs, such as *merely* and *mostly,* are portable words that can be moved around in sentences to express various relationships and emphases. In conversation, *only* often comes early in the sentence (I'm *only* thinking of you) as a signal of what is to come, irrespective of the meaning. In writing, it's preferable to keep the adverb closer to what you want to modify and accentuate. Compare:

> Only I am thinking of you.
> I'm only thinking of you.
> I'm thinking only of you.
> I'm thinking of only you.
> I'm thinking of you only.

In your own writing try such adverbs in different places in the sentence until you have the emphasis and rhythm you want.

past participles as modifiers: In speaking, combinations such as *air conditioned, tossed salad,* and *prejudiced attitude* run together, and the past tense indicators (the *-ed* sounds) get lost. But be sure to spell the words with all the letters, even if the *-ed* for the past tense isn't pronounced distinctly.

not: air condition   toss salad   prejudice attitude

She is *prejudiced* [not *prejudice*] against men with long hair and moustaches, even though she realizes that her *prejudice* is irrational.

precede/ proceed: To *precede* [*not* spelled *preceed*] is to *go before* or *ahead of* in *importance, rank, place,* or *time.* To *proceed* is to *go forward* or to *continue an action or process.* Peace *precedes* war in our national value system, but we nonetheless *proceed* in our military buildup.

real (as an intensifer): In casual speech some people like to use *real* instead of *very* or *much*. He's *real* handsome. Stick to the latter terms in formal or general writing. He's *very* handsome.

set/sit: *Set* usually requires an object. *Set* the scales near the dieter. *Sit* does not usually require an object. Day after day, Mme. Defarge *sat* [not *set*] and knitted.

split infinitive: The "rule" against splitting an infinitive was designed to keep the *to* next to the verb—*to sleep soundly, to wave frantically.* However, as may be seen in the above discussion of *only*, there are other options, depending on your meaning. *To strongly emphasize* the verb, as in this sentence, put the adverb between the *to* and the verb. To emphasize the adverb, put it before or after the infinitive or the object of the verb.

then/than: Then refers to *sequences,* either of *time* or of *cause and effect.* The princess kissed the frog, who *then* turned into a prince. *Than* is used in comparisons: bigger *than,* less *than,* better *than,* worse *than.* . . .

through/thru: In formal writing, use conventional American spelling for all words written for an American audience. Overly simplified spelling (*nite, foto*) may be appropriate for flippant ads, but it's too casual for most college writing.

who/whoever, whom/whomever: *Who* and *whoever* are nominative forms used as the *subject* of the clause in which they appear. *Whom* and *whomever* are objective forms used as the *object* of a verb or a preposition. Identifying the subject of each clause should enable you to tell which form to use.

(*We* voted for the person) (*who* campaigned the most honestly).
(But public *policies* depend on) (*whoever* gets elected).
(The *person* [*who* has the most votes] will gain in power and prestige.)
(The *candidate* [for *whom* we voted] was elected.)

who's/whose: *Who's* is a contraction of the subject and verb combination *who is.* *Who's* going to cook the artichoke? *Who's* going to eat it? *Whose* is a possessive pronoun. *Whose* paycheck will buy the groceries?

will/shall: Most Americans use *will* to indicate both *determination* and *intention,* regardless of what the "rules" say. I *will* run in the marathon tomorrow, and they *will,* too. For unusually dramatic, emphatic, or formal occasions, we now use *shall* in the first person, singular or plural. We *shall* overcome.

-wise: This is a suffix added to nouns or adjectives to form adverbs indicating *manner, direction,* or *position: clockwise, edgewise.* When used in the sense of *with reference to* (*travelwise, coursewise, incomewise*) it will sound jargony and offensive to many readers *stylewise.*

you're/your: Like *who's and whose, you're* is a contraction of the subject-verb combination *you are. Your* is a possessive pronoun. With *your* speed and *your* stamina, *you're* bound to win the race.

SPELLING

Like it or not, the quality of your writing (and sometimes, unfortunately, even of your mind) may be judged by the accuracy of your spelling. Although you won't need to worry about spelling on a first draft, when you revise you will need to check in an up-to-date college dictionary words of which you're uncertain or which you chronically misspell. Your most serious problems aren't likely to be new or difficult words; those you'll look up. Rather, the troublemakers are likely to be more common words, homophones (words pronounced the same but spelled differently—*to, too, two*), or words in which the pronunciation gives insufficient or ambiguous clues about the spelling. *Harass,* for instance, has one *r* and two *s*'s while *embarrass* has two *r*'s and two *s*'s—and it's *embarrassing* to spell *harass* wrong.

When you find alternative spellings given (*cargoes, cargos*) use the first, preferred spelling. Assuming that you're an American or are writing for an American audience, be sure to use American spelling. If you adopt British spelling (*cheque* instead of *check, honour* instead of *honor*) you'll appear artificial.

Suggestions for Improving Your Spelling

In spite of numerous exceptions, two-thirds of our words employ conventional and predictable spelling patterns. Even with words that don't, there are systematic ways of trying to cope with the irregularities.

1. *Keep a pocket-sized notebook of words you commonly misspell. Group the words* not alphabetically but *according to the type of problem they represent,* one problem to a page. Identify each group by the nature of the problem; beneath that write the solution (or alternative solutions); then list the problematic words. Put related problems near each other in the notebook so you can compare the difficulties and the solutions. Add new words to the appropriate categories. If there are exceptions to the solutions, note these and learn them as exceptions.

Your aim will always be to learn the underlying pattern and to categorize the solution so you can think in terms of groups of related words, rather than single words in isolation. Analyzing your reasons for misspelling certain words can help you do this. Among the questions you can ask yourself are:

Is the misspelling related to the pronunciation of homophones (*coarse/course*)?

To the mispronunciation of words (*axed* for *asked, heighth* for *height*)?

To the confusion of one word with another that sounds similar (*eminent/imminent*)?

To the confusion of one word with another that looks similar (*loose/lose*)?

Failure to recognize the consistent patterning of a prefix or suffix as it appears in various words?

Here are several examples of the way your sample spelling notebook pages might look.

PROBLEM: How do I decide whether a word is spelled *ei* or *ie*?
SOLUTION: Remember the rule, "*i* before *e*, except after *c* or when sounded like *a*, as in *neighbor* or *weigh*."

I *BEFORE* E	*EXCEPT AFTER* C	EXCEPTIONS
achieve	deceive	[note: all these exceptions
believe	receive	are spelled *ei*]
grief	conceive	either
yield	ceiling	foreign
		leisure
		weird

PROBLEM: How do I decide whether to retain or drop the final silent *e* when adding a suffix?

SOLUTION 1:   Retain the final -*e* before a suffix that begins with a consonant.

SILENT -E	*RETAIN* -E *WITH SUFFIX*	EXCEPTIONS
love	lo*ve*ly	[note: All omit the
move	mo*ve*ment	final -*e* before the
nine	ni*ne*ty	suffix beginning with
		a consonant]
		jud*gm*ent
		tru*ly*
		a*wf*ul
		arg*um*ent

SOLUTION 2: Drop the final -*e* before a suffix that begins with a vowel.

SILENT -E	*DROP* -E *BEFORE SUFFIX*	EXCEPTIONS
love	lo*vi*ng	[note: all retain the final
move	mo*va*ble	-*e* before the suffix
believe	belie*va*ble	beginning with a vowel]
		mil*e*age
		notic*e*able
		cano*e*ing

PROBLEM: How do I form the plural of nouns ending in -*y*?
SOLUTION 1: If a consonant precedes the final -*y*, change the -*y* to *i* and add -*es*.

SINGULAR *FINAL* -Y	*PLURAL* *I PLUS* -ES	POSSIBLE PITFALL
copy	cop*ies*	*not* copy's
lady	lad*ies*	*not* lady's
navy	nav*ies*	*not* navy's

SOLUTION 2: If a vowel precedes the final -*y*, add -*s*.

SINGULAR *FINAL VOWEL* + -Y	*PLURAL* *FINAL VOWEL* + -Y + -S
attorney	attorn*eys*
donkey	donk*eys*
journey	journ*eys*

PROBLEM: How do I tell whether a word is spelled with an *ar* or an *er* when they're pronounced the same?
SOLUTION: Memorize the spellings, by similar groups.

AR	ER
sepa*ra*te	despe*ra*te
burgl*ar*	cemet*er*y
alt*ar* (religious platform)	alt*er* (change, transform)
hang*ar* (for airplanes)	hang*er* (for coats)
station*ar*y (not moving)	station*er*y (letter paper)

PROBLEM: How do I form adverbs from adjectives ending in *-l*?
SOLUTION: Keep the *-l* and add *-ly*.

accidental + *-ly* = accident*ally*   hint for remembering:
general + *-ly* = gener*ally*   all the endings are *ally*
frugal + *-ly* = frug*ally*
essential + *-ly* = essenti*ally*

2. *Learn common spelling patterns.* Many one-syllable words are spelled consistently when incorporated as syllables of longer words.

day: *day*break, *day*dream, *day*light, *day*time, Mon*day*, yester*day*

Words that rhyme are often spelled the same except for the initial consonant.

*b*in, *d*in, *f*in, *g*in, *k*in, *p*in, *s*in, *t*in, *w*in (*-in* is the basic spelling pattern)
*b*un, *f*un, *g*un, *n*un, *p*un, *r*un, *s*un (*-un* is the basic spelling pattern)

These words are often spelled the same when incorporated into longer words, as: *fin*ger, *kin*dred, *tin*type, *gun*nery, *nun*nery, *run*way, *run*ner.
Words with the same vowel sound are often spelled the same except for the initial consonant. Or they may have two or more common spellings. If so, learn the variants by groups of similar spellings.

b*each* (sand), br*each* (break), l*each* (water action) [*ea* is a common spelling for the vowel sound]
b*eech* (tree), br*eech* (bottom), l*eech* (parasite) [*ee* is another common spelling for the same vowel sound]

Learn some common derivatives in which the base words are spelled the same: *beach*comber, *beach*head, *breech*es, *breech*cloth. You can find them easily near the base words in the dictionary.

3. *Beware of possible pitfalls.* Some of the most common are identified below. Although you will want to be alert to their existence, you will need to check your dictionary for the spelling of problem words.
Word endings. The following vowels are often pronounced alike, which makes the spelling confusing. When in doubt, look them up.

ENDING	SAMPLE WORDS
-able, -ible	(More English words end in *-able*—*agreeable*—than end in *-ible*—terrible.)
-al, -el, -il, -le, -ile	fin*al*, ang*el*, civ*il*, mirac*le*, wh*ile*
-ance, -ence	brilli*ance*, differ*ence*
-ant, -ent	pleas*ant*, pres*ent*
-ar, er, -or	regul*ar*, play*er*, mirr*or*
-ous, -eous, -ious, -uous	nerv*ous*, gas*eous*, delic*ious*, decid*uous*

Homophones. Homophones (words sounding the same) are words with similar sounds but different spellings as well as different meanings. (Others are discussed in *Usage*, pp. 369–375.)

> *advice* (noun)/*advise* (verb)
> *break* (fracture)/*brake* (slow down)
> *elicit* (draw forth)/*illicit* (illegal)
> *flout* (defy)/*flaunt* (display)
> *insure* (indemnify)/*ensure* (guarantee)
> *lessen* (reduce)/*lesson* (teaching)
> *loose* (slack)/*lose* (misplace)
> *pray* (beg)/*prey* (victim)
> *weather* (atmospheric state)/*whether* (if)
> *which* (that one)/*witch* (sorceress)

Plurals

Nouns whose singular ends in -ch, -s, -sh, and -x all form plurals by adding *-es*:

> *church/churches, box/boxes*

Nouns whose singular ends in a consonant plus -o form plurals by adding *-es*:

> *hero/heroes, tomato/tomatoes*

Nouns whose singular ends in a vowel plus -o become plural by adding *-s*:

> *ratio/ratios, studio/studios*
> Exceptions: *altos, pianos, sopranos*

Words with alternative plural spellings. Use the preferred spelling, whichever one your dictionary lists *first*.

> *cargoes/cargos*   *zeros/zeroes*

Compound nouns (nouns made of more than one word) *form their plurals in the way the last word ordinarily does*, by adding *-s* (*break-ins*) or *-es, -ies* (*language laboratories*), or using another regular plural form (*council women, field mice*).

EXCEPTION: When the first word of the compound pair is the key term, pluralize that instead. To pluralize the second term is likely to change the meaning. Most dictionaries spell out these exceptions.

fields of vision	(not *field of visions*)
sisters-in-law	(not *sister-in-laws*)
men-of-war	(not *man-of-wars*)
rights-of-way	(not *right-of-ways*)

Nouns with foreign plurals. As a rule, it's safe to use English plurals for foreign words, rather than trying to pluralize them as the original languages would: *cactuses, ratios, sanitariums.* Again, check your dictionary. Greek and Latin derivatives whose singular ends in *-is* regularly form the plural by changing the *-is* to *-es: analyses, crises, theses.*

EXCEPTIONS: But these common foreign plurals still prevail:

Singular	Plural
criterion	*criteria*
datum	*data*
phenomenon	*phenomena*
stratum	*strata*

PUNCTUATION

Punctuation marks are the traffic signals of writing, directions the writer gives to readers so they will know where to stop, start again, pause, and how to control the rhythm and emphasis of sentences and words. Although they're little marks and unobtrusive (as one student writer has observed, "Commas are so cheap!"), if used appropriately they can enhance the meaning of the words, without either overwhelming them by excess or being so sparse that the meaning is unclear or ambiguous. The following conventions of punctuation are offered here to help you answer the basic questions, What punctuation marks will help my readers to understand my meanings? my emphases?

Period   .

1. *The period is used as end punctuation:*

at the end of a declarative sentence, i.e., a sentence that makes a statement.

Every May, Cal Tech students play elaborate pranks.

at the end of an imperative sentence, i.e., a sentence that expresses a command, request, or plea.

On May 7, all seniors must leave campus by 8 a.m.

at the end of indirect questions.

An innocent transfer student asked what kinds of pranks were played.
(Contrast this with the direct question: An innocent transfer student asked, "What kinds of pranks are played?")

2. *The period is used after many abbreviations:*

degrees: B.S., M.A., M.B.A., Ph.D., M.D.
titles: Mr., Mrs., Ms., Dr., the Rev., Jr., Sr.
states: Ariz., Mich., N.H. (but not with postal abbreviations preceding zip codes: AZ, MI, NH)
bibliographic citations: anon. (anonymous); i.e. (that is); p., pp. (page[s]); vol., vols. (volume[s])
numerical designations: a.m., p.m., m.p.h., B.C., A.D.

3. *Three spaced periods constitute an ellipsis . . . and signify that something has been omitted from a quotation.*

Original: Cal Tech students, embracing their history with a vengeance, have a long-established tradition of pranksterism.
Elliptical version: Cal Tech students . . . have a long-established tradition of pranksterism.

To indicate that material has been omitted at the end of a quoted sentence, use four periods—add the period that ends the sentence to the three of the ellipses.

Original: The classic prank is to disassemble a senior's parked car and reassemble it in his dorm room, where he will find it with the motor running.

Elliptical version: The classic prank is to disassemble a senior's parked car and reassemble it in his dorm room. . . .

Question Mark ?

1. *The question mark follows a direct question,* wherever the question ends in a sentence.

Question form: Can one lose weight on a diet of steak and chocolate?
Statement-form question: You call that a diet?
Tag question: You expect me to take you seriously, don't you?
Question within a question: Why don't you ask yourself, "Are chocolate and steak low-calorie, or are they simply my favorite foods?"

2. *A question mark in parentheses (?) indicates doubt.*

The steak-and-chocolate diet was developed in Mesopotamia around 400 (?) B.C.

BEWARE: Avoid using doubting question marks as a form of sarcasm. Experts (?) have denounced the steak-and-chocolate diet. It's better to express your doubt in words.

So-called experts have denounced the steak-and-chocolate diet.

Exclamation Point !

Exclamation points indicate particularly strong emotion (Oh! Alas!) or emphasis:

All violators will be prosecuted!

BEWARE: Use exclamation points sparingly; too many will make your writing appear childish! or naive! Instead, try to use words and sentence structures that will provide emphasis without requiring the extra jolt of the exclamation point. Or several—which will be even more shocking and distracting to the readers!!!!!

Semicolon ;

The semicolon, more emphatic than a comma but less emphatic than a period, has several functions.

1. *A semicolon can connect independent statements (clauses) that are closely related,* as when:

one statement explains the other.

Save water; shower with a friend.

one statement balances or contrasts the ideas of the other.

To err is human; to forgive, divine.

2. *A semicolon can show the main divisions in a series punctuated by commas* and indicate where one grouping ends and the next begins.

In the Great Rose Bowl Hoax, when Cal Tech pranksters switched stunt card instructions for the University of Washington cheering section, the Washington director watched, aghast, as his signal to spell "Washington" produced "Cal Tech"; as a Cal Tech beaver materialized instead of a Washington husky; and "Buy bonds" came out "Buy blondes."

BEWARE: Semicolons, like any other form of punctuation, can be overworked.

Semicolons are not substitutes for colons.

Wrong: Student pranks may be divided into three categories; those at which everybody laughs, those at which only the pranksters laugh, and those at which nobody laughs.
Right: Student pranks may be divided into three categories: those at which . . . .

Semicolons are not substitutes for commas; don't use a semicolon to separate an independent clause and a fragment.

Wrong: The point at which a prank turns into vandalism is subtle; because the incidents are so variable.
Right: The point at which a prank turns into vandalism is subtle, because the incidents are so variable.

Colon :

A colon has a variety of uses.

1. *A colon can introduce an explanation or amplification.*

There could be no doubt that she was a wealthy woman: her Porsche, her Pekingese, and her penthouse broadcast the not-so-subtle message.

BEWARE: Don't let the colon separate important sentence elements that belong together, such as a preposition and its object, an infinitive and its object, or a verb and its object.

Wrong: On vacations she particularly enjoyed traveling with: her fiancé, her Head skis, and her matched leather luggage.
Right: Either eliminate the colon in the above sentence, or add another object of the preposition:
On vacations she particularly enjoyed traveling with three indispensable entities: her fiancé, her Head skis, and her matched leather luggage.

2. *A colon can also introduce:*

a series of elements	In addition to her wealth, she had a number of assets: beauty, brains, and enormous energy.
quotations	As Samuel Johnson observed: "It matters not how a man dies, but how he lives."
a subtitle of a book or article	*From Private Vice to Public Virtue: The Birth Control Movement and American Society Since 1830*

3. *A colon can separate:*

the hour from the minute in time: 10:45 a.m.
the salutation of a business letter from the body:

Dear Sirs or Mesdames:

the place of publication from the publisher's name, in footnote and bibliographic entries:

Phoenix: Put Put Press, 1982.

Comma   ,

Commas provide less emphatic separation of sentence elements than do either semicolons or periods. They are generally used to clarify meaning by enabling the reader to group related words or to keep more isolated words separate. Commas often signal convenient places to pause when you're reading a sentence aloud.

1. *A comma preceding a coordinating conjunction (and, but, or, for) is used to separate independent clauses in a compound sentence.* (A semicolon without the conjunction can do the same thing.)

John enjoyed hang gliding, and as a consequence he often jumped off cliffs.

BEWARE: If you're joining two independent clauses with a comma, be sure to include a coordinating conjunction. Otherwise you'll end up with a comma splice—two sentences that look as if they should be separate, but are joined unnaturally by a flimsy connection.

Wrong: John enjoyed hang gliding, he often jumped off cliffs.
Right: John enjoyed hang gliding, *and* he often jumped off cliffs.

EXCEPTION: You can sometimes use commas without coordinating conjunctions to connect a sequence of several *brief,* closely related, independent clauses.

He jumped, he glided, he flew happily ever after.

2. *A comma is used to separate introductory words, phrases, or clauses from the main clause.*

After studying, she always had a snack.
Even though she knew that overeating causes obesity, she couldn't keep away from desserts.

EXCEPTION: You can omit the comma if the introductory word, phrase, or clause is brief and the meaning is clear.

Eventually she had to come to terms with the problem.

When in doubt, leave the comma in, especially if to omit it would make the sentence ambiguous or confusing.

Confusing: After eating a candy bar is a pleasant alternative to a nap.
Better: After eating, a candy bar is a pleasant alternative to a nap.

3. *A comma is used to separate words, phrases, and clauses in a series.*

Among her favorite mementoes of her freshman year were a battered biology textbook, a stuffed wombat, and a mysterious envelope with her name in calligraphy.

EXCEPTION: Some writers, journalists in particular, omit the final comma in a series, before the conjunction. This is acceptable if you do so consistently, and the resulting sentences are not ambiguous.

Ambiguous: Favorite party drinks are sparkling cider, white wine, soda and whiskey.
Does *whiskey and soda* refer to one drink or two?

BEWARE: Avoid an excessive number of commas.

Excessive: Today, among the most delicious, party foods are creamy, almost runny, brie, French, if possible, tangy, but not hot, guacamole, and pita, a flat, round, Middle Eastern, bread with a pocket.
Better: Today, among the most delicious party foods are creamy, almost runny brie (French, if possible); tangy but not hot guacamole; and pita, a flat, round, Middle Eastern bread with a pocket.

4. *Commas are used to set off nonrestrictive clauses.* A nonrestrictive clause is not essential to the meaning of the main clause; it could be omitted and the sentence would survive in grammatical construction as well as in meaning. So it functions as a parenthetical element, interruption, or afterthought. Consequently, a nonrestrictive clause should be set off on both sides by commas—unless it comes at the beginning or end of a sentence, where it gets only one comma.

Herkimer managed to indulge in ice cream binges, though no one else knew about them, by sneaking to the freezer every night at 2 a.m.
Like other chocaholics, Herkimer was miserable if only vanilla remained.

BEWARE: Do not use commas to set off restrictive clauses. A restrictive clause is necessary to identify, explain, or describe the noun it modifies. If it were omitted, the meaning of the sentence would be lost or considerably altered.

To eat chocolate ice cream *in the quantities Herkimer consumed* required the unusual ability to estimate *how many calories he could burn off through strenuous exercise.*

Both italicized portions are restrictive appositives, necessary to identify how much ice cream Herkimer ate and what his unusual ability was. If these were deleted, the remaining structure wouldn't make much sense:

To eat chocolate ice cream required the unusual ability to estimate.

5. *Commas are used to set off parenthetical elements,* single words or groups of words that interrupt the sentence with an explanation or an aside. The portions of the sentence before and after the parenthetical (as in *parentheses*) elements fit together in meaning and in grammar. In addition to nonrestrictive clauses (see *4* above), such parenthetical elements may be:

a name in direct address:

You, *Henry Higgins,* claim you can teach a flower girl to speak like a duchess.

a modifying phrase:

Eliza Doolittle, *a spunky but uneducated Cockney lass,* was the one Higgins agreed to teach.

an inserted question, aside, or exclamation:

Higgins, *it appears,* never learned to consider people's feelings as well as their accents.

a conjunctive adverb:

Eliza, *however,* ultimately learned more than the linguist taught.

BEWARE: Unless you are using commas to set off parenthetical elements (including nonrestrictive clauses), don't insert com-

mas between main sentence elements, such as subject and
verb, verb and direct object, or verb and complement.

verb   object

Wrong: Eliza recognized in her heart, the nature of Higgins's
boorishness.

If you pause after *heart* in reading, you may be tempted to insert a
comma; avoid temptation so that the verb will be more strongly
connected to its object.

6. *Commas are used to separate items in*

> *dates:* October 12, 1492
> *addresses:* 302 Mill Neck Road, Williamsburg, Va. 23185
> *numbers of more than four digits:* 561,324,187

Apostrophe   ʼ

Regular singular possessive. An apostrophe plus -*s* [ʼ*s*] usually forms
the possessive of a singular noun whether or not the noun ends in an
-*s* sound.

a year's time	the lady's car
Keats's poetry	the boss's schedule

EXCEPTION: The apostrophe alone [ʼ] can be used when the addition
of an ʼ*s* would result in three -*s* sounds, hard to
pronounce.

Moses' commandments   Odysseus' journey

Regular plural possessive. An apostrophe without -*s* [ʼ] forms the
possessive of a plural noun that ends in -*s*.

two years' time	the Jones' party
the ladies' car	the Marx brothers' comedy
	the bosses' schedule

EXCEPTION: An apostrophe plus -*s* [ʼ*s*] forms the possessive of plural
nouns not ending in -*s*.

the Women's Movement   the children's hour   the people's choice

Possessives of pronouns. Pronouns that are already possessive do not take an apostrophe in either singular or plural.

his	ours
hers	yours
its [don't confuse this possessive	theirs
form—*no* apostrophe—with it's,	whose
the contraction of *it is*]	

NOTE: Some indefinite pronouns form possessives in the regular way, by adding *'s*.

one's   anyone's   another's   somebody's   nobody's

Some indefinite pronouns, however, are made possessive only in the *of* form.

RIGHT:	*WRONG:*
of each	each's
of all	all's

BEWARE: In compound possessives, only the last name takes the possessive form.

Shreve, Crump, and Low's account
Abbott and Costello's comedy

Apostrophes with letters or numerals

Apostrophes are used to indicate that letters or numbers have been omitted in contractions.

isn't	I'll	class of '85
can't	we're	blizzard of '08
didn't	it's [for *it is*]	[but omit the apostrophe
won't		in spans of dates,
		1851–54, or spreads
		of pages, pp. 178–85]

An apostrophe plus -s ['s] is used to form the plural of numbers, letters, and words used as words.

Figure 8's are harder to skate than figure 2's. It's even harder, on skates, to dot all the *i*'s and cross all the *t*'s.
Writers have to be careful with the little words, the *and*'s, *but*'s, and *or*'s.

Dash —

Dashes can be substituted for other internal punctuation marks—commas, semicolons, or colons. Despite their versatility, use them with restraint or your writing will look slap-dash.

1. *A dash can be used to indicate an abrupt break or interruption in thought.*

Drunk drivers are unsafe at any speed—until they get out and walk.
Jason always told the truth—at least I thought he did—until I caught him in a boldfaced lie.

2. *A dash can emphasize an important idea or create suspense or irony.*

A man's best friend is his—credit card.
After hearing a tremendous clatter in her kitchen, Jody walked bravely toward the noise, ready for a confrontation, only to discover—muddy footprints and an open window.

3. *A dash can replace a comma in setting off parenthetical material, for greater emphasis.*

Each partner needs at least three qualities of mind—trust, forbearance, and love—for a happy marriage.

4. *A dash, instead of a colon, can introduce a series.*

Every truly educated person needs to know the following—how to swim, type, drive a car, and balance a checkbook.

Parentheses ( )

Parentheses have the effect of subordinating the material they contain, so their interruption is less distracting than that of a dash. But, as with dashes, what is tolerable in moderation becomes offensive in excess.

1. *Parentheses can enclose added information or ideas that clarify, supplement, or explain the main point of the sentence.*

To students of the 80's, the mystique of the 60's (the heyday of the Civil Rights and antiwar movements) is almost inexplicable. How many people under twenty-five today even know what

Woodstock (the site of a marathon rock concert) was, let alone what it symbolized?

2. *Parentheses can enclose cross references.*

Even the literature about the 60's was unconventional and idiosyncratic (see discussion on p. 22).

3. *Parentheses enclose publication information about books.*

A fascinating view of the 60's is provided in J. Anthony Lukas's *Don't Shoot—We Are Your Children!* (New York: Random House, 1971).

It's preferable to avoid situations that involve putting parenthetical material inside other parenthetical material, but sometimes footnotes or other references involve this.

J. Anthony Lukas's "Two Worlds of Linda Fitzpatrick," a portrait of a girl who alternated between posh Greenwich, Connecticut, and New York's sordid East (Greenwich) Village, won a Pulitzer Prize. (See "Linda," *Don't Shoot—We Are Your Children* [New York: Random House, 1971], pp. 157–189.)

NOTE: To eliminate double sets of parentheses, which are confusing, use brackets [ ] instead of the innermost parentheses.

Brackets [ ]

1. *Brackets enable you to insert your own words—explanations, corrections, supplements—into a quotation.* Because brackets signal the words that you as a writer have inserted into those of someone else, you can't substitute parentheses for brackets; parentheses denote the words of the original speaker or writer.

"The heroes of the sixties were Abbie [Hoffman], Fidel [Castro], and Ben [Spock]."

2. *Brackets also enclose* [sic] (*Latin "thus"*), *which you can insert into the original quotation to show that an error is the fault of the original author rather than yourself.*

The inscription on the ancient map read, "Americca [sic]. Discovered by Christopher Columbus in 1493 [sic]."

Hyphen   -

1. *The hyphen can divide words at the end of a line, only between syllables.*

>   manu-script   build-ing

2. *The hyphen can connect the parts of some compound words.*

>   daughter-in-law   even-tempered

Many compounds, however, are either written as separate words (*rocking chair, roller coaster*) or single unhyphenated words (*baby-sitter, roommate*). *Hint:* The more familiar the word is, the more likely it is to lose the hyphen.

NOTE: Compound adjectives are hyphenated *before* the modified term, but usually not afterward.

>   a high-priced diamond   a free-lance photographer

The following conventions can help you determine where the divisions should come, though you may prefer simply to check the dictionary for proper syllabification.

> *Divide words between the prefix and the root.*
>   anti-dote   bi-lateral   circum-navigate
> *Divide words between the root and the suffix.*
>   independ-ence   young-ster   loveli-ness

BEWARE: *Do not divide one-syllable words.*
>   wrong: on-ce   br-eak   thr-ough

> *Do not separate a single letter from the rest of the word, leaving it either at the end of a line* (o-nly, a-lone) *or at the beginning of the next line* (env-y, Horati-o).

Slash   /

1. *A slash can separate alternative word choices.*

For centuries, philosophers have been discussing the mind/body problem.

2. *A slash can indicate line divisions in short quotations of poetry that aren't set off separately.*

> For instance, experts have long noticed the political connotations of "Humpty Dumpty sat on a wall,/Humpty Dumpty had a great fall."

Quotation Marks " " or ' '

1. *Quotation marks enclose the words of a speaker.*

> Mme. Jeanette Picard, the first woman to ascend to the stratosphere, commented, "We always take a bit of angel food cake. We never know who we might run into up there."

2. *Quotation marks enclose quoted material incorporated into the main text, up to fifty words of prose, or one or two lines of poetry.*

> When Benjamin Franklin wrote "Early to bed and early to rise, makes a man healthy, wealthy, and wise," he could not have been thinking of students who have to study for final exams.

NOTE: *Use single quotation marks for a quotation within a quotation, even if you have to change the original punctuation to do so.*

> As Jean Jacobs observed in *The Paradox of the New World*, "Benjamin Franklin's advice of 'Early to bed, early to rise' assumed an agrarian society whose work patterns were determined by the hours of daylight."

BEWARE: Do not put quotation marks around indirect quotations. Friendships are made, not given, says Jane Howard, and from the best of them we create communities based on attraction and affection.

Note also the conventions of quoting prose passages of more than fifty words or more than two or three lines of poetry.

Generally, tie the passage into your text by introducing it with a colon, less often with a comma or with no punctuation at all. Don't precede the quotation with a period.

Indent the entire quoted prose passage ten spaces from the left-hand margin; indent three additional spaces at the beginnings of paragraphs.

Space poetry quotations exactly as in the original.

Do not enclose the indented quoted passage in quotation marks.

3. *Quotation marks can be used for special emphasis, substituting for italics to call attention to words as words.*

> The term "quark" was coined by James Joyce in *Finnegan's Wake*, and then adapted to physics by Murray Gell-Mann.

You may occasionally want to put quotation marks around a word or phrase to indicate, by this emphasis, that you disagree with what it implies.

> Hitler's solution to "the Jewish question" was genocide.

This punctuation is equivalent to prefacing the term in question with "so-called," as a substitute for the quotation marks.

> Jordan went to the movies with his "wife."

BEWARE: This derisive use of quotation marks is often a cheap shot. It's fairer to explain why you object to the term in question, especially if the objection isn't obvious, than to damn the term with quotation marks.

> Jordan went to the movies with his girlfriend.

4. *Punctuation of titles should distinguish between works that are shorter than whole volumes and book-length works.*

Quotation marks are used to enclose the titles of works shorter than whole volumes—articles, essays, stories, songs, poems of less than book length, paintings.

> Van Gogh's painting, "Sunflowers"
> Eudora Welty's story, "Why I Live at the P.O."

EXCEPTION: Don't put quotation marks around the titles of your own essays unless they contain quotations or other titles.

> My-thology—and Yours
> Braid: Three Strands of Yarns in Joyce's "The Dead"

Italicize (do not put in quotation marks) the titles of whole volumes—book-length poems, operas, newspapers, movies, magazines, journals.

William W. Warner's Pulitzer Prizewinning book, *Beautiful Swimmers: Watermen, Crabs and the Chesapeake Bay* (Boston: Little, Brown, 1976), evocatively follows the seasons up and down Chesapeake Bay.

Quotation Marks and Other Punctuation

1. Put commas and periods *inside* quotation marks. Always.

As Mae West said, "Too much of a good thing is absolutely splendid."
"Too much of a good thing is absolutely splendid," said Mae West.

2. Put semicolons and colons *outside* quotation marks.

"Too much of a good thing is absolutely splendid": those were Mae West's immortal words.
Mae West's immortal words were "Too much of a good thing is absolutely splendid"; I sighed in agreement as I devoured my fourth piece of chocolate cake.

3. When you are quoting an exclamation, a question, or an interrupted statement, put the exclamation point, question mark, or dash *inside* the quotation marks.

"Too much of a good thing is absolutely splendid!" she exclaimed with a lascivious wink.

If the exclamation point, question mark, or dash is *not* part of the quotation, put it outside the quotation marks.

As we were discussing excesses, she interrupted—"Absolutely splendid"—and I agreed, overwhelmed by the thought.

4. In general, except for the practices identified in 3, the end punctuation in a quotation yields to the punctuation your own writing requires. For example, if you're quoting material that ends with a period but your sentence continues on after that, delete the period and replace it with your own punctuation.

"Nothing exceeds like excess," my exhibitionistic friend was fond of saying.

5. Footnote numbers ordinarily follow all other punctuation at the point where the quotation ends. They may occur in mid-sentence as well as at the end.

Gresham's law, "Bad money drives out good,"[7] has been recently supplanted by "voodoo economics."[8]

6. When you incorporate a quotation into your text (without setting it off by indentation) and follow it by a reference in parentheses (pp. 72–73), the parenthesis should come *after* the final quotation mark but it should come *before* the comma or period of the main sentence.

When Franklin Roosevelt said of the Depression in 1933, "The only thing we have to fear is fear itself" (*Presidential Papers,* p. 176), he could not have been referring to the 1970's fiscal policies, sometimes labeled "voodoo economics" (Bush, p. 221).

Conventions of Punctuating by Typewriter

1. Put punctuation marks immediately beside the word they precede or follow, without leaving a space.

EXCEPTION: Ellipses, where each period is preceded by a space.

". . . the startling . . . mysteries of outer space."

2. Double space after each period, exclamation point, or question mark.
3. Single space after commas, colons, semicolons, closing parentheses, brackets, and quotation marks. However, if this punctuation is immediately followed by another punctuation mark, type them with no space between.

"Absolutely splendid," she said.

4. A hyphen is a single -. A dash indicating an interrupted thought is two hyphens with no space between.

It was--my God--an octopus!

A dash replacing an omitted word consists of four unspaced hyphens.

The mystery guests, M. ---- and Mlle. ----, spoke eloquently.

5. Don't leave space before or after hyphens, dashes, or apostrophes unless the apostrophe ends a word or the dash is substituting for an omitted word.

6. Don't substitute parentheses for brackets. If your typewriter lacks bracket keys, draw in the brackets by hand [   ].

MECHANICS
Capital Letters

sentences   Capitalize the first word of every sentence, or word or group of words written as a sentence.

Who was that masked man I saw you with last night?
A stranger. How exciting!

poetry   Capitalize the first word of each line of poetry unless the poet (yourself or someone you're quoting) intentionally avoids using capitals.

Ethics are the shadows cast
Of men's behaviors from the past.

direct quotations   Capitalize the first word of a direct quotation if the original was also capitalized.

She sighed, "First it was jogging, then it was tennis, now it's hang gliding. What next?"

titles and subtitles of works (books, magazines, essays, chapters and chapter subheadings, movies, songs, poetry, operas, plays)   Capitalize the first letters of the first, last, and other important words of titles and subtitles of works written in English. Capitalize the first letter of a subtitle. Other words—articles, prepositions, conjunctions—are not capitalized unless they have unusual significance or occur first, last, or at the beginning of a subtitle.

War and Peace; The Saturday Review; Uncle Tom's Cabin, or, Life Among the Lowly [*Among* is capitalized because it is an important word in this context.]

EXCEPTIONS: Some scientific disciplines use a different system of capitalization in bibliographies and other citations. If you're writing for such fields, look at samples of published writings or consult specialized style manuals.

Foreign publications may use different systems. If you're quoting titles without translating, copy them exactly.

proper nouns and proper adjectives   Capitalize names or nicknames of people, literary characters, specific animals.

Eudora Welty, Babe Ruth, Oliver Twist, Secretariat (the race horse)

Titles that precede a proper name or stand for a specific person.

General Eisenhower was President of the United States.
Previously, the General was president of Columbia University.

CAUTION: When a title does not precede a proper name or substitute for it, but refers instead to the larger occupational category, do not capitalize it.

The university presidents assembled at Hot Springs, Arkansas.

However, the titles of some high offices are routinely capitalized.

the President of the United States, Secretary of State, the Queen of England, the Pope

Capitalize family relations when they're part of a name or title or used in direct address, but not otherwise.

Mother Theresa   "Oh, Mother . . ."   My mother and I went shopping.

sacred names   Capitalize titles and pronouns referring to the deity.

God   the Lord   He, His, Him   the Virgin Mary   Buddha

Capitalize but do not italicize titles of sacred books.

the Bible   the New Testament   the Koran

specific places   Capitalize names of specific places.

Emporia, Kansas   Vietnam   the Western World   the South

CAUTION: Don't capitalize compass points that simply indicate a general direction.

We trudged *west* for miles, buffeted by a subzero *northeast* wind.

specific businesses, organizations, institutions, and their formal subdivisions   Capitalize the important words.

Bah, Humbug Exterminators   Case Western Reserve University
The University of the South   the United Nations
Phi Beta Kappa   the Fine Arts Department
the Engineering School

CAUTION: Don't capitalize informal or general groupings, or institutions meant in a general sense.

university libraries   the middle class   the deserving poor
colleges of technology   exterminators

historical events, eras, movements   Capitalize the important words.

World War II   the Vietnam War   the Civil Right movement
the Middle Ages   the Renaissance   the Enlightenment
the Depression

names of days, months, holidays   Capitalize the important words.

Sunday   July   the Fourth of July   Christmas   Ramadan
Chanukah

CAUTION: Do not capitalize seasons or the numerical parts of dates.

last summer   the eleventh of July   January twelfth

Italics

Italic is a thin typeface, slightly slanted to the right, as is the type *in these words*. In printing it is used to set off words from the customary typeface, known as roman. In a manuscript (handwritten) or typescript (typewritten) you can achieve the equivalent by underlining the words in question. <u>Think or thwim!</u>

emphasis   Italics can emphasize key words and expressions.

He said he ordered *two* flounders, not *three.*

CAUTION:　Supply emphasis with italics when this will clarify your meaning. But use italics sparingly, or you'll give the impression that you're angry or shouting.

Guenivere *told* the waiter she wanted *seconds*, but *this* was *incredible!*

When you (rather than the original author) emphasize quoted words with italics, indicate your contribution in parentheses following the quotation.

Mme. Jeanette Picard said of her stratospheric balloon ascensions, "We always take *angel food cake,* never knowing who we might run into up there" (emphasis added).

word as word　Italics can identify words considered as words. So can quotation marks.

Does *corroborate* have the same meaning as *verify?*

foreign words　Use italics to designate foreign words not yet adopted as common English expressions, and for Latin or other scientific names.

The *au pair* girl enjoyed *la dolce vita.*
Australian marsupials include the kangaroo (*Macropus giganteus*), the koala (*Phascolarctos cinereus*), and the wombat (*Vombatus hirsutus*).

When in doubt, consult a dictionary. Many borrowed words, including a number of common Latin abbreviations, have become sufficiently common to be written as regular English words.

auld lang syne　laissez faire　arpeggio　arroyo　ex post facto
cf.　et al.　e.g.　f., ff.　i.e.　vs.

CAUTION:　If you use too many foreign words that require italicization, your writing is likely to sound snobbish.

titles　Use italics for titles of whole works.

books: *Sons and Lovers*　　*To the Lighthouse*

EXCEPTION:　Use roman type for the Bible and its divisions—the Old Testament, Acts.

plays: *The Little Foxes*   *The Elephant Man*
films: *The Gold Rush*   *2001: A Space Odyssey*
magazines: *Scientific American*   *Ms.*   *College English*
newspapers: the *New York Times*   the *Washington Post*

EXCEPTION: When one title includes another that would ordinarily
be italicized, don't italicize the second title.

The Significance of Shakespeare's Hamlet: *The Anguish and the
Ecstasy*

vehicles   Use italics for the names of ships, planes, trains, rockets, and
other individually named vehicles.

U.S.S. *Missouri*   *Delta Queen*   the *Orient Express*   *Pioneer 10*

NOTE: Names of shipping or railroad systems, airlines, automobile
companies, brands, and models are not italicized.

Chesapeake and Ohio   American Airlines   Ford Granada

Abbreviations

Abbreviations, shortened forms of words and phrases, are used to
save time and space, but only under certain conditions, as convention
dictates. In conversation and in some kinds of scientific and technical
writing they are common. In highly formal writing, they are less
frequent. In most general-purpose writing the following types of
abbreviations are common.

Titles and degrees

Use Mr., Messrs., Dr., Ms., Mrs., Mlle., St. *before* proper names;
use Jr., Sr., M.D., M.S., Ph.D., LL.D., and comparable abbreviations *after* names. All of these abbreviations are followed by
periods.

NOTE: Do not use such abbreviations independently or redundantly.

Appropriate: Dr. Samuel Johnson   Samuel Johnson, M.D.
Inappropriate: Dr. Samuel Johnson, M.D.   The *dr.* is in.

If you use Ms. to avoid indicating a woman's marital status, use it to
refer to both married and unmarried women.

Appropriate: Ms. Keller and Ms. Macy
Inappropriate: Ms. Keller and Mrs. Macy. In this context people will interpret *Ms.* as *Miss.*

Names and acronyms (words formed from the first letters of names) *of organizations, government agencies, technical terms.* Most of these are ordinarily written without periods.

organizations: ACLU, AMA, ASCAP, NOW, SPCA, UNICEF
government agencies: FBI, IRS, NASA, OMB
technical terms: ACT, ACTH, DNA, ICBM, SALT, SAT

NOTE: In many contexts it is helpful to your readers to spell out each unfamiliar term once, the first time you use it, before abbreviating subsequent references.

first reference: deoxyribonucleic acid (DNA)
subsequent reference: DNA

When in doubt, spell out what you think will be unfamiliar.

Terms customarily abbreviated

date: B.C.   A.D.
times: a.m.   p.m.   EST   CST
some units of measurement: mph   mpg   rpm   rps

NOTE: Use these abbreviations *only* with numerals, and *not* independently.

Appropriate: 468 B.C.   A.D. 1066   10 a.m.   12:15 p.m.,   EST
38 mpg
Inappropriate: In the a.m. the car gets good mpg.

some Latin terms: e.g.   et al.   etc.   i.e.   viz.
some places   Some places are commonly referred to by abbreviations:

U.S.A., D.C., U.S.S.R. Other places, U.S., N.M., Ore. are abbreviated in bibliographic references and sometimes in other contexts; check a model.

NOTE: In general, the following types of words are not abbreviated in the body of an essay, though they may be abbreviated in bibliographic references:

given names: Jonathan   Henrietta
months, days of the week: September   Saturday

some units of measurement: feet   meters   seconds   gallons
academic courses: political science   chemistry [except for R.O.T.C.]

Numbers and Figures

In general writing, it is customary to write out numbers that can be expressed in one or two words. Written-out numbers are called *numerals*.

eighty-eight   twenty-nine cents   ten votes   a million dollars

Figures are used with larger numerals.

888    $42.73   74,629 votes   115 mpg

To make figures plural, add either -*s* or -'*s*.

two 10s   several 100's

When the number is written out, don't use an apostrophe.

EXCEPTION: Figures are preferred in most

scientific and technical writing: 76 psi
newspapers for all numbers over ten: 14 soccer players
contexts that would otherwise involve mixing figures and written-out numbers. Use figures exclusively.
Most adult women weigh between 90 and 150 pounds.

However, to avoid strings of confusing zeros, as in round numbers of millions and billions, the larger term may be written out, but preceded by a numeral.

$28 billion [or twenty-eight billion dollars]

Always write out numbers beginning a sentence. If the number is long, try to rework the sentence and put the number later, where it can be expressed as a figure.

Inappropriate: 25-35 hours credit per year is an average full-time college course load.
Appropriate: The average full-time college course load per year is between 25-35 hours credit.

Figures are ordinarily used for the following.

sums of money, decimals, and percentages:

$18.99   17.76   12.2% (or 12.2 percent)

dates and hours when followed by a.m. or p.m., except in highly formal contexts, such as wedding and graduation announcements:

September 12, 1983   12 September 1983   September 12th
11:15 a.m.   12:00 p.m.   5:45 p.m.

NOTE: Use numerals to designate whole hours, without minutes, before *o'clock, noon,* and *midnight.*

five o'clock   twelve midnight

mailbox numbers, apartment numbers, street numbers, zip codes, telephone numbers:

108 Wakerobin Drive,   Apt. 4-A,   St. Louis, Mo.   63105,
tel. 314-721-2856

NOTE: Spell out the names of numbered streets.

7 Fifth Ave.   33 Third St.

However, if a numbered street is designated by a compass direction, write out or abbreviate the direction and use a figure for the street name, as long as the resulting address is clear.

201 East 82nd St.   or 201 E. 82nd St.

volume numbers, chapter numbers, page numbers (see Chapt. 13); *acts, scenes, and lines of a play:*

Ham. II. iii. 27-31 means Shakespeare's *Hamlet,* Act Two, scene three, lines 27-31
II Sam. iii 4 means The Holy Bible, Second Book of Samuel, Chapter Three, verse 4

INDEX

Boldface indicates definition of topic or central discussion of it.

A

abbreviation, **401–403;** acronym, 402; degree, 402; names of terms and organizations, 402; places, 403; titles and degrees, 401–402; when to avoid, 401–403

abstract diction, **167–169**

acronym, **402;** punctuation of, 402; when to spell out, 402–403

active voice, 173, 364–365

ad hominem argument, 275

adjective, **360;** comparison of, 360–361; in description, 220; irregular forms, 361

adverb, **361;** as movable word, 373; comparison of, 362–363; forms of, 362; from adjectives, 378; in description, 220; meaning, 362; sentence connector, 368

aggravate vs. *irritate*, 370

all ready vs. *already*, 370

allusion vs. *illusion*, 370

almanacs, 318

a lot vs. *allot*, 370

among vs. *between*, 320

amount vs. *number*, 370

analogy, **51–53;** in argument, 283–284, 302–306; in single case argument, 306–307; to develop ideas, 52–53

analysis: as essay mode, **236–250;** book review, 243–244; questions to aid in, 237–239; research report, 245–250; scientific paper, 245–250

angry vs. *mad*, 370

apostrophe, **388–389;** to form plural possessive, 388; to form singular possessive, 388; to indicate omitted letters or numbers, 389

argument (persuasion), **259–260;** as essay mode, 259–309; *ad hominem,* 275; assertive, 284, 291–298; authority in, 269–270; by analogy, 283–284, 302–306; by cause and effect, 284, 298–302; checklist for Determining Argumentative Propositions, 285; contradictory evidence in, 273–274; emotional appeals in, 267–268; evidence in, 268–274; generalizations in, 263–264; handling objections, 273–274, 292–293; language in, 274–276; oversimplification, 264–265; personal experience in, 269–270; providing sufficient options in, 264–265; relation of writer to audience, 265–268; selecting arguable issue, 260–261; thesis, 263–264; *tu quoque,* 275–276

article, as part of speech, **368–369**

article in edited collection, citation of, 332

assertive argument, 284, **291–298;** Checklist for Writing an Assertive Argument, 292–293

atlases, 318

audience, **33–38,** 42; adapting language to, 155; assumptions about writing, 35–37; biases, 34–35; educational background, 34; "general," 33–34; interests, 35; introductions to appeal to, 111–116; reactions to writing, 62–63; writer's assumptions about, 33–35

author, *see* writer

B

balance in sentence structure, **135–137**

begging the question: in argument, 264–265; in examination, 251–257

bibliography, appended to essay, **333–337;** form of, 334–335; sample entries, 334–335; sample research pa-

ABOUT THE AUTHOR

Lynn Z. Bloom is currently Professor of English and Chair of the English Department at Virginia Commonwealth University. She earned a B.A. (Phi Beta Kappa), M.A., and Ph.D. from the University of Michigan. Her most recent awards include a grant for the U.S. Office of Education as Co-Director of the Eastern Virginia Writing Project, College of William and Mary; a National Endowment for the Humanities grant as Associate Editor (with M. Briscoe) of *American Autobiography: A Bibliography, 1945–1980* (University of Wisconsin Press, 1982); and a grant from the Writing Center of George Mason University for research on the composing processes of anxious writers. Her research interests are reflected in this book, *Strategic Writing;* in an advanced composition book, *Contemporary Writing: Advanced Modes and Models* (1984); in *Doctor Spock: Biography of a Conservative Radical* (1972); *Forbidden Diary* (1980), and in numerous articles and reviews.

Most of this book was written—and rewritten—when Dr. Bloom directed writing programs at the University of New Mexico, and at the College of William and Mary. The author lives in Williamsburg, Virginia, with her husband, a professor of social work, and two college student sons.